RELIGION REINTERPRETED

RELIGION REINTERPRETED

by

Hale Michael Smith, M.D.

www.penmorepress.com

Religion Reinterpreted by Hale Michael Smith

Copyright © 2022 Hale Michael Smith

All rights reserved. No part of this book may be used or reproduced by any means without the written permission of the publisher except in the case of brief quotation embodied in critical articles and reviews.

ISBN-13:978-1-957851-00-6(HardCopy)
ISBN-13: 979-8-9855298-0-7(Paperback)
ISBN-13:-979-8-9855298-1-4(E-book)

BISAC Subject Headings:
PHI036000   PHILOSOPHY / Hermeneutics
PHI038000   PHILOSOPHY / Language
REL051000   RELIGION / Philosophy

Edited by Chris Wozney

Cover Illustration by
The Book Cover Whisperer:
ProfessionalBookCoverDesign.com

Address all correspondence to:
Penmore Press LLC
920 N Javelina Pl
Tucson AZ 85748

Dedication:

Dedicated to you, dear Reader

TABLE OF CONTENTS

Editor's Note	viii
First Words from the Author	1
Prologue	9
Chapter 1: In the Beginning…	37
Chapter 2: The Will of God	43
Chapter 3: God's True Name	58
Chapter 4: Cost and Sacrifice	68
Chapter 5: Being and Its Aspects	78
Chapter 6: Emergence of Divinity: God as "I AM"	83
Chapter 7: Zoroastrian Roots	87
Chapter 8: Prologue to Existence	94
Chapter 9: Guiding Principles	100
Chapter 10: Existence	129
Chapter 11: The Light Boundary	139
Chapter 12: Ideas	153
Chapter 13: Angels	168
Chapter 14: Awareness	193
Chapter 15: What is Religion For?	212
Chapter 16: Comments of Genesis	248
Chapter 17: Two Brothers	274
Chapter 18: How Christianity Became "Christianity" with Quotation Marks	294

Chapter 19: Christianity without Quotation Marks	309
Chapter 20: The 4 Gospels—and Others	326
Chapter 21: Perception	347
Chapter 22: Being Human	357
Chapter 23: What Does All This Mean for Me?	389
Last Words	405
Chapter Appendix: The Enneagram	406
Bibliography	439
About the Author	447

Editor's Note

For nearly 40 years, Hale Michael Smith was one of my dearest friends. First he was friends with my stepfather, Myron Becker, even though they were a generation apart in age. Both of them had driven taxis in New York City to pay for college. Both of them had entered the medical profession: Myron as an underage Navy corpsman in 1942, Hale as an older than usual medical student at Georgetown University. When Hale was invited to our home for dinner, conversations were usually about medicine and philosophy, especially the philosophy of dimensions, interspersed with reminiscences of their various taxi driving adventures. Hale became the older brother I'd grown up wishing I had.

Over the years, we continued having conversations. He introduced me to some of his favorite books, including *A Wizard of Earthsea* and the extraordinary four-volume Anthony C. Yu translation of *Journey to the West*. In return, I would explain aspects of fairy tales based on my own readings.

We usually lived very far apart, and sometimes years passed before we'd see each other again, especially after I became an Army medic, but that never seemed to matter. When one of us needed a friend, the other was there. At least, I hope I was there for Hale the way he so often was for me.

About 45 years ago, Hale began writing down his questions and ideas about religion. For the rest of his life he worked at clarifying, expanding and refining what he wished to communicate. No matter what was happening in his life, this project was the central thing. Nothing stopped him from working on it, not even a crashed computer that wiped out years of work. I have 5 crates filled with printouts of earlier drafts of sections of this book. If I still had access to my old emails, I'd have 20 years of communications from Hale, with variant chapters as he wrote them. He never thought he actually finished, at least, never for more than a few days at a time. There was always more to say. He did tell me several times he felt that writing this book was what he was truly born for.

When he realized he might die before completing his project, he asked me to be his executor with respect to this one thing. Our mutual best friend, Robert Beeson, helped make it possible for us to meet one last time and plan out a campaign of editing and publishing his book. A decision was made to leave certain repetitions in place, so that certain ideas would be presented together whenever they occurred. It was also agreed that I could interpolate passages that were not in the 2019 manuscript, based on my recollections of conversations and emails.

It should be noted that this is not an academic book in the sense that the author is focused on conducting research and providing point by point references. Rather, this is the sharing of decades of pondering. The authors who are quoted and the books that were influential are listed in a bibliography at the back.

It has taken longer than we originally intended, because Life sometimes has a way of throwing obstacles in one's path. But thanks to Robert Beeson, Robin Smith, and Juanita Smith, this book is seeing the light of day.

First Words from the Author

*Western and Eastern religions; the effects of interpretation;
a vivid dream; "Flatland"; a joke*

This book is an effort to reinterpret religion. This effort applies most of all to Christianity, the religion of my upbringing, which, along with the Judaic and Moslem faiths, is focused on compliance with the dictates of an autocratic God. The Religions of East Asia tend to be different in that they are more focused on the human ability to witness a higher order Reality directly for themselves. Many scholars would say that this approach was originally true of the three Abrahamic religions as well. What we have seen historically is that *any* religion is susceptible to distortions driven by fear, and the desires of some to control others by means of fear.

Western Religions have all too often been reduced to following rules of behavior that will enable one to avoid the displeasure of that autocratic god and his so-called representatives, who abrogate to themselves powers of life and death. The *why* behind these rules is largely forgotten, and sometimes the original rules themselves are forgotten, or changed. As a result, those laws have slipped into irrelevancy for more and more people. It is not the case that more and more people lack faith, but that more and more people realize that their spiritual life is not adequately addressed by fear-based and rule-based religions. And yet, for most of human history, Religion was a primary agent of civilization and the art of living together in groups, and that's something we need to recover.

At an early age I was badly disappointed by what I was taught in church. But in moments alone, I was fascinated by the questions of why I was here, and how everything fit together into something that made sense. And it seemed to me that religion ought to address these questions. Later, as a teenager, I became aware of the seemingly great differences in what people believed to be religion. Then, in college, an inorganic chemistry class led me to become a Religious Studies major. That may seem an odd tack to take, to use a sailing metaphor, but the notion came to me that without understanding how this world came to be *as it appears to be*, I had no chance understanding anything about religion or reality. The primary tack I took was to identify and question the assumptions underlying whatever I was looking at.

The idea that any religion represents a direct dictation from God is almost irrelevant, because from the moment you read or hear that supposed dictation, what lands in your mind is your interpretation of it, filtered through the interpretations of whoever wrote it down, and again of whoever translated it, unless you are reading the original language, which most of us are not. The weak link in this system is humans with their perceptions and interpretations, not God. Change the assumptions that underlie interpretations, and you change the resulting interpretation.

What most of us are told to believe and take on faith as Holy Scripture are *interpretations* given for those scriptures over the last two millennia. Scripture and interpretation are never the same thing. Even so, any questions raised about interpretation will be misperceived by many as an attack on scripture. But questioning or attacking the validity of the Holy Scripture of the three Abrahamic Religions is the very last thing on this author's mind. Let me say again, at no point is it my intention to attack Scripture, only to examine interpretations and assumptions. And yes, I am well aware that this book is also and only an interpretation of some aspects of Scripture.

HALE MICHAEL SMITH, M.D.

Allowing a negative reaction to any statement made in this book to sidetrack you from understanding that statement would be a kind of error I am asking readers to make an effort to avoid. Undertaking this project was hard enough without dreading the blowback of willful misunderstanding. If I write something that seems just flat wrong to you, please allow me time to explain. At the same time, I acknowledge that what seems true to me, based on decades of study and experience, may simply not be recognizable as true to some readers. It may even be wrong, although I have done my best to avoid errors of comprehension and reasoning. But I am not setting out to offend anyone. If what I share has relevance to you, then I dare to hope the years I have labored on this project were not wasted time.

If I may offer a recommendation based on my own experience: as you read, allow yourself quiet periods so something deeper than the surface of yourself has a chance to digest what you've read. In each of us, there's something which could never be completely cut off from its Source, whether you call that Source God or Reality. But to hear it, you have to tune out the TV that's almost always left running in your head.

I hope only to offer a way to look at things, all with the aim of helping the Prodigal Son in each of us to find his or her way back home, back to God.

I had long wondered why the religions of the Far East seemed so different from the Abrahamic religions of Western Eurasia. The divisive yet widespread notion that only one group of people had been given the truth by God, while everyone else would be left to rot for eternity, had never sat well with me. Instead, I wanted to understand what lay behind all religions, and why Religion had taken so many seemingly different forms. Furthermore, I wanted to understand how Science fit into the overall picture. During my undergraduate years of a Religious Studies major, the notion had come to me that one had to understand *why* Man was created in order to explain religion. And to understand *why* Man was created, one would have to understand how this entire Universe was created, and why it came to be the sort of world it now seems to be. The world we see around us is not the world one would expect to have been created by a Perfect and All-powerful God. And yet, something in me simply was not persuaded by the arguments of atheists. I had an unshakable feeling that *something* was Real, and that there were reasons for reality as we experience it to be the hash it is.

In 1987, I was sent to Tulsa, Oklahoma to pay back the Government for underwriting my medical school education by working at a clinic in an underserved area. That summer, I had plenty of time to speculate on these questions. One week, I started having insights. Somehow, there seemed to be more depth in almost everything I saw or thought. If I attempted to say anything to anyone about what I was experiencing, I had the overwhelming feeling that, in the mere act of putting it into words, I was squashing something flat which was otherwise three dimensional. In other words, I was crushing out of existence some important dimension of whatever I was trying to convey.

By Wednesday I was actually becoming frightened, because whatever was happening to me was beginning to interfere with my ability to deal with my patients, and even to drive safely. I sat down and did an inventory of everything I had ingested over the last week, on the assumption that I might be hallucinating because of some food allergy or medication. The only thing I could come up with that was out of the ordinary was that, on the previous Saturday, I had started taking Medrol for an inflammation. It's a steroid, which starts with a high dose (60mg), that the user titrates down each day by 10mg for six days. I knew that steroids sometimes lead to hallucinations, but that had never happened to me before, and nor has it ever happened since. But the Medrol was the only thing I could fix on, so I stopped taking the rest of the doses. It wasn't the safest thing to do, prematurely stopping the steroids, but I was becoming desperate. And sure enough, things quickly quieted down.

I spent that Thursday contemplating everything which had happened to me that week, and what it might mean. The fact that steroids seemed to have triggered this didn't necessarily mean that the insights I had gained were invalid. Blaming everything on the steroids somehow seemed insufficient. By the time I got home from work I was still dealing with a lot of emotional turmoil, and having no one close to talk to in Tulsa at that time, I called my former girl friend in Washington, D.C. She was a nurse, and we had been together for the three years of my post graduate residency. While we were talking, she reminded me of a dream she'd once had, which she had already told me about. At that time, the significance of what she told me had gone right past me. This time it didn't.

While my friend was a Nursing student, she had an unusual dream—a vivid dream. It was about her favorite patient at that time, a woman in her seventies who was dying. This patient had spent her life as a pediatrician, and had gone to medical school at a time when a woman was uncommon in the profession. In my friend's dream, she went into this patient's room only to be confronted by a couple who presented themselves as this patient's uncle and aunt. (My friend noted that they didn't seem that old.) They told my friend that her patient had died during the night, and was sorry that she had been unable to properly say goodbye and thank

RELIGION REINTERPRETED

my friend for the care she had shown. They then told my friend that the deceased patient had left to my friend a gift, specifically, an Amaryllis that had been in her room.

My friend didn't think much of the dream upon awaking, but it was so vivid she did not forget it, either. And when she got to work that morning she also wasn't entirely surprised to discover that the patient had indeed died overnight. Furthermore, the Amaryllis was still there in the emptied room, so my friend gathered it up to take home. What is significant is that the room *had already been stripped and cleaned* for new patients, and theoretically at least, the Amaryllis should have been removed. To explain why the Amaryllis was still there, my friend pointed out that it wasn't in bloom and it therefore looked like a flowerpot with nothing in it but dirt. (An Amaryllis is a bulb plant, and when not in bloom it shows little or nothing above ground.) Even so, the people cleaning the room should have removed it.

It was here that a light went on in my head, because while her explanation made factual sense, that dream she'd had was far too specific to be dismissed as trivial or simply imaginary. While very intelligent, my friend was not given to philosophical speculation, neither was she mendacious (inclined to falsehoods). It was, therefore, right here that I began to understand that there were at least two levels of "truths" for explaining most things in this world. Her explanation for why the Amaryllis had been left in that room was like me assigning to the steroids the responsibility for my experiences and insights of that week. Both explanations were what I would now call "Flatland" explanations which, while valid, didn't explain the sense that something very different and very important had also been involved in these events.

Flatland is a book I had read as a teenager. Written by a British mathematician named C.H. Hinton, it is a metaphorical story about a literal Square, a four-sided geometric figure who lived in a flat two-dimensional world, populated by other two-dimensional figures like himself. They are able to explain everything in terms of two dimensions. No other dimension is necessary to explain reality. Therefore, it is a major problem for our Square when one day he has an unexpected encounter with a Sphere who is transiting through his two-dimensional world, and who tells him about the three-dimensional world. Because our Square is unable to visualize what he is told by that Sphere, he simply cannot believe him. The Sphere then transports him into the world of three-dimensions. This radically alters our Square's perceptions, including his prejudices. But when he returns to his world of two-dimensions, he is unable to explain his experience to others.

Now, you don't get into or through medical school without taking science seriously. Science is very good at explaining *how* things happen. With sensitive enough instruments, we can measure qualitative differences in brain waves and assign names to the range of frequencies that correspond to vivid dreams with spiritual and religious content. But *why* things happen is a whole other dimension. In what follows, I hope to share the ideas, insights, thoughts and experiences that are my best effort to explain *why*.

But first, a joke.

One day, the Devil was feeling bored and restless. He decided to have some fun. He opened a golden chest, the chest that held everything he had managed to bring with him from Heaven, and took out something that gleamed and shone. Then he manifested himself on Earth, and dropped the shining thing on the ground alongside a busy street. Then he waited and watched.

Many people passed by the shining thing without noticing it. Eventually, however, a man saw it, stopped, and picked it up. His

RELIGION REINTERPRETED

face became illuminated. Just before he rushed off with the shining thing clutched to his chest, the Devil whispered in his ear.

Well pleased, the Devil returned home.

When one of his slaves asked about his day, the Devil told what he had done.

"But Master, what was it you let drop on the ground?" the slave asked.

"It was a bit of Truth," the Devil replied.

"But Master," the slave exclaimed, bewildered, "it is said that Truth will set Men free. Why would you give Truth to Mankind?"

*"Aha!" replied the Devil gleefully. "What I dropped was only a **piece** of Truth, but what I whispered in his ear was... it was the **whole Truth!**"*

HALE MICHAEL SMITH, M.D.

PROLOGUE

*The meaning of religion; the purpose of religion; a joke;
the Land of Nod; "primitive" religions as intuitive knowing; ADAM;
zero; beginnings contain results; the dilemma at the heart of Creation;
assumptions; more about ADAM; cosmology; the etymology of "repent";
the purpose of this book; faith; how science fits in; Will*

This book is a reinterpretation of Religion, of why Religion exists, of why it's important, and especially of what the true aim of almost every genuine religion is most likely to be. It's also intended to show that the major world religions are not intrinsically in conflict with each other, nor even in competition; instead, each of the major world religions has something critically important to add to our understanding of the whole. This book is therefore not intended to convert anyone to anything, but only to demonstrate in a concrete way how we each of us, as Man, has a very necessary part to play in the one great effort which must eventually be made by all of us together, if we are to accomplish that purpose for which we as Man were intentionally created, and intentionally thrust into such difficult circumstances as we find ourselves in, here in this fractured world.

In addition to debugging Religion, this book has much to say addressing that greatest of anomalies, Man. In this vast Creation only Man needs Religion, because everything else in this universe actualizes its function. We ask, "Why are we here? What are we

RELIGION REINTERPRETED

here for?" Religion was originally the source of answers to these questions.

Fewer and fewer people know what the Latin-derived word *Religion* actually means. The old English word for religion was the word c*reed*, which literally means *belief*, and that's pretty much consistent for the word for Religion in most European languages. But the specific word "Religion" is actually far more insightful.

At ten years of age I asked my Baptist Sunday School pastor what the word religion actually meant, and he replied that no one knew. At that precise moment I realized I would unfortunately learn nothing at that church. So I stopped going to that church. But in my teenage years, having acquired an interest in linguistics, I found the answer to my question by simply opening up an etymological dictionary. The center of gravity of meaning in this word *religion* lies in the second syllable: -lig. It comes from a Latin word which means "to tie", as in tying your shoes. In anatomy, ligaments are the straps and bands of tough collagen which tie muscles to the bones they're intended to move. This word "-lig-" takes part in many English words, like *obligation* and *allegiance*, just to name a few.

The word "Re-lig-ion" means *tying back together something which has come apart*—with a strong connotation or implication that the separation was somehow improper. Given the context for religion, that separation must somehow be related to the real intention behind the word *atonement*, which by itself simply means "Becoming At-One" with someone or something other. (The notion of somehow "atoning" for some sin in order to redeem yourself is largely a misunderstanding, something we'll speak about later.) Religion is aimed at reaching a return to Oneness with God.

So then, why is finding one's purpose in being separate, unique, "special" in some way, so often the goal in human affairs?

HALE MICHAEL SMITH, M.D.

That's another question this book will attempt to illuminate. Here's a hint: whenever you find yourself facing a paradoxical conundrum, you are really, really close to understanding the heart of the matter, whether it is the nature of light (is it a wavelength and/or a particle?), the nature of our Human purpose (oneness and/or individuality?), or even the nature of God (ONE and/or ALL?)

All of these questions demand a context if they are to be properly answered, and for most of us it needs to be a new context. The reason for the need of a different context is because for most followers of the Abrahamic religions, God is only understood as being an Autocrat; a benevolent one, perhaps, but absolute in His demand for loyalty and obedience in behavior, thought, and belief—very much like a political dictator. The price for violating any of that is believed to be some sort of punishment, or even destruction. But why should it be like that? Why should so many people believe that the major religious issue is that we are on trial for our lives, simply for being born? Is it possible we've misinterpreted something along the way?

Over a lifetime of dwelling on these questions, I have come to agree with the conclusions reached long ago by the founding prophet of one of the earliest revealed religions: Zoroastrianism. And that conclusion—in my interpretation— is that this Creation came along with an unavoidable price. However, a means to make a correction was finally discovered, but it was indirect, because it involved the need for reliance by that ultimate Cause (God), on help from a relatively independent agent to accomplish it. And that independent agent would be us: Man. Probably sounds preposterous, I know. But this interpretation of Zoroastianism does lead to an explanation for why such a creature as Man exists. And it isn't based on an idea that Man in inherently "fallen" or that human suffering is all Woman's fault, or that God abandoned us, or that some of us will be Saved and the rest Damned to Hell. It's based on an idea that Man has a necessary and important role to fill, that it isn't always easy, and that mistakes can and will happen. But what can Man possibly offer the Infinite in the way of aid? What is it about Man that we would be given the most precious thing in the whole of creation to share as our own: a potentially free and independent Will, the very something that is God Itself?

Developing a context for new answers to these questions will demand patience on the part of the reader. "Returning Back to Singularity with God" is the true theme of this book. Ultimately, nothing real can ever be permanently lost or left behind. Whatever is genuinely real must eventually return to the Singularity of God, because that was the original Creation.

Patience is called for, because not everything will initially seem to be pertinent to religion, starting with the following "joke" which is actually a teaching story, like the parables of the New Testament.

"A man was walking home late one night when he passed a dark side street. Down that street, he saw a neighbor searching for something under a lone street lamp. He asked the neighbor what he was looking for, and when the other man said he was looking for a wallet he had lost, our good neighbor decided to help.

However, after an hour of searching had passed fruitlessly, he finally asked the other man if he was sure he had lost his wallet here under this street lamp. The other man then said, "No, I actually lost it on the other side of town." At which point our man asks in great frustration, "Why then are we looking for it here?"

The other man replies: **"Because the light is better here."**

HALE MICHAEL SMITH, M.D.

Most of us are in search for something. It's as if we each had a hole within ourselves which we need to fill, whether by means of religion, or family, or work, or love. Yet for too many of us, there seems little point to our lives other than trying to survive, attempting to stretch out our short lives here on this planet for as long as we can, simply because it's all that we know.

For most of us, it's impossible to imagine that this "streetlight" might refer to our minds, to our own subjective way of perceiving the world, and that this might possibly be inadequate by its very nature.

This book aims to demonstrate that all genuine religions consistently start with leading one to understand that we rely on the wrong mind (the wrong "light") to illuminate what we search for and how we search. In other words, the assumption that our ordinary everyday mind is an appropriate and adequate means for this search can only lead one to the "Land of Nod", as expressed in Genesis 4:16. And for the record, the word "Nod" means "wandering" in Hebrew. In other words, the curious consequence for Cain having "murdered" his "brother"—I'll explain the quotation marks in a later section—was to be exiled into a land of blind and fruitless wandering. If that is what our lives feel like, we may have something fundamental in common with Cain, even when we have never murdered anybody, least of all a brother.

I actually started college as a Linguistics major. While this book will demonstrate that Linguistics is still important to me, especially etymology, I eventually found it too confining a subject for the sort of private questions I was still asking. I therefore left Linguistics, and went through Psychology, Sociology, Anthropology, Philosophy.—which meant I spent more time in college than my classmates did. Most of them were starting careers while I was driving a taxi in New York City to pay for those extra semesters. But I saw something in a Chemistry class that caught my imagination. It had something to do with the whole being more than the sum of its parts when elements combined to form molecules. And from there, my next turn was to Religious Studies.

In my new major, I shied away from modern "Christian" Theology because, as it was being taught, the focus was on the history of denominational differences and dogmatic answers to questions. Had our instructors presented the teachings of some of the older denominations, such as Eastern Orthodoxy or Benedictine, I might have joined one of these orders; as it was, it was decades later that I came across these traditions in their depth and spiritual robustness.

Instead, I focused on other religions of ancient Eurasia, especially in their earliest, most "primitive" forms. I sought to find what they held in common, whatever that might be, before each became encrusted with their own idiosyncratic forms of dogmatic inertia. Religions tend to become ossified in the externals—the forms of proscribed patterns of thought and behavior.

The result of that sort of ossification has unfortunately once more raised its ugly head in Egypt as Radical Islam (ISIS). A number of Coptic Christians were murdered on their way to worshiping the approach of Easter. Historically, ISIS's "Christian" counterparts have similarly shed much blood in the hard game of "My God is better than your God." And much harm is still committed in the soft game of "My version of God is better than your version of God."

It eventually came to me that these older religions were not nearly as "primitive" as they were labeled. Here's an example. It is the creation story of the ancient Kurds (the Medes of old), among whom are the Yezidi of Northern Iraq, who still follow their ancient ways.

In that ancient religion, far older than Islam, Christianity, and possibly even Buddhism and Judaism, the Universal Spirit, whose name was Xwede—a name which meant "He who created himself"—created a shining Pearl and placed it on the back of a bird named Anfar. When Anfar eventually decided to fly away, that pearl fell off its back and smashed when it hit the ground. Xwede then created six very high-order helpers to manage and develop the Pearl's fragments into this fractured world called the Universe. The very highest of these "six beyond-ordinary" Beings was Melek Taus, the Peacock Angel, who didn't actually create this Universe, but he did give it the form it now has. This is why Melek Taus is associated with the planet Saturn, traditionally the god/planet of Time, Form, and Limits among old world peoples. Unfortunately, this association resulted in the misguided local belief that the Yezidi are devil worshippers, the consequences that they are persecuted and subjected to genocidal extremism by people who forget their own religions' injunction to love their neighbors, even neighbors of other religions, as was the case in the parable of The Good Samaritan.

It seemed obvious to me this "smashed Pearl" business was a story of the Big Bang, the explosion of that Primordial Singularity which, according to science, was the source of this Universe. The central image, of a sudden explosion, fragmentation and spherical scattering of matter, was intuited and described allegorically as a pearl by the ancient Kurds.

In the not unrelated Zoroastrianism religion of the Persians, the creation of this existing world was depicted as a trap set by the creator god Ahura Mazda, a trap which both fascinated, contained, and limited the mischief of his Inverse twin, Ahriman—and think of Ahriman as Dark Energy, the energy of separation that destroyed the Primordial Singularity and which is still attenuating this Universe we find ourselves in. The original, single, primordial destruction is recapitulated over and over again as Ahura Mazda creates and Ahriman subverts or destroys his twin brother's works.

As for the six great beings which oversee this fractured world of existence, Zoroastrianism calls them the Amesha Spenta, the six Divine Sparks of Ahura Mazda. And we find them within the Bible as Seraphim or, in Genesis, Chapter One, as the Elohim—the actual Hebrew word used in the Torah. Elohim is a plural, or composite god, for "Elohim" is a plural word. "They" are responsible for guiding the evolution of life. This information has become obscured for English speakers who only read the Bible in translations that do not accurately translate plural and singular words and pronouns.

I eventually began to realize more and more that there would be little which could be understood about religion or mankind unless one had some solid notion about how this world came to be and why, and especially about why we are here. Why should this world seemingly be so imperfect if it was created by a perfect, all-powerful, and all-knowing God? And what is our part to play in all of this? The so-called primitive creation stories were in fact profound cosmological statements. But how could this knowledge be available to them, even assuming it was correct?

So let's now look at this problem in this manner, starting with this fact: Man's body is without question an animal, no more or less so than any dog, sheep, panther, or horse. Throughout this book, it's intentionally referred to as our "Human animal body", explicitly understood to be the outcome of 500 million years of evolution (without specifying where or to what extent Wallace, Darwin, Lamarck, Ardrey and others were correct or in error)—with much tweaking by the Elohim. (There's the "intelligent design".) But what kind of animal can imagine such things as a world full of invisible Beings with Universe-wide purposes? Or that the moon is a place one can go to, from which to take pictures of Earth, and figure out how to do this? Not even the most intelligent, tool-wielding, social animals do this; which in turn means that something entirely other had to have been added to the mix called Man, something able to see abstractly. This Human animal body simply cannot be the Adam which was directly created by the God "I AM" in Genesis Chapter Two.

Scientists are explicit about being very aware that something extraordinary happened to Mankind about 100,000 years ago, something that strongly differentiated Homo Sapiens Sapiens from Australopithecus, Homo Sapiens Neanderthals, and all other hominids populating regions of the planet. Something catapulted Homo Sapiens Sapiens' ability to think abstractly far beyond that of even the most developed hominids.

As for intuiting what was impossible to learn factually about the origins of the universe, I simply assume that intuition was given to ADAM along with whatever else was given to ADAM in that first "breath" of awakening. Full knowledge of everything was given as part of that first awakening "breath", and came along with ADAM when our incarnation into these human animal bodies took place. We actually came here knowing everything, absurd as that must sound. But as our inner connection between that awakening breath and our acquired, externally oriented, everyday personas began to weaken and fray, we began to lose full access to most of what we knew. The knowledge which came with us to this world eventually was sequestered in cultural forms to avoid becoming completely lost. Those cultural forms were those of religion and language.

RELIGION REINTERPRETED

To reiterate, this book is an attempt to present Religion in a "different light." Some content may contradict what you already think and believe to be important and true about Religion. Only your own reflection on those assumptions will enable you to understand what your own thoughts and beliefs actually mean, but first those assumptions must be brought out of the background and into the foreground of your thoughts. If reading this book accomplishes nothing more than that, I hope it proves helpful.

Again, this book is not intended to convert anyone. Whether or not you change your thinking or beliefs about Religion is your concern alone. In our own way, we each of us seek to find that Pearl of Great Price or its equivalent, however we think or believe that to be, either from what we have been taught or what we have intuited. And we all have our favorite street lamps under which we believe that Pearl will, or at least can, be found.

The Secret of Zero

We usually start counting with the number One. Seems ordinary enough. However, if you think about it, what that number One actually means is that you already have something, a whole something which can be counted. The number One is like an actor who's already behind the curtains, just waiting to come out to take a bow. Zero is the empty stage. Starting with Zero is actually an example of how Potential precedes Actuality.

So, just what is this potential that comes before that actual Whole something that the number One represents? In the ordinary world of material things, Zero means that there's nothing explicitly there yet, and we have a couple of names for that: Zero and Null. The word Zero derives from the Arabic word "sifr" (also the origin of our English word "cipher", which came to mean both "secret" and "empty"). The word Null comes from the contraction of the Latin expression "ne-ullus" ("not-any").

These names work for the world of ordinary material objects, but in Mathematics, Physics, and Finance, the question of what Zero means isn't always so straightforward, because Zero again represents potency, the possible. In Math or Physics, having a Zero is like having credit. That "credit", while being nothing in itself, can yet be called an "implicit something" because you can borrow from that credit. If, for example, you borrow a dollar, you now actually have both a dollar, an explicit something, but you also have a debt of equal amount, and that debt is an explicit nothing. As a consequence, you might therefore say that the Zero represented by your empty pocket or wallet is a sort of Latency, because even though nothing objective is there, you aren't yet in debt, and you have the possibility, the potential of borrowing something. Borrowing that single dollar means taking an explicit something from that implicit something, now leaving behind an explicit nothing.

So you might now ask, "So what does this have to do with Religion?" Well, one of the fundamental axioms of this book is precisely that Potential precedes the Actual. This axiom is well known in certain circles, and now it has been made explicit that this important axiom also applies to Religion. All our myths and creation stories which begin with darkness and void, or nothing, acknowledge this, but how often do we see this as Zero? Now we can. And now we can describe Creation as the act of subtracting or extracting One from Zero, where Zero is the potential, the implicit All, and the positive One is the Actual, the explicit something: such as the Biblical Light that now takes the stage. Correspondingly, the remaining minus One is also actual, as the Biblical Dark: the explicit nothing left behind. So therefore, Zero has everything to do with Religion, because most Religions begin their Creation stories with a great Zero, a great Void, Abyss, Emptiness, or Nothingness, from which the Creation is drawn. The real meaning of the Greek word "Chaos" just like the related word "Chasm", is that of a great Void, a great Abyss; the modern meaning of chaos as "disorder" is a secondary, newly acquired meaning. In Zoroastrianism, this great Void was called the god Zurvan, whose name meant "Infinite Time". Notice the similarity in sounds of Zurvan and the Arabic word for Zero, "sifr". In terms of phonetics, the words seem to have the same root, transformed by substitution ("v" becomes "f") and reversal displacement ("r-v" changed to "v/f-r"). In fact, there was also a heretical version of Zoroastrianism called "Zurvanism" where Zurvan was the true beginning of everything. To be frank, the Cosmology to be presented in this book is by far more Zurvanism than orthodox Zoroastrianism; the difference will be explained in the Chapter devoted to Zoroastrianism.

But those readers who belong to the Judeo-Christian tradition need only read the first three verses of Genesis to see how this subtracting something from Zero is important, because the very second verse in the Bible reports that there was Void. This means that there was nothing solid (read "objective", in the sense of being solidly real) anywhere. This is immediately followed by a referral to a vast ocean (also read: "non-objective", in the sense of being dreamlike, such as being too fluid to be solidly real). Many traditional creation stories start with just such an Ocean, and with a bird being sent by some Deity to dive to the bottom of that ocean to find and to bring back some mud, which then becomes the first dry ground (the first solidly objective something). And this is precisely how I believe that these stories are intended to be understood: that the true creation was that of bringing forth the first objective (read: explicit) something out of the implicit something (out of the previous more dreamlike void, the fluidic dream world if you wish).

In Genesis, the separation of the Light from the Dark is precisely such an example of the removal of an explicit something (= the Biblical Light), from the implicit Something of the Zero (= the Dream, the Primordial Chaos), thereby leaving behind an explicit nothing = (the debt, aka the Biblical Dark). This is of critical importance because that resulting Biblical Light had in fact to have been the True Creation, that of Absolute Reality (the true start of everything objectively real). The later business about six days with a seventh of rest was something else entirely, a diffraction or unfolding (aka evolution, which literally means much the same thing) of that secondary structure, the Firmament. This Firmament was in fact Existence; aka this Universe, and it was a Boundary state between the Light and the Dark, partaking of both (by being in between the waters below and those above).

But everything started with that separation of the Light from the Dark, including those problems unavoidably brought on by that separation. Why unavoidably? That Light was the Positive One, the explicit something that was subtracted from the Zero, that Implicit Something that was the Ultimate Source of all potential for everything genuinely Real, and which therefore was prior to everything else. The Dark which was left behind by the extraction of the Light was not some great evil as many people might suppose, but it was a great debt, a great Negative One which had to be accounted for. And keeping that Jewel of Light (Reality) intact without losing it back to the debt (Dark) is the real source and meaning of everything that has since followed. Keeping the (Biblical) Light intact was the real problem which the Creator had to deal with because both that Biblical Light and the Biblical Dark together were together Itself as the Primordial Chaos. The Creator couldn't simply do away with what was part of Itself, part of Its own Absolute Omega Transfinity.

There will be further elaboration about this in the section "Emergence of Divinity". There, we will see that the only thing that makes sense is to assume this new Creation, the Biblical Light, was in fact the Creation of everything objective: potential preceding actuality. Reality is the source of Existence; Reality cannot be some fixed object, but instead must be the infinite potential for all that can genuinely be. Existence is the stage whereon the potential that is Reality can become actual (something you can witness or experience), thereby allowing the infinite variety contained within Reality to manifest itself.

Later, an attempt will be made to explain just what is meant by Will, and why Will has intentionally been equated with Zero. This is not intended to suggest that there is no self-aware, self-directed, Intentional Cause as the Source of everything (aka God). To the contrary, equating that Source to the number Zero only means that this Ultimate Source of everything is not something material, and is beyond all definition and attribution. (It's this very transcendence that Islam rightly emphasizes.)

Religion is widely understood to be a correcting and healing agent, one aimed at healing a major breach in the Creation, by correcting both Man, and also this world we live in. The next question naturally is to ask just what needs to be corrected (healed) and why. This book is also based on the premise that the beginning of something contains within itself the final result (essentially, a variation on Potential preceding the Actualization). Therefore, this book assumes that the answer to what needs correction and why, is to be found in how Man and this world came to be. And we have already suggested that there was an intrinsic problem in the Creation at the very beginning: the Biblical Dark. And although this "Dark" was not intrinsically evil, it still represented an unavoidable incompleteness in some sense, as the explicit nothing left behind by that creation (by the removal of the corresponding explicit something from the implicit nothing, the Primordial Chaos).

The standard answer that evil spoiled everything simply doesn't hold water in the face of a God which is unquestionably absolute in its foresight, power, and goodness. Some other sort of snag in the creation must have kept what might have been perfect from being so, and it had to have been more subtle and insidious, but also able to answer No! in some meaningful degree in response to the Yes! given by God. This suggests that the Biblical Dark had to have been in some sense equal in force to the Biblical Light, and yet, the only thing which could possibly be equal to God would have to be God Itself. How to reconcile this seeming dilemma?

This book will attempt to unearth many likely snags to achieving a perfect Creation, by attempting to follow the Creation from a state of Primordial Chaos (emptiness, abyss, Void, our Zero) to ourselves and to this world we inhabit. We will attempt to do this by showing what assumptions are needed to make walking that path feasible. And unfortunately, these assumptions will unavoidably clash with many of the assumptions which have long been taken as true, and which are responsible for the unsatisfactory standard interpretations of today's Abrahamic religions. You know, those three Western-most Asian religions of Abraham, each of which claims exclusivity in being God's last word, and yet who paradoxically are at perpetual war with each other... all in God's name of course.

RELIGION REINTERPRETED

<u>Assumptions</u>

You may ask, "Why assumptions?" Assumptions are needed for interpretation. Nothing in this world of Man (again, called "Flatland" in this Book) can be known directly, a truth which will be well demonstrated before this book is finished. But for a simple example of how interpretation is unavoidable in everything, think about the fact that there are no colors outside of your head. Colors are interpretations your brain has learned to make over 400 million years, interpretations of a very narrow range of colorless electromagnetic waves. Specifically, three different groups of frequencies of light—those we experience as red, green, and blue, exactly like your color TV—correspond closely to three specific chemical pigments in the nerve cells of your retina, that can respond to those frequencies. The colorless responses made by those retinal cells is all there is to anything objective called color. The rest is but an experience of the interpretations made of those colorless nerve impulses, interpretations bequeathed to you by biology, and organized into tidy groups by your native cultural upbringing. You see only a fraction of the spectrum of colors that birds and insects see (whose color spectrum includes the color ultraviolet), and your dog only sees a fraction of the spectrum you can see (whose color spectrum does not include green, and therefore no yellow or orange), even though all of you are looking at the same outside world. Therefore, if even your sensory world is but an interpretation, how can reading something written by Man or even by God be otherwise?

But don't misunderstand what's being said here. The problem with our interpretations doesn't lie in the source of the message. For example, even though I grew up in a Judeo-Christian context typical for Black American culture, and even though I'm personally certain that Wahabist Islam has gone off the rails much like Christianity did during the Inquisition, still, I'm still quite certain that the Quran Itself was a valid transmission from above, just as was also true of large parts of the Jewish and Christian Bibles. The problems begin instead with the receptions and interpretations made by Men who have quite different agendas, as for example, when people believe they've been given permission or even an directive by a valid scripture to go out and force the conversion of others to their religion. When compulsion is resorted to in Religion, a misunderstanding very grave has occurred in what is otherwise God's word, because it contradicts the very free Will we each were intentionally given by God, needed to make possible the correction of that which ails us all in this Human world called Flatland.

This question about assumptions is far more important than most people realize. The wrong assumption about what something means can easily skew everything you read in that scripture. Again, the interpretation is the problem, not the scripture in question itself. One must recognize what one's assumptions are if one is to have any chance of finding one's way to an interpretation of those scriptures which actually helps. For example, many people bemoan the many seeming contradictions in the Bible and therefore deny the Bible's validity, while many others refuse to acknowledge those contradictions as being significant, or even as being real, and instead continue to hang onto them unchanged, while thinking their tenacity in their unexamined belief is proof of their faith and a substitute for a need to understand what they read or hear. In such a case, that sort of "faith" is merely a house built on sand. In truth, by far most of those seeming Scriptural contradictions are actually indicators that you're intentionally being told something that's difficult if not impossible to put into direct and ordinary everyday language, and that you'll have to really work to understand what's really at stake in that piece of Scripture.

RELIGION REINTERPRETED

<u>Hint</u>: The word "Intelligence" itself literally means: *the ability to read "between the lines"* (inter—legere in Latin). In other words, "Intelligence" is the ability to see beyond the apparent, beyond the obvious; the implicit behind the explicit; to be able to see the potential behind the actual.

For a fairly transparent example of how a "less than adequate" assumption can badly skew things, let's speak for a moment about a certain long-held belief about ADAM. For the record, in this book, when that single name alone is spelled in full capitals, this author is speaking specifically and exclusively about the ADAM as created directly by the Lord God (God as "I AM"), specifically in Genesis 2: 7, and NOT about the later, much diminished Adam of Genesis 3: 21 who stumbled out of Eden with his female better half, Eve. It's an unwarranted and unsupported assumption that the two "Adams" are the same entity.

Typically, everyone rightfully believes ADAM to be the first Man in some sense. But there's more than one way to understand exactly what this *"being the first"* means. As it happens, most people assume this ADAM to be the first concrete male Human Being. And as a consequence of this, we are almost forced to believe by later Biblical statements that the "Woman" drawn from the rib of ADAM, must therefore likewise to be the first concrete female Human Being.

These two assumptions, millennia old, immediately result in a seemingly unavoidable contradiction between Chapter One of Genesis, where Man, both male and female, appear together as the last to be created in the order of all created material life on Earth, and Chapter Two of Genesis, where ADAM is created before all other living things, and is believed to have been created separately from the female of our species, who by herself alone is then the last to be created. In addition, note that ADAM is created in Eden (Ideal Existence) in Genesis Chapter Two, in contrast to Chapter One of Genesis where surprisingly, there's no mention of Eden. Standard Theology has no real answer that I know of that makes any real sense of these seeming contradictions. They are explained away as two different and contradictory traditions that were incomprehensibly put side by side. And yet there's an easy answer to all of this, one that doesn't gloss over the obvious seeming discrepancy between the first two chapters of Genesis by ignoring it, but instead explains it. It's also one that's believed by this author to be the correct interpretation, even though it forces everything else up a very different path, one both more interesting and insightful than the standard and accepted interpretation based on a concrete male Adam.

In order to start straightening things out, we have to first understand that the Elohim (the Hebrew name given to the literally plural or composite "god" of Genesis Chapter One), was something distinct from that God named "I AM" (literally the "Lord God" of Genesis Chapter two), which directly created ADAM. This, the seeming suggestion of polytheism, is critically important to this entire story, and will be explained/defused elsewhere in this Book. Here I will simply point out that God as "I AM" is not a God to be worshipped. There is only "I" here, but no corresponding "ME" to receive that adoration.

Next, and most importantly, in order to reconcile Genesis Chapter Two with Chapter One, you only have to let go of the assumption mentioned first above, that ADAM was a concrete male. In this Book, ADAM is considered to be an "Idea" (and an Intention). Specifically, ADAM is considered to be the original Idea of Man as a Universal class of Beings within Existence. What this accomplishes is that ADAM becomes the first Man by becoming the infinity of all possible manifestations of Man, without much regard to the specific type of material body. Ours on this planet are called human, and have human animal bodies. But this universe is vast, and there are an infinite number of possible varieties of bodies for Man. This Ideal ADAM is something that the first Man is normally assumed to be in almost every other traditional culture on this planet: androgynous. This simply means that the Idea of Man is properly just as much female as it is male. Because this Ideal ADAM is an Idea and not a material thing, we can dispense with the extra pairs of arms, legs, and genitalia that are so often portrayed in other cultures to convey the dual gender nature of this first Man, such as Gayomart in Zoroastrianism. And notice: all of this is legitimate because ADAM was created in EDEN, in Ideal Existence, and not on this concrete earth.

This assumption of an Ideal ADAM has another advantage: It clears up the seeming contradiction in time-lines between Genesis Chapters One and Two. How so, you ask? Well, in order to begin or start some project, any project at all, you must first intend it and visualize it (which is the real reason why ADAM was first). And here, we return again to the significance of Zero, the implicit something that is the potential that precedes the Actual. You simply cannot build or make something without some Idea of what you wish to do, and how to do it. This had to be true even for God, who first announced an intention to create a Man that most resembled Itself, before starting to actually do so. Therefore, what Genesis Chapter Two is actually telling you and me about ADAM is that ADAM (or more specifically, an animal body to serve as the material vehicle for ADAM) was actually the ultimate goal of all material life on this planet. ADAM, the Idea of the Ideal Man, was the intention of creating a material Being which could bear the "spirit" (the "Will") that is God alone within itself, for a critically important task, as this book will demonstrate. However, that creating *process* involved generating the many forms of life endemic to this planet until a suitable precursor finally appeared (the primates). But ADAM was the Idea, mind and intention that preceded this many millions of years process, starting from the earliest time that the first bacteria began to transform this planet into something more than mere rock. It was a grand experiment for the Elohim to arrive at a body for that Idea called Man that was a "best fit", which is why there were several types of hominids along the way.

Note: Science does not pretend to be able to address the question of disembodied intentions, which is why it rightfully doesn't attempt to address the question of God in Man's creation. It therefore primarily addresses only the question of *what* happened and *how* it happened, and not the question of *why* it happened.

A question remains: if ADAM is as much female as male, then what or whom was extracted from that rib? I'll leave that for the reader to ponder for a while. It took me more than 40 years to see an answer, and it makes sense to give the reader a chance to find the answer for himself or herself.

A working Cosmology

The first aim of this book is to establish a working religious/scientific Cosmology, to serve as a reference for reinterpretation of Scripture. A reference Cosmology is one which addresses both Religion and Science, because anything addressing Reality must address both Religion and Science if it is to be genuinely complete. This Cosmology assumes the real creation was that of Reality, the infinite potential for anything and everything. And the key feature of Reality is its very Oneness, literally, its Singularity. Evil per se only comes into the picture in this infinitesimal Human world of Flatland. The fundamental problem for the cosmos cannot be sin, simply because nothing but Man is able to sin (intentionally make a wrong choice). You need a free will to be able to sin, which is why predator animals who kill by design and necessity don't sin in their killing. Instead, the major problem for this Universe is the tendency it has to break down and disperse. In that context, the rupture and dispersion of Reality (the Big Bang), which thereby created this Universe (Existence), was actually a temporary expediency intended to temporarily contain that Dark (Energy, aka the Biblical Dark of Genesis 1:4), which is precisely what the Zoroastrian religion implies in the trapping of Ahriman. In turn, Existence provides a context wherein ADAM can work. In other words, Man is the collective One True (Prodigal) Son sent by God to save this world (the Creation), which is what Religion actually informs us. In short, a complete Cosmology must also include the Why, as that which explains the What and the How.

With an established picture of existence, we can proceed to better speak about what our role in all of this might actually be, and what the end point for us is likely to be. In the process, we'll also dig up many of the assumptions responsible for interpretations of religion we've long taken for granted, like the one that we only need "to believe", regardless of whether what we believe makes any sense or not. We seem to have forgotten that we've been blessed with a brain that can add 2+ 2 and arrive at the correct answer of 4; and therefore, any time someone or something demands that this ability be discounted as invalid, it should at least raise a question in our minds before we agree to go along gullibly.

Then again, there are several places in Scripture where what is written makes no sense because something has been altered, intentionally but wrongly. A little etymology will help us here with an example, because in Christian Gospels, the word "repent" is more often than not an error, by its replacement of the word that was actually used in the Gospels. While it's true that "repentance" was widely used by John the Baptist, it's also true that Jesus mostly used an unrelated word, if the literal Gospels are themselves to be believed.

The word "repent" comes from both Greek and Latin, and is a word fundamentally based on the central syllable "-pen-". That syllable is also the source of our English words "pain", and "punishment." What this adds up to is that repentance is concerned with behavioral control by means of inducing discomfort, fear, and regret (aka pain). John the Baptist certainly preached this. But did Jesus do so? The word actually used by Jesus in the original Greek Gospels was the word "meta-noia". This Greek word literally means finding "a higher grade of mind", a "mind beyond one's everyday mind". Basically, Jesus is telling us that we must use a light other than and superior to that of the street lamp which you've been searching under for whatever it is you've lost.

How did we go from a message of metanoia to an unrelated one of "be sorry for your sins, or else you're going to Hell"? Well, remember that the Council of Nicaea was organized by the Emperor Constantine, specifically to organize Christianity under a single roof. And the reason for this was Constantine's need for population control, read: behavioral control. This politically motivated repentance wasn't the Christianity that Jesus preached. Instead, Jesus preached the Christianity of finding your way Back to God. It was the priests who decided to emphasize sins and buttressing the Empire of Rome. And sure enough, the Church of Rome, and most of the later Western Protestant Churches, pursued this line of social control by means of fear. In so doing, each and every one of them succumbed to the very temptation that Jesus Himself defeated and refused while in the Wilderness: the lure of Temporal Power.

All three of the Abrahamic religions have fallen badly short with regards to the real purpose of Religion: leading us back to God. Again, it's not the original messages of the founding prophets that failed. It's the misguided interpretations thereof which serve other purposes: usually power and wealth. In this context, the Catholic Church, in spite of doctrinal problems such as their opposition to contraceptives in an already overcrowded world, and the unnecessary mandate of celibacy on ordinary priests (with the obvious, unfortunate consequences for little boys), is actually one of the lesser offenders, seeking at least to be of some genuine comfort to people through charity and good works.

What then is the purpose of this book?

Basically, it's an attempt to dis-inter the deeper story intentionally hidden within the overt historical narrative of the Judeo-Christian scriptures, and to remind us that this Flatland world is not our true home. It does this by attempting to demonstrate how one can start from Zero and Primordial Chaos, and end up with this world we see, in the process showing 1) why this world (this Creation) is seemingly so imperfect, 2) why we were created, and 3) where we should be headed. It's surprising how well most of the world's major religions align when seen in this context. But accomplishing all of this is not something for those who simply seek to be told what to believe. Jesus warned people He didn't come to bring Peace, but Division. I'm no Jesus, but I'm hoping to leave the reader with concepts which seem so reasonable that they can't simply be easily rejected, even when they superficially seem to contradict what the reader already believes. I want these new concepts to be pieces of a puzzle that the reader keeps moving around in his incomplete picture of Religion, in an attempt to find where those new pieces properly fit in, or whether they fit in at all.

In other words, you the reader will have to make some genuine effort to understand just what's being spelled out in the Book, because the very last thing this book is intended to do is undermine Religion, or even any specific religion. Any genuine God would have to be rational, if for no other reason that we can be rational by that same God's intention. As a result, interpretations which demand that people be punished or even killed for being "disbelievers", should be reviewed very carefully. Such demands are usually misinterpretations of demands really intended to target aspects of one's own mind. Faith without the contemplation that's needed to understand is merely ordinary belief, a form of spiritual decomposition akin to Alzheimers, with much the same end result.

In any religion, Fundamentalism actually celebrates the supposed superiority of its "beliefs" over obvious fact. But ordinary belief is really nothing more than the habit of a set of acquired interpretations. What we grow up believing would have been so very different if we had instead been born to the family next door. It would have been even more different had we been born to a family on the far side of the planet. Ordinary belief is the hand you were initially dealt by your family and your culture. Turning that hand into genuine faith is a game which requires investment of genuine interest, genuine effort, and persistent learning.

Genuine Faith actually comes from being able to see Reality directly. By its very nature, such Faith implies little or no conflict with the facts of this material side of the Creation. The ordinary inability to distinguish between Reality and appearances is precisely the meaning behind the story about our having eaten from the "Tree of the Knowledge of Good and Evil." This very lack of certainty about which is which, was actually the intended consequence of our intended incarnation into these Human animal bodies spoken about in Genesis 3: 21. This book is literally saying that we were tricked into making the mistake which got us kicked out of Ideal Existence, i.e. the Garden of Eden. Things wouldn't have worked otherwise, as this book will eventually demonstrate. (The Quran also takes this position. This author came to this conclusion independently by simple logic.)

Basically, this book is being written for those potential readers who feel there must be something genuine about Religion, or at least that there must be some genuine purpose for our existence. How to align a nagging sense of there being a real meaning and purpose behind this life, with the all too obvious appearance of senselessness that's so pervasive today? We seem to be born for no purposes beyond those which we can find for ourselves in this life, and our deaths all too often seem to have even less meaning than our lives. We all seem to have a hole, a Zero, an implicit something (or worse, an explicit nothing), where a Soul, an explicit something, should be.

This book might seem to be a mere intellectual exercise in speculation by many, but nothing could be further from the truth. I have lived and breathed these questions and the answering ideas for decades. This author makes no claim to any revelation comparable to those of the Prophets, but the implications to be drawn from what is presented here may yet contribute to the health of this experiment called Mankind. This book is an attempt to present a coherent way of understanding why we are here, and why this world is like it is. It assumes that we were created to fulfill a most important purpose, and that every one of us as Man is the very same One Son sent by God to save this world (Creation). Only by the process of accomplishing our individual contribution to this task do we accomplish our Salvation (our permanent release from this world which allows us to Return completely back to the ultimate freedom that is God). In our collective efforts to accomplish this task, we either learn to swim together or we sink together. Unfortunately, this branch of Mankind called Humanity is presently sinking.

Where does Science fit into a book about Religion?

Genuine Science attempts to deal with the Actuality that is this material world, calling that Actuality "reality." Much of what Science has so-far learned has far more genuine bearing on Religion than most people even begin to realize. One firm place where Scientific Cosmology intersects with this Religious Cosmology has already been mentioned, and that is that the Creation, Absolute Reality, the Biblical Light which was separated from the Biblical Dark, is to be identified as that Primordial Singularity which exploded or expanded (the Big Bang), resulting in this world of staggering diversity. It's opposite, its "Inverse Twin" of Zorastrianism, the Biblical Dark, "the Illusion of Discontinuity", is Dark Energy.

Absolute Reality was never some fixed thing, it is always the entirety of potential within Primordial Chaos, which could be organized as a singular, coherent whole, in other words, a Cosmos. The Big Bang merely made that potential available in separate combinations, analogous to the separate colors one needs to paint a picture, or the separate commands a programming language makes available that enables one to write a program for a computer, or the many elements available to compose different molecules. In other words, God created an open system of possibilities which were left to interact, randomly to a large extent, to see what would happen.

Later on, the term "logoi" will be discussed, a term for that which allows these possibilities, themselves being the "Thoughts of God".

The present conflict in words and deeds between the Judeo-Christian West and Islam is itself a contradiction of the meaning of the word Religion (which again, literally means "to tie back together"). What sort of God would pick sides in such a conflict? To a deity capable of creating a Universe this stupendous, with a radius of 13.8 billion light years, our conflicts can only be absurd and stupid, even less than bacteria-like. And yet, the Cosmology to be presented in this book stresses that Man was created for a critically important Cosmic reason, and no Man is expendable for that very same Cosmic reason. Why else would God "stoop" to share that which is most intrinsically Itself (Will), with every single Man, whether Female or Male; Black, Red, White, Brown or Yellow; Human, or some species from another planet?

It's precisely this very presence of Will which most defines Man, and all religious morality about how we ought to treat one another stems from this simple fact.

CHAPTER I

IN THE BEGINNING…

In the beginning; boundaries and limits; infinite reduction; linguistic note on energy; logoi; the <u>Philokalia</u>; quoting <u>The Gospel of Thomas</u>

"In the Beginning, there was nothing", and yet, in some sense, that nothingness did have to be something. This is the paradox inherent in almost all Creation stories.

Each possibility is paired with its own opposite, which essentially cancels them both. It's precisely this canceling out of every possibility by its own opposite that produces the seeming emptiness of the Primordial Void (Chaos). This state of pregnant emptiness is represented in some creation stories as a boundless ocean which just happens to be there, or as a void, as in Ginungagap of Norse mythology, which exists between the opposites of ice and fire and mysteriously generates antagonistic entities, including primordial gods. The early Chinese called this Transfinite Emptiness the nameless Tao which both was and was not, both at the same time. If God is not a created being, then what is God? To envision unbounded potential and unbounded possibilities comes close. God is the Infinity which is the reciprocal to Zero, which is also God. Even closer would be to see God as a self-directed Cause which was not an effect of some previous Cause. The Kurdish title for the Primordial Universal Spirit, Xwede, means "He who created Himself." The Greek philosopher Aristotle, in his *Metaphysics*, Book 12, portrays God as "Thinking Thinking Thinking"—ie, that which creates itself.

God is not some great invisible Being, because to be a Being is to be this-and-not-that. In other words, Being is a sort of limitation, while God is implicitly and intrinsically beyond any limits. To be something, any something, is to have limits that define you. This is the real reason why the Abrahamic religions have always been so adamant against graven images (that prohibition is very much misunderstood nowadays, because fixed thoughts about what God is and what God wants are far greater offenses than those made of stone or ceramic).

A simple choice to become Real in some sense is perhaps as close as we can come to explain the Creation, but even that wasn't straightforward. It entailed a complication, even for God, precisely because there is nothing other than God.

Boundaries and Limits

There is a theory in modern scientific cosmology called "M-Branes", which assumes that two multidimensional sheets of energy collided, resulting in the Singularity. My objection to this theory is that it's another example of Infinite Regression, where one proposes an explanation of one thing by resorting to something that is itself equally in need of an explanation. With M-branes my question is, where did these multi-dimensional sheets of energy come from? There seemingly needs to be an already well formed Cosmos for them to even exist.

The ancients left us with a well-known warning against resorting to Infinite Regression. It's the image of the Earth being supported in space by four huge elephants, which in turn are supported by a tortoise, and that tortoise is carried by a tortoise, which is carried by a tortoise, which is carried by a tortoise, which is…. Most people seem to think that this image represents how the Earth was actually believed by the ancients to be suspended in Space. This author believes that this image was more likely a warning about the futility of Infinite Regression. "Tortoises all the way down!"

The only rational thing I can think to say is that one seems to find this Infinity of potential only when nothing else is around, in other words, when there's a Zero of some sort.

The subsequent self-bifurcation of that pool of Primordial Potential into two essentially opposite reciprocals, (the Biblical Light opposing the Biblical Dark), was the actual Creation. All separation and dispersion is the manifestation of the Biblical Dark, now to be defined as the "Illusion of Discontinuity." The fundamental conflict within the Universe (a word which literally means "turning as One") is the tendency to become and remain One (aka Love), versus the tendency to disperse, attenuate, and individualize, in other words, to separate from each other and from God. This is not possible in reality, there being no such thing as an "outside" to God, which is why the Biblical Dark is Maya, the Buddhist principle of illusion.

This illusion of discontinuity is not to be automatically equated with evil. In the creation story of Zoroastrianism, the creation of this Universe was intended to trap and circumscribe this tendency to separate. At the same time, this tendency is the very prism that diffracts the singular potential of Reality into the diversity of beauty that this Universe exhibits, in its many forms. This reflects the fact that the Biblical Dark is ultimately no less part of God than is the Biblical Light. The control of this force was the power given to Melek Taus, the Peacock Angel (aka Chronos/ Saturn), which was necessary to give form to Existence to enable it to function properly as a self-maintaining entity.

A linguistic note about Energy

Energy is the potential to do, to change, or to become something in this material world. The word "energy" derives from the Greek, and literally means "in-work." The Greek "-erg-" of energy is cognate to (and very much the same word as) the English word "work". Being cognate means that both words, the Greek and English, were once literally the same word when the earlier common mother language, called "Indo-European", had yet to split into its many daughter languages. It should also be noted that in Physics, the equations for calculating the amount of energy that is available are exactly the same as the equations that measure the amount of work that is possible to be done with that available energy.

In turn, the word "potential" came to English from the Latin word "posse" which meant "to have power; to be able", itself derived from the even earlier "potis", meaning "a master; one who is able"—one who has potential, and "works it out".

Will and Logoi.

How does Will fit into an image of an "Ocean of Nothingness" aka Chaos? Here's where that sleight of hand comes into play, speaking about something which can't actually be spoken about. It depends on separating two things which aren't actually separate. In short, if there genuinely is something properly called Will (and this author does make that assumption), then that Will absolutely depends of the potential, the options, available to it. For example, assuming that I as a Human Being do have a free and independent Will, this still doesn't mean that I can choose to live my life backwards from old age to youth. That possibility is simply not available to me, whereas the possibility of treating other people decently is well within my capacity to do, in spite of how my upbringing may have programmed me.

Resorting to Will as an explanation for the origin of everything does not mean that one has found some piece of solid ground for our tortoise to stand on. We still can't explain from where that latent potential, which was the Primordial Chaos, came from. We can only choose to say that it was already there in some sense, and thereby save ourselves from that fruitless exercise in futility, aka Infinite Regression. This means that there's simply no way to prove "objectively" that God is Real. Thinking in those terms is no less a fool's errand than is Infinite Regression.

What itemizing this Primordial Potential into logoi allows one to do is to differentiate that Potential into discrete units of just what is specifically possible, and also of what opposes every such unit of possibility. This word, the plural of the Greek word "logos", was defined in the *Philokalia* as the "inner essences or principles; the thoughts of God."

The *Philokalia* is an extensive collection of the writings of the early Church Fathers, most of them from before the separation between the Eastern Greek Orthodox and Western Roman Catholic Churches. These writings are not part of the more recently discovered Nag Hamadi Gnostic writings, yet they also describe a Christianity far different from what's presented today. They point to a Christianity based on Metanoia, not on need for "repentance".

As for representing Will, I can only resort to logion #50 of *The Gospel of Thomas* (translated by Hugh McGregor Ross). There, as in the canonical Gospels, Jesus is giving his disciples instructions as He sends them out to pass on His teachings:

RELIGION REINTERPRETED

"Jesus said: If they say to you: 'Where are you from?'

Say to them: 'We came from the Light there, where the Light was, by Itself.

It stood boldly and manifested Itself in their image'.

If they say to you: 'Who are you?'

Say: 'We are His sons and we are the chosen of the Living Father.'

If they question you: 'What is the sign of your Father in you?'

Say to them: 'It is a movement and a repose (a rest).'

CHAPTER II

THE WILL OF GOD

*Creation as a game; Cantor's transfinities;
Gödel's Incompleteness Theorem; poets intuit the truth;
Significance of the Number Three; fictitious components; pi;
the meeting place; the Reconciling component; triads;
Man as a vertical triad; Man as inverted triad; gender and triads;
a caution; self; return to God*

The Creation as a Game.

The Creation, the bringing forth of both Absolute Reality (the entirety of all potential) and Existence, can be understood as being a game. This is not in the least intended to imply anything trivial or inconsequential about the Creation. Instead, it's intended to emphasize the importance of rules, laws, and conditions that make Creation what it is. This notion first came to my attention in my late teens when I first began to read about Gurdjieff. Early on in St. Petersburg, Gurdjieff made the point to his group that in a card game, "even God cannot beat the ace of trumps with an ordinary deuce." Gurdjieff's point was simple: *that to break the rules that make a game what it is, is to change or destroy that game.* Therefore, even God cannot break the rules (God's own Rules or Laws),

RELIGION REINTERPRETED

without changing or destroying the game which depends on those rules.

Of course God as "I AM" could do so, but that would defeat whatever purposes there originally were for Creation. This also means that any direct intervention by God (as "I AM"), must be both limited and very strategic in its nature, and the possibilities for doing so must be inherent in the structure of creation.

Hennce, this material world, which is referred to in the Lord's Prayer as "Earth" in the phrase "on Earth as it is in Heaven", is governed by the laws of cause & effect, the laws of physics. Ours is not a world manipulated and managed in every detail by the so-called "Will of God". That is why the Lord's Prayer asks that this earth become more like heaven, where God's Will is done.

The Will that is God (God as "I") created Reality, therefore, it's only the Will that is God which determines what is Real. This point is of extreme importance in understanding religion, because it means that whatever does not derive directly or indirectly from the Will that is God simply cannot be Real. And God interacts only with Reality. This material world, called "earth" in the Bible, along with all of its problems, cannot be Real for God, as God defines that term, because what God wills has so little sway here. What this further implies is that, for this very same reason, *sin and evil cannot be Real*. They cannot be Real unless God created them, which God did not. Instead, they can only be *actual*. How this state of affairs came about where that which is not Real (as God would define that term), could seem to have such a big stake in God's Creation, is a major part of what this book is about.

Cantor's Notion of Transfinities.

The term Transfinity was coined by the 19th century mathematician Georg Cantor, who demonstrated that there is an ascending order of ever more encompassing infinities. I have already referred to "I" as the Omega Transfinity. And the Creation, which is to say, the newly minted Cosmos, would therefore be the next lower order, the Penultimate Transfinity: the entirety of all Real logoi (the Biblical Light) and all rejected logoi (the Biblical Dark).

The lowest order Infinity is known as Aleph Null. This is the ordinary Infinity such as "all even numbers" or "all possible butterflies". It refers to something very specific, because it is the order of infinity right next door to the finite entities of the finite material world.

The Incompleteness Theorem of Kurt Gödel

In the early 1930s, a then obscure German mathematician who was a friend of Einstein, Kurt Gödel, proved that no system (mathematical or otherwise), can within itself prove the validity of those axioms (assumptions) on which that same system is logically based. This proof was heartbreaking for many mathematicians, including one Bertrand Russell who was in the process of writing his *Principia Mathematica*. A corollary to that theorem states that there is a limit to the number of basic axioms that any system can incorporate, before additional axioms unavoidably begin to contradict the previous axioms that were the basis on which that system was originally founded.

This actually explains why the Primordial Chaos which, because it literally included *all* possibilities—even contradictory ones—could itself never be an Objective Something. Every possibility (every logoi) was canceled out from within by its own corresponding contradicting possibility. God as "I" couldn't include every possibility (every logoi) into its new Creation if that Creation was to be a self-consistent Whole, a Cosmos, instead of being self-contradicting Chaos. This is part of the reason why there had to be a separation of Light from the Dark in Genesis 1:3.

RELIGION REINTERPRETED

In surveying the "infinite waters" of Genesis 1:2, the "Spirit of God" was likely designating what each of these infinite logoi would represent, and subsequently cherry picking those logoi which together could be safely included into Its new Creation. But this internal "movement", resulted in two groups of mutually exclusive logoi: those part of the new Cosmos, and those antithetical to that Cosmos. This was the separation of the Light from the Dark.

Now, the Good Book says that the Light was called "day" and the Dark was called "night." You can take that literally if you wish, but it begs the question of what day and night mean when there's still no planet Earth, nor a Sun to provide light. This Cosmology assumes that the better interpretation of that Light would be "awake and aware", and for the Dark would be "asleep and unaware."

The necessarily rejected logoi (the Dark), would now be a negative, a deprivation, and a lack: another secondary level penultimate Transfinity of logoi, a secondary chaos in the sense of disorder, inherently opposed to Creation.

Note: Traditionally, poets have the ability to intuit the truth. Goethe has Mephistopheles say to Faust, speaking on behalf of all that was excluded: "I am a part of the part, that was once the whole." In *The Brothers Karamazov*, Dostoevsky describes a meeting between Ivan and the Devil, in which the Devil admits he is a trickster. He describes his exclusion from Heaven and his longing to be welcomed home by God, but how that return would unmake the Universe. There it is in a nut shell!

The critical significance of the number Three

The number three comes up in the context of Religions too often to be merely accidental or coincidental. Gurdjieff referred to the Law of Three as "one of the two most fundamental Laws of World-Creation and of World-Maintenance." I believe law is expressed in how Will operates within the Creation. The very act of creation was a result of a fictitious "self–trifurcation", a splitting into three components of that single and Singular Primordial Will which is "I". The three parts, of course, are the selected logoi of order, the contradictory logoi of disorder, and God Itself. I call the tri-furcation fictitious because God, whether as "I" or as "I AM", ever remains One, containing all.

It might help to understand the fictitious part if you think of Creation as divine theatre, with fictitious roles assigned, and a writer-director who likes his actors to improvise.

<u>The three (fictitious) components of Will.</u>

This Law of Three can be called the Law of "We Two Oppose, yet We Three Cooperate." This means that the first two "components" of Will oppose each other to make a polarity, a contrast, a contest, an opposition or even an impasse. It takes a third component for there to be a resolution, a Reconciliation. A contest or polarity is like a tug of war: it's implicitly linear. Whatever resolves this opposition must be outside of that linear contest, something intrinsically independent of both opposing parties which transforms the linear contest into a two-dimensional triangle. Sometimes that extra dimension is hard to discern, in the same way that a square will look like a line if you only see it edge on. A tug of war may be won by one side because they trained harder or smarter, and that extra effort is the third thing. Or the winning side may have had an advantage of ground or even of wind.

Every aspect of creation, therefore, takes <u>three specific, different</u> and most importantly, <u>independent</u> components to compose something. Traditionally, the symbol for the triad is a triangle represented by the number 3; however, I believe that a more fitting number than the number 3 would be the transcendental number PI: 3.141592654.... The reason for this belief is simply that any whole is invariably greater than the sum of its parts. Hence, the Law of Three is also symbolized by the circle as the symbol of completeness, of Wholeness, and even of Holiness. It's the symbol of the Creation itself.

As for the names of these three "fictional" components of Will, I most prefer the titles and the corresponding numbers given them by Gurdjieff:

1st) the Holy Affirming
2nd) the Holy Denying
3rd) the Holy Reconciling

Other names would do nearly as well, as for example:
Positive / Negative / Neutral
Acting / Reacting/ Responding
Thesis / Antithesis / Synthesis

Affirmation can be thought of as the push that triggers or kick-starts something, whereas the Denial is the push-back which opposes the initial push. Here is Isaac Newton's Law that every action must have an immediate, opposite and equal reaction. These polarities and oppositions have no intrinsic resolution. Something from the outside must intervene, if that contest is to be resolved into something beyond a meaningless impasse. (Think of all those arguments about politics that go nowhere.)

The Reconciling component is usually the least obvious of the three. To give one simple example, for many years I was able to see that the act of walking involved the pushing with one's feet

(Affirming), against the push-back friction of the ground (Denying). And by the way, the above is a great example of why the Holy Denying is every bit as important as is the Holy Affirming. You only need to try to walk on ice to understand this. Driving on ice is an even more emphatic (if riskier) example.

However, the question of what constituted the necessary third, Reconciling component long remained a mystery for me. Finally, I suddenly and unexpectedly realized that one can't walk buried in sand, and is only barely possible to walk in water that's up to one's neck. In other words, the Reconciliation of the action vs. reaction of walking, was simply that it was possible! The Holy Reconciling component was to be found both in my body's ability to balance and in the medium in which this transaction of walking could take place. The interesting thing here is to realize that the Reconciling component comes both from within and from without.

The Meeting Place

The catalysts of chemistry and the enzymes of biochemistry are the most obvious examples of the Law of Three for someone trained in the sciences. Catalysts and enzymes make things happen, that either wouldn't happen at all or would otherwise take a much, much longer time. Another way of visualizing the Reconciling component is what I call the Meeting Place. For example, think of the different possible types of meeting places available to people of the opposite sex, and the different types of liaisons that different types of meeting place can catalyze.

In a case like this, the first of the two components would be the Affirmation of a wish to connect with another person. In opposition to that would be the Denial component, such as fear of strangers (and fear of their motives), as well as concerns over the suitability of a liaison based on differences in education, money, race, religion, etc. It's because of Denial that simply walking up to a stranger on the street and introducing yourself out of the blue almost never works.

Some short term liaisons are catalyzed by money, aka prostitution. The bar scene is usually not much better; it can occasionally result in some something positive, but it takes the additional catalyst of patience, where two people are willing to take their time and talk extensively. The work-place can also be a positive catalyst, but there's usually much to lose if a liaison should fail.

Much better are the meeting places based on common interests and hobbies. Here the mutual interest (bird-watching, parachuting, church, etc.) is the Reconciling component, providing an alternate focus for the attention of both parties.

The very best connections of all are often mediated by a trusted, mutual acquaintance. Trust reduces the degree of opposition, reduces the intensity of Denial between the two parties, very much like catalysts and enzymes reduce the resistance to interaction in a chemical transaction.

Also of note, chemical catalysts and enzymes typically cycle through a series of transformations, only to return to their original configuration, which usually allows them to continue to catalyze further reactions. Something very similar can be seen in meeting places and in shared interests. Bars are cleaned and readied for the next night. Board games like chess, checkers, Monopoly, etc, are put back in their boxes until the next Game Night.

The Reconciling component of Will can reduce the tension of opposition between Affirmation and Denial, however and importantly, it doesn't completely eliminate it. Instead, that remaining "tension" is somehow locked up as part of the final product. This is an important notion, because the Reconciling component for the

Primordial Creation, for that original Cosmos which is Absolute Reality, has its own name. It is known as "Impartial Divine Love", and it's this which remembers all Reality is One, a Whole, a <u>Singularity</u> in fact! Here is also one of the places where Religion and Science agree. Every religion I've encountered emphasized the transformative power of God's love, and most of us experience this love through a sense that God sees us, always, and always cares. In science, this very phenomenon is called The Observer Effect: the observer affects what is under observation. We can see this effect in nearly all our relationships. One very clear example: a teacher's positive regard can inspire students, whereas negative expectations usually discourage students, unless their own self-regard is stronger, or someone else sees them in a good light.

It should already be possible to foresee in this Law the reason and purpose behind the appearance of that ultimate of anomalies: Man. It is by reason of our appointed task of playing the Holy Reconciliation that only Man (Human or otherwise), among all created Beings and things was intentionally given a potentially independent Will.

Horizontal versus Vertical Triads.

What I call a level or horizontal triad is one where all three components have the same force and status. An example of such would be a relationship between two or more people (friends, coworkers, spouses) based on mutuality, not on dominance or possession. Mutuality means that the Will of both parties is always equally respected. Even though one partner will usually know something more about a particular subject than the other, mutuality remains the center of gravity of their relationship, the Reconciling component between them. Especially since the other partner is sure to know more about some other subject! The individuals are equal partners, even when temporarily allowing the appropriate one to lead according to circumstances.

<u>Addendum</u>: Obviously, children cannot always be allowed a say in every decision. However, even in cases of urgency, it's still very important that they understand that they are not simply being overridden, that they will be listened to as soon as that proves feasible. They also have a right to expect that some attempt will be made to explain things to them as time allows. A healthy independence in Will must always be nurtured in children for their future well-being.

Then there are vertical triads, with an intrinsic ranking between the three components, which in to say, a hierarchy. Vertical triads have a tendency to shift, as the "power" seems to flow from one component to another. To take a ready example: I may think that my will power— this is not the same thing as Will—is the Affirming component and the top dog when I resolve to lose some weight. I plan a regime of sensible eating and exercise. The Denying component consists of my habits, and I expect them to submit and cooperate. I plan that the Reconciling component will be my daily check-in with supportive friends. And for a few days it goes very well. My will power is strong. I exercise, I eat carefully. But then there is a party, and I am invited. Now the Reconciling component is very different from my circle of supportive friends. (It's a different meeting place.) Here are all my favorite drinks, lots of tasty foods, and a birthday cake. Suddenly, the Denying component has all the force of an uprising, and the formerly submissive habits stage a coup.

A correct example of a vertical triad is a master instructor, the students, and the discipline being imparted.

Of far greater importance than periodic (weekly) episodes of publicly "praising" God (something that the Creator of this unimaginably stupendous Universe doesn't really need from us), is Religion's genuine purpose, which is to lead each of us to discovering and understanding our status as one of God's Sonship. Speaking directly, we were created to play the role of the Prodigal Son. We were created to play the role of the independent Holy Reconciling between the Affirmation of the Biblical Light, and the Denial of the Biblical Dark. *God sent His Only Son (Man) to Save the World* (aka the entire Creation). This is why understanding this Law of Triads is so important.

Gender and the Triad.

This subject calls for a bit of caution, because words can be so easily misunderstood and misrepresented. It's for this very reason that I prefer to use the terms Holy Affirming and Holy Denying/Holy Receiving rather than "Active" and "Passive", because the word "Holy" underscores the fact that both components are equally good, equally necessary, and equally Holy, instead of implying that the second component is wrong or sinful because it counters the first. This is critically important when applied to male and female Human Beings.

Each and every Man is properly a Horizontal Triad in the sense that both the masculine (Affirming) and the feminine (Denying) sides of Man are equally necessary to the wholeness of every individual, regardless of the gender of their Human animal body. Beyond that, both genders (and their input) are equally necessary to a healthy society, whether that be a society of two, or a society of many. One need merely look at our world over the last few millennia to see how forgetting this truth (with the resulting male dominance) has been such a disaster for Humanity. It's important to remember that dominance by any component turns a level or horizontal triad into a hierarchical one.

And yet, every Man is properly a Vertical Triad. The Idea (the Spirit) of Man, ADAM, is the single Affirming component for each and every Man. Our differentiation and individuality as Human Beings is below at the level of our individual True Soul, which is our Reconciling component. Below that is our Denying component. Some religious teachings say it is our bodies, our "flesh" which houses the Denying component, and we are supposed to resist and struggle against our fleshly desires. Alternatively, Carl Jung presented the idea that there is a collective Human unconscious, which includes collective memories, and some of these need redeeming or rethinking—in a word, Metanoia. It seems to me that each of us needs to see and name our respective Holy Denying. I do not think it is the same thing for every person. I also think it changes over time.

Unfortunately, our local branch of Mankind called Humanity is abnormal, because for Humanity as a whole, our functional Affirming component is that which should be our Denying one. Globally, we are led by what is "lowest" in ourselves, by the "worldly mind". For some, the dominating "worldly mind" consists of appetites, desires, and habits. For some of us, it is what we fear others will think of us, what they will do to us. For some, it is family expectations. Some of us are addicted to our emotions.

Hint: think The Seven Deadly Sins, then add fearfulness, gullibility, self-righteousness (which is a form of Pride)....

The reason we are inverted is because we are cut off from the higher portions and functions of ourselves, and this is a major problem. As a result, this entire experiment of Man on this planet is in doubt. Man's ultimate reason for having been created was to function as the Independent Holy Reconciliation between the inner Affirmation that is God as "I AM", and the Denial that is the Illusion of Discontinuity (the Biblical Dark). This places Man's status in the Hierarchy of Existence, in between God as "I AM", and this lower, "sub-luminous" half of Existence known in the Lord's Prayer as "earth." What this means is that both male and female are equally the "Holy Feminine": passive or receptive when inwardly facing God; and both are equally "Holy Masculine": active when confronting this world over which we've been given stewardship. Being male or female has nothing to do with what is properly (and essentially) our spirit within. It only marginally has anything to do with our True Soul. This understanding will be important when we attempt to correct certain long held mistaken interpretations of Genesis.

<u>Aside</u>: The term "psychology" literally means, the "study of the soul". This book takes this meaning literally. However, contemporary Psychology is more the study of neurological hardware (brain circuitry), and of its behavioral software (our programming by our culture, by our society, and by our personal history). The author agrees with Dr. Maurice Nicoll who once said *"The true psychology of an acorn must start with the fact that its proper destiny is to become an oak tree."*

Traditionally, and by reason of his physique, the Human male is primarily tasked with confronting the outer world. In so doing, the male is literally looking at the external world from the same direction as does "I AM", which is to say, looking outwards and downwards as would the Holy Affirming. This is the basis for the male's tendency to look at everything as a tool and instrument, and to even give them feminine names and assign them feminine pronouns. But this is only the Human male's role in Existence, and not the Human male's essential role of facing inwards towards "I AM". In contrast, the traditional female role is care of the home. The deeper meaning of this is that the Human female, both existentially and essentially, looks inward towards "I AM". This is why the female tends to see everything as being alive, and therefore as worthy of care and preservation, unlike the male whose overt role in Existence is contrary to his essential inner role. But the Human female must also be able to deal with the outside world as needed, because she too is Man. And finally, no Human Being is completely on one side or the other of the male-female spectrum, and both aspects are absolutely necessary for being a whole Human Being.

Note: This existential male/female duality is the point to the myth of Theseus and Ariadne confronting the Minotaur, where Theseus defeated the monster, and Ariadne held the thread to lead them both back out of the Labyrinth. Both together represent our Human Soul.

The female's role is the more fundamental and important of the two, because "I AM" alone is absolutely Real, whereas Existence and everything therein is only relatively or conditionally real. "I AM" alone is the ultimate and absolute Holy Affirming. Man (both female and male) can only ever be the Holy Feminine (Denying) before God, which literally means we must be "open" to God. This explains the alternative name for Holy Denying, which is "Holy Receiving".

Before God, we can only be the instrument and the recipient. This truth is explicit in genuine Islam, for the religion's very name for itself means "submission". (*Islam* comes from the Arabic word *salaam*, which is equivalent to the Hebrew *shalom*, and means peace, acceptance, and submission. SLM is the Semitic tri-consonant core of all three words.)

A special caution.

The fact that this second component of Will bears the name Denying and is associated with the Sacred Feminine must *never* be a justification to label the female portion of mankind as inherently wrong (evil), or as being secondary or inferior.

Remember this the next time you drive too fast on a slippery road and then have to stop suddenly. The critical importance of the (feminine) Denial, as spoken by the now absent friction of the road surface, will become "screamingly" obvious to you. You absolutely need the "No" just as much as the "Yes", if you are to achieve anything at all.

To identify Denial with the Sacred Feminine, really means that more often than not, the female will preserve the sanity that males so easily lose about what is most important, and about what must be conserved, nurtured, and protected. The Sacred Feminine is actually that "No", that voluntary, self-imposed limitation by "I", that gave us this Creation in the first place. This is why the words *mother* and *matter* have a common etymological origin.

Another useful image for the critical necessity of the sacred Feminine (the Holy Denying), would be that of an automobile engine's flywheel. It's the very nature of the inertial flywheel that makes it possible for the erratic (male) explosions in the piston chambers to be translated into useful work. One without the other (acceleration without being reconciled with inertia), renders the whole affair impotent and useless.

At that critical moment when the Soul of all Mankind descended to the border of this concrete material world, it had to split into the two genders because of the necessity of becoming embodied (as the newly incarnated Adam & Eve; Genesis 3:21) in forms that could procreate. When this came to pass, the male part didn't walk away with all of the Affirmation, nor was the female part left with all of the Denial. The respective proportions were just about 50-50 for the two genders.

<u>Addendum</u>: Paradoxically, one thing that the necessary balance between the two genders means is that "nagging" is actually what a female is properly supposed to do, *as long as it's done consciously, and not simply out of a habit of being negative*. And those males who are at least partially aware will usually recognize this, even if they only rarely welcome it. Such relatively awakened males will usually understand that a female's so-called "nagging" is a necessary impetus when they have become too comfortable in their own inertia. Women should and must take over this role of Affirmation, when men have abandoned it.

For myself, personally, it was a girlfriend's "nagging" which finally forced me to follow through with a dream to get into Medical School, even though I didn't really believe it to be possible.

As gender roles become more fluid, it falls to each of us to recognize when someone else is "nagging" us for our own good.

Returning Back To God is ultimately the task of stripping away each layer of Self in succession until nothing other than that Pearl of Great Price you bear deep within remains as WHO you are. And for certainty of clarity, all of what you are, from Human animal body to ADAM, derives from and belongs to Existence: "dust to dust". Only that which is WHO you are as God's One Son, and not "what" you are as an individual, as an existing creature, was ever meant to Return Back to God. This is also how we Reconcile the contest between Reality and Illusion, between the Biblical Light and the Biblical Dark, and thereby save the World (the Creation) as we were created and sent to do.

CHAPTER III:

GOD'S TRUE NAME

"God" as title; etymologies of god; singular and plural; God as "I AM"; an image

<u>The term "God" is really a title</u>

The names we typically use for everything are actually designations. They are verbal signs which we have collectively agreed to use to refer to / to point to the many things, both concrete and abstract, that we encounter in this world or within our minds. However, these "names" usually say nothing intrinsic about what that which they point to, actually is. For example, English speakers use the verbal expression "water". "Wasser", pronounced "vasser", is the German equivalent. Spanish speakers say "agua"; French speakers say "eau" (pronounced "oh"); and Japanese speakers say "mizu" (the final 'u' being an unaccented vowel sound very much like the 'e' in "Apple"). All of these words are but designations for what is scientifically designated H2O, the name that actually best describes what is being referred to.

I do in fact believe there to be a true name for God, one which, much like H2O, does describe what it *refers* to. And I'm just crazy enough to believe I know what that name is. You too can easily see it; it's actually also your own true name, because both are one and the same, as we will eventually see. But for the time being...

Etymologies.

The English word *God* is itself derived from an older Germanic word. I've seen the reconstruction "ghutom", which supposedly meant something like "the invoked one", or, "the Supreme Being which we call upon". (C.S. Lewis may have known this when he wrote *The Pilgrim's Regress* and addressed a heartfelt prayer to "Not to that which I think Thou art, but to that which Thou knowest Thyself to be".)

b) The Latin "Deus" (the source of our words *divinity* and *deity*) holds a very interesting promise. This is because it ultimately derives from an ancient Indo-European word reconstructed to an approximate form something like "diwos", which had the basic meaning of "to shine." "Diwos" has many derivative in its daughter languages such as:

The Sanskrit titles "Deva" and "Dyaus" ("Dyaus" being the very same name as the two well-known following names of both the Greek and Roman supreme god).

The Greek "Zeus." There is also the Greek word "Theos" (as in the English word "Theology", which also comes from "diwos".

The Latin equivalent is the "Ju-" of "Ju-piter" (literally, "Ju-Father" or "Father Zeus"). There are also the derivative English words "Jove" and "jovial."

In addition, there's the feminine name "Diana" who was the Roman Goddess of the moon. This name was also derived from "diwos".

All of these titles for God are cognate descendants from the single Indo-European word "diwos", and they all originally meant "the god that shines in the sky." This connection between light and "higher beings" has further implications because of something very important in this Cosmology, something referred to as the Light Boundary.

The Slavic and Indo-Iranian languages form the Eastern branches of Indo-European languages, and they have a title in common for God. In the Slavic languages, it's "Bog"; in Bulgarian "the Bogomils" means the "Lovers of God". The Indo-Iranian Sanskrit equivalent was "Bhaga", as in the *Bhagavad Gita*, the "Song of God." And I believe the Iranian (Persian) equivalent is "Baga". As best I can tell, all of these words originally had a meaning akin to that of the English title "Lord".

Originally, in Old English, the expression that eventually became our Modern English title "Lord", was the compound word "Hlaf-Weard", which literally translated meant "Loaf-Warden." Its more Modern English translation would be the "Guardian of the Bread." In other words, a "Lord", or a "Bog / Bhaga" originally meant "the one who possessed, guarded, and distributed the wealth", the "bread" in both its literal and present day slang meanings.

An older name for God was "Zurvan", a Persian name which meant both "the Void", and "Infinite Time".

The Kurdish title for the Primordial Universal Spirit, "Xwede", meant "He who created Himself."

g) I have no insight into what might be the deeper meaning behind the standard Semitic expression for God, "Aleph-Lammed", (Hebrew, and AL or EL by spelling). However, what is very significant is that the first letter "Aleph", and the Arabic equivalent "Alif", are in fact intrinsically silent, unlike the corresponding Greek derivative, "Alpha". (Aleph was sometimes but not always assigned vowel sounds, but also often stood for nothing more than a glottal stop, if even that.) A silence to indicate God? That is wisdom, subtle and profound.

In the first Chapter of Genesis, the Hebrew word for God is *Elohim*. This word features the initial "Aleph-Lammed" This "AL" is also found in the Arabic name for God, *Allah*. Allah does not refer to some "different" or specifically "Islamic" God, but to the very same God that both Jews and Christians pray to.

The Hebrew "Elohim" is striking for a very important reason. First, the final "-im" demonstrates that *Elohim* is in fact a **plural** word, not singular. That it is used with a verb in the third person **singular** means that the Elohim **acts as one**. I have been told that, according to ancient understanding, Elohim's plurality represents "God Our Father and God Our Mother". Subsequent emphasis on a purely (merely) masculine nature for God and a singular, masculine pronoun are inaccurate translations. (The writer T.H White knew the truth of this and used the pronoun "They" for God in his book for children, *The Sword in the Stone*.)

In contrast to Elohim, the name used for God in the second Chapter of Genesis, YHWH, (here spelled left to right for English readers), refers to something very different. What this must actually mean is that two very different entities are being referred to, in spite of the monotheistic protests this assertion will likely raise. But this explains why it was a shocking thing to announce, in Deuteronomy, "Hear, Oh Israel, the Lord thy God, the Lord is One!" This was an attempt to convey a paradoxical quality of God.

<u>My own preferred name for God</u>

Explaining this will not be as straightforward as it might seem it should be. We Westerners are used to thinking only in terms of one single God. But I've found that I've had to make distinctions among differing manifestations of that Singular Deity for the sake of clarity. And I'm not the first to do so. I believe it was William Tyndale (died October 6, 1536), the English reformer who was the first to translate the Bible into English directly from the original Hebrew Bible (Old Testament), and from the original Greek (New Testament). He encountered a similar problem confronting the implication of two different gods in the first two chapters of Genesis, something formal Theology still refuses to acknowledge as meaning what it actually does.

Names are very important in the Torah, the first five books of the so-called Old Testament, and they must be taken seriously by anyone who really wishes to understand what the Bible is telling us. One cannot simply disregard the fact that *Elohim* is a plural form of *Aleph-Lammed* (AL or EL). Tyndall certainly knew this. But it's also likely that Tyndall had concerns about how persons wedded to a monotheistic interpretation would react to a literal translation. Given that heretics were still being burned alive, and monotheism was the prevalent interpretation of the Bible, he had reason to be concerned.

RELIGION REINTERPRETED

Some theologians have postulated that two entirely distinct traditions, an "Elohimic" one for Genesis Chapter One, and a "Yahwehan" one for Genesis Chapter Two, were juxta-positioned (placed next to each other). Unfortunately, most people refuse to notice that you literally cannot align the timelines of Creation between the first two chapters of Genesis in a manner that makes any sense.

Tyndall resolved this seeming discrepancy as follows. For the Elohim of Chapter One, he used the simple term "God." And then, for the YHWH of Chapters Two and Three, he used the term "Lord", or the expression "Lord God." And when the King James translators of the Bible made wholesale use of the Tyndall version, they simply followed his example, and no one was the wiser. But once again, I believe that it's not that difficult to resolve this paradox in a manner which reconciles the seeming discrepancy. This corrected interpretation was given when we discussed ADAM in the Introduction.

I've made a distinction between God before the primary creation, and God after that primary creation. And just why would this be necessary? Well, I believe there was a critical adjustment, really a "Great Sacrifice" which God as Absolute Will chose to make, an adjustment that resulted in a change in Its own name.

It was for this reason that I initially chose for God as Primordial Will a name used by Carlos Castaneda: "INTENT". I personally love this name, but eventually (and reluctantly), I came to understand that this would be far too abstract for most people. By the time the year of 2012 rolled around, I decided to replace this with the only name which I believe the Primordial Chaos could have for Itself. And just what might that name be? Well, I am certain that God's true name for itself can only be "I", pure and simple.

The fundamental equation is that "I" = Absolute Will = God as the Primordial Chaos. The transition from God as "I", to God as "I AM" (YHWH) is the adjustment (Great Sacrifice) referred to above. This transition, along with its corresponding moderation of name, was a response made to mitigate the major problem that arose as a consequence of Creation. However, I will say here that the "I" of both manifestations are one the same, just to make clear that we are not speaking about two different gods.

But there is in fact one other entity that has possession of this name "I" as part of its own name. That entity is ADAM, and by extension, every one of ADAM's embodied manifestations: Man. This too will be elaborated on elsewhere. For now, please try to understand that the privilege of having been given this name "I" as our own, is very much the *single most important thing* that must be understood about Man, about each and every one of us. It's the very reason for our creation, and the reason for our task within Existence as *God's One True (if Prodigal) Son*.

For the moment, to encapsulate the above:

God as "I" = the Primordial Chaos = Absolute Will

God as "I AM" = Will plus BEING

Elohim = the council of Seraphim appointed to be the Overseers of Existence. It may be that *Elohim* corresponds to the East Asian concept of Yin and Yang; to the Hindu gods, three pairs of male and female deities: Brahma and Saraswati, Shiva and Parvati, and Vishnu and Lakshimi; and to the 12 Greek Titans, who also came in pairs (syzygies) of male and female.

<u>A few last things to be said about God as "I".</u>

"I" is the "Active Side of Infinity", a great expression borrowed from Carlos Castaneda. There can be no intrinsic limits, restrictions, or boundaries of any sort that bind "I", other than such which are *entirely self-chosen and self-imposed by "I" Itself.*

"I" is the Unique Subjective, which can only know, and never be known. This is to say that "I" can never be used in the accusative case, because beyond any notions of grammar, "I" can never be the direct or indirect object of any outside action.

Grammatically, the Indo-European captures in form this stark distinction between the first person singular Nominative pronoun "I", and the first person singular Accusative pronoun "me". This has to have been a stroke of genius. Not all language families make this distinction. But there's a world of difference between "I" and "me".

The human "I", <u>when we speak from the true center of ourselves</u>, is the very same "I" that is God.

Paradoxically, this "I" we each bear, is only ever truly Itself when it is spoken in complete alignment with Itself as "I AM" (YHWH). "I" can never be genuinely in opposition to Itself. Such a "worsted" (twisted) Will has a different name: "ego." For any of us to speak this name which we are privileged to share with God as "I AM", from that which is trivial, shallow, or partial, or from whatever is negative, hateful, and false, is in fact what it genuinely means to use God's name in vain (in emptiness).

<u>An image</u>

The question of whether someone (king or prophet), is a man or a god has been around for a long time, and has always been very dicey. The men who declare themselves gods on earth usually cause a lot of trouble and death.

We already have enough people running around mistaking themselves for a god, from tyrants to madmen. So here is an antidote. This image is offered as something to focus on, the better to understand our connection to the Divine, and our relationship to each other. The image is that of a wagon wheel.

This wheel's outermost rim is our outermost being, because it's the part that touches the ground. It includes both our human animal bodies and our legitimate worldly minds, which are the basis for our socially acquired sense of self, our Personality.

The inmost rim holds the axle. This inner rim is ADAM, our universally shared spirit, created for a specific purpose.

The intermediate spokes represent our souls, our distinctiveness as individuals. Nearest the center, they are nearly touching; as they extend outwards towards the rim they diverge.

The egoism of the outer rim is forever attempting to pass itself off as our inner center, but don't let it, and this happens every time you say "I am this" or "I am that." Freedom starts when you begin to keep separate WHO you are from the *what* you are.

This entire Wheel represents your created Being, all of what you are. The most important part of this image is that central-most hole, the emptiness or Zero where the axle would go. This is the seat of your Will.

The space at the very center of the wheel is empty, because only nothingness is large enough to include the infinity that is God. (This corresponds to the design of the Ark of the Covenant.) Be sure to leave that Zero empty in your thoughts, because no man is a god, not even Jesus of Nazareth. This confusion about Jesus resulted from him having sold all that He had in His purse, all that He was. That meant that there was nothing left other than that central emptiness, that central Zero. That was more than enough for him to seem god-like to others. The possibility of our becoming like Jesus "and more so"— His own words, not mine!— rests in remembering our wholeness, and the emptiness at our centre.

CHAPTER IV

COST AND SACRIFICE

The passive side of infinity; sum of all logoi; fundamental math of creation; creation of reality; Atonement; the great triad; the semblance of separation and enmity; Second Great Sacrifice; Will plus BEING; ADAM, the only Son

The "Passive Side of Infinity"

The title given to Primordial Will by Castaneda's teacher, Don Juan, was "The Active Side of Infinity." Well, the "Passive Side of Infinity" correspondingly seems to be a good name for the Creation. The new Creation was the passive yet objective result of the act of intention by the Primordial Will that is God as "I". Because "I" is an entirely *self*-directed Cause which is *not* the effect of some prior Cause, we can do little more than speculate as to why this project of creating Objective Reality was ever undertaken.

However, one thing that we can know for certain is that bringing the Creation forth was not accomplished for free. This may be a surprising concept, and yet, the Orthodox Christian Church is quite explicit in acknowledging this, stating: *"The Whole of Creation rests on a Sacrifice made by God."*

HALE MICHAEL SMITH, M.D.

<u>The Creation as the sum of all of God's Thoughts (Logoi)</u>
The Course of Miracles has something relevant to say about the Creation. It's one of the more eloquent statements I've ever read on the subject, and it presented itself to me one evening when I simply allowed the book to fall open where it would. Strangely, I had read the entire text of that book at least three times, yet I had no memory of ever having read this short paragraph. So much for being awake to what I've read. But to quote:

> *Creation is the sum of all God's Thoughts, in number infinite, and everywhere without limit. Only Love creates, and only like itself. There is no time when all that it created was not there. Nor will there be a time when anything that it created suffers any loss. Forever and ever are God's Thoughts exactly as they were and exactly as they are, unchanged through time and after time is done.*

One critically important point being made in this statement is that Reality is permanent! This also means that whatever is genuinely Real, is always conserved! Conversely, whatever is perishable and subject to loss could never have been Real in the first place, except in seeming. The implications of this on Religion are far-reaching, and help to answer many religious questions that presently seem to be unanswerable for many of us. The saints (of any and every religion) understand this, which is how they can be fearless and loving even in the most adverse situations, even in death.

It's here that the Holy Reconciling can be seen by its other name: "*Impartial Divine Love.*" Everything genuinely Real (as seen by the Creator), is always connected to everything else Real, regardless of appearances within Existence. Another way to say this is that the Primordial Singularity even now remains intact, something that Jesus tried many times to tell us (Matthew 3:2; and Mark 1:15).

What this also means is that Existence at its best, is only partly or relatively Real. If Reality remains as an inviolate One, then Existence can only be a compromised Reality. I cannot at this point even begin to explain how important this is to understanding Religion. But it does explain the real meaning of the word *Atonement*: "At—One—ment."

Atonement is actually the counter-current to Creation's diversity of Existence, a movement into increasing differentiation and dispersion (like the spokes of a wheel which spread away from each other as they leave the hub). *Atonement* would be the corresponding inbound process of focus, of concentration; becoming again One with God, One with each other, and one with the entire Creation. In other words, *Atonement* echoes the meaning of the word *Religion* itself.

Aside: A useful image here would be to insert all five of your fingers into a bowl of water, but only up to the first or second knuckle. Then, imagine you are a microbe whose entire world consists of the two-dimensional surface of that water (without an above or below). How likely is it that you would ever recognize that those five circles of flesh, made by your fingers as they intersect the surface of that water, are in fact intrinsically connected and share one life? This is precisely why the Prophet from Nazareth insisted that we *be charitable to* (love) everyone, including those we believe to be enemies.

So why is there even the semblance of enmity? Why is there the appearance of separation, of "otherness"? Precisely because "I" could never be in contrast to itself without bringing forth an "other" which was yet part of Itself. Creation came at the price of separating out part of the original logoi (the Biblical Dark) from the new Creation (the Biblical Light). Hence the Incompleteness Theorem of Kurt Gödel.

Thus, the act of Creation actually boiled down to elementary arithmetic:

$$0 = (+1) + (-1)$$

Zero (ALL) equals Creation (the Biblical Light) AND what is excluded from Creation as antithetical (the Biblical Dark)

Conversely,

$$0 - (+1) = (-1)$$

Creation (+1) was subtracted from the Primordial Chaos (Zero), leaving behind a remainder (—1): a residual and opposite negation.

This composed a Triad, where the Light constituted the Holy Affirming, and the Dark constituted the Holy Denying, and the Will that is God as "I" played the role of the Holy Reconciling. However, this situation was unstable, because the new Creation needed to be able to stand on its own and persist without the danger of remerging with its "Inverse Twin", the Dark. This made the second "Great Sacrifice" necessary.

A Reminder: It's important to remember before proceeding that Will and the availability of options (logoi), stand together as One. There can be no meaningfully effective Will without the availability of choices. Likewise, the availability of choices (logoi) is meaningless without Will, without the ability to choose from among those options and act on them. The seeming distinction between Will and the options (logoi) it has available is but one of the many unavoidable artifacts of our type of perception. This is not a condemnation of our usual mode of perception so much as it is a reminder that we are not all-encompassing in our vision and understanding.

An image of the Creation which came to me a long while back is as follows: Imagine an infinite expanse of simple (neutral) gray twilight, essentially, the "waters" of Genesis 1:2. Next, imagine that all of the brightness of that twilight is gathered together into one place, thereby leaving everything and everywhere else as complete darkness. This was the true Creation. In Genesis, God is reported to have said, "Let there be Light!" In the Quran, God (Allah) is reported to have said, "'BE!' and it was!"

Next, this emerging collective of Light, the Holy Affirming of Creation, was reinforced by the gift of substantiality, of becoming something substantial courtesy of the Holy Denying (analogous to how matter can be defined as inertia). Those logoi of the Biblical Dark were not so endowed, and could therefore never manifest as Real but only remain as Illusions. These were now Chaos in its secondary sense as disorder and undoing.

<u>The Creation of Reality meant the Creation of everything that might ever be Real.</u>

That Singularity which was the locus of the Big Bang was the potential for everything which exists today, and in no way does this conflict with Genesis. The story of creation in six days is the story of how the potential unleashed by the Big Bang unfolded (evolved) stage by stage into this actual world of Time, Space, and Things (aka, sub-luminous Existence).

Seeing God's primary creation as that of everything that *could come to be*, removes any conflict between religion and science, creation and evolution. This flexibility is also far more consistent with life experiences, where there are usually more ways than one to arrive at a given goal.

Another way to picture this: This image just came to me, and it might just help. It's a picture analogy. Remember that logoi are the thoughts of God, those possibilities available to the Will that is God. After the separation of the Light from the Dark, they now came in two primary flavors: those which were Real, and those which weren't. We now change the word logoi into that of letters, like our English letters A, B, C.... With this, the real Creation was the act of choosing an Alphabet of letters which would be Real from the total group of all possible shapes and sounds, and laws of possible (pronounceable) combinations. Just by this simple act, you've automatically created everything that can be spelled out, in any way that is possible. God didn't have to write out every possible word. All Darwin did was show how some of God's words morph over time (Grimm's Law), how some living being changes its appearance and function over time, and might even transform into a new living being with a new name.

5) The Second Great Sacrifice: Why God as "I", Chose to Become God as "I AM".

This issue is critically important, because it is the beginning of the explanation for why this world we know is not absolutely perfect. It also answers the question which will present itself to anyone familiar with Exodus 3:14-15: "If God *is* "I", then where did

God as "I AM" come from?" The claim has already been made that this modification of God's name "I" was in fact the result of an adjustment which "I" chose to make for the sake of the Creation. Furthermore, the claim has been explicitly made that in spite of this "adjustment", that the "I" (the Will) that *is* both God as "I" and God as "I AM" *is* One and the Same, and therefore both are still the same single God.

However, this adjustment led to a voluntary relinquishment (Sacrifice) of the full functional Absoluteness possessed *by* "I". And this points to something of incredibly serious import about this transition of God as "I" to God as "I AM", from the "Primordial Godhead" to the subsequent Lord over the created world (the Demiurge).

Creation essentially meant a "*self*-bifurcation" (a self splitting into two) by the Primordial Chaos, by that Omega Transfinity of logoi which in its entirety constituted God as "I". This act of creation meant that there were now two opposite and incompatible groups of logoi, only one of which could be designated as Real (the Light). This Light consisted of all logoi which together could support a Singular Self-coherent Whole (a Cosmos), whereas the Dark consisted of all logoi, all potential which were intrinsically incompatible with this new Reality. And this created a novel problem for "I", because the second group of incompatible logoi (the Biblical Dark of Genesis 1:3), was still "half" of *Itself* as "I". The consequence of this was that there were now two dangers. The first of these, as mentioned above, was that these two newly separated groups of logoi might merge back together, thereby reconstituting the original Primordial Chaos at the expense of the brand-new Creation. "I" would have to take protective measures if the new Creation were to be kept intact.

This is analogous to modern Physics, specifically concerning the spontaneous appearance of a particle out of a vacuum according to Heisenberg's Uncertainty Principle. The nature of the ensuing problem of keeping the newly formed particle without losing it to its negative counterpart is essentially the same.

But there was another danger inherent in this division of the Omega Transfinite logoi into two incompatible groups, because it meant a potential division in Will, in "I" *Itself*. In other words, there was the danger of "I" becoming divided against *Itself*, and this was the direct reason for this "Second Sacrifice", also called here the Great Sacrifice. In response to this danger, "I" had to have chosen to separate *Itself* from the second and rejected group of logoi in the only way It could, in order to avoid the risk of becoming a single (and Singular) Will in conflict with *Itself*. In essence, "I" would henceforth have to deny *Itself* of any and all access to those rejected logoi.

This voluntary withdrawal of all Will from the Dark, from the rejected "half" of *Itself* which could never be safely included into the new creation, meant that from now on, "I" *would have access only to those logoi that were part of its Creation*. And this is how God as "I", became God as "I AM" (Will plus BEING).

I know of no scriptural support for this theory, which doesn't mean they don't exist, merely that I haven't read as much as I would have liked. The only support I do have is Occam's Razor, because nothing else makes as much sense.

This is incredibly important to the story of creation, because it means that God as "I" voluntarily "hobbled" *Itself* so that an ordered Creation could manifest. At the same time, the other logoi could never be destroyed. The true Absoluteness of "I" remained intact, even while it's "effective" Absoluteness didn't, because of this voluntarily self-imposed abstinence. And as a result, "I AM" would now have to be strategic and indirect in Its methods and actions, acting through the accepted logoi. Which is to say, the Dark "half of *Itself*" logoi would have to be rendered impotent in some manner which worked around the Dark's fundamental invulnerability. How this was eventually accomplished is the ultimate reason for the intervention of that insulating boundary phenomenon that Genesis calls the Firmament, and which in this book is called Existence. And as is pointed out in Jewish commentaries, this Second Day of Creation is *not* blessed by God; it is the only day of the seven not so blessed. It is a *necessary* act, not a good one.

Later, it is the literal inspiration of Spirit, God's breath, that awakes ADAM out of a state of inert stupor (mere potential) into the awareness that ADAM was in fact alive as God's True One Son. In other words, Spirit, the medium for Will within the Creation, is the true animating agent for that former Pinocchio which became the living spirit of each and every one of us, the source of our Souls. As for the Biblical Dark, the withdrawal of that same Spirit by God as "I" had the opposite effect: it rendered anti-being soulless. To understand what this means, think of this: an earthquake or a fire that destroys your home aren't evil in themselves for one simple reason, they aren't acts of Will. Evil, as we sense and recognize it as a wrongness, is the alliance and involvement of Human Will with the intrinsic tendencies of anti-being which are counter to the Atonement. This essentially means that we Human Beings have only ourselves to blame for the genuine evils that haunt us here in this Flatland.

Along with anti-being's containment within Existence, there is the need for some additional and independent means of Reconciling this conflict between the Affirmation of the Light and the Denial of the Dark (between being and anti-being, between Singular Reality and Illusion of Discontinuity). This necessity was the reason for the creation of that single greatest anomaly within the whole of Existence: Man, who unlike everything else, was given to share that Free and Independent Will that was God Itself.

As Christian doctrine states, "God sent Its only Son (Man) to save the world" (the Creation).

CHAPTER V

BEING AND ITS ASPECTS
"Allah said, 'BE!'"; BEING as Sophia; etymological aside; a quote from Jean-Yves Leloup

"Allah said 'BE!', and it was!"

This command "BE!" is far more interesting than might appear at first sight. One can think of its result, the Creation Itself, as a standing wave, which is an oblique way of saying that the result of that command is simultaneously a Noun and a Verb. A standing wave is set up in some medium, inside of some chamber; that wave itself has a wavelength which is a whole-number division of that chamber's linear dimension. That wave will continuously reflect back and forth inside of that chamber without chaotically or destructively interfering with itself. Assuming one can see that wave (in dye-colored water, or in a vibrating guitar string), that wave will appear to be a sine wave which seems to be standing still (as if nothing is happening), even though it is actively reflecting back and forth.

Likewise, the new Creation was the result of God's command, and constantly being upheld and energized by the very same command, just as if the command were being given again and again from micro-moment to micro-moment. The new Creation was a definite something, yet that "something-ness" persisted only because it was being continuously upheld by the intention that is God as "I". This is why it's being calling a standing wave, instead of some static object. And if you think about it, this ambiguity of simultaneously being both noun and verb applies to practically every usage of *to be*. This implicit activity in being a standing-wave reflects the fact that the entire Creation is alive.

This new Creation, BEING (Absolute Reality), is the Singular Whole of <u>Reality</u> and of <u>Goodness</u>. Furthermore, it is also the Singular whole of <u>Awareness,</u> of <u>Intelligence,</u> and of <u>Life</u>. And finally, BEING is the locus of Infinite <u>Impartial Divine Love</u>.

Goodness means that nothing about Reality is intrinsically harmful or destructive to Itself.

Impartial Divine Love means that everything Real (as God defines that term), is bound to everything else Real, in spite of appearances within Existence.

<u>An important note</u>: This is what Jesus meant when He said that *"the Kingdom of God is at hand."* That statement had nothing whatsoever to do with future Time! Instead, it meant that God's Kingdom is always and forever Here&Now! Unfortunately, as we normally are, we lack any meaningful awareness or understanding of this. Our perceptions and experiences in time are transient, whereas Reality is eternally Now.

BEING is our Queen Sophia (Divine Wisdom); the Creation is the feminine half of Divinity, the "consort" of "I" from the very beginning. Because BEING is Absolute Reality, it's also the mother and source of everything Real within Existence. Wisdom is the firm Intelligent awareness of what is Real and True and Good, as well as what is Alive. BEING is therefore the ultimate *At-one-ment* (Singularity).

Etymological aside

As an undergraduate, I spent one semester attempting to learn Sanskrit. I failed the course, but I did come away with two discoveries that had a major impact on my understanding of this subject matter. In Sanskrit, the words for "Truth" and for "Goodness" are both derivatives of the Sanskrit word *as* which means "is".

Satya: The Sanskrit word for Truth. Something is genuinely True when and because it is genuinely Real.

Sattva: The Sanskrit word for Goodness. Something is genuinely Good when and because it is genuinely Real.

Most people who are likely to read this book will recognize this latter word as part of the word Bodhisattva. A Bodhisattva is a Buddhist saint who has voluntarily chosen to postpone entering into Nirvana. This voluntary postponement enables that particular saint to continue to work for the salvation (the full awakening) of all sentient Beings within Existence. Jesus of Nazareth fits this description as an Intermediate between ourselves as Humans and God as "I AM".

The word Sattva actually derives from the participle of the word *as* and is thereby equivalent to the English verbal participle, "being", as in the expression: "being a doctor, he felt obligated to help the injured man." The actual Sanskrit participle is *-sant*. It's more recognizable to speakers of English in its Latin equivalent *-sent*, (Latin, like Sanskrit, is an Indo-European language). This participle appears in numerous English words like es<u>sent</u>ial, es<u>sence</u>", pre<u>sent</u>, repre<u>sent</u>, and so on.

All of the above made me wonder whether English, itself an Indo-European language, might still have a word corresponding to Satya or Sattva. It took me twenty-five years to stumble across that word: sooth. Sooth means Truth, as in the word "Soothsayer", and it too derives from the word "is." As for the verb "to soothe", it probably originally meant to "put someone at ease by telling the truth", but eventually dropped the part about truth, finally coming to mean just "putting someone at ease." It's a good example of "meaning drift" in words.

A quote from Jean-Yves Leloup
This quote is a commentary found in Mr. Leloup's translation of and commentary on *The Gospel of Mary Magdalene*.

> *The Good is the manifestation of the famous Triad of the ancient philosophers: goodness, truth, and beauty. The Good in this sense does not have evil as its opposite, for it means the unity of these three, the One that embraces the multiplicity of all qualities through which it is expressed.*
>
> *What does goodness become when separated from light, consciousness, and truth? A softness that is the gateway to hypocrisy and compromise.*
>
> *What does truth become when separated from goodness, love, and beauty? A hardness that is the gateway to fanaticism and persecution.*
>
> *What does beauty become when separated from truth and goodness? Art for art's sake, an aestheticism that is the gateway to a brilliance which clarifies nothing.*
>
> *Beyond the Realm of opposites, the Good is the One, the doorway to Being. This Being can only manifest in a*

heart, body, and mind that have been emptied of all illusion and presumption; for it cannot fit into the straight jacket that they offer.

> *" This is why the Good has come into your midst*
> *It acts together with the elements of your nature*
> *So as to reunite it with its roots. "*

CHAPTER VI

EMERGENCE OF DIVINITY: GOD AS "I AM"
Aleph vs AlephBeyt; the persona of "I"; God as a Self; mass noun, common noun; Spirit

Aleph vs the AlephBeyt

Aleph is the first letter in the Hebrew alphabet (Alif in Arabic). This letter became Alpha when the Phoenicians passed the Semitic alphabet onto the Greeks. However, unlike in the Indo-European Greek, and later Latin, the Semitic letter Aleph / Alif was never permanently the sound of "Ah" as in "Father" or as in the Arabic "Allah." This is why it sounds like "E" in the word Elohim. The letter often remains silent, unpronounced. For this reason of being both first and silent (non-objective), Aleph is presented as another name for God as 'I' (as Primordial Will alone). The Creation was that of everything objective, and therefore of everything Real. However, the Great Sacrifice meant a joining of God as "I" to its Creation. God as "I" thereby became God as "I AM", now also known as AlephBeyt", (yes, our Alphabet). "Beyt" (or Bet, or Beth as in "Beth Israel", the house of Israel), means house, or container, and became the second letter 'B' of our Alphabet.

RELIGION REINTERPRETED

"I AM", the Persona of "I".

"I AM" is the *persona* of God as "I". This word *persona* comes from Latin. It was the name of the mask worn by actors in the Latin theater, and its etymology is straightforward. "Per-" means "through", and "-sona" means "sound." Hence, the per-sona was a mask because the sound of the actor's voice came through it. Understanding this has a meaningful bearing on the derived words "person (-hood)" and "personality".

A person is a self, the Reconciliation of WHO you are with what you are, with what you do. Therefore, while God as "I" is not a Self, God as "I AM" is. I understand that this distinction between two versions of the same God might seem confusing to most people, and also probably seems unnecessary to most. But without it, there's no chance of explaining why this existing world seems so imperfect. One need merely ask, "Why would a supposedly all-knowing and all-powerful God create such a seemingly flawed world as this one?" to see the point being made here. Blaming these flaws on sin and evil is no answer, because if you start out with nothing other than a single God, only that God can then be responsible for such imperfections, including those of evil, and of any such evil Beings that might be. And that's nonsense. Neither can Humanity's so-called sins transform God's Creation into a travesty, unless one believes Man has the power to veto God. None of that makes any sense, but there is an answer to these conundrums.

God as a Self

God as "I" was not (nor could be) a Self. God as "I" has no attributes whatsoever, not even such attributes as being Real or of existing, and is therefore something entirely unavailable to us. However, this is not the case for God as "I AM".

"I AM" is Absolute Will joined with Absolute BEING (with Absolute Reality). Understanding theses differences enables us to say something about the Gods of the major Religions. It promotes understanding (and civility and tolerance) to remember that these all indicate the same Singular Deity, just differently named, emphasizing various aspects, and not different Deities.

The most prominent "God as Self" to someone of the Judeo-Christian traditions, would be the Tetragrammaton, God as YHWH (called "Yahweh" or "Jehovah." But YHWH is actually a formula, not a title). This is the God who gave Its name "I AM" to Moses on Mount Horeb. This same God is called Brahma by Hindus, the great Creator Self of the Universe. Another name is the Zoroastrian God Ahura Mazda.

The name Allah, on the other hand, seems to place the emphasis on the "I" of God. Islam seems to focus far more on the ineffable and unimaginable transcendence of God, which of course is absolutely true. Perhaps one way to understand the difference would be to remember that God as "I" created Reality (the Allah who said "BE!", and It was!), whereas it is God as "I AM" Who protects that Reality with the interposition of Existence (the Biblical "Firmament"). The latter version, while still the same God, yet seems to be somewhat closer and more familiar, that's all.

"I AM" is Spirit

Absolute Will ("I") needs no medium to function. Thus, "I" was able to act freely by intention alone, to create Reality. However, within the Creation itself, Spirit is the medium for Will. This is simply another way of saying that Will only acts through what is Real, because Spirit is nothing other than "I AM", pure and simple. However, this notion can lead to confusion, because we are used to thinking in terms of individual "spirits." There is a Universe of difference between "Spirit", and being "a spirit."

The difference between a mass noun and a count noun

Spirit is universal because it has no limits. In the statement "water is wet", *water* is a mass noun because all water everywhere (that isn't frozen) is wet. However, one must often speak of a specific quantity, parcel, or portion of a mass noun. In such a case, one must then resort to using an appropriate quantifier, as in such expressions as "a glass of water", "a gallon of milk", "a truck load of dirt", or "a moment of time". We also use verbs in their singular form for mass nouns, as when we say water (rice, mud, air) *is*, and not *are*.

Occasionally, mass nouns are turned into count nouns to emphasize categories, or differences in space and time: "the waters of the Nile", "the Seven Seas".

In contrast to mass nouns, there are the count nouns. These are individualized objects. These include most everyday items such as bricks, stars, bugs, dreams, and words. Unlike the mass nouns, count nouns have genuine plurals. If you are ever in doubt of the difference between the two types of nouns, simply think of "beans and rice." Beans are count nouns whereas rice, for whatever arbitrary reason, is treated as a mass noun, even though rice consists of many individual grains. (Grass is usually another mass noun. We "cut the grass" when we mow the lawn.)

So now it's considerably easier to explain the difference between Spirit and being "a spirit." Spirit is a mass noun because it has no form, no boundary, no limits. The only Spirit is God as "I AM". In contrast, "a spirit" is a denizen of Existence with a sense of self.

CHAPTER VII

ZOROASTRIAN ROOTS

Zoroastrianism, the duo-theistic religion; dualism; the inverse twins, Ahura Mazda and Ahriman; Zurvan; the Merciless Heropass; the Amesha Spenta; the unequal equation; Man is part of the equation

Zoroastrianism is possibly the oldest of the revealed religions. It certainly has had a historical influence on the three Abrahamic religions. It was the Zoroastrian Persians who freed the Jews from their exile in Babylon, and subsequently returned them to Palestine, under the tutelage of Ezra. This just happened to occur during the same general period of time that the Torah (the five books of Moses) was being set down in written form. And the wise men who read the stars and traveled to Jerusalem and eventually Bethlehem were Zoroastrian.

The historical founder of Zoroastrianism was Persian prophet Zarathustra (the name "Zoroaster" is the Greek form), who lived in Central Asia and who died in the city of Balk, which still exists today as a small village located in present day northern Afghanistan.

Zoroastrianism was neither monotheistic nor polytheistic, but was instead duo-theistic. In its Orthodox form, there were postulated two primordial gods. As presented by Dr. R. C. Zaehner, the reason for this arrangement was that the Zoroastrians could not accept the notion that a good god created a world such as ours, one filled with evil. Because evil was an obvious fact, there had to have been two separate gods: a good god who was responsible for the good in this world, and an evil god that was likewise responsible for the harm. To their way of thinking, this evil god had to be able to enforce its will in the face of opposition from the good god.

This is NOT how Judaism viewed Satan, and neither was it the view of Islam, which regarded Satan as an obedient servant of God with very specific tasks and responsibilities. Allotting equivalence in power to God and some devil was part of the reason why the Catholic Church relentlessly hunted down the believers of the so-called "Cathar Heresy". (The horrible Albigensian Crusade in Southern France, with the subsequent Inquisition, got its start as persecution of Catharism.) However, a notion of "Inverse Twin gods" is not that far from many present day Christian views, which regard Satan as a genuinely real menace to be feared, and the opposite of Jesus.

The many spin-offs of Zoroastrianism, such as Manichaeism, Mithraism, Gnosticism, Bogomilism in the Balkans, and Catharsis in Southwestern France, tended to be dualistic. There was even a subsidiary notion that the spirits of "good men" were trapped in evil, material bodies. This dualism contaminated Christianity with an ambivalence about (and aversion to) bodies and the function of sex. And unfortunately, since people tend to assign blame to others rather than acknowledge their own faultinesses, all too often according to a defense mechanism called Projection, women were historically equated with "evil" matter, "evil" sexuality.

My understanding of original Zoroastrianism, however, is very different from these polarized derivatives. Duo-theistic Zoroastrianism postulated a conflict between two primordial Spirits, not a conflict between spirit and matter. As a consequence, matter and the material world per se were never considered by the Zoroastrians to be intrinsically evil. To the contrary, matter was considered to be a good, or at least neutral, creation of the good god Ahura Mazda, and sexual reproduction was a good (or at least a neutral) part of creation.

3) The Zoroastrian Creation Story: the Inverse Twins.

Now to get to the main point. In the orthodox Zoroastrian creation story, there were two primordial gods. They were twins, but they were inversely opposite to each other in nature. One of the twins was named Ahura Mazda, the god of Goodness, Light, and Intelligence. His twin and moral opposite was named Ahriman, the god of evil, darkness and ignorance. These twin gods were separated by a Void (a Chasm) named Zurvan, a name which in Persian also meant "Infinite Time".

As the Zoroastrian creation story goes, Ahura Mazda knew about the existence of his opposite, because Awareness and Intelligence are attributes of Goodness (it still seems to work that way today). In contrast, Ahriman possessed neither attribute. However, the dormant Ahriman did eventually learn of the presence of his twin, and he attacked his twin in a blind rage. Neither one could defeat the other because they were equal in strength. After considerable struggle, Ahura Mazda did manage to temporarily put his opposite number down by reciting the Ahunvar, a prophecy about Ahriman's eventual but certain defeat. This prophecy caused Ahriman to swoon and drop once again into a coma, this time for 3,000 years.

During this interlude, Ahura Mazda thought hard about what he might be able to do to avoid an eternity of such fruitless conflict.

He finally came up with a stratagem which I personally like to call "Operation Tar Baby" (as in the story about Brer Rabbit and the Hungry Fox). Ahura Mazda created a stunningly beautiful and perfect, shining world. Ahriman did eventually re-awaken, and when he saw this new world, he attacked it, making every effort to defile it. Ahriman introduced the lie, anger, and despair; disease and death; and he polluted fire, which was sacred), with smoke.

Now here's the catch. When Ahriman turned to leave this new world after having defiled it, he discovered that he was now trapped therein. He was stuck, just as Ahura Mazda had foreseen. There followed an extended period of time (still in progress today), during which Ahriman, who could never be destroyed, would nevertheless be slowly neutralized. In other words, he would be slowly rendered harmless. In addition, Ahura Mazda's beautiful creation (including Mankind) would eventually be fully redeemed and restored, because Ahura Mazda knew his creation to be fundamentally good. Remember this, because it means that no one can ever be lost in the long run.

To aid his effort to redeem his Creation, Ahura Mazda created several helpers, the first being the Amesha Spenta. These were the six Divine Sparks of Ahura Mazda (for all practical purposes, the equivalent of Seraphim). Ahura Mazda also created Gayomart, the first Man. And like the Greek "androgyne", *this first Man was equally female and male, together as One*, possessing two pairs of each limb and both sets of genitalia. Also of great significance, Ahura Mazda showed Gayomart the struggle that was about to begin, and the price that Gayomart would have to pay for its own involvement as the center of this struggle—his&her death. Ahura Mazda then gave Gayomart the choice of whether or not to help. (Free Will, anyone?) And Gayomart voluntarily jumped into the trenches.

Gurdjieff's "Merciless Heropass."

When I first read the allegorical book *Beelzebub's Tales to his Grandson*, I was startled and somewhat offended by the notion that God might find Itself in a bind because of some difficult aspect of Creation. However, I couldn't simply dismisses the notion outright. It had left me too unsettled. And as it turns out, this was the most important reason that a distinction between God as "I" and God as "I AM" is necessary.

God as "I" could never be in need of anything. All possibilities were available and inherent. However, by the disavowal of anti-being (the Biblical Dark), God as "I" chose to invest in and *limit Itself* to the logoi made available to Creation, in order to avoid the specter of being a divided Will in opposition to Itself. God as "I" thereby became God as "I AM". As a consequence, "I AM" was now incomplete and limited, compared to the Primordial Omega Transfinity of "I". This meant a measure of restriction in God's freedom to act directly. And yet, BEING (Reality) still had to be defended against being destroyed by remerging with its Inverse Twin, anti-being.

This new lack of freedom was actually analogous to becoming a parent. Conceiving a child can be accidental, but becoming a genuine parent is only possible through an act of Will, because it means voluntarily choosing to put the needs of the offspring before one's own needs or desires. And the nature of this problem was such that even God would need help in this struggle with what was essentially *part of Itself*.

Therefore, and because Existence had to be as independent as possible, its development and management was largely turned over to that very highest order of created Beings, the Amesha Spenta, also known as the committee of Seraphim. And collectively, this governing group was named the Elohim in the Torah. This "executive congress" was also the basis for the ancient Kurdish "Cult of Angels". This seems to have been a very common notion in antiquity: that God as "I AM" is relatively remote or removed from the day to day affairs of Existence. In the context of this Cosmology, this remoteness reflects the fact that because of the intrinsic status of Existence as part of the Reconciliation of the conflict between the Affirmation of BEING ("I AM") and the Denial of anti-being, Existence had to largely remain a hands-off affair for God as "I AM".

Thus, it fell to the Elohim (as Natural Law), to manage the organization of Existence. But looking deeper into this situation, we see that the Elohim were "all of the King's horses, and all of the King's Men, which couldn't put Humpty Dumpty back together again." A semi-independent WILL was needed, a representative of God as "I" as WILL; without an agent of "I" as "WILL", all of Creation is like the sum of 0.3333... + 0.3333... + 0.3333..., which only adds up to 0.9999...., which does not quiiiiiiite equal 1 Whole. Something like Man, a special yet universal class of Being within Existence, was created to play the role of the independent "Holy Reconciling" in the Creation.

<u>But why resort to Zoroastrianism?</u>

Yes, Zoroastrianism is no longer a major world religion by today's standards. But I personally believe that it got closer than all the rest to the heart of things, when it came to explaining why this world is like it is. One aspect of Existence is to be a beguilement, a distraction and even a school for the Spirit of Ahriman. This is important because what any given religion demands of a Man depends on what that religion believes to be the problem with this world. For example, modern Christianity assumes sin is the primary problem, and therefore demands that its followers renounce sin. Buddhism renounces ignorance and "waking sleep", and therefore works instead to awaken and enlighten people.

Zoroastrianism explains that we as Man were intentionally created to participate in an effort to safeguard Creation. This is a far different proposition from the notion that we were sent here to demonstrate that we ignorant brats can indeed behave properly, with the threat of an eternal beat-down as the price of our failure.

Man is an active part of the equation

Man is presented as having a genuine purpose for having been created. This alone doesn't yet explain exactly what our special task is, but it's the start. And regardless of what that task will prove to be, it was important enough for the Creator to share Itself in a way not offered to any other part of Existence, not even with the Amesha Spenta, the Seraphim (angels).

CHAPTER VIII

PROLOGUE TO EXISTENCE

Adding Existence to Creation; etymology of re-lig-ion; Looking Back: "God is a Point"; Kurdish creation story; several potential problems attending reinterpretation this side of the light boundary; in summary

<u>What is Existence? Why was it added to the Creation (added to Reality)?</u>

One of the more difficult notions of this reconstructed Religious Cosmology to convey to the reader will be this seemingly strange notion that Existence, this Universe we inhabit, was not itself the primary Creation, and is in fact something quite different from that Creation, which is Reality. Existence and Reality are related, but are quite different things, and this point is central to understanding why we are here, and even to understanding exactly what our own "Salvation" actually means.

Existence, this Universe we inhabit, is actually a modification made to the Primordial Creation (Reality). And this modification began with the manifestation of materiality, of boundaries and differences. Existence is a "World", a context for and a realm of many. And if this doesn't seem important or relevant, simply remember what the word "Re-<u>lig</u>-ion" means: "tying something back together (that once was One)." In other words, the fact that God's fundamental Creation, Reality, seems to have come apart in some fashion, must have some bearing on why this world is how it now seems to be, and why we as Man are here.

<u>Looking back</u>: In the later years of my undergraduate experience, I went to this one party up on the hill on the East side of town one Friday night. Afterwards, I left the party and spent the night walking around the Hill till sunrise, thinking about many things. This is where I first began to understand that dimensions, measures of separations, ultimately had to be illusions, virtual distances like those seen in a mirror (and yes, this actually became more important for me to contemplate than searching for ladies at the party). I had just for the first time seen that God could never be separate from anything (at least from anything Real). This meant that God could not be subject to dimensions, which in turn meant that God had to be a point in some sense, something of zero dimensions—and this, by the way, is the key to understanding what "going through the eye of the needle" means.

That following Monday when I returned to my job, I put a note on the notice board that said "God is a Point." Didn't get the reaction I expected. This had to have been about mid 1972.

Why would the Primordial Creation (the Biblical Light) have been made to be, or at least allowed to become, fractured? Especially since that fracturing represented an intrusion to some degree of the Biblical Dark into the Biblical Light? It might seem that our Omnipotent Creator should have been working to avoid just such a result. The voluntary disavowal of the Biblical Dark in the Great Sacrifice had only rendered the Biblical Dark unable to act on its own by its own "Will." To put it in the form of a paradox: anti-being did not cease to be.

An aside: I had once thought that the stuff called anti-matter might actually fit the bill for anti-being. However, to the best of my knowledge, it would be theoretically possible to construct an entire Universe almost identical to our own, using only the anti-matter equivalents to what we think of as matter. For this reason, anti-matter won't do, simply because anti-matter is a "differentiated something", while anti-being is an "undifferentiated nothing."

Let's review how this event was regarded and explained in earlier religions. The Kurdish creation story started with the Universal Spirit having created a shining white Pearl which was then placed on the back of a bird named Anfar (Unfortunately, I don't know what the name Anfar might mean). Anfar eventually took flight, and the Pearl predictably fell off, smashing into pieces. And one has to assume that this was the prior intention behind placing the Pearl where it could only fall and smash into pieces, because it was immediately placed in the care of six Great Beings which had been created by the Universal Spirit for just this very purpose: that of organizing the fragments of that Pearl into a self-sustaining world. In the Persian Zoroastrianism, Ahura Mazda created a perfect world with the aim of trapping, interring and interning his inverse twin Ahriman, as an internally disruptive element. Having done so, he created six Great Beings, the six divine sparks of Ahura Mazda, together known as the Amesha Spenta, in order to help him to manage this world, newly (intentionally) defiled by His evil twin counterpart, while that evil was slowly neutralized over time.

Existence is like a progressively graduating (step by step) band of grey that seems to stretch from the Absolute White of Reality (including all colors), and the Absolute Black (the absence of color). This means that the upper region of Existence, the "waters above" of Genesis, is closer to Reality than is the lower region of Existence, the "waters below", which is descendingly closer to Illusion. This is absolutely central to understanding both Religion, and ourselves as Man, because, even though Man was created on the uppermost side of town (Existence), we were eventually tricked into dwelling on the wrong side of the tracks, so to speak. This is because we were intentionally created to be the Prodigal Son. Salvation is therefore finding your way back home… once you figure out just what home is, and just what has to be done to get there.

<u>Several potential problems attending this reinterpretation of Religion</u>
Central to this Cosmology is the notion that Man was intentionally tricked into dropping into this lower half of Existence where illusion reigns over Reality. Only here, below the Light Boundary, is where the so-called "knowledge of good and evil" is possible, precisely because being confused about which is which ("good and evil", or "Reality and Illusion"), was an absolutely essential precursor to the task which Gayomart/Adam undertook. The deception that put us here was in no way done out of malice, nor as some punishment. Rather, it was done because God as "I AM" needed our help, (absurd as that must sound), because of God's very own Law of Triads, which demands an Independent Reconciling element.

The belief that the Bible is meant to be understood literally has been an enormous tragedy. Something is read and interpreted, leaving people with a fixed picture, and they go away believing that they understand something. But the Bible is more like those pictures which consist of layers, and if you can change your focus it will give you an entirely different picture than the one you started with. That other picture was always there, but it was needing a change in your focus of mind (aka Metanoia) to become apparent. For example, very few people ever notice that the story of Creation in Genesis is presented twice, from the perspective of the sub-luminous portion of Existence in Genesis Chapter One, and the hyper-luminous portion of Existence in Chapter Two. Chapter One is about the creation of Life in this material world of Time and Space, whereas Chapter Two is about the Creation of Ideas and of Intentions, in the abstract but more Real World.

In summary

In summary, Existence seems to be an intermediate condition that works to keep anti-being sequestered within the Creation, for much the same reasons one might keep anti-matter safely sequestered within some unusual container, such as a magnetic bottle, to prevent BEING and anti-being from merging and unmaking Creation. The effects of anti-being on BEING are apparent but muted. Because of the rupture and fragmentation introduced by what is called the Big Bang (we really don't know the form this event took), anti-being is sequestered in the midst of what was formerly a Singular Reality. The result was that potentialities became actualities, Reality became a World. The resulting Existence is an infinite collection where nothing is ever complete, but instead, is always becoming.

The notion that anti-being is sequestered with Existence should raise another question: why doesn't this forced proximity not result in the destruction of both conditions, both the Light and the Dark by their mutual reduction back to the Primordial Chaos? There's an answer that will be presented in the Chapter MAYA.

HALE MICHAEL SMITH, M.D.

The firmament of Genesis is the boundary between Ideal and concrete Existence. This sub-luminous world is more illusion than not. Speaking metaphorically, that's essentially the price paid by Existence for Ahriman's (the Biblical Dark's) containment here.

Each one of us, as "sons of Adam and daughters of Eve", is the door-way that makes it possible for the Will that is God to enter this sub-luminous world in a meaningful way.

CHAPTER IX

GUIDING PRINCIPLES

Cartography of dimensions; unfolding existence; Creation as a cascade; Great Octave; the Paraclete; interrupted hierarchy; origami; significance of number seven; Looking Back: experiment with strobe light; word origins of Do-RE-Mi...; the actuality of hazard; the Four Elements; phase transitions; etymological aside; the light boundary; the golden ratio; four realms of Existence

<u>Cartography of dimensions</u>

To simply say that "God and Heaven are up there, and I'm down here," is nowhere near informative enough. So let us start with something already stated.

BEING, aka Absolute Reality, is everything, everywhere, and everywhen. There's not even any nothingness beyond God.

The entire Creation Itself is but a thought in the "Mind" that is God. This is why for God everything Real is always immediately present without any "there vs here" or "then vs now." Existence is something like the virtual image of your bedroom when seen in the bedroom wall mirror. The furniture you see, along with their arrangement in space and the distances between them, seem very real and they can even be measured in the reflection. But they are only virtual measurements. Those virtual distances are, however, a good example of what this Cosmology calls Actuality: that which presents itself to you as real within sub-luminous Existence, regardless of whether it is genuinely Real or virtually real, or a full blown illusion. In other words, actual appearances can vary vastly in their degree of Reality.

The majority of the presentations of Existence in this book will largely be vertical scales where Divinity ("I AM", the Source of everything), is at the top, and anti-being (oblivion, and hence nothing) is at the bottom. This is primarily because this format is the most amenable to print. In other words, these word maps will mostly present Existence as a vertical Hierarchy, where *higher* means greater proximity to God (ever greater proximity to the Central unity & reality, and "proximity" in awareness to the Source of Everything), and where *lower* means ever greater dispersion, illusion, and "distance" in awareness from the Source of Everything. It also equates that which is *higher* with that which is more *interior*, and that which is lower with that which is more exterior. In other words, increasing distance from the top (from the Center), also means that things spread ever more apart, like the spokes of a wheel spread apart as they approach the outer rim of a wheel. All together, to approach closer to the truth would mean to see that which is highest as being closer to the center of the whole, and that which is lowest as being further to the outside, more external.

But in spite of this vertical representation of Existence, a sphere, or better yet, an eleven-dimensional hyper-sphere, is the more correct presentation of God as "I AM" as the ultimate center of everything. What this means is that everything that exists is a result of a creative movement outward from the most Central point, out from that inmost Source, as I came to realize and understand while learning to fold Origami. This progressive radiation and dispersion outwards is actually what Evolution means. But always remember, there is no true outside to God for anything to expand into. This entire subject of Cartography is a result of the limits of our 3-dimensional, brain-dependent awareness (literally, our worldly mind).

Etymology: The word "evolution" itself ultimately comes from the Latin *ex-voluere*, which simply means "to roll or unfold outwards." The *voluere* part has given English many words like revolve, involve, revolt, vault and interval.

The easiest way to understand evolution is to see the act of creation as the "energy of activation" in physics and chemistry. Evolution is then a resulting transformation which spreads outwards. And as for that which is unfolding? It's potential. However, how that potential gets expressed depends on what the conditions will allow.

The unfolding of Existence was the spreading, unfolding, expenditure of that penultimate Transfinite potential inherent in BEING. The claim made by this Cosmology is that it subsequently went through eleven primary stages (or deflections), and then rebounded backwards in direction from which it originally came. In other words, what was originally an outwards movement of increasing dispersion and entropy eventually rebounded at the extreme distant limit (anti-being), reversing course to become an inbound and upwards, and uphill, movement of concentration and integration. This rebound is known as "Atonement", the Return to Oneness with God. Again, we are once more confronted with the meaning of the word "Religion."

It makes no sense to me to think that God individually fashioned every single quark and lepton which, in aggregate, comprises this stupendous Universe. Nor does it make sense to believe that God choreographed everything that would happen. Such would make Man's supposedly free and independent Will, meaningless. Rather, it makes far more sense to understand that all which could be, all which could ever happen, was created together all at once as potential, as possibilities, and then largely set free to play out as it would. And this scenario is consistent with what is said in Genesis Chapter One.

Creation is a Cascade: the progressive expenditure of Potential for the Actual

The effect of the Big Bang on that Primordial Singularity, while fundamentally fictitious, yet had the effect of allowing the Real logoi the ability to manifest.

That first act, the true Creation, is formulated in the Quran as "Allah said 'BE!', and it was." And in Genesis, its formulation was "And God said, 'Let there be Light!'" In other words, all Real potential was established all together at once, "in the Beginning." This separation of the Biblical Light from the Biblical Dark, was analogous to separating two magnets which were initially in contact with each other, or, like climbing up to a high roof top and standing on the edge. In both cases, one has created potential, a tension where before there was none. For the magnets, they will now seek to rejoin each other. As for standing on the roof top, the gravity of the Earth seeks to pull you back down. In either case, the pull one feels is the energy, the potential that's now available. Likewise, the division of the Primordial Chaos into the Light and the Dark meant that now something could happen.

In this Cosmology God as "I AM" _directly_ created "Six Divine Sparks" which were then left in charge of the overall management and development of Existence, including the staged evolution of material Life. In addition, as is pointed out in Genesis Chapter Two, God as "I AM" also <u>directly</u> created one additional Seraphim: ADAM. ADAM, the eternal Idea of Man (equally female as male), is the 7th member of the Elohim, echoing the Fundamental Origin of God as "I AM" above. Thus Man is made in the image of God, and is a co-creator of many parts of Existence, such as naming the animals demonstrates. Only ADAM (however ADAM manifests on worlds throughout Creation), can accomplish that which "all the King's horses and all the King's men" (the Amesha Spenta), could never do: play the role of the *independent* Holy Reconciliation, and "put Humpty Dumpty back together again", even though no Man is a God.

A clarification

To use the analogy of music, consisting of vibrations which naturally organize and which in the West we describe in terms of Octaves (and those readers already familiar with the cosmology presented in such books as *In Search of the Miraculous* will recognize the analogy). The Great Octave is Creation as a Whole, where Reality is the Fundamental Origin, the Note DO; the complementary lower Note DO is anti-being and the illusion of discontinuity, the Biblical Dark.

The Second descending Octave is actually a sub-component of the first, because it's contained entirely within the entire Note SI of the Octave of Existence. It's at this highest level that God as "I AM" is able to <u>directly</u> shape Existence, creating specific Ideas in order to influence or intervene within Existence. Below and beyond this level, God as "I AM" must use some intermediary to affect things. Why would God be restrained in this way, you might ask? Simply because to side step Note SI to order to intervene at some lower level (at some lower Note), would necessitate destroying everything in between to reach that lower Note. This is why something analogous to that intermediary known as the Holy Spirit (aka the Advocate / the Paraclete) was needed.

<u>Note</u>: In Physics, this is known as the problem of an interrupted Hierarchy. Imagine the problems you would have if we had a second brain in our bodies, a second brain which had been independently wired and programmed to present itself to the outside as the true you. It would act as a random switch in your nervous hierarchy. (And in fact, this is not that far from our actual situation.)

Importantly, God does have direct contact with that which is Spirit within each of us as elements of ADAM. But unfortunately, only the rarest of the rare among us has any genuine direct connection with that which is ADAM within ourselves.

However, what God does not have is contact with the sub-luminous portion of our total Being. Quite simply, God has no contact with, nor can God even speak with that self in us which is based on our Human animal body's worldly mind. And this is unfortunate because for the vast majority of us now present on earth, only the worldly mind is active within our animal bodies, which are in no way intrinsically bad or wrong in themselves. This is not some aspect of ourselves that supposedly seeks only to sin; the giant nerve ganglion that sits between your ears was intentionally designed to see this material, animal-grade world we live in as real, and you'd be unable to live without it. But this ordinary, everyday mind was never designed for Religion. It only understands this physical world we seem to inhabit.

But to continue, God as "I AM" directly created an intermediate agency for the maintenance of Existence: the Elohim, the source of Natural Law. But be clear, the Elohim are not genuine

RELIGION REINTERPRETED

Gods, for one very simple reason: Whether individually or as a Collective body, the Elohim do not have a free and individual Will of their own. Only one element of this secondary Elohim Octave has Will: God's True Son, made in God's Image: ADAM. This Sonship extends to every single one of ADAM's embodied progeny, aka to all Men, of this or of any other planet.

Among other things, this scenario means that God as "I AM" did not create every specific item on this Earth. That was mostly left to the Elohim, as Chapter One of Genesis describes. For example, the forms taken by living things were explicitly fashioned stage by stage in Time, each stage depending to some degree on those forms preceding it.

Origami

I started seeing the world in this manner while still in college. A Chinese girlfriend one day sent me an origami sitting crane, hung within an icosahedral cage made of toothpicks which she had taken the time to construct. I was deeply fascinated by (and also deeply grateful for) this gift, perhaps because of my long-standing geometric bent of mind. So I carefully removed the Crane, and carefully unfolded it to see how it was done, then carefully refolded it and replaced it into its cage. The toothpick cage is long gone, but the last time I checked, I still had that folded crane (after almost 50 years).

Not long afterwards, while looking through my favorite local corner bookstore on Thayer Street, I found a book on Origami written by a sociology professor at my University, a Dr. James Minoru Sakoda. I never took one of his courses, but my memory is that he would fold paper while lecturing. That following summer, I taught myself to fold from his book, either at red lights while driving a yellow cab in Manhattan, or, while on the subway & LIRR to and from work. (I'd give the pieces I folded to those people who were too curious not to look, yet who were also not forward enough to feel free to admit that they were interested in what I was doing.) Later that year after returning to college, I was able for a short time to associate directly with Dr. Sakoda himself and he taught me several new folds, like his lotus with 16 separate petals. My big regret is that I've forgotten one fold he taught me where he would somehow pull out the center of a fold, with a result that looked like a lady's ballroom gown as she spun in a turn (an eight-sided helix).

As I learned to fold, I began to see things I didn't expect to see. One of the first realizations was the simple recognition that each of these diverse forms started with a simple square piece of paper. I began to understand that these beautiful folded items were explicit expressions of the possibilities intrinsic to the square shape. And your square piece of paper doesn't have to be more than the tiniest of fractions off of true to make the folding of most of those forms impossible. This intrigued me because it meant that the infinite number of folds that were possible with that square shape (or with any starting shape) were dictated by the lines of potential intrinsic to that shape (lines like a square's diagonals). And yet, the square shape itself was the most mundane, unassuming, and most (to my way of thinking) boring of shapes. This proved to be a perfect example of how non-obvious and unexpected potential can lie right under our noses in almost everything, no matter how dull and ordinary it might seem.

I next began to understand that the process of folding towards any particular form, was actually a sequence (a cascade) of trade-offs, of actualizations, of implicit potential for something ever more explicit and more actual. As one progressed with some particular sequence of folds, you would progressively narrow down the number of forms you could still make. In other words, each step in a sequence of folding traded off a measure of the total potential of that square shape, the potential for all of the things that you could possibly still fold. What you got in return was something ever more specific.

For example, if you were attempting to fold a bird, you would move past the sequence of folds where you could make a star, a flower, or an insect. In Origami, any branching node within any established sequence is called a base, the best known of which are the simple bird and frog bases, because of the several forms they directly lead to.

This trade-off of potential for specificity would continue until you would eventually reach a point where the potential along one's chosen sequence of folds was basically exhausted, and the only possible changes remaining were essentially cosmetic ones, such as changing the size of the beak or the curve of the wing on the bird you've just produced.

Note: Applying this perspective to the evolution of the Human physical form allows one to see the genuine significance of our so-called races of Mankind in their true light as mere cosmetic variations on an established underlying and essentially identical form.

I eventually began to understand that this was the manner in which the evolution of Existence worked. The whole of Existence was organized in just this fashion, from the absolute and entirely implicit potential of BEING at the top, cascading down through the many branch points in the hyper-luminous "Realm of Mind" until one reached the concrete specifics and concrete particulars that would be found in the lower, sub-luminous levels of material existence. This process of evolution therefore followed the path of an inverted tree, in other words, our "cascade."

HALE MICHAEL SMITH, M.D.

The significance of the number Seven

While Existence has already been described as being analogous to a band of gray, incrementally progressing from the absolute white of BEING, down to the absolute black of anti-being, an additional factor modifies Existence, transforming that "smooth band of transitioning gray" into something much more like a spectrum of color, or like a musical scale.

One possible name for this additional factor affecting the unfolding (aka evolution) of Existence might be the "Law of Selective Self-Reinforcements and Selective Self-Cancellations". Another possible name (which means much the same thing), might be the "Law of Harmonic Self-Interaction". However, it's already known simply as the "Law of Octaves". However named, the impact of this Law of Octaves means that Existence is *not* a simple smooth progression. Rather, Existence is lumpy, irregular, and seemingly asymmetric, because it tends to be emphasized in certain places and deemphasized in others, by self-reinforcing and self-canceling interactions. Existence spreads BEING out, just as a point of white light is diffracted (spread out) into a band of color (the color spectrum), by passing it through a prism.

Looking back: An opportunity to experiment

I am the son of a composer, and I was exposed from a very early age to a lot of music, first to "Formal" music (my father's idiosyncratic name for Classical), and not too long after to Jazz. Later came R&B, and then a fair amount of Rock and Folk music in college. Even later came Celtic and New Age. I've always had some access to a piano. I never learned to play well, but I could at least experiment on it. I had a few years of formal music theory while very young, and even a few years of violin (which I detested).

RELIGION REINTERPRETED

Music, in particular its structure, has always fascinated me. So it was no surprise that when I began to read the writings of Gurdjieff, there was already in place an eager audience for his teaching about Octaves. But I also learned something during my premedical studies, when I chanced to have an opportunity in a junior college lab to play with a one-speed electric motor, along with a variable speed strobe-lamp.

When I was a kid, I would often wonder why, during cowboy movies, the spoked wheels of wagons and stage-coaches so often seem to be turning in reverse as they sped off in some direction. Now, in the lab, I was able to re-create and study this appearance because I was able to digitally control the rate of strobing of the lamp. I could make the strobe-lamp flash on and off as frequently or as infrequently as I wished.

The entire room was otherwise absolutely dark; the only light came from the flashing of the strobe lamp. The motor ran at a fixed speed. And I was able to fix, to that motor's axle, something lightweight but rigid, and at a right-angle to that axle (I used a pencil). In this darkened room where the only light came from the strobe-lamp, I was able to play with the *appearance* of the pencil as it spun around, as I varied the rate of the strobe lamp flashing.

<u>Note</u>: This would be an excellent Middle School classroom experiment to help kids understand this world we live in.

To start, when the strobe-lamp flashed on and off exactly as often as the motor made a single full rotation, the result would be the *appearance* of a stationary pencil. This was because the lamp would light the pencil at the exact same point in its rotation. Remember, the room was otherwise completely dark. This was effectively the Note DO.

Next, if the strobe lamp flashed on and off exactly twice as fast as a the motor turned, it would illuminate the pencil twice during each full rotation of the motor and its pencil. That same pencil would then appear to point in opposite directions (exactly 180° apart).

For the strobe lamp to flash on and off exactly 3 times as fast as the motor turned, the pencil would appear to be pointing in three directions, as if forming an equilateral triangle, with angles of exactly 120° degrees. Likewise, a 4:1 ratio of strobing and motor rotations produced the appearance of a square with 90° angles. And yet, there was only ever the same single spinning pencil.

The reader will now notice that I used the word "exactly" in cases above. This is because if the strobe-lamp flash rate was even a tiny amount off, the figures described by the pencils would seem to rotate.

For example, if the strobe lamp flash rate was just the tiniest bit *slower* than the motor's rate of turning, each time the strobe light illuminated the pencil, that pencil would have gone slightly further than a full turn. The end result would be that the pencil would appear to be rotating forward. And if the strobe rate was just a tiny bit *faster* than the motor's rate of rotation, it would catch the pencil just before it would complete a full rotation, and that pencil would then appear to be rotating backwards.

This meant that those moving pictures where the spoked wheels of wagons appeared to be going backwards were cases where the scene was being filmed frame by frame at a rate slightly faster than the wheels of the wagons were actually turning. In other words, each film frame would catch the wheel just before the spokes completed a full turn— actually, before any given spoke could rotate to the place and replace the adjacent spoke which had previously been there during the previous frame.

But there was more to discover here. As I slowly increased the rate of flashing of the strobe lamp from the starting rate equal to that of the motor's rotation, I began to see and understand the how and why of the DO-RE-MI-FA-SOL-LA-SI-DO notes of an Octave, and in a way not taught in my much earlier music theory classes. (The reader will also noticed that the original "SI" was used, and not the relatively recent "TI", the change having been made for clarity in hearing.)

When the rate of strobe lamp flashing was exactly nine times for every eight rotations of the motor, you would see nine pencils, each exactly 40° apart from each other. (Does the Biblically educated reader suspect that this 40° might correspond to the meaning underlying many Biblical stories?) The nine appearances of that pencil would describe the nine-sided polygon known as the Nonagon.

This nine-to-eight frequency ratio defines Note RE, whose frequency is invariably 9/8 the frequency of the fundamental, the Note DO. In other words, if the motor was rotating at 24 times a minute, and the strobe lamp was flashing 27 times a minute, they would produce this nine-sided figure. For Note MI (strobe rate of 30 to 24 rotations), I would see five pencils (a Pentagon), because there would be five flashes for every four rotations of the motor, and Note MI = 5/4.

And so on. One sees seven pencils when the strobe lamp flashes at 42 times a minute, because 42/24 equals 7/4. The lamp will be flashing on seven times for every four rotations of the motor.

The traditional Octave (whether of seven or of twelve notes) is composed of notes for which the frequencies are those wherein the only numerical factors are the first three prime numbers after the number One: "Two", "Three", and "Five." Every new odd number frequency that appears in any such Octave becomes the origin of a new branch Octave. This vastly increases the overall complexity of the whole affair. And there are those other prime numbers: 7, 11, 13, 17, 19, 23, and beyond. These represent Octaves composed of notes not fully compatible with the primary starting one. However, they are still just as real in spite of their seeming incompletion.

The Religious Origin of DO—RE—MI...

It turns out that the DO—RE—MI... labeling of the notes of the seven Note musical scale, had their origin in Christian monasteries, when the language in use was Latin. (Another remove from the language originally spoken by Jesus.) Here's where those names came from:

DO—DOMINUS—"Lord"—Divinity (= God as "I AM")
SI—SIDERA—Stars—Existence (the Universe as a WHOLE)
LA—LACTEA—Milk—world of Galaxies (the Milky Way)
SOL—SOL—Sun—each individual star
TRITONE
FA—FATES—The Fates—the World of Planets
MI—MICROCOSMOS—Nature—world of a planet's surface
RE—REGINA DE COELI—Queen of the sky—the Moon
DO—DOMINUS— Under-lord—Anti-being

Descending vs. Ascending Octaves

A Descending Octave is a Creative, Evolutionary Octave. In turn, an Ascending Octave is one of concentration, of Atonement, unlike the dispersion of Evolution in a Descending Octave. Atonement is a motion towards increased concentration, where the initial outward thrust of Creation must be reversed if one is to Return home to its Source (the Oneness of Divinity).

The "gap" between Note SOL (ratio 8/5), and Note LA (ratio 5/3), is the existential basis for that asymptotic break-point known as the Golden Ratio = 1.6180334.... Looking at the frequencies of the two Notes that bracket this "gap", relative to that of the Fundamental (Note DO), reveals why: the numbers 3:5:8 are part of the Fibonacci series that the botanist Fibonacci originally discovered in nature. (There's also a good chance that the lower MI-FA "gap" is related to this as the square root of the Golden Ratio.)

This Fibonacci Point at SOL-LA is the true half-way point of an Ascending Octave. There's also the Tritone, which is more the geometric half-way point between that initial frequency of Note DO and its Octave frequency. It's that number two that introduces the square root of two, which forces the Tritone to be an irrational number, making the true Tritone completely incompatible with all of the other ratio-based (rational) Notes of an Octave.

These two "half-way" points are represented on the Human animal body itself. The Tritone corresponds to the geometric half of the full height of a normal Human body, that height divided by two. This human Tritone is normally located at our crotch, the point where our thighs join together with each other and with our torso. However, our Fibonacci point is our true center of gravity, located just a couple of centimeters south of our navel.

For those familiar with Hinduism, this following diagram corresponds to the Samkya system of Hindu philosophy, although the true source of this Diagram for myself was simple Physics.

Divinity ("I AM")
Gap "The Eye of the Needle" (SI-DO)

Existence— Realm of MIND
The Light Boundary (the Fibonacci point SOL-LA)
Realm of ANIMATION
Realm of INERTIA
Oblivion— MAYA

There's one other example which I can present, something I saw decades ago, but didn't understand until very recently that it too was a qualitative Octave. It's the progression in scale from an autonomous single cell organism to an entire multi-cellular organism, both of which represent a comparable degree of autonomy and self-sufficiency, which the intervening levels of tissues and organs do not have. The following should make sense to most people, in spite of being incomplete:

DO—an animal body (maximum autonomy)
SI—
LA—organ systems (nervous, digestive, endocrine, etc.)
SOL—organs (brain, lungs, skin)
FA—
MI—tissue types (nervous, muscle, connective, etc.)
RE—tissue colonies
DO—a single eukaryotic cell (maximum autonomy) such as a paramecium or amoeba

Note: Animals like sponges score at best at the level of colonies (Note RE). Fungi and Cnidaria show some differentiation of tissue types (perhaps Note MI). The Human Body is a mammalian animal body, one which was intended to anchor us within this sub-luminous world. Why this was done is of great importance, and will be explained later. However, simply recognizing that our Human bodies are in fact animals is very, very important. This is why Man is defined as ADAM embodied. To be "incarnated" literally means to be "encased in meat."

The Actuality of Hazard (Chance)

The subject of Hazard is fundamental to Existence, and this is as good a place as any to say something about it. But first we must say something about Hazard itself, and its purpose in Existence. I am in tremendous debt to J. G. Bennett for his insight into the incredible importance of Hazard to Existence.

For "I AM", Absolute Reality is a single perfect thought. For hyper-luminous Existence, the infinite logoi of that single thought have been expanded, becoming the differentiated totality of every specific Real possibility, arranged in every possible combination. Hyper-luminous Existence is the World of Mind, the "Matrix of Ideas". It's analogous to that organic matrix of nerve cells which comprises our brain. Those Minds, themselves Ideas, are the eternal bearers of the specifics borne within that infinite thought that is God as "I AM".

It's only within sub-luminous Existence that what "is" in Eternity, must "become" in Time. Above in hyper-luminous Existence, every possible outcome that could result from some line of happening is present, along side of every other possible outcome, all in Eternity. In contrast, below the Light Boundary, the norm is that only a very limited number of possible outcomes can become actual at any one time, for any one observer. The awareness that is possible down here has contracted to the degree that the actualization of the many possible outcomes for any line of happening are very limited, and more often than not seem mutually exclusive. All of those outcomes are there, but only a very few can become actual for any given awareness. This is how both Free Will and Hazard can combine with Predetermination:

Everything which could ever possibly happen is predetermined in hyper-luminous Existence, whereas whatever actually does or can happen for any given observer, happens in sub-luminous Existence.

Hazard is an extension of the Heisenberg Uncertainty Principle, the idea of there being "play" in the system. Sub-luminous Existence is where no event entirely contains within itself the certainty that it will actualize the outcome or purpose that engendered it. Every event within sub-luminous Existence depends on a confluence of conditions. For example, pollination doesn't occur if the wind isn't blowing, or if birds and bees and bats aren't present. Or think of the times you meet someone and feel a potential connection, or see how they could become a friend. Maybe you even exchange contact information… but you may never speak or see each other again, and that potential never "folds" into a shaped, actual relationship. The fluidity of uncertainty combines with the predictability of Cause & Effect, so there can be play in the entire system, while yet being securely enough connected together to avoid having everything unpredictably fall apart.

The SOL#-LA "gap" is the Hazard of a switching yard. It represents the need for a course correction, followed up by the need to walk that extra mile. A seed that results from a successful pollination may well germinate and grow. But it might end up as food for some animal, or, it might rot because it can't germinate where it fell, or it might sprout and then die from the lack of necessary sunlight and water. Or it might get crushed.

When Human Will is part of the equation, points of Hazard represent Temptation. Altogether, the presence of Hazard is an important clue to why this sub-luminous Realm was able to become the sort of place that it is.

The Law of Four (The Four Elements).
Having discussed the significance of the Number 3 (Triads) and of the Number 7 (Octaves), it's time to speak about the significance of the Number 4. This is usually known as the Four Elements in the West. However, the true meaning of this concept was lost long ago, as the understanding of the true meaning of the word *Intelligence* began to flatten, thereby becoming transformed into literalism.

Etymological definition: *Intelligence* and *Intellect*
Both words come from the Latin *inter-legere*. "inter-" means "between" or "among." The second part, "-legere" originally meant "to gather together", as in the modern English word "to co<u>l</u>lect." However, it also came to mean "to read", as seen in the English word "lecture". Most likely, this had something to do with the monastic practice of daily lectures where everyone in the monastery gathered together for the daily reading, but I'm not sure. However, as a result, the word *Intelligence* referred to the ability to *read between the lines* or *to see (relationships and potentials) among what is gathered together*. *Intellect* accordingly came be understood as the means to be intelligent.

Being able to "read between the lines" means that one can see what is implied, indicated, inherent, or potential. It means the ability to see beyond the form into the substance, the meaning of the issue at hand. Thus, when literalism began to trump intelligence, it saw only the "four elements" as if actual substances were the topic of concern, whereas The Law of Four is really the notion of Triads applied to Being. The number 3 is odd, whereas Being tends towards even divisions, consistent with being binary. It's also a sliding scale (a scale of relativity), and that is the crucial notion which literal interpretations completely lost. In other words, "Fire" refers to whatever is the most active and initiating "element" in a given situation, and "Earth" refers to whatever is the most resistant or passive "element." Then there are two middle (Reconciling) "elements" of which "Air" is the more active, and "Water" the more passive. (Using fire to smelt metal from rock was an alchemical process, rendering the solid metal temporarily liquid and separating it from the rest of the rock.)

Speaking of Binary, this pairing of the notions of "active vs passive" by using a plus sign (+) for the first and a minus sign (-) for the second, can help explain the four "elements." For an example of how this works, we'll use the four states of matter and of movement.

Fire (+ / +)… (active outwardly/active inwardly)…plasma
… Control
Air (-/+)…(passive outwardly/active inwardly)…gas
… Acceleration
Water (+/-)…(active outwardly/passive inwardly)…liquid
… Change (Velocity)
Earth (-/-)…(passive outwardly/passive inwardly)…solid
… Inertia (location)

Note: A change in Location per unit Time = a Velocity (aka Speed, hence, Activity, and Change).

A change in Velocity per unit Time = an Acceleration (= changes in speed and/or in direction).

A Change in Acceleration per unit Time = Control, which implies Purpose, hence Intention.

RELIGION REINTERPRETED

If readers are only familiar with three states of matter: solid, liquid, gas, the fourth state is plasma. Plasma is a gas which is so energetic, so heated, that the electrons of the constituent atoms have been torn away (ionized). As a result, the gas is electrically charged. Even though this concept is not as familiar to the public as those of ordinary gases, liquids, and solids, by a considerable margin most of the matter of this Universe is normally in a plasma state. We see a gigantic ball of plasma every time we look at the Sun, and we see a tube full of plasma every time we turn on a fluorescent lamp (it's the ionized plasma which emits the light). Even lighting a fire can generate a small amount of plasma.

Looking back: I first came up with this scheme while trying to answer a knotty question on the final exam for my Course in the Religions of India in college. The question was: "Why in Buddhism would Mind be considered active, and Body be considered passive, whereas in Hinduism it is the reverse, with Body being considered active and Mind being considered passive?" My answer was that I saw that Mind is active (Fire) in the sense that it directs the Body, and yet it is passive because it just sits there (Air), while the Body (Earth) actually responds by doing (Water) what the Mind directs it to do.

It's because of this schema of the Four Elements that Jesus (while speaking to Nicodemus in John 3: 5) referred to the need to be "reborn in Water".

An only half-silly example of the Four Elements would be the command crew of the original *Star Trek*. Although the entire bridge crew contributed to the success of this series, it was the fourfold command structure which made it work so well. And a big part of the reason for this seemed to me to lie in the fact that each of them represented one of the four channels that Man possesses for knowing this world. However, I have no notion of whether the characters were designed in that manner intentionally, or not.

Fire—Intuition—Captain Kirk
Air— Ordinary intellect— Executive/ Science Officer Spock
Water—Emotion/ Feeling— Medical Officer McCoy
Earth—Sensation—Chief Engineer Scott

<u>Phase Transitions</u>

Everyone who has ever seen water freeze or boil away has witnessed phase transitions. The three ordinary phases of matter are well known to everyone: solid, liquid, and gas. The expression *phase transition* describes a transition between phases, because there's always an energetic tax involved.

Imagine you are driving along a turnpike which charges you one-half dollar for every mile (or kilometer, choose your unit of measurement) you drive. Then you come to the border with another state (or country), and you suddenly discover that you have to shell out an additional $80.00 just to cross the line into that next state, where you now have to pay a full dollar for every mile on that turnpike. That's a phase transition.

The word *centigrade* means "one hundred grades" or "one hundred steps." This is because the temperature range between that where water freezes and that where water boils is divided into 100 steps, with the freezing point of water logically set at 0°, and the boiling point set as 100°. This is far more simple than the Fahrenheit system. (Dr. Fahrenheit set Zero at the lowest temperature he could manage in his laboratory manipulations of water, alcohol, and salt.)

Etymological aside: The Latin *centum* and Germanic *hundred* mean the same thing. The Latin *cent-* was originally pronounced *kent-*, which better demonstrates the relationship to the Germanic *hund-*, which had undergone the phonetic changes described by Grimm's Law.

Next, we learn about a cubic centimeter: a cube with each face measuring one square centimeter. The volume of this cube is the well known "cc" one so often hears about in medical dramas. One cc of water also defines the weight measure known as the gram. In other words, one gram of liquid water by weight equals one cubic centimeter of water by volume.

Now this is very important: *adding one calorie of heat energy will raise the temperature of one gram of liquid water one degree Celsius. Likewise, removing one calorie of heat energy from the same one cc of liquid water will drop that water's temperature one degree Celsius.* For water that is frozen or steam, a change of one degree temperature only involves an exchange of one-half calorie of heat.

Take ice at any temperature, and warm it. Every gram of ice will cost you one half-calorie of heat energy until its temperature reaches 0°. However, to change that ice into water at that very same temperature of 0°, you will have to add an additional 80 calories of heat energy for every gram of that frozen water. And the price is even more steep if you wish to boil that same water, because then, the Phase Transition price will not be 80 calories per gram, but 540 calories per gram. This is why heating water up to boiling is so energy expensive.

The Light Boundary is the phase transition between the hyper-luminous Ideal Realm of Existence, and this sub-luminous material

Realm of Existence. As a parting shot of sorts for this Chapter, here's the definition of a Realm:

A *realm* originally meant an "area ruled by a King." The word derives from the French *Roy*, from the Latin *Rex*, all of the way back to the original Indo-European *Reg*, which meant "straight." Its many cognate descendants include the English word "right", the German word "reich", the French word "region" and many Latin derivatives like regular, regulate, direct, and erect.

In this book, the word "Realm" refers to a domain within which a single overriding principle or quality, speaks for the whole.

Phase Transitions applied to the Realms of Existence

We return to the "graduating band of gray" motif, which stands as an analogy for how Existence is organized. With this motif, Existence is at all levels a mixture of both BEING and anti-being, a Singular Absolute Reality somewhat lost in the Illusion of Discontinuity (of having been fragmented, itemized). Furthermore, as Existence unfolds and seems to expand outwards away from the center, away from God as "I AM", the dilution of Reality by illusion increases as a function of that distance… hence, the increasing darkening of the gray.

This means there must be a 50%/50% point along this progression that is Existence, where Reality and illusion are in some sense equal in their respective contributions. And this point would represent a Phase Transition.

An interrupting Apology in Anticipation

As the above was written, I was hit by the image of some joker seizing on the schema as a justification for disparaging the "Browning of America". With myself being 75% non-caucasian, this would represent an agonizing irony. Therefore, I wish to offer a disavowal and an apology for any such misusage to every genuinely sober reader before hand.

If Existence is looked at as an Octave, then one could be forgiven for thinking that this 50%/50% point, the Light Boundary, would be found at the geometric 50%/50% point of an Octave, the Tritone. This Tritone is the true geometric center of an Octave. In a sub-luminous (quantitative) Octave, the frequency of this note is that of the Fundamental (Note DO), multiplied by the square root of two (1.41422...). Being mathematically irrational, that note is incompatible (disharmonious) with the other notes. However, it seems to me that the actual break point is at the SOL#-LA gap. The reason for this is that Existence can be said to be top heavy, in the same way that a sword is haft-heavy. In other words, if one attempts to balance a sword on one's finger, the point of balance will be skewed closer to the handle than to the sword's full length arithmetic half-way point, because the handle is usually heavier than the blade. As regards Existence, only Reality has any "weight." Anti-being, as illusion, has none, and this is why Existence can be said to be "top-heavy" because the proportion of Reality within Existence increases, the closer that part of Existence is to full Reality itself. This is also why the 50%/50% point of balance is neither at the arithmetic nor the geometric center of an Octave.

Instead, this ever so critical 50%/50% point seems to be an Asymptote found somewhere between the traditionally natural semitone at SOL# whose natural (numerical) frequency is 8/5 times the Fundamental, and Note LA proper whose natural frequency is 5/3 times the Fundamental. Those two ratios, 8/5 and 5/3, are both part of the Fibonacci series of numbers which tend towards the irrational number 1.618033989... the Golden Ratio. Furthermore, (and

I've only just this minute thought of this, on 6/24/14), the major Phase Transition below the Light Boundary, the MI-FA gap labeled as the "Animation Boundary" on the diagram below, could well be the square root of the Golden Ratio (1.27202...), which does in fact fall between Note MI (5/4 = 1.25) and Note FA (4/3 = 1.33333...).

The Golden Ratio:

The Golden Ratio is the ratio between the diagonal of a Pentagon, and its side (which means that you see this proportion every time you see a five point star, such as those on our American flag). Nature seems to greatly favor this ratio, for it shows up again and again in body proportions.

The Fibonacci series is the series of whole numbers discovered by the Renaissance Italian botanist Fibonacci, in his study of plant proportions (points of branching; flower spirals; etc.). The specific sequence is as follows: 0, 1, 1, 2, 3, 5, 8, 13, 21, 34, 55, 89, 144, *ad infinitum*. Each number is the sum of the two preceding numbers. Dividing any two adjacent numbers will tend ever closer to the irrational number 1.618033989....

There are two further major Phase Transitions. The first is that between Divinity and Existence proper. This would be the DO-SI gap of a Major scale. In this Cosmology, this most significant Boundary has been given the name "The Needle's Eye." It could just as easily have been given the name of "The Gate to the Kingdom of God" or "The Gate to Nirvana". Only WHO you really are, which is you as Zero ("I AM"), can pass through that "eye". This means leaving all of what you are as an existing Being (the "riches" that are your individual self) behind.

The second Phase Transition is within sub-luminous Existence, and has yet to be mentioned in any detail. It's referred to above as the Animation Boundary, the MI-FA gap in the overall Octave of Existence. This Phase Transition is quite simply the separation between animated living organic matter, and inert matter coupled with the physical energies. Combining several previous charts, we now have:

HALE MICHAEL SMITH, M.D.

THE FOUR REALMS OF EXISTENCE:

Fire— DO—God as "I AM"—ABSOLUTE REALITY

> <u>The Needle's Eye</u>

Air—SI— The Elohim EXISTENCE
Realm of Mind (the Living Ideal)

LA Hyper-luminous

> <u>Light Boundary</u>

Water—SOL Sub-luminous—Realm of Animation

> Tritone

FA Living material beings

> <u>Animation Boundary</u>

Earth—MI—Realm of Inertness—Organized inert matter

RE—Disorganized inert matter

> Barrier to Oblivion

MAYA—lower DO—anti-being / illusion— OBLIVION

RELIGION REINTERPRETED

<u>An aside</u>: I have always found such neat encapsulations of complex concepts (such as above), most suspect. Now, having done much the same myself, I can only hope that my results fare better under the scrutiny of others.

At any rate, the very lowest "Boundary" is that which separates Existence from anti-being proper, here labeled as "Oblivion." Obviously, it was given this name because nothing lies below and beyond Existence (which itself is not really "outside" of "I AM"). However, this additionally means that nothing which has even minimal reality as part of what it is, can pass this Boundary. Reality is always conserved, and there is always some reality to everything which genuinely exists, however minimal. Because of this, this Boundary is more properly the place of Rebound.

CHAPTER X

EXISTENCE

Recapitulation; firmament; sacred constructs; Maya, the illusion of discontinuity; anti-being not equated with evil; metaphor of emulsion; Planck's Space and Planck's Time; "Thirty spokes share the wheel's hub"

Recapitulation

As explained earlier, the primordial act of Creation was equivalent to subtracting a Positive One (a Real something), from the Zero that was the Primordial Chaos. The remainder was the residual Minus One, in effect, a "negative nothing." However, there is more to the "Great Sacrifice" than simple arithmetic. The withdrawal of all Will from this residual negative "half" of Itself meant that beyond being a negative nothing, anti-being was now a "sterile void" (an expression borrowed from Jean-Yves Leloup). This means that the totality of its logoi forever lost any meaningful possibility of ever being or contributing anything Real to the Creation. But just as importantly, it also meant that neither could anti-being ever be a "self", because it would no longer be animated by Will, by God as "I". From that point on, its negative influence on the Creation would only ever be a passive one of condition, of a tendency towards "not being" like that of erosion, or better yet, like a general tendency towards entropy or of attenuation. Its deleterious effects on the Creation forever lost the possibility of being an active act of Will... with one partial exception (Man).

This means that the notion of there being some "devil" in active and willful opposition to God as "I AM", is nonsense. <u>*There is no Will other than that which is "I"*</u>. However, it is also true that at this sub-luminous level of Existence, the general, and legitimate self-maintaining functioning of Existence can and often does seem to work against the spiritual growth of individuals. For example, it's very difficult to resist "being a lemming" in this world, which is to say it's difficult to remain a genuine individual who owns his or her own True Self. It's hard to climb uphill, here in Flatland where there's this tremendous gravity of Illusion. There's also this overwhelming tendency towards psychological inertia that siphons off our own personal efforts to retain an inner direction. Most Human culture actually feeds on the dispersion of our inner, psychic, life energy, meant for our inner growth. But nothing is wasted in this Universe. You'll be surprised by what it is that consumes this otherwise lost psychic energy of ours.

The rendering of anti-being "inanimate" so to speak, only partially diminished the danger it posed. More had to be done to safeguard the Creation from that residual "inverse twin." This was the reason for the interposition of the Biblical Firmament as a barrier between the "waters below" (the collective of all now rejected logoi), and the "waters above" (the collective of all Real logoi). In other words, that Biblical Firmament refers to and essentially is, Existence.

<u>Etymology</u>:
Firmament comes from the Latin *firmus*. It means that something is "strongly set in place". English has several words that de-

rive from *firmus*, one of which is the word "farm", which probably came from the time when farming was a legal (firmly upheld) contract between a Lord which owned the land, and the peasant (farmer) who actually worked that land. But there are two other, unexpected words derived from that same original Indo-European root, and which came to English from two different Indo-European sister languages. One is the Greek word "throne", which can be said to have meant something like "political power firmly set in place." And just as surprisingly, the other is the Sanskrit word *dharma*, which can also be also said to have meant something like "divine or spiritual law, firmly set in place."

In spite of its "firmness", Existence alone was insufficient as a means to neutralize the danger that anti-being posed to BEING. Existence mostly contained it, but Existence alone is basically a great machine, or better yet, a great self-sustaining organism which, like any living Being, maintains itself by means of innumerable circulating feedback loops. Depending on the context, we might call those feed-back loops physics, ecology, metabolism, etc. But this was not the expression of Will needed for true Reconciliation, because neither Existence nor the governing Elohim had an independent Will of its own. To connect this general notion of the ultimate insufficiency of Existence by itself, with regards to the role of being the Holy Reconciling, to an earlier formulation:

"All the King's horses and all the King's men,
Couldn't put Humpty Dumpty back together again!"

This is meant in all seriousness, and nursery rhymes like this one will pop up again in this book, because they are ofttimes "Sacred Constructs", intended to pass on esoteric teachings (or comment on politically hot issues) while evading the wrath of both

Western Churches (Catholic and Protestant). The words of this nursery rhyme were, oddly enough, the way my own subconscious made clear to me that all of the self-maintaining mechanisms of Existence, plus the active efforts of the Elohim, are insufficient to recover the state of Atonement (of original wholeness). So, again, God sent Its only son— Man (EVERY SINGLE ONE OF US)— to save this world.

I want to say more about the nature of our "smashed" Humpty Dumpty (Existence). A whole, undamaged Humpty Dumpty egg balanced (precariously) on a wall is, to my way of thinking, remarkably similar to a pearl balanced (precariously) on the back of a bird. And the explosion that results from the (inevitable) fall corresponds to the Scientific notion of the Big Bang.

Definition: Sacred Construct

This is my loose translation of Gurdjieff's term *Legominism*. There was an enormous amount of important knowledge which was left to us by our ancestors, much of which is hardly recognized for what it is. For example, it can be demonstrated that the twelve known language families of Humanity must have been the work of actual schools. Their basic grammars were almost certainly intentional constructs based on an understanding of where, how, and why we exist. This will be spoken of in greater depth later on.

But languages are not the only Sacred Constructs left to us. Certain nursery rhymes fall into this category, many of them rendered necessarily "silly" by the vigilance of the Inquisition. The DO-RE-MI system of Music was another. And Sacred Constructs also include much ancient Art. For example, I remember a large wooden statue of the Buddha in the hallway at the Rhode Island School of Design. I was looking at it one day when I quietly realized that I had suddenly understood how to "sit" in a manner that allowed both my breath and my attention to naturally drop into my lower abdomen, without any force, tension, or stress on my part.

The Illusion of Discontinuity in Existence

Space is the context for things, whether animated or inert, whereas Time is the context for change (events). And Eternity, an all encompassing NOW, is the context for non-material Mind (aka Ideas) Recognizing this leads us to the meaning of the word Existence.

Existence comes from the Latin word *ex-sistere*, which means to "stand out", or "to stand forth", "to emerge." It's basically the Gestalt concept of foreground versus background. Something has an individual existence or presentation because it can be separated or isolated out from everything else in the awareness of some mind. For that moment, that individual item becomes the foreground, while everything else becomes or remains as the background.

In other words for Existence, the Oneness (Singularity) that literally defines what Reality is has "been lost sight of" and seemingly been replaced with the multiplicity made possible by a limited and ever changing focus. Things seem to have become distinguishable from other things, depending on your depth of focus. It's conditional actuality; it has no reality of its own separate from your focus. This is so very important to understand.

Awareness is actually the true key to understanding Existence, because the multiplicity that makes Existence what it seems to be, is in fact impossible, *except in seeming, in appearance alone*. And this is precisely why this Path of Returning to God is called Religion, retying back together what has been sundered.

MAYA is the name of the Hindu god/goddess of Illusion (and also known as the more negative MARA). Anti-being is Ahriman trapped and fuming within Ahura Mazda's beautiful secondary Creation, the existing world. Whether you name the resistance to Return Maya or Ahriman, or regard it in simply in terms of physics, it remains that Existence overall is always as much illusion as it is reality, and this is why Existence at any level is never absolutely Real, but is instead "relative", or "compromised" reality, having dimensions (aka degrees of separation). Anti-being manifests as the illusion of discontinuity.

Anti-being is not to be automatically equated with Evil

This must be understood and remembered. There is no separate and independent evil Will. Anti-being is only illusion, the overall tendency towards separation, dispersion and entropy. Only Man can actualize those possibilities known to us as evil (to any degree), because other than God, only Man has an independent Will. It's precisely because "I" withdrew itself from the rejected logoi of anti-being (the Great Sacrifice) that evil can never be genuinely Real. In giving Man the Will that was Himself, God left one thing only entirely beyond Man's reach: God retained for Itself alone the decision about what would always be Real, and what would never be so. Made in the image of God, we do actually have access to those Rejected logoi of the Biblical Dark, but that's as far as it goes. As a result, in spite of all the damage we do to each other and to this world, it's never Really permanent. It only seems so, and that is our salvation. We do pay for such mistakes, but no one pays forever, such as by burning in hell, and that's because of a strange line of logic. It will be presented in the appropriate place.

Nothing produced by someone given to illusion or evil can have any Real effects, any genuine effect on anything Real. At most, anti-being only makes evil seem possible (and even desirable), but even then only as an *"actuality"*, never as a Reality. This is also why evil cannot touch hyper-luminous Existence, the so-called Ideal or "real" World.

Something else must also be clarified here. The fact that anti-being, the Biblical Dark, was originally an equal part of God as "I" does not mean that God as "I" was ever part evil, or even part illusion. Those logoi were rejected only because they were the opposite of the selected logoi, and as long as they were all equally real as part of God as "I", there could be no "AM", for they continuously and eternally canceled each other out.

And in spite of everything so far said, there is actually a positive side to anti-being (in its guise as the Peacock Angel). Specifically, the need to "distract" anti-being is responsible for all of the beauty found in the form of the natural world we see. Existence is like a stage whereupon the many logoi of BEING/ Reality can separate and recombine into smaller sub-maximal units, thereby demonstrating their possible combinations in this material world. The beauty of a sunset, of a flower, or the stunning beauty of a woman's face and form, is genuinely Real, even though the material structure on which that beauty is draped is short-lived.

<u>Existence as an emulsion of BEING and anti-being.</u>

A reasonable question has yet to be answered: "If anti-being is so antithetical to BEING (to Reality), then how does it seem to co-exist in such a seemingly stable intermix with that which is Real within Existence? I don't have a complete answer to that, except to say that Existence isn't a completely stable mix. For example, that's why we have an expanding Universe. It's also why we have such things as Time, entropy, erosion, decomposition, and exhaustion in this lower material half of Existence, all of which are something so very different from the eternal Here&Now that is hyperluminous Existence.

An aside: I had already come to the conclusion that most of the negative effects of anti-being were primarily restricted to the subluminous part of Existence, which is to say to the material and quantitative part. It was only in the excellent book *The Other God* by Yuri Stoyanov, which is about the dualistic religions, that I got confirmation on this matter. Until then, I had only surmised that Ahriman's negative effect on Ahura Mazda's creation were specifically confined to the material half of Ahura Mazda's perfect world (and trap).

A partial answer to the question posed just above is that Existence may be understood to be "emulsion." For those who don't know what this means, we should first digress by describing two different types of mixtures: solutions and suspensions. Basically, a fluidic solution is where something is dissolved, broken down to either the atomic or molecular level. Everyday examples of this are sugar in water, salt in water, and water in air. Water dissolved in air is that solution we know as humidity. Metal alloys are actually solutions, examples of which are iron plus carbon which combine to make steel, and copper plus tin which combine to make bronze.

In contrast, a suspension is where something mixed in a fluid cannot be broken down to the atomic or molecular level. Muddy water is an example, as are apple cider and milk. Another example of a suspension is a cloud, which is where the amount of water dissolved in the air is more than that air can hold. That water will then precipitate out of solution as water droplets suspended in the air. This means that a cloud is a suspension of water in air.

An emulsion is a type of suspension. Perhaps the best known one would be mayonnaise. Vinegar and oil do not normally mix. Hydrocarbons like oil don't usually dissolve in fluids which ionize, like water or vinegar. You cannot blend them into a solution because neither will dissolve into the other. Instead, the best you can accomplish is to turn them into a suspension. This means that to get an emulsion, you have to start by breaking up both the oil and the vinegar into very, very tiny droplets of each, producing a suspension. Vigorous shaking accomplishes this, as we can see with vinaigrette salad dressing.

To get an emulsion you also need something additional, a stabilizer to keep each component from separating and recombining with like droplets. In the case of mayonnaise, that stabilizer is egg. The egg protein essentially behaves as an edible soap which encapsulates the tiny particles of both the oil and the water, restraining unlike droplets so they can't rejoin with like droplets. Otherwise, after sitting for a while on a shelf, you'd find yourself with a layer of oil sitting atop a layer of vinegar.

An aside: soap works because its molecules have one end which ionizes, and the other which doesn't. The non-ionizing end sticks to the dirt or oil, while the ionizing end sticks to the water.

Applying this to Existence, the tiniest unit of "Being" is called Planck's Constant, after the discovery made by the 19th century scientist Max Planck, who discovered that the wavelength of light always increases or decreases in discrete whole number units. Thus Planck's Constant is not really so much an object as it is a unit, of action or of measurement. The corresponding minimal units of anti-being are presently known as Planck's Space and Planck's Time.

RELIGION REINTERPRETED

The question arises as to how this emulsive analogy applies to hyper-luminous Existence. The most likely answer is that logoi are the analogous equivalents to Planck's Constant.

One other question might be raised. If this sub-luminous Universe is a suspension, then why does it seem so clear? The answer is that it isn't. It's full of dust, gas, and plasma. Beyond that, with continued expansion it has become diffuse. One can read through muddy water that's been allowed to settle, or which has been sufficiently diluted with additional water. That sufficiency of dilution only began to occur for our Universe approximately 380,000 years after the Big Bang, before which the entire Universe was a solution of energy. It was so dense and energetic that for the above mentioned period of time the rampant energy was unable to settle down into discreet atoms, thereby allowing the transmission of light through the intermediate space.

Courtesy of the Tao Te Ching:

To end this Chapter on a high note, here's a relevant quote from the *Tao Te Ching*, Chapter 11, demonstrating the interaction of Discontinuity with Reality within this existing world.

> *Thirty spokes share the wheel's hub; it is the center hole which makes it useful.*
>
> *Shape clay into a vessel; it is the space within which makes it useful.*
>
> *Cut doors and windows for a room; it is the holes which make it useful.*
>
> *Therefore profit comes from what is there; Usefulness from what is not there.*

CHAPTER XI

THE LIGHT BOUNDARY

"All turning together"; infinities, asymptotes, and limits; reality vs. actuality; multiverses; looking back: parallel lives; rupa vs. arupa; what defines forms; speed of light as a barrier; time shifts approaching the light speed barrier; Time as dimensional flattening; changes in mass approaching the light speed barrier; changes in space; simultaneity and life reviews; an analogy; the light boundary as event horizon

Why a Boundary of Light?

For a long time I was struck by Einstein's discovery that light, or more precisely the speed of light, was an upper limit of some sort for the material world. The notion that nothing with mass could reach that asymptote begged for some kind of explanation, especially in the context of this stupendous Universe. The very name "Uni-verse" means "One turning", or, "All turning together." In other words, the Universe is a whole in some sense. And yet the speed of light, fast as it is, is nowhere near fast enough to be the means by which the Universe can be a Unity.

For example, light takes 8 minutes to reach us from the sun's surface. Yet from any distance at which our entire solar system could be seen in its entirety, one would be hard pressed to see that gap between the Sun and our home planet. And from any distance at which the Milky Way could be seen in its entirety, our entire solar system would be indistinguishable, too small to be visible. In other words, there must be something far beyond the speed of light able to connect this Universe together if it is to be a whole, a "one turning together." So why do we not know of it?

The claim has been made in this book that Reality is Penultimate Transfinite potential. This is based on the assumption that the original (Primordial) Creation is comprised of the potential for everything that could ever be Real (being half of the Omega Transfinite potential of the Primordial Chaos, aka God as "I"). Reality as such infinite potential would allow for anything and everything Real to be, and to come into existence in its own way, and at its own time, in its own context.

But the world we ordinarily know is not one of infinities. Does this therefore mean that this world is not Real? In fact it does. Although Science will object, Religion has been saying this all along. But we are locked into our senses for defining what is "real" to us. This sub-luminous, finite and quantitative world is on the far side of the Light Boundary from Divinity, from God as "I AM", the very Source and Meaning of Reality. Should it therefore be a surprise that no direct evidence for God has ever been discovered in this material world? Looking here in Flatland for proof of God is worse than attempting to illuminate an entire mountain at night by holding up a hand held match.

Definition of Asymptote

An asymptote is a border of infinity when it's approached from the direction of the finite and quantitative. An asymptote is a mathematical term which refers to a limit of whatever sort, which can be approached to any degree of proximity, but which can never actually be completely reached. The temperature of absolute zero is one such example. Likewise, irrational and transcendental numbers (like pi) are also asymptotes for our digital system of whole numbers. You can get as close numerically as you wish, but you never reach a final number or repeating pattern. For this finite and quantitative world, Infinity itself is the ultimate Asymptote, in whatever context infinity is found.

A very important note: Before we go further, I wish the reader to be clear that *physical light itself is not the cause of this Boundary*. The limited velocity of light, along with all of the other effects of that limit, is an effect of whatever it is which restricts electromagnetic radiation to its well known velocity. My personal best guess is that it's some dimensional divide that limits light to that velocity (as per Dr. Lisa Randall of Harvard), something perhaps analogous to the bending and diffraction that light undergoes when entering water from the air.

2) Reality versus Actuality

In this Cosmology, sub-luminous Existence is considered to be "Actuality", the "actual world", instead of being the relatively diminished "reality" of hyper-luminous Existence. Actuality is whatever actually presents itself to some observer. Whatever it happens to be, it will usually seem real enough, even though illusion rules at this lower level of Existence. And this too is part of what Religion tells us (simply remember what the Lord's Prayer says about God's Will, heaven and earth). The loss of our ability to distinguish even compromised reality from illusion is the real key to understanding what really happened to us in that "eating the forbidden fruit" event, thereby giving us the "knowledge of good and evil" which made both illusion and Reality seem equally real to us.

Beyond this, however, consider this additional issue. In almost any situation, there are more than one possible outcomes or consequences. All of these possibilities are real, in the sense that they genuinely exist as possibilities. But more often than not, these possibilities are mutually exclusive. For example, in the coin toss before a football game, it's possible for either team to win the toss, but not both together. It's therefore not possible for both teams to simultaneously receive the first kickoff. Both possible outcomes are equally real as possibilities, yet only one of them can become actual for that specific game. When scientists only consider the actual to be real, they are unable to postulate a higher-dimensional level of Existence wherein all possibilities are retained and conserved together as a whole.

The potential ramifications of this are staggering. For example, here's part of the explanation for the multiverse hypothesis. Every possible type of Universe, and every possible variation within any given Universe, resides as real potential in hyper-luminous Existence. It's only in sub-luminous Actuality that these possibilities become mutually exclusive and actual for some observer.

The fact that different observers experience the same actuality in very, very different ways and have very, very different interpretations of what actually happened is the threshold to first perceiving and then comprehending the reality of mutually exclusive, simultaneously real possibilities. Even in our own minds there is a hyper-luminous and sub-luminous boundary. The more partial we are to self-justification and judgements, the more illusions we propagate; the more willing we are to live with truths, including the truths of not-knowing, the more hyper-luminous our minds and lives become.

But if this is still a problem for you the reader, then simply recognize this: nothing Real is ever separate for (or from) "I AM".

God is where everything both is and starts. For God, everything Real is never other than Here&Now: the beginning of Creation, the formation of the Earth, the dinosaurs, the Roman Empire, and your first breath are all equally Here&Now for God. Existence is the external elaboration in time and space for potential realities.

Looking back: I first began to notice the uncertainty about Actuality when I was ten years old. I had been playing all day with my childhood best friend, Gregory C. Watson (at the time of this writing, the Secretary of Agriculture for Massachusetts under Governor Deval Patrick). Going to bed that evening, I suddenly began to wonder what time it might be for Greg. For all I knew, he might already be waking up next morning in his awareness, in his actuality. I believed that I would only know where he was on our parallel time-lines when we again met up, thereby aligning our individual time-lines. However, I now understand that even meeting with Greg (or anyone else) does not mean that our awareness of our mutual actualities are actually aligned. It's certainly easier for us not to think about something like this, but none of us really has any certainty of whether someone else's own present moment is the same as our own, or not. (I was a weird kid.)

More than once, I have had the distinct sensation that the conversation I am hearing and experiencing is not the conversation and experience other people are having.

Rupa versus Arupa

Distinctions such as those between exterior and interior, form and substance, appearance versus reality have no meaning above the Light Boundary, for the Light Boundary is where such distinctions begin. This is an important point made in the religions of India (Hinduism, Buddhism, Jainism), with the words *Rupa* (form) and *Arupa* (without form).

This divide first occurs at the Light Boundary, where the external seems to divide from the internal. It is precisely this delineation of what something is that accounts for things becoming finite and quantifiable. We look around our room and see every separate object because we can isolate each one out from the overall context of the room. If there were no outlines for each, it would be impossible to isolate anything out from its background. Such is the nature of Flatland.

Hyper-luminous Existence is the domain of Ideas, whereas sub-luminous Existence is the domain of things, whether animate or inert. It is the limitation of having an outline which defines the latter, and these outlines allow for such questions as "who", "what", "which", "where", "when", and "how much" to have meaning. But Ideas too are distinct from one another, even though in a different way. In this regard, I can only offer the analogous example of the color spectrum. On such a continuous color spectrum, it's impossible to delineate exactly where red ends and orange or magenta begin. However, I can point to where red seems to be at it's maximum, and the same for orange or magenta. In other words, Ideas are defined by their center of gravity, by what we might call their center of greatest concentration/meaning. What this allows for will be discussed in the next chapter about Ideas.

Einstein's Light Speed Barrier

As mentioned at the beginning of this chapter, I long pondered why the velocity of light should be the upper limit for anything with mass (in contrast, photons of light themselves have no mass), and therefore an upper limit for the existence of matter (and by extension, this entire material world). The velocity of light is the asymptotic upper limit for the maximal speed at which matter can travel. But this also means that there have to be other velocities in some sense, above and beyond that of light speed. For example, in the initial period of the expansion of Existence out from God as "I AM", there was what in Science is called the Period of Inflation, originally postulated by Dr. Alan Guth. This initial inflationary period saw the Universe expand at a rate far higher than light speed. Specifically, it was empty Space (anti-being) itself which was expanding, and dragging everything else along with it.

The second thing that came to mind in this regard was the property known in Science as "non-locality", also known as "Entanglement." Einstein himself called it "spooky action at a distance." This refers to the proven fact that two particles tied together by their origin will share linked properties, such as opposite spins. Until observed, the spin of either is uncertain. However, once you determine the spin of one of those two particles, the spin of its partner can be instantaneously shown to be the opposite, regardless of any intervening distance. In other words, there is a communication here which does not depend on light. This presents a big problem if Time & Space are your only definitions of reality. However, if your definition of Reality starts with the Oneness (the Singularity) of BEING, then everything Real is by definition already connected with everything else Real, without regard to physical distance, and despite its seeming projection into "Flatland", aka sub-luminous Existence.

Approaching the velocity of light

The speed of light is the upper limit to our finite quantifiable world. Time, mass, and space as we know them disappear entirely as this limit is reached, and we do not directly know what is to be found beyond this boundary. Understanding what happens as we approach light speed is instructive, even though the velocity of light is the very best example of an asymptote. While we can approach it as arbitrarily close as we wish, we can never completely reach it... as ordinary finite material Beings, that is.

Changes in Time as one approaches the speed of light

As a mass approaches the velocity of light, time for that mass increasingly slows down. This is not apparent to the mass itself. Were the mass in question a space ship with passengers, no one aboard would register any change in the rate of the passage of time, which is to say that their clocks would not seem to them to run any slower, nor would they themselves seem to age any slower. It would only be on their return to Earth that they would realize that they had aged at a rate much slower than those they left behind.

This is called time dilation or time expansion. Time, and therefore, the rate at which change occurs for an observer at light speed (were that possible for mass—our space ship—to reach that speed), would cease to exist as a dimension of perception, because Time would have become an infinite Now— what we call Eternity. Anything we would then think, feel or do would all be part of a Now without a before or an after. This is very different from the usual notion of Eternity, that of an endless calendar and extension in Time.

An endless Now might seem appalling, like being suspended in oblivion. However, I have reason to believe that this expanded experience of Now is not something frozen, even though I can't yet completely put it into words. For now, I would call it the experience of an increased depth and density in the Realness of something. And if this sounds corny, one need only speak to someone who's had the experience of time slowing down, like a soldier during his first encounter with actual combat, or, with anyone who has witnessed something both dramatic and totally unexpected. Change is actually only a superficial surface phenomenon, and its diminishment allows one to witness the Reality around oneself in far greater detail. Besides, Eternity (in some ultimate form) is how "I AM" (God) sees everything, so it can't be that bad.

Time is really the symptom of an awareness too limited to witness everything as a Whole, as an entirety. In such a state, we can only know things as a series of cross-sections of themselves, like the continuous frames in a moving picture. Time is the experience of becoming, as opposed to that of being. It's a dimensional thing, but I don't believe Time to be an independent dimension. Rather, Time is a consequence of the dimensional "flattening" of the awareness of an observer.

Changes in mass as one approaches the speed of light

Keeping in mind that mass is really the manifestation of inertia (the Holy Denying), the mass (inertia) of any matter increases as one approaches the velocity of light. Part of this increase is due to the energy one must continuously add to continuously accelerate (further speed up) that mass, because that energy itself adds to that mass. This is why a fast moving bullet or car does more damage than a slow moving one of equal rest mass. But in our far from light speed worlds, such increases are negligible. The resulting infinite increase in a mass which is approaching light speed, however, is not negligible. The greater the build up of mass, the greater the energy will need to be added to further speed up the mass. One of the reasons that light speed is an asymptote is because of the infinite energy needed to reach it. This is borne out everyday in particle accelerators, even in the new one at CERN, Switzerland, where enormous energy is needed to move infinitesimally small particles like protons to a velocity anywhere close to light speed. Only particles without mass (without any inertia at rest), like photons of light, can actually move at that speed. Paradoxically, those particles are only actual when they move at light speed. Otherwise, they don't exist.

The increase in mass when approaching light speed must be a "bunching up" of the Higgs Field in some sense. The same must be true for the gravity which creates a Black Hole in the collapse of a star. The light boundary is a dimensional divide, below which are too few dimensions to allow the Higgs field itself to remain a Singularity. It must be analogous to the contrails trailing an airplane wing because of the localized drop in air pressure the wing tips cause.

Changes in Space as one approaches the speed of light

This is another part to the reason why our mass becomes infinite as it approaches the velocity of light. Einstein pointed out that in the attempt to do so, space begins to contract along the direction that mass is traveling. Actually, this happens with any spatial translation, which is to say with any ordinary motion of any ordinary object. It is just that spatial contraction remains too small to notice until one has begun to closely approach the speed of light. But to be even more precise, it's not so much Space which contracts as it is our mass which is traveling that contracts. For example, a spaceship traveling at a high fraction of the speed of light would look visibly shorter to an outside observer. However, someone traveling inside of that ship or alongside of it at the same speed would not notice any change, just as they would not notice any change in the passage of time.

In essence, the object in question would pancake, but without spreading out to the sides. The two dimensions perpendicular to the line of travel would remain unchanged. Taking this to its logical conclusion, and restricting ourselves to spatial dimensions alone, were an object to actually reach the speed of light, it would essentially become absolutely two-dimensional. However, as I will speak of in the chapter about Dimensions, I believe that the dimension of Space that seems to have been lost would in fact only become implicit. Replacing that lost dimension of Space would be that which was formerly the dimension of Time, now expanded to infinity.

Life Reviews: examples of Simultaneity

Changes to Time, Mass, and Space while approaching light speed happen simultaneously in all three media. This proves to be a frequent problem in explaining things, because that which is simultaneous can only be approximated by sequence. Failing to recognize this is the reason for the confusion surrounding the Life Reviews reported in Near Death Experiences.

Science and Medicine are on the slow track to accepting that such experiences might be genuine; they continue to insist that there must be some as yet unknown brain function responsible for them. However, as a former (and humble) internist who has run his share of resuscitation attempts, I know that the only part the brain could possibly play in such experiences is that it's shut down and temporarily non-functional. (In other words, it's not getting in the way.) Besides, there's a limit to how long the brain can be deprived of air, if it is to return to unimpaired function. Even in cases of cold-water drowning where the brain can withstand hypoxia beyond the usual four minute limit, there still is nowhere near enough time spent in the near death state for one's brain to sequentially witness one's entire life by means of ordinary memory.

The brain is a mechanism which works sequentially in time, but it's out of action in a Near Death Experience. A Life Review is a "release phenomenon" of some sort (meaning that the cessation of conscious brain functioning releases something else to replace it). Life Reviews are instances of Simultaneity in Awareness, examples of an awareness able to witness one's entire life as a single whole without reference to time. One sees one's entire life in detail as a single Now. It is only when returning to our everyday brain-mediated awareness that we are forced to remember (and speak of) that experience in sequence. Such an extended Now is proof that one has jumped up a grade in Awareness, and is therefore a full Note up in the Hierarchy of Existence. The crucial proportion is:

Time is to Eternity as Sequence is to Simultaneity.

<u>The light boundary's placement in the octave of Existence (the Fibonacci breakpoint)</u>

For the typical major scale, the highest frequency gap is between Notes SI-DO. This corresponds to the gap between God (Absolute Reality), and Existence, in a descending Octave. The lower Frequency gap is between Notes MI-FA, which in this Cosmology is called the Animation Boundary because it separates animated (living) matter from inanimate (inert) matter. However, there's a third gap.

The light boundary corresponds to the gap found in the Enneagram (see Appendix) between Notes SOL-LA. However, more precisely, it's found between SOL#—LA. The ratio of note LA to its (lower) fundamental is 5/3, whereas the ratio of the half-step lower note, SOL#, is 8/5. In other words, this is the Fibonacci (Golden Ratio) break point in an Octave, and by extension, in Existence. And again, we find this point to be musically as well as mathematically asymptotic, as we follow it down the spiraling rabbit hole of fibonacci ratios: 13/8 -> 21/13 -> 34/21... etc..

The Light Boundary: the "Event Horizon" for BEING

It was the summer of 2010 when, thanks to the Science Channel, I first learned about the "Holographic Principle" for explaining this Universe, as developed by Dr. Leonard Susskind. It was a Cosmological principle developed to reinforce and preserve the scientific axiom that information is never lost in this Universe. It was a means to demonstrate that even a Black Hole does not destroy information. Instead, that information is retained on some Cosmic Event Horizon.

It was only after I was able to grasp a small bit of what Dr. Susskind was talking about that I realized just what that Event Horizon had to be in the context of this Cosmology. It could only be this postulated light boundary, and the Singularity which corresponded to that Event Horizon could only be the Primordial Singularity, BEING, aka Absolute Reality, and therefore God as "I AM". Furthermore, Dr. Susskind's Holographic Principle suggests that information is more fundamental than the material structures of this sub-luminous Universe, which is also to say that this material world is *not as real as that information*. Exchange the word 'Information" with the word "Idea", as used in this book, and one begins to see the connection.

The light boundary itself acts as a sort of pin hole camera through which "information" (the collective of Aleph Null Ideas), is projected outwards in some sort of inverted fashion. This inversion is manifest as the illusion of reality that this material Universe seems to posses. At any rate, because this Universe is supposedly a projection of information, the Holographic Principle, like this

RELIGION REINTERPRETED

Cosmology, is also saying that this material Universe is in truth more Illusion than Real.

The implications are staggering. Furthermore, they correspond to the implications embedded in the Lord's Prayer. Those implications are that this sub-luminous World is largely outside of the direct influence of God as "I AM". God only operates here through the heart of Man... WHEN OPEN.

A caution: Dr. Susskind has not been contacted regarding this supposition of mine. It's doubtful that he would readily ascribe to the assumptions of this Cosmology. Therefore, he cannot be called into question or held responsible regarding the conclusions that I have written into this book.

CHAPTER XII

IDEAS

Fundamental units; the experience and the metaphor of schizophrenia; spalling; etymologies of "idea"; height and seeing; idolatry in religion; names; naming Man; true names; matrix of ideas

The fundamental units of Existence

Existence is predicated on the illusion that Reality (BEING) is discontinuous, separated in some sense. Such a seeming is only possible because Awareness, one of the seven fundamental aspects of BEING, is susceptible to anti-being, and therefore to appearances. The consequences that such incomplete Awareness has on Reality is the reason why Existence is referred to in this book as "compromised", "conditional", "relative", or even, "defective"—meaning, not bad or wrong, but merely incomplete.

It is postulated that "I AM" (or possibly one of the Seraphim of the Elohim) triggered the seeming expansion and transformation of Reality into Existence by creating "Ideas": individualized packets of Universal Spirit (God as "I AM"). To be certain this is clearly understood, understand that God as "I AM" is Spirit, and is only ever Spirit in the Absolute sense. But God as "I AM" is never "a spirit." Being familiar with this concept is important, because it is also the difference between the "Absolute Heaven" as the ultimate

Singular Kingdom of God (as in "the Kingdom of God is at hand"), in contrast to the relative "heaven" known as Paradise (the relatively perfect world that is Hyper-luminous Existence). Our absolute Return to the former is both Nirvana and that which Jesus called "threading the Eye of that Needle", the true and ultimate destiny for every individualized manifestation of God's True One Son (every son of Man, male or female), thereby leaving the whole of Existence entirely behind. This is not our true home.

But to return to the primary point of this Chapter, Ideas (also known in this book as Ideal Beings) are the true building blocks of Existence. Ideas are the denizens of hyper-luminous Existence, which means they too are Infinities.

Ideas are not mutually exclusive from each other; their essential compatibility is what makes Existence possible. Recollect that everything inherently antithetical to a sustained Existence had to be excluded in the Great Sacrifice. The identity of individual Ideas is an Identity by Inclusion, an Identity defined by how much you include in overlap. Another way to express this is to say that they are not externally circumscribed like the entities of the sub-luminous realm, something known as Identity by Exclusion (an Identity defined by what you are not). There's no differentiation of form versus substance above the light boundary.

The basic issue involved here is the fundamental and ultimate incompatibility between (sub-luminous) Precision and (hyper-luminous) Accuracy. In a sub-luminous realm it is possible to be quite precise and still be inaccurate. I can say that it is precisely 11 hours, 35 minutes, and 16 seconds of the clock; but what if my clock is set inaccurately? Any "precise" delineation can be done arbitrarily, but it can nevertheless be unreal. Ideas, however, have a reality of quality, not of quantity, and can only and ever be true to themselves. Furthermore, every Idea is connected to (and merges with) all other Ideas, forming a Matrix in fact.

Ideas are individualized packets or parcels of Spirit. This is to say that each Idea is a *specific formula of logoi*. The transfinite logoi which collectively comprise the Singularity that is BEING (Reality) are the fundamental building blocks for every individual Idea. This notion is not unrelated to the notion in modern Physics, that there is but one of every known sub-atomic particle. This is not to say that in this entire universe there is literally but one electron. Rather, because every electron so absolutely identical to every other electron, it makes sense to think of each as a lower dimensional projection of the very same single electron, no matter how many of them there seem to be numerically. From a religious standpoint, this would be to say that God does things but once. An example would be a perfect phonetic alphabet where there is just one symbol for one basic sound, even when that sound is used over and over again in innumerable words or names.

Schizophrenia as the means of Creating a World

In spite of the explanation about how Ideas overlap each other, each Idea does have a sense of its own individuality, a sense of being itself. And the process by which this was accomplished by our Creator, (or perhaps by the Peacock Angel) can be called "Induced Schizophrenia". To explain:

<u>Looking back</u>: My first clinical rotation in medical school (summer 1980) was a two week stint on the Psych ward at the VA Hospital in Washington D.C. Like everyone else, I had already attended the prescribed lectures in Psychiatry and Psychology. However, I had come away from those lectures believing that the diag-

nosis of Schizophrenia was an ill-defined grab bag of symptoms. The word itself, "schizo-phrenia" does literally mean a "split mind", but not in the sense of a split personality. And in spite of the lectures, I didn't understand exactly what was supposedly "split" from what.

I spent two weeks listening to the inmates of this ward, who had been diagnosed as being schizophrenic. They spent much of their time attempting to explain and justify why they believed they were hearing voices (there seems to be some fundamental human need to explain and/or justify everything we believe). The typical scenario they presented involved having had miniature radios implanted in their teeth (or in less accessible parts of their anatomies), very often by some spy agency. While I was disbelieving of their scenario stories, I had no doubt of the subjective reality of their experiences of hearing the "voices". The reason for this was a similar though brief episode in my own life, during the last couple of months of my first semester Anatomy class, one and a half years earlier.

Intellectually, Anatomy class had been a fascinating experience. At the same time, it was a horrifying shock at some deeper emotional level, to dissect the body of another human being which was like every other human animal body, including my own and those of people important to me. I won't describe the awful experiences I was confronted with in that lab, except to say that there were times I almost had to literally drag myself into that lab by grabbing my own collar. My consumption of meat dropped off sharply (as did my interest in sex), as typically happens to many medical students.

By November, I was beginning to hear voices telling me that I was going to die. Importantly, these voices did seem to be coming from outside of myself, and they increasingly plagued me long into

December, getting ever more insistent. The only thing that saved me is that I never once believed that they were genuinely coming from some outside source, as opposed to being my own thoughts. One night in late December while attempting to study for final exams (alone in my apartment), I got angry and answered those voices back by yelling out loud at them, "Even dying doesn't take forever!" By that I meant that I could endure the transition of dying, simply because even that would have a discrete end point (a great idea for a good, Poe-like horror story, that of someone endlessly trapped in the middle of the process of dying. Be my guest if you wish to try your hand at it). I never heard another voice after that. I also did very well on the finals in Anatomy.

Because of that experience, I was able to take those patients seriously, even though I had yet to understand why (or how) this was happening to them, or why it had happened to me. By the end of the two weeks, I did begin to understand what it was that was split for them. These patients had aspects of themselves which they couldn't accept or even acknowledge as being part of themselves, and as a result, they rejected those unacceptable thoughts and feelings by contracting their own sense (awareness) of their own selves. You could illustrate this process by having a number of dots on a piece of paper (which represent thoughts, feeling, impulses, fears, wishes, etc.) and then circling a number of them. That circle would now represent "ME". Now draw a smaller circle within the original one, leaving some of the dots within the first circle outside of the new smaller one, and that smaller circle would now represent the newly schizophrenic "me". Those rejected thoughts and feelings were then experienced as coming from the outside… something I could well understand. This contraction of self occurred as a result of the pressure they felt themselves to be under; leaving parts of their own minds "outside" initially seemed to be a release or escape from the unacceptable, but the excluded, rejected thoughts and feelings did not cease to exist. And this was the "split-mind" of schizophrenia.

The metallurgic and military term "to spall" comes to mind. This occurs inside of an armored vehicle when a fragment of metal is flaked off from the inside of the armor wall, as a result of an impact to the exterior of that tank's armor by some projectile. The original projectile will have no need to actually penetrate the armor of that tank in order to kill the crew, because that spalled fragment within will do the dirty work for it by ricocheting throughout the tank's interior. In the case of schizophrenia, unwanted thoughts and feelings are spalled off of one's contracting sense of self, and are subsequently experienced as coming from some independent outside source.

It was at this very moment of insight, long before there was any thought that I might write a book, that I saw something else. I immediately saw that a similar contraction of awareness would have to be responsible for making this world of Existence. In other words, a localized (and ultimately illusory) contraction of awareness around a chosen set of logoi, within the entire Set of all Real logoi which together comprise BEING, would end up producing an Idea, while at the same time producing a world external to that Idea. Those logoi and Ideas now outside of that specific recipe would now be experienced as the sort of external context we think of as a World.

The interconnection of all Ideas fits into this picture like my name does with all other names. The individual letters of my name are used in other names without blurring my individual Identity. It's the same with logoi. This motif of Identity by sharing basic elements extends throughout Existence. It's a strong argument against the belief that God would have resorted to creating every single little item individually, instead of creating the basic system, and then letting it unfold on its own.

And Existence is precisely that, a world with an almost infinite number of levels, populated by an infinity of centers of awareness. It's a world which is the result of a sense of "me", being embedded within a context of "not me". In contrast to this localized experience of what seems to be myself alone, everything else now seems to be out there (outside of me), in some sense. However, the very notion of an outside or elsewhere is an illusion, from the standpoint of "I AM" that is. This is why religions speak about Atonement, about Returning to being One with everything and everyone else, with all of nature and this entire Universe. Unfortunately, this is usually understood as little more than sentiment, or as simply being forgiven for sins. In genuine fact, it's the admonition to be At-one in one's awareness, because ultimately that's the true state of affairs. For us as Man, it means an expansion of consciousness back to where it once again includes everything and everyone as part of itself.

This is how we simultaneously fulfill both our designated purpose of acting as the Independent Reconciliation between the Affirmation that is God as "I AM" and the Denial that is the illusion of Discontinuity, as well as finding our absolute Return back to God.

So why the word "Idea?"

The word "Idea" is derived from an Indo-European word reconstructed as "weid" (and presumably pronounced as "way-eed"). This single word included a number of meanings which have become separate words in the daughter languages of Indo-European. In formal Linguistics, such a cluster of meanings is known as an "etymon", and it is precisely because of the original etymon of

RELIGION REINTERPRETED

"weid" that the word Idea was chosen as a replacement for the word "spirit" when describing hyper-luminous Beings, individualized parcels of (Universal) Spirit. In other words, "Ideas" are here used as the count noun version of the mass noun "Spirit." To give you the reader some notion of the etymon for the word "weid:"

1) The Sanskrit title for the earliest Hindu religious texts was the Vedas. There was also the later Vedanta. These texts were the truths as "seen" by the Indo-Iranians, which had been revealed to them by the gods. I believe the Persian "Avesta" also qualifies.

2) One of the two postulated meanings ascribed to the Celtic title Druid is that of a "powerful seer": *Dru-uid*. ("uid" is pronounced "w-ee-d")

3) The Latin "uidere" means "to see." It's the source of numerable English words such as: "view", "vista", "video", "visible", "visa", and "evidence", just to name a few. The Romans tended to be very concrete in most things. They pronounced "v" as we pronounce "w".

4) The Germanic cognates are also considerable. In modern German, "Wissen" (pronounced "vissen") is the word meaning to "know a fact." "Wissenschaft" is the modern German word for Science.

5) The Normans (Germanic Vikings, "Northmen", who settled in Normandy France) gave English the word "guide." A French word starting with "gu-" is almost invariably a borrowed Germanic word beginning with a "w-" (having been changed to look more

French). Hence, a "guide" (uid) is someone who "sees" the way, and can therefore direct you to or along it.

6) English has its own direct Germanic descendants of "Weid." They include the words "wise", "wizard", "wit", "witness", and "wisdom".

7) The English word "idea" comes from the Greek "idein", to see metaphorically, unlike the literal Latin. There's also the Greek word "eidos" which gave us "eidetic", "ideal", "idyllic", and the word "idol".

All of the above is quite a lot to have come from the original word "weid".

The point to this exposition is to recombine into one meaning, the notions of seeing both literally and metaphorically, along with the notions of knowing and understanding. An Idea is therefore intended to be something seen/known/understood as a whole, "all at once" in a sense. An analogy to what we are groping for here would be to picture that someone is traveling along a path. Walking along that path is like thinking about it, in that you take note of what you encounter in sequence, as you continue to walk. Then again, a concept is like having a map for that path. You can visualize the overall form of how that path wends its way through the landscape. But to actually see the entire path all at once means getting above it in some sense, without having to chop it up into pieces arranged in a sequence, like you do for thinking. "Being above" is a metaphor used very often in the Bible to indicate an elevated level consciousness. Above, you can see the entire path and understand it all at once as a whole. Therefore, the notion of "height", of an elevated awareness from where you can take in everything, is very important to this notion of "seeing".

For a similar reason, height is also a theme in the Bible. It's why Moses encountered God on a mountain top, why the Transfiguration of Jesus also occurred on one, and why the Last Supper took place in an upper room. Conversely, it's why Jesus encountered insanity and "demonic" possession in people after coming down from hillsides and mountains. He was returning to this Flatland, which is still mostly insane.

About idolatry.

The average American thinks of an idol as something made out of rock, ceramics, or even drawings. However, the true meaning of an idol is that it is a "dead idea". An idol is literally an Idea/notion which has become a fixed, rigid, sub-luminous affair, suffocated of any true life by its entrapment in its form by the worldly mind. The external form of that Idea has replaced its inner meaning in priority. For example, most "-isms" are Idols, because most "-isms" become ends in themselves. Communism was certainly an "-ism", but the same is true for Capitalism. At present, even to raise the question of whether Capitalism is or is not appropriate for certain situations is considered anti-American by many. As a result, services essential to life like education, postal services, health care and support for the elderly are under threat because some believe they should be subjected to motivations of profit, with profits increasing as services diminish. This is an example of genuine Idolatry.

Another damaging idolatry for Western society: the elevation of Jesus to the status of deity. This status was established as the foundation of "Christianity" by Constantine, primarily for political reasons. Historically, calling Jesus a deity helped proselytizers "equate" the "new God" Jesus with any of several gods of antiquity, who were gods and sons of gods. But Constantine had another motivation. For centuries, Christians had been persecuted by the Roman Empire for not agreeing to the supposed "divinity" of the Emperor. In a time of great internal turmoil, Constantine and his bishops "solved" things by substituting Jesus as the "divine" emperor.

This has long been considered to be an Idolatry by both Judaism and Islam, and I feel them to be correct on this issue. This Cosmology is based instead on the notion that *no man is a deity, even though every Man does have divinity as the very core of WHO he or she is (but not of what he or she is)*. This confusion of having "I AM" as the true center of every individual with "being a god", was the cause of elevating the prophet Jesus to the status of being a god, and it very badly compromised His true message, and ever so many people have died as a result. There's much more to this, which will be addressed in the section on Religion.

But as another example of Idolatry, there's the present day effort by militant Islam to force the world to conform to Islamic beliefs and customs (much like the effort of "Christian" Europe to convert traditional people during the age of colonization). In both cases, forced conversions are made under threat of harm or death; there is nothing voluntary about them. But true metanoia, genuine Return to at-one-ment, is a voluntary process or event.

Names

Hyper-luminous Existence is also the realm of true names. Earlier, when speaking about the titles we have for God, we referred to the chemical formula for water, H2O, as an example of a true name. Readers of Tolkien may recall Treebeard's explanation of Ent names. True knowing is only possible at the hyper-luminous level of Existence, because true knowing involves no intermediate agency such as sensation or thought. At these levels of Existence, everything is known directly, because what is "seen" is the true name and nature of each being, as expressed by its unique formula (recipe) of logoi.

In this context, Man is anomalous because there are five pyramidal levels of any Man's "true name." The very lowest level of these is that of any Man's planetary species. For we here on Earth, that species is called Human. Etymologically, that title, along with the word "humility", derives from the Latin word *humus*, which literally means "soil". This explicitly means that our Human bodies are derived from the basic material of the surface of this planet Earth. Our Human animal bodies are our basement self.

Importantly, what this means is that Man's Human animal body is simply that: a modified animal, just as Science correctly asserts, and again, something that was created separately from that Idea of Man, ADAM. Having dissected a human body in medical school, I can confirm that this is not merely theoretical. Animals are made of meat; spirits are not. There is less than 2% genetic difference between ourselves and our nearest animal relatives, the Chimpanzee and Bonobo. Like every other animal, we must eat, breathe, urinate and defecate, as well as copulate in order to sustain our numbers. And the equipment for doing all of these things is similar to the corresponding equipment of all other mammals. And finally, upon dying, our bodies rot, as animal bodies do. There should be no sense of shame or disgrace about this, nor in accepting that it took the Elohim billions of years to accomplish this work of organic art by the slow processes of mutation and adaption. Nothing in Time & Space pops into existence fully formed; we are born after nine months of transition from a start as a single cell. This is what Genesis Chapter One is explicitly telling us in the original Hebrew.

Our bodies have very little genetic variation between any two randomly selected Human individuals. What this means is that even at this lowest and most differentiated of levels, we are, everyone of us, very much alike. This alone should highlight the stupidity of racism in its myriad of manifestations, because in every meaningful way, we are born, live, and die in the same manner. In essence, we all share the same genetic Name.

The next two levels up of our pyramid of selves, are those of our two souls: a sub-luminous material soul, and a hyper-luminous "True Soul". It's too early to go into specifics here, except to say that these are the locus of our individuality, in other words, our selfhood beyond the accidents of our socialization.

ADAM is the single Idea that includes each and every one of us. ADAM is the entire alphabet of Man. Someone's True Soul is essentially their true name as drawn from that alphabet of Mankind. In Genesis, this was what was drawn from Adam's rib—a more concrete and specific (individualized) version of ADAM. The sub-luminous material soul is the connection needed between our True Soul and our material (read "animal") being.

True names

Ultimately, a Man's Truest Name is "I AM". Finding this Pearl lost within our total Being, and allowing all else to be sold off, is how we both perform our designated task as Man, and, how we accomplish our Return Back to Singularity with God. But this Return is one of awakening to the fact that in Reality, we never left. In leaving Existence behind, we leave illusion behind.

But this notion of the true name of something is why, in early cultures, true names were protected by giving the individual a different name for general use (a designation). This is also why individuals who are very close to each other tend to have private names for each other which are often more appropriate for that other person by somehow striking much closer to the central essence of that person (even nicknames like "Stinky").

<u>The matrix of Ideas, the foundation of Existence.</u>
The entire collective of Ideas which together comprise a dense multi-dimensional structure can be called the Matrix of Ideas. Even though Ideas are individualized to a degree, they are in no way as discretely individualized as material beings and things tend to be. All Ideas are connected together as part of the larger whole, each Idea being connected through this Matrix to every other idea in Existence, even when only seemingly indirectly (Julia Sets).

Another name would be the Matrix of Every Real Possibility. The entirety of every Real possibility in this entire Universe, over the entire period of its Existence, is permanently present as a single composite whole at the hyper-luminous level. Within Existence, this potential is spread out and expanded (aka diffracted). For example, the possibilities intrinsic to the "Idea of Branching" thereby allow plants to spread out; allows for river (drainage) systems and river deltas; allows there to be circulatory systems; cascades of water down a rock wall; evolutionary patterns of animal and plant divergence; computer programs with branch points determined by the result of previous calculations; and family trees, just to name a few of the infinite possibilities.

Another example would be how the Idea of translation (moving forward), and the Idea of falling (moving inwards towards the center of a gravitational field), combine to produce the Idea of orbiting, when the two Ideas balance each other.

Ideas, like their source, are alive, intelligent, and self-aware, but to us they can seem to be abstract entities. They can be understood as being "Natural Law." Natural Law is the primary manifestation of this Matrix of Ideas. This manifestation includes laws of physics, chemistry, biology, geology, and of mathematics, laws which are usually only believed to be mere, inert abstractions. Here in Flatland that may seem to be an adequate description, but the inability of modern Man to sense the aliveness of Ideas is, sadly, an indication of diminished intelligence.

CHAPTER XIII

ANGELS

Elohim; Xwede; the white pearl; Melek Taus of the seven Archangels; the Amesha Spenta, the six divine sparks; Seraphim; ADAM / Gayomart; an infinity of shadows; triads and octaves; linear permutations and metaphorical astrology; "acquiescing elegantly to the solicitations of Infinity"; spirit in the jar; semi-permeable membranes; ADAM's role; "bad angels"; etymology of "demon"; idea of Mother Nature

Angels?

It was only when I began to seriously contemplate just what the title "Elohim" might mean, and wondered why it would be a plural word, that I began to think about Angels. This title for the God in Genesis, Chapter One is the Hebrew plural version of the Semitic name for God, "AL" (Aleph-Lammed). Had it been translated literally into English, the only appropriate English word for Elohim would have been "gods". But that would have led to Theological mayhem in Christianity.

J. G. Bennett once interpreted the Elohim to mean "the powers of God." Accordingly, angels together as a collective could be understood as analogous to that collective of nerve cells which we call our brain, except that this angelic, Cosmic Brain is in charge of the entire body of Existence. Playing the role of individual nerve cells in that collective would be the individual Ideas of the Matrix.

Years after having made this equation between the Elohim and the Matrix as the governing principle of Existence, I learned that this is precisely the point made in the ancient Kurdish religion called "The Cult of Angels" (the Yazdani). Because the Kurds (Medes) were themselves part of the Iranian overthrow of the Babylonians, I no longer accept that such a parallel confluence of meaning between these two traditions, the Semitic and the Iranian, could be accidental.

The highest of Angels must be far more than mere messengers, which is what the word "angel" actually means in the original Greek. The higher Angels are usually considered to be "pure spirits" because, unlike the lowest orders of ideas, they tend not to have any intrinsic connection with any specific material entity or process, the day to day management of Existence.

Angels are alive, intelligent, and self-aware, and for us they can seem formidable, which is why the first words an Angel utters so often are "Fear not!" But there's something very important to remember. In spite of the tremendous Beings that they are, Angels do not possess independent Will. Angels do not have an independent initiative. Because of this, their "selfhood" can have the experience of "me", but not of "I", except as it is supplied by God as "I AM", something called in this book displaced "I". As such, Angels are like high ranking military officers which, while competent in their profession, are yet beholden to civilian authority for their initiative. This lack of independent initiative is the precise reason why "all the King's horses and all the King's men" could not, by themselves, put Existence back together again. This is why Existence alone was insufficient to be the primary instrument for Reconciling, neutralizing, anti-being.

"I AM" is too transcendent to fit into this tiny bottle called Existence, which is why the Matrix of Ideas is responsible for insuring that "all the trains run on time" here in Flatland. "I AM" decides where those trains should ultimately go; the Elohim was left responsible for the task of the unfolding and development of this material Universe. This is the real meaning behind the "six days" with a seventh "day of rest"— a day, an interval, a "reset" in which to remember "I AM". This is the answer to such questions as "How could Evolution be true if God created everything?"

Well, God (as "I") absolutely did create everything when God created Reality as the sum of all possibilities. The actual forms these possibilities would take are variable, depending on the subluminous context they eventually inhabit, which is the primary point to Darwin's explanation of evolution. It's just like the route you take to drive to work everyday, which you will change if road construction makes your usual route more difficult to use. You changing your route is an example of adaptation to prevailing conditions. Likewise, life changes according to conditions. At the same time, I am personally certain that there have been episodes of intentional intervention (by "I AM") in the unfolding of life on this planet, especially where it concerns Man, as will be described later.

It is important to understand that Existence, much like our own individual bodies, is designed to work largely by itself on its own accord. You don't need "I AM" to directly determine every little change that occurs in this world. Similarly, by their very design, our bodies know how to develop from a completed (fertilized) single cell, how to continue to grow to maturity, both before and after birth, as long as they are fed and cared for. God (as "I") absolutely did create everything Real; God (now as "I AM"), also designed Existence to mostly work on its own. The manifestation of the collective intelligence within Existence was the evolution of life, as loosely directed by the Elohim (aka the Yazdani), via the Matrix of Ideas.

This alone explains the difference between Chapters One and Two of Genesis in the Torah/ Bible, while at the same time allowing for and validating a Scientific knowledge of Evolution, which we still do not fully comprehend. I suspect that both Lamarck and Leibniz have been unduly ignored.

About the Kurdish Cult of Angels

In the study of the world's religions, this title, The Cult of Angels refers specifically to the very ancient religion of the people known as the Kurds, who presently inhabit Northern Iraq, Northeastern Syria, and Southeastern Turkey. They are not Semites, but are instead an Indo-Iranian people more closely related to the Persians. In the West, one of their present day sub-groups are the Yezidi, at the time of this writing, under threat of annihilation by Sunni militants in Iraq. In their traditional religion, the *Melek Taus*, the "Peacock Angel", is a far less demonic Satan responsible for the creation and maintenance of this material world. Unfortunately, that reverence (which is a form of respect, not to be confused with worship), has long led the neighboring locals to incorrectly believe that the Yezidis are "devil worshipers", and therefore "infidel" candidates for genocide.

For a long time, I mistakenly believed the religion of the Yezidi to have simply been an offshoot of the ancient Persian religion of Zoroastrianism. It was only in February of 2014 that I learned about their Cult of Angels proper, and about their creation story, which I have mentioned earlier.

RELIGION REINTERPRETED

To paraphrase that Creation story, everything started with *Xwede* (aka "the One who created himself"), also known as the Universal Spirit (comparable to the Great Spirit of several First People religions in North America). Xwede created a White Pearl (the Cosmic egg) which was placed on the back of a bird named Anfar, also created by Xwede. However, when the bird Anfar took flight, the White Pearl fell off its back and smashed. Xwede, while all-encompassing, was too detached to be directly involved in the material world, for which reason a Heptad of seven Seraphim was given the responsibility for the evolution and governing of the material world. Melek Taus was the first and foremost of the seven Archangels to emerge from the eminence of Xwede. Melek Taus corresponds to the Greek Chronos, (and the Roman Saturn), who brought order to Existence after blocking potential disruption by his father Ouranos (Uranus).

I find it difficult to believe that there isn't some validity behind the notions presented by their creation story. Just such a ruling congress of Angels, given responsibility for governing the material world of time and space, corresponds so closely to the notion of the Elohim in Genesis, Chapter One. I believe both to be essentially the same story, harkening back to something that was once far more commonly understood by ancient Humanity. Also to be considered is the reference to the "Sons of God", God's council in Job 1: 6, which included Satan. Another scenario is that the notion of the Elohim arose in Judaism due to the interaction of the Babylonian Hebrews with the Medes.

This notion of a collective governing body of a very high order of created Beings is also likely to have been the original basis for the polytheism for the early Semitic and early Indo-European peoples. There are indications of such day to day polytheism coexisting with the belief in an ultimate God in the Old Testament. Rachel takes "the household gods" with her when she goes with Jacob. And this co-recognition of an Ultimate God and of Beings of Agency (the Elohim and Angels as God's intermediaries for Creation and World Maintenance, the household gods at the more personal and material level), makes perfect sense. I have consistently made the case that Existence was created to be an intermediate between the Light which is "I AM", and the Dark that is the Illusion of Discontinuity (anti-being). In essence, Existence is a perpetual motion machine which in some manner compensates for any erosion of BEING due to its continued and unavoidable interaction with anti-being. And for Existence to play the role of Reconciliation, even if imperfectly, it must function as independently as possible of "I AM". But "all of the King's horses and all of the King's men" alone are still insufficient for repairing the White Pearl.

That task belongs to ADAM, as God's True One "Prodigal Son". It's for this very reason that "I AM", while detached from the day by day workings of Actuality, is anything but detached from Its embodied Echo, Man, trapped so far away from Home in this painful, confusing sub-luminous labyrinth.

The six linear Permutations.

In its strictest sense, the title Elohim refers to those seven primary Ideas directly created by God as "I AM". And the first six of those primary Ideas were the six Seraphim, collectively denoted here by the title given to them in Zoroastrianism, the Amesha Spenta, the six divine sparks (helpers) of Ahura Mazda. In the Judeo-Christian tradition, they are the six-winged Seraphim (the "Radiant Ones", from the Hebrew *seraph*). These six are the very highest order of Angels, the six Angels closest to God, fundamental to everything about Existence which followed. These were those

Ideas with the most extensive portfolios of logoi, so to speak. Of all created Beings, these six are the closest to "I AM" in Transfinite scale. I like to think of them as being analogous to very large buttress roots like those so often found supporting the trunks of tall trees where the soil is shallow (like in rain forests). However in this case, these "root" Angels support the entire inverted tree of Existence by being embedded in the infinitely deep soil that is "I AM". And it's from there that they cascade "downward" from God, combining and recombining to result in all lower order Ideas until the Light Boundary is reached.

The seventh such fundamental root, a central taproot, is called ADAM (or Gayomart, if you wish to continue with the Zoroastrian system of naming). This taproot would lie at the center of the six buttress roots of the Amesha Spenta, and would itself be the mirror image within Existence of God as "I AM".

Let's first assume that the creation of BEING (Reality) actually came to pass as it has already been presented in this book. Primordial Will ("I"), is said to have divided the Singular Will which *is itself*, into three components: #1 (the Holy Affirming, the Biblical Light); #2 (the Holy Denying, the Biblical Dark); and #3 (the Holy Reconciling, Existence). This configuration can be visualized as a two-dimensional Triangle. If *the order of these three components* becomes important, you have six possible linear (one-dimensional) permutations: 123, 132, 231, 213, 321, and 312. The dimensional shift this demands is being emphasized here, because it's a drop-away from the *whole* of something to dimensionally deficient *cross-sections* of that something. It's this dimensional "drop" which makes Existence so different from Reality.

An analogous example can be easily provided to demonstrate how this works, this dimensional breakdown of the One ("I AM") into Six permutations, continuing downward through hyper-luminous Existence, all of the way to the Light Boundary. This example starts with an ordinary cube, a source of light, and a wall onto which one projects shadows of that cube— in effect, two-dimensional cross-sections of that cube. There are an infinity of potential cross-sections of the cube, but there are only three primary or fundamental cross-sections, which together define the entire range of the others. In other words, that infinity of shadows can be shown to range between the three fundamental shadows.

The first and most obvious shadow (cross-section) would be a square. This is achieved by aligning the light horizontally so that its central axis is perpendicular to the wall it strikes. Next, one holds the cube so that its faces too are perpendicular to the central axis of your light source. If done correctly, your result will be a square shadow. However, if you align your cube so that the central axis of light passes through a pair of opposite corners (where three square faces meet), your shadow will instead be a six-sided figure: a hexagon. And lastly, if you align your cube so that the central axis of light passes through the center of a pair of opposite edges (where two square faces meet), the resulting shadow will be a root-two rectangle. Such a rectangle is where the short side corresponds to the length of the cube's square faces, and the long side corresponds to the length of the diagonal of those square faces, in a ratio of 1 to 1.1412.

The suggestion being made here is that, as the number of dimensions involved decreases, the number of cross-sections of some whole entity inversely increases... at least up to a point. God as "I AM" is a Singular entity without internal divisions. However, the six Seraphim are in some sense the projection of "I AM" down onto that multi-dimensional "screen" we know as Existence. They are not themselves gods, even though they've sometimes been thought of as such, owing to their collectively assigned task of being the guardians and governors of Existence... the Elohim.

Gurdjieff, who presented these six permutations to the West via Ouspensky's book *In Search of the Miraculous*, called them the "Six Basic World Processes". (Parenthetically, this means that none of this was ever my own original crackpot notion. Instead, I've spent forty years of my life contemplating this schema in my effort to understand it). Therefore, here in their glory are the six Amesha Spenta (permutations) to the best of my understanding, along with their Seventh Note:

DO— Divinity ("I AM")
==
SI—(3-2-1) TRANSCENDENCE: True Creativity; Metamorphosis; Freedom; Serendipity, Sex as it is meant to be

LA—(3-1-2) DOWNGRADE: Form; Order; Limits; Structure; Reduction; Death

SOL—(1-2-3) ANABOLISM: Endothermic Transactions; Growth; Accumulation; Teaching

FA—(1-3-2) CATABOLISM: Exothermic Transactions; Acceleration; Effort/Struggle; Destruction

MI—(2-3-1) ORCHESTRATION: Adaptation; Communication; Healing; Invention; Patterning

HALE MICHAEL SMITH, M.D.

RE—(2-1-3) UPGRADE: Digestion/Diffraction/Distillation; Purification; Refinement; Learning; Submission/Faith when genuine and voluntary

DO— ADAM

Venus, which is missing from the above sequence, is really the Idea of Connection, and is therefore an echo of the Holy Reconciling, of Impartial Divine Love… at least in the Old World. In the Americas the symbology was different; Venus was the god of War and harbinger of Destruction. The New World Venus essentially replaces Mars as the Principle of Effort, Struggle. And getting married is the beginning of the _struggle_ by both parties to adapt to the close proximity of another person. The New World Venus essentially replaces Mars as the Principle of Effort, Struggle.

It's worth noting that the sequence 123 (the one permutation wherein each number coincides with its most natural place), is in the position of the dominant of a musical octave. The major fifth is the note most in harmony with the fundamental, after the octave.

You also have here the foundation for the meaning of the planets in so many of the Old World Pantheons, and the meanings of the planets in astrology. In the diagram above, the planets would be (respectively from SI to RE): Uranus, Saturn, Jupiter, Mars, Mercury, and Moon. One doesn't need to believe in astrology to see this symbology extends beyond religion. For example, this same symbology can be demonstrated to be the basis for the original Indo-European system of noun declination, just as other aspects of this Cosmology can be demonstrated to be part of the Original Indo-European grammar. For one example, the triad of traditional voices: active, passive, and the middle voice, the last of which is now extinct in English, save as the lingering reflexive. In classic

Greek the middle voice is quite evident, and there are even words which are "transgender", having a feminine/passive article and a masculine/active declension.

However, to continue. Here are examples that have helped me clarify my understanding. But first, allow me to explain that the place value of each numeral of a triad indicates how they interact. Remembering that the numerals 1 corresponds to Energy, 2 corresponds to Matter, and 3 corresponds to Form, then the first place corresponds to what we start with, the second place corresponds to what is encountered, and the third place corresponds to what results.

<u>ANABOLISM and CATABOLISM: Permutations 123 and 132 (Jupiter and Mars).</u>
These two are taken together because they were most easy to explain, in contrast to each other. (I figured these out long before the others.)
Anabolism, P123, it is most easily explained as energy (intention) directed at some material, to produce some intermediate form. One example of this would be building (energy as work) a house out of wood and bricks (raw materials) to produce a place to live (the resulting form). Another example is chlorophyl using sunlight (energy) to convert water and carbon dioxide (raw materials) into a molecule of stored energy: glucose (one of the forms of the many sugars). Important to understanding this latter example is to recognize that the energy which was provided by the sun is now literally locked up in form of this new molecule. That sun energy is now the new and larger electron shell which encompasses the entire molecule, thereby making that glucose molecule an individual something in itself.

<u>A linguistic note</u>: This process of anabolism means growth and accumulation, because energy must be added step by step. But growth also means an expansion outwards as things accumulate (as all of us older than 30 all too well understand). This is why in linguistics, it is associated with the Ablative Case in the noun declension system. This declensional case indicated expansion, and also the source of something. In such sentences as "She came out of the house" or "This letter is from Mom" or "This table is made out of wood", the prepositional phrases "out of" or "from" replace what was originally a change in the suffix ending to the noun. The Ablative therefore best equates to the meaning of Jupiter in Astrology.

As for process P132, Catabolism, a form is destroyed. Fire burns wood, releasing heat and light and producing ash— remember, the tree grew from the light and heat of the sun, and matter from the soil. Buildings (3) are intentionally (1) demolished and reduced to rubble and opened space (2). In a controlled, regulated process, each cell in your body "burns" glucose enzymatically. The resulting energy can be transferred to the molecule ATP (adenosine tri-phosphate), the currency of cellular metabolism.

<u>UPGRADE: Permutation 213 (Moon)</u>

To the best of my memory, this process, P213 (Note RE), was originally presented as digestion. The basic notion was that food "submitted" itself to the digestive enzymes of the stomach, and in that way was upgraded into a form which the body could absorb and then use as food. But since food doesn't go out of its way to be digested, this example always seemed to me to be a rather thin gruel for an explanation of what this permutation represented. Something made me look closer at the number 2 (raw material), and its placement in the number one spot, the one of initiative. And for some reason, I then thought of Learning.

RELIGION REINTERPRETED

Learning is fundamentally different from being taught (P123). While both involve a teacher transferring knowledge to a pupil, genuine learning entails the pupil (#2), the "raw material", *voluntarily submitting itself to the teacher* (#1) in some fashion. Instead of merely sitting there, the pupil itself takes the initiative to learn. And most teachers will affirm that a pupil who *chooses to learn* will always outstrip one which merely allows itself to be taught. The willing, attentive pupil is "upgraded" as a result.

And upon subsequent reflection, I finally understood the original example, involving food. The trouble I'd had was a result of modern convenience.

Before we got our food at markets, we had to gather and hunt. And the best gatherers and hunters have, across cultures and geographies, spoken of an essential *relationship* between what was gathered/hunted, and what did the gathering/hunting. Plants produce tasty nectars and fruits that are the epitome of "Eat me!", calling out to bees and other creatures, including human gatherers. In her book *Always Coming Home*, Ursula Le Guin described a custom of saying, "For your life, my words" before harvesting anything. As for hunters, First People hunters described a process of waiting for the moment of recognition, of knowing that this particular animal has agreed to sacrifice itself to become food.

The critical thing about this process is this notion of voluntary submission. Quite simply, in relation to God, all Human Beings are the Holy Denying/Holy Receiving. This means that we can never compel God to do anything; we can only ever respond to God. And yet, we do have an independent Will. We can refuse, or we can engage. We can even elicit something from God. If the reader will pardon the implicitly sexual metaphor, we can "become open". A man or woman giving someone their phone number, or accepting an invitation to dinner, are appropriate as examples of "opening".

HALE MICHAEL SMITH, M.D.

Castaneda's Don Juan said something very appropriate in this regard about Man when submitting to God:

"Choice, for Warrior-travelers, is not really an act of choosing, but rather the act of acquiescing elegantly to the solicitations of Infinity."

This notion of voluntary Submission is the very "center of gravity" of genuine Islam, but it's just as important in Christianity and Judaism. Millions of people go to Church, Mosque, or Synagogue every week, but *"acquiescing elegantly to the solicitations of Infinity"* does not mean just sitting there and allowing our religion's "milk" to be pumped into our mouths, even when it's become rancid. When we allow our perceptions to be actively "digested" by genuine instructions, those teachings separate the subtle from the dross within ourselves. In truth, the initiative to genuinely understand what your religion is attempting to teach us must come from the individual itself, if it is to amount to anything more than Pavlovian beatification. And as history demonstrates, simply swallowing what others "feed" us without the effort to digest it, is usually quite harmful.

Note: It is most important that this submission, *regardless of the religion in question,* be voluntary on an individual's part. It is an individual's choice to open, to submit, if that act is to be one of substance, and not of sham, meaningless appearances. The real goal of submission, regardless of the religion in question, is the inner transformation which takes a person well beyond the specific proscriptions of that religion. Proscriptions are there to make a person behave as he or she would if they were already at a certain degree of spiritual accomplishment. On reaching some higher level of transformation, such behavior comes of its own accord, because one directly sees what is involved, and why such behavior is correct. None of that works unless it is voluntary. Unfortunately, human beings of more than one faith have forgotten this, which is why there has been so much violence in the last two millennia. *When respective religions are genuinely understood*, different faiths are actually very much the same religion, and are valid paths to God. Their seeming differences are simply sub-dimensional cross-sections of the singular Path of Return to God.

Addendum: It's not accidental that the Moon, as the receiver of light from the Sun is Note RE (Regina de Coeli), and is therefore also the symbol of Islam. Astrologically, the Moon refers to the passive-most part of our Being, as for example our habits, and whatever else is the line of least resistance for us. Linguistically, this is the Accusative case, which is the recipient of action: "I brought *the bouquet of flowers* home."

DOWNGRADE: Permutation 312 (Saturn) "Spirit in the Jar"
This permutation is perhaps the most slippery of all to understand. It was originally presented to my group as meaning "Degeneration", and this bothered me, because I couldn't understand why God would include such a seemingly negative process as an intrinsic part of Existence. I simply couldn't accept that God would create something that was intrinsically bad or negative. However, this is actually much the same question that has bedeviled Western religion: Why should this world be so much less than perfect? Why should everything deteriorate over time? Why should there even be the experience of harm or evil?

To simply say that an angel named Satan rebelled doesn't help, because an omnipotent and omniscient God should have known all things beforehand, and could therefore have nipped that rebellion in the bud, before it spoiled Creation. God would be left holding the bag as the responsible party for having created evil, and for having allowed this blight to continue.

<u>Etymological Definitions</u>: The names for those seeming opponents to that which can have no opposition, God, are themselves of considerable interest, and will be presented below. For the moment, however, the problem of Satan's other name, Lucifer, must be addressed, because the very name "Lucifer" literally means "He who bears the Light (of God)." I wonder how many people ever genuinely question why this should be so?

Just what could reasonably be the upside to 312? The above title, "Spirit in the Jar", is an allusion to a well known Irish tune. "3-1" can be understood to mean either "encapsulated Spirit" or "encapsulated Light", or even "encapsulated Life." It's this encapsulation, this trapping of Spirit by form, which leads to the name Lucifer, "that which bears the Light". In this sense, every Idea, every Angel (every individualized portion of Spirit), is actually a "Lucifer", including even ADAM. Here is the problem engendered by Separation, Distinction, Differentiation, and Individuality.

Existence is predicated on the Singularity that is Absolute Reality having become fragmented. And for every fragment, whether Ideal or material, to remain something separate and specifically itself, is to be an individual, which means to be something "other" than everything else. It therefore also means to be demarcated off in some sense. For the Ideal Beings which constitute the hyper-luminous portion of Existence, this demarcation is minimal and implicit. However, from the Light Boundary outwards, demarcations become explicit by means of that which we call form—including color, shape, function, etc. And the question which arises is whether this form, this external boundary, is a guardian or a prison guard? This is actually the very same question as to which name best applies: Lucifer or Satan?

Our month of January was named after the Roman god Janus, the two-headed guardian of the gate. January also happens to be the month of Capricorn, the Astrological sign ruled by Saturn, the planet most associated with limits, outline, structure, boundaries, and what they can safely represent. Linguistically, this is your Indo-European Locative declensional case, which refers to location in time or space.

The proper purpose of a living cell's membrane is to protect the internal order of that living cell by isolating it from the external, surrounding environment. And as guardian of that internal order, the cell membrane has the task of deciding what can enter from the outside and what has to remain outside, or be pushed outside from within (Janus as guardian). Nothing within Existence can be complete within itself; it's in this mutual dependency that we see the conflict between guardian and the guard. The wall which defines an individualized dominion must be "intelligently" semi-permeable. If it allows everything in, the cell will be destroyed in any number of ways: viruses, bacteria, even too much water. If the membrane allows nothing in, or out, the cell will firstly starve, and secondly choke to death on its own waste products. (If you doubt your dependency on the rest of the world, try holding your breath for five minutes and see what happens.) For anything or anyone to be entirely cut off from the rest of this world means to die, and that is the true meaning of the final "2" in this permutation, the reduction of Spirit, light, and life to simple raw materials, such as happens when some animated material Being dies, and subsequently decomposes. When Lucifer becomes Satan (when the guardian becomes a guard instead), the light within grows dark.

We see a comparable degeneration in Religion when Ideas become dogma. An Idol has already been defined as a "dead Idea," which is what happens when transmitting the teachings in the most literal terms has become an end in itself. It has become something rigid in our minds; the "letter of the Law" has replaced the spirit of its inner meaning and intent. When unthinking obedience to religions' forms has become the primary end in itself, then the real point to Religion (and to all commandments), dies. Recollect that Jesus freed the woman condemned to be stoned to death for adultery.

This therefore is the underlying meaning of Permutation #312. Limitations and differences make individuality (and therefore Existence as a whole), both possible and viable. And yet, when boundaries, restrictions, separations and differences become an end in themselves, what's alive inside is smothered and therefore dies. Thus, individuality and separateness must always remain carefully porous, even though intelligent assessment is always more difficult than simply laying down a set of laws as being absolute. That's the price we pay for a free and independent Will. When Permutation 312 is functioning as a guardian (Lucifer) and not as a guard (Satan), careful and inwardly honest judgement is always an intrinsic part of its function.

For those familiar with Astrology, this is precisely why Saturn is exalted in the sign of Libra, the sign of deliberation and judgement, the symbol for which is the Scales of Balance.

There's another aspect to this Linear permutation (312), one that concerns how we perceive the world we seem to live in. Revisiting something said above, a cell membrane properly functions by deciding/limiting what can enter and what cannot, and determining what can or must leave, and what can't or must not. In effect, this membrane imposes order. In a similar way, our minds determine what we are and can be aware of, what we ignore or dismiss, and what we allow ourselves to wonder about. If this isn't clear, think of winter. For people who are warm and comfortable, the beauty of snowflakes is a matter of delight. For scientists, their crystalline forms are a subject of interest. For a tracker, it is the prints left in the snow that matter. For a skier, different kinds of snow affect speed of passage and safety. But what significance can snowflakes have for some animal?

One day in my third year of college, I returned to my apartment to find my cat asleep on top of a pile of text books on my table. There was nothing usual in this, yet this time, something stopped me. I noted that this cat had no notion of how much knowledge she was lying on, and yet as far as she was concerned, her world was complete. Even if she could understand English, there'd still be no way I could convince her that there was so much more to the world than she was aware of, as demonstrated by those books that were presently her couch. I immediately recognized that this applied equally both to my fellow Man, and to myself.

Even among human beings in what is assumed to be a shared culture, the filter of each mind will emphasize and de-emphasize different cultural elements, making for different world views, resulting in differing political stances. This is why what's so very important among people is the effort we make to see the world through someone else's eyes. It's so much easier to oppose another's view and attempt to change it, than it is to make the effort to stand in their place and look around, and within.

In summary, it seems that this linear permutation 312 fundamentally has something to do with controlling and directing the illusion of discontinuity. This is necessary if Existence is to have some degree of order. Lucifer's seat on God's board of advisors would seem to have some merit after all.

ORCHESTRATION: Permutation 231 (Mercury)

With this Triad, 231, the breakthrough for understanding came for me with a redefinition of the number 1 in the final position. Instead of calling it Spirit, Light, or Life, I suddenly thought to call it Wholeness. In this manner, 231 could be understood as some raw material submitting itself to a pattern, resulting in a whole greater than the sum of the original parts.

However, this Permutation often carries with itself the sense of a return to some previously established status. For example, when the "raw material" happens to be injured or diseased organic tissue, then submitting that tissue to the pattern originally proper to it results in healing, a return the Wholeness. The words "to heal" and "health" are themselves derived from the word "whole". Continuing with this line of reasoning, communication is the means to social wholeness, and adaptation is an adjustment made to one's environment. Inventions are usually an adaptation of some sort.

The god Mercury (Hermes) has the responsibility of communicating the higher pattern of intention to us.

TRANSCENDENCE: Permutation 321 (Uranus)

Transcendence means moving above and beyond the limits of form, beyond the limits of being a particular something. This process is listed last because until now (10/ 10/ 2015), it's remained beyond my reach to explain using the format by which the other five have been explained, and it still largely is. However, at this moment I can at least say that there are forms, patterns, which allow Being to go beyond itself, on the Return Back to God.

RELIGION REINTERPRETED

On the surface, this permutation seems to be very much like the permutation 231, Orchestration. But that process was a return to something already established. In contrast, 321 is more like a prison break, a movement beyond the limits of the original pattern to something entirely new, an elevation of some sort like a caterpillar becoming a butterfly, becoming something very different from what it was before. This is also why sex, a genuinely creative force, is so very different from the simple fission of cells and primitive multicellular organisms, or parthenogenesis, as occurs in some advanced multicellular creatures, like certain lizards which can still reproduce asexually. Unlike fission or parthenogenesis (the latter word literally meaning "birth from a virgin"), sex means a re-shuffling of genes, and represents potential novelty (the unexpected = Uranus) for each new offspring, which even includes the possibility of becoming a brand new species.

Triad 321 is actually the basis for Heisenberg's Uncertainty Principle, because it means that Existence always carries within itself a "crack", an opening whereby the unexpected can enter, something brand new, something outside of the limits of strict Cause & Effect. For the most part, this means randomness or "play" in the system. But this very same "looseness" or "swerve" (a nod to Lucretius here) or "play in the system" also allows Intention to quietly sneak in when and where it so chooses, without compromising the ordered nature of Existence. It's unfortunate that with 321, I can't further demonstrate how that specific number sequence means what I sense it does, except to say that the # 1 in the final position in this particular permutation, means more than a simple return to some original wholeness. Instead, it points to a movement of Atonement, of moving beyond the reality of boundaries and forms. It is an unwinding.

ADAM as the Seventh Member of the Elohim, and the Octaval echo of Note DO (God as "I AM")

This is a speculation of mine, one without any corroboration from anything I learned from the Gurdjieff Work (the source of these six permutations). This Octave of six Ideas has its origin in God as "I AM", the upper Fundamental Note DO. As the lower Octave DO, ADAM is essentially "I AM's" echo (counterpart) within Existence, God's reflection or projection into Existence, so to speak. Another way to say this is simply that ADAM was made in God's Image. ADAM is therefore God's doorway to direct influence into those reaches of Existence.

The absurd notion of "Bad Angels"

Angels and other high level Ideas are not automatons. Their intrinsic self-awareness and intelligence allows them to perform the functions they were designed for without the immediate oversight of "I AM". This goes far in explaining the messenger aspect of angel when speaking for God to Man. The lack of independent Will precludes any notion of some literal rebellion by Angels. Besides, a little common sense makes obvious why this is nonsense.

We Human Beings inhabit this sub-luminous material world, and are ordinarily cut off from being directly aware of the Infinite Presence that is God as "I AM". This capacity is what we struggle to recover when we begin our effort to Return to our Source. In contrast, all Ideas are hyper-luminous (above and within the Light Boundary), which means that they are blind to the immediate presence of God. Their very moment to moment existence is that of a living thought in God's mind. It's difficult to believe that this wouldn't be a deterrence to any rebellion. The whole point to the notion of "bad angels" is instead to be found in the Human need to explain the seeming short-comings of this world, and of ourselves

RELIGION REINTERPRETED

as Man. (A psychologist might describe this as the defense mechanism called Projection.) A little etymology may be useful here:

"Demon": Derived from the Greek "daimon", which originally meant a protective spirit. It seems to come from the Greek expression "daimoni", which means "I distribute." For the Greeks, a daimon distributed a good fate. Then the Romans got hold of that word and flipped the meaning to being "that which distributed a bad fate." (This is consistent with the Romans' tendency to brutalize, or brutally simplify, ideas. No other people in recorded history equated the irrational number pi (3.14159…) with the numeral 3.)

"Devil": This English word is derived from the Greek "diabolos". This was originally a compound word. The initial 'dia-' means "across", just as in our words "diagonal", and, "diaphragm." The second half, "-bolos", comes from the Greek word "ballein" which means "to throw." We find that word in the English word "ballistic", and in the name of that Argentinian hunting tool, the "bolo." Altogether, the title "dia-bolos" (and therefore the title "devil") means "he who throws across", in other words, "he who obstructs." Sounds much like the job description for the Hebrew Satan in the Biblical Chapter of Job.

Islam does not accept the notion that Angels have a Will independent of Allah. Iblis, who rebelled by not bowing to ADAM was a Djinn, not an Angel. (Although this begs the question, how did the Djinn arise?) The Christian devil seems to be an almost direct transfer of the Zoroastrian Ahriman, who was co-equal with their good god Ahura Mazda, and therefore a genuine threat to beings who inhabit the sub-luminous realm. The demons of, say, Tibetan

Buddhism, are meant to symbolize negative psychological factors, and not independently "real" external Beings.

The subject of how Man's Will can seem to be distorted, even though it is the same Will that is God, will be further explored in the Section about Man. In the meantime, however, it should be noted that devils and demons are uniformly represented in art as evil, out of control animals. There's a reason for this which is important to keep in mind. Our Human body is literally an animal. In that alone, there's nothing intrinsically good or bad. Properly speaking, we should treat our bodies the way a cavalry soldier treats his horse, doing whatever is needed to keep it healthy, satisfied and ready to serve as it was meant to. However, the role our animal part properly plays in our lives is that of the Holy Denying. As such, our animal side is also the resistance which each of us needs to work against, if we are to reach our destiny as God's Prodigal Son.

The very fact that this sub-luminous material world seems to be reality to us is due entirely to our identification (our confusion) of ourselves as being this body. Remember that the "I AM" within is our Real Identity as Man. However, our awareness and direct contact with God's True Son within (ADAM, and beyond that "I AM") is ordinarily not part of our comprehension.

Devils and demons are represented as "bad animals" because when our material goals and passions rule us, which is to say that when our animal side becomes an end in itself, then our purposes become contrary to the purpose for which we were created. More will be said about this later. Meanwhile, a supporting statement to this line of logic, from logia #7 from the Gospel of Thomas:

RELIGION REINTERPRETED

1) Jesus said:?
2) Happy is the Lion which the Man will eat,
3) and the Lion will become Man;
4) and cursed is the Man which the Lion will eat,
5) and the Lion will become Man.

The Angel Gaia

Before leaving the subject of Angels, there is one in particular I wish to acknowledge. It's the Idea associated with this specific planet Earth, long known as "Mother Nature", but now also known as Gaia. This is our own specific representative from the Elohim, the immediate Idea / Angel which was given the task of guiding the progression of Life on this specific planet so that it could produce a material organism suitable for embodying ADAM.

Gaia accomplished her task by being an "intelligent catalyst". She "arranged" certain conditions which would increase the odds that certain changes would take place, thereby guiding animated material life on this planet towards certain ends. And it was definitely a process of experimentation (one only need witness the many side-branches of hominids to recognize that our forward progress was one of groping). An example of this arrangement of conditions would be Man's upright posture, which I personally believe was due to an extended period during which we resided in water. The present day Afar triangle seems a likely place to me, during some period when it was a shallow salt lake, as per Elaine Morgan of Wales. I find her reasoning compelling, assuming that the crocodile population was limited. In addition, the available seafood would have provided considerable fatty acid for brain development.

CHAPTER XIV

AWARENESS

Personality; thoughts as things; attention; degradation of awareness; heightened awareness; mindfulness makes Religion possible; birthright, Cain and Abel; sentient light; time bodies; why time matters for Man; samsara, wandering, the land of Nod; multiverses again; many mansions; a joke; dimensions and black holes; Mandelbrot set; iterations; "He Who Created Himself"; holographic cosmological theory; aleph-null scaffolding

<u>Acquired personality</u>

Our brains are the basis for our worldly mind, the basis for our personality. *But our personality is mostly acquired software.* It is mostly the product of our socialization, and that modifies how we interpret and experience our sensations, thoughts, and emotions. It's for this very reason that the religions of East Asia have typically considered our everyday thoughts to literally be things. We are now, finally, closing in on something directly important to Religion.

This Human animal body and this material world it inhabits are not intrinsically wrong or sinful, but both are more illusion than real. As for our worldly mind, it's necessary to us, if only to keep our bodies alive in this material world long enough for us to achieve something here. However, this same worldly mind is not capable of guiding us on our effort to Return back to God. It was not designed for that, but unfortunately, it's the only mind that most of us know about, and our typical understanding of Religion is limited to what our worldly minds can "understand". Are things beginning to become more clear now?

We were intentionally sent into this sub-luminous labyrinth as the Prodigal Son, to find our way Back to God. This is the Real meaning to Salvation. But this starts with acquiring a grade of awareness higher than that which the ordinary functioning of our brains can provide. Finding it starts in that sort of *active awareness* we call *Attention*. Attention is directed awareness, properly directed by one's own Will. Without our Will's active involvement, our attention will only ever be passively drawn away from ourselves, and passively directed by some influence outside of ourselves, and this is a very big part of our problem. The vast majority of our lives is spent with our attention being sucked away by something outside ourselves, which is how animals were designed to live. Attracting our attention is the aim of all advertisements and sports. Disasters and fame capture our attention. The very word to "entertain" literally means to "hold in between", in other words, to suspend or interrupt something—our Return. The same is true for the word "diversion", which means to be "turned aside from your purpose or chosen destination."

This is not an indictment against having fun or enjoying oneself. Play is an essential part of living and growing. But a life of unending, relentless distraction is not how a Man was meant to be, because *when you live your life in this manner, Nature actually cannot tell the difference between you, and any other animal!* This has far more bearing on Human history than anyone realizes.

We do not usually notice that which is most important in our lives: ourselves. We are not aware of our breathing, the feel of our clothes on our bodies, the play in our muscles, how our voice sounds when we speak, or even what we are really saying when we speak. And because we don't notice ourselves, we don't really notice each other. As a result of this state of our "waking sleep", most of our memories of our lives are little more than bookkeeping.

<u>Mindfulness</u>
Buddhism calls the augmented state of awareness Mindfulness. *It's the consistent, immediate awareness that "I am", and that I am alive moment to moment, simultaneous with whatever I am doing, whatever I'm feeling, whatever I'm thinking, and of whatever is happening around me.* Gurdjieff called this sort of Noticing: "Self-Remembering", and any notion of spirituality without a consistent measure self-remembering is simply fantasy. That's because without this, there's no *you* available at home to account for yourself, or to hear God's efforts to reach each and every one of us. God does not and cannot speak to the worldly mind and its artificial sense of self (the personality), which we usually believe to be ourselves.

When we are young, this ability and state of Noticing is most apparent. But unfortunately, by the time we've reached puberty, such inner life has mostly eroded to nothingness. By this time in our lives, we "know" what cups, rocks, paper and everything else, are, and so we no longer notice what we encounter. We are strongly discouraged from stopping to notice, to wonder, to marvel. Such "marveling" might diminish our ability to function efficiently! Unfortunately, something very important in us depends on just such direct experiences, and will eventually become moribund when starved of them.

I find that there's a peculiar taste to these moments, especially when they appear unexpectedly. (They rarely last for long without some practice in holding a place in ourselves open to such experiences.) Typically, I'll be involved in doing something, or thinking about or feeling something, and suddenly I seem to "Wake up!" This seems to happen most often when I'm looking at something or someone. Everything suddenly seems so much "brighter", as if brand new. The world around me suddenly seems more dimensional. But what makes such a moment so peculiar is the question that comes along with this change in perception: "I've been looking at this for some period of time, so why does it seem that I'm just now seeing it?"

As I said earlier, our typical memory of the events of our lives is mostly bookkeeping. I remember that I was at such a place, doing whatever I was doing. However. if a sufficient being-grade of Noticing was present in that past moment, one's memory of that experience would be vivid, fresh.

Sudden emergencies can have a surreal flavor to them, a sense of heightened awareness. Soldiers often experience this when facing their first battle, when the possibility of actually being killed is no longer a theoretical abstraction. The resulting question for them is almost invariably something like: "How in the hell did I get myself into this?"

Peter Kingsley spoke about this in his book *Reality*, when he spoke about what the Greeks called "mêtis", a certain type of enhanced alertness and awareness where one can competently juggle many balls at one time. One is wide awake, but not limited to the usual ordinary thinking, which is far too slow. The present day slang for something like this is called "being in the zone", and such experiences of heightened awareness are definitely exhilarating, especially when we are extraordinarily active. However, as a constant state of Being, Noticing usually begins as a deepening quietude where one becomes increasingly centered, while remaining completely in touch with whatever one might be doing, and with whatever might be happening within and around oneself. This state is that which is proper for Man in his should-be natural state. Unfortunately, it's now something to aspire to, and it is only achieved as the center of gravity of one's Being gravitates inward, which only becomes possible with considerable and persistent intentional effort.

Living without Mindfulness

So Noticing, or Mindfulness, is the proper condition for Humans, and it is the mind-state that makes genuine Religion possible. It is very different from the worldly mind, which is necessary to living on this planet's surface. Unfortunately, we have collectively fallen from what should be our natural state. And this fallen state is described over and over again in the Bible, first as Adam's exile from Eden, and then again and again in the relationships between siblings, usually (but not always) two brothers.

Cain and Abel are the first of at least seven Biblical "Two Brothers" stories (sometimes it is more than two brothers, as with Joseph and his ten older brothers). As with most Biblical stories, these are usually believed to have been literal history, and in some, if not all cases, that is entirely possible; however, their Real import and significance is psychological. In each of these stories, it is the younger brother (or sister, as with Leah and Rachel,) for whom the "Birthright" is destined, not the older one. This is because these two brothers represent our two sub-luminous minds: the first born being the worldly mind, the second born (and yet the more fundamental of the two) being the true mind of awareness. It's only this "younger" mind which can genuinely connect with one's True Soul (the Birthright). In the story of Cain and Abel, Cain literally murders his younger brother; figuratively speaking, our worldly mind, our programed, socialized, personality mind, murders our natural mindfulness. The real meaning of Cain being condemned to wander is that our worldly mind is completely insufficient for guiding us to anything more than what an animal would seek.

One unfortunate consequence of this "fall" from our natural condition is that we've fallen deeper into the sub-luminous Realm (where illusion takes precedent over Reality), than we were ever meant to, the effect of which is to increase the importance of separation. This is why we find ourselves where anti-being has priority. Were enough of us consistently functioning at the higher Being-Grade where the proportion of illusion is substantially less, most of the major problems of this world would be worked out overnight. But unfortunately, for the most part, we see everything quantitatively, and are concerned only with acquiring whatever we can get for ourselves, for our offspring, and for our tribe, without concern for who else loses as a result. This is the result of living only in the basement of ourselves.

<u>Sentient Light</u>

By far most (if not all) traditional cultures and world religions speak about there being a type of light which is both alive and self-conscious. This light is often accessible to young children; some degree of meaningful detachment from the world, even some spiritual development is generally needed for an adult to be able to perceive this light directly. When this living light is associated with an individual, it's usually called a halo or an aura. When it's associated with some other sort of Being, animate or otherwise, it's usually a sign that some message is intended for the perceiver in question, such as the burning bush encountered by Moses on Mount Horeb. And when this light is perceived by someone everywhere they look, the entire world is seen for what it really is: alive and very self aware. Such a perceiver will have genuinely crossed some important boundary in her or his inner life.

Importantly, this would be the place we visit at the end of that dark tunnel we seem to transit when leaving this world. And this sheds important "light" on something which medicine continues to struggle with: the Near Death Experiences that so many people so consistently report when they temporarily die. Scientists and doctors tend to dismiss these experiences for the very simple reason that, without a functioning brain, how can there be any genuine awareness of anything? The brain is certainly out of the picture when these sort of experiences happen. But whatever it is that so-often floats above a person's body in times of great distress, thereby watching one's body below lying (struggling) in that bed or gurney, or in a bomb crater, is no longer overwhelmed by the brain's vertebral Being-Grade of Awareness. In other words, these experiences must be a release phenomenon of some sort. None of these experiences would be possible were there not something else besides the brain involved. And this "something else" is not as limited in time as the brain is.

Remember that at normal room temperatures, the brain can only be deprived of oxygen for perhaps four minutes if you wish that patient to return neurologically intact. In cases of drowning in cold water, you might be able to stretch that to thirty minutes. However, even thirty minutes (not to mention only four), is nowhere near long enough to think through every single moment of your life, as these patients consistently report having done. (This is called by many the Life Review.)

Time Body

There's actually a simple explanation for this, and that has to do with dimensions and the existence of a Time Body.

Just think about this planet Earth we sit on. We know this Earth to be spheroid in 3-dimensions. But in four dimensions, with the fourth dimension being Time, the Earth is a coiled sheath around our Sun, with seven other major planetary coils and an almost infinite series of sheaths which represent the moons, astroids and planetoids. The Earth we can visualize is but a three-dimensional cross-section of its four-dimensional Time-body, directly analogous to the two-dimensional, cross-section circle you would see if you cut in half a garden hose or ball. Everything in this world is a cross-section of some higher entity. This is even true for a mountain, which never seems to move, or for a broken down car that sits in your drive-way until rust overwhelms it. This is the additional dimension of Persistence, which seems temporal to us, but which is spatial in a higher dimension.

At a higher dimensional level of awareness one can see the entire Time-Body as an intact whole. And this is the key to these Life-Reviews. In such an experience, one's entire life, everything which has happened, every thought, feeling, action, is experienced as a single all-encompassing Here&Now. Everything of life that has so far been lived is simultaneously available to one's direct (and expanded) awareness. It's only on returning to one's body and its brain functioning that one is once again forced to think about this experience sequentially, conveying a linear memory. Understandably, such patients are usually much too preoccupied with what has just happened to themselves, to be concerned with arguing with doctors about the validity of those experiences.

HALE MICHAEL SMITH, M.D.

Time

Ultimately, all dimensions are illusions because they all represent the seeming separation into parts of that Singularity which is Absolute Reality. Time however, refers to the specific incompleteness which is experienced when individual entities are themselves experienced incompletely. Another way to formulate this particular type of experience of incompleteness, would be to call it the "experience of becoming", in contrast to the "experience of being." For example, our experience of our 3-dimensional Human animal bodies is really an experience of becoming, because we experience this body as growing up, and then as growing old, and eventually dying. This is the "experience of becoming" that we associate with time because we experience our bodies as successive and sequential cross-sections of our fundamentally more real Time body.

Change itself is a distinct dimension of Time. Below the Light Boundary, there are too few dimensions to allow the complete Being of anything to be directly perceived as a whole. This is why Time "stops" at the velocity of Light.

On our scale, Time-Bodies are not material objects like a rock, a planet, or a snake. And yet, they are more substantial than mere intellectual, abstract exercises. There are myriad examples and accounts of people, usually hunters or trackers or scouts, who could perceive at least small portions of Time-Bodies. They could track an animal on the ground or a bird in the air by seeing not only where it had been but where it had gone. Even partial or occasional perception of Time-Bodies explains a great deal of genuine psychic phenomena.

Hyper-luminous Ideas have a wholeness and reality that is independent of whether or not they manifest in "the real world"—that is to say, in the sub-luminous world. People who are idealists know this. For some people, just knowing that true love is possible is so comforting that they can forego relationships that fall too short of the ideal and wait for something good to present itself— or not. It's really only for Man that there's any significance in whether any given specific possibility is ever actualized or not. *This is precisely why only Man is really aware of Time!* This critically important fact has been largely overlooked by those who question what Time means, and whether or not Time is real. It matters nothing in the greater Universe whether Schroedinger's Cat remains alive or not, because both results exist in the totality of all possibilities, and both outcomes lead to different but equally valid histories (actualizations, versions) of this Universe. But Time matters for us, because in the exercise of Will we can select, determine, and change which possibilities become actualities. This very rarely happens; most of us live lives of being buffeted about, sucked into experiences, ring-led by desires, or moved by countless social pressures. But the infinite arrays of possibilities include possibilities of Mindfulness, of Noticing, and of behaving in ways that lead to developing a presence of a higher order of Being.

For man, the significance of Time lies in finding those traces of actualization which will eventually lead one out of this sub-luminous labyrinth, something the religions of Southern and Eastern Asia call "escaping Samsara." Otherwise, one will simply continue to eat and be eaten by life. While we remain in ignorance of our true "raison d'être" we are merely marking time towards no particular end other than entropy. We lose ourselves, and our potential selves, in Illusion.

Samsara is usually understood to mean the "wheel of birth, death, and rebirth." But its original meaning by etymology was that of "wandering through"! In this regard, the reader will recall what was said about the land of Nod to which Cain was exiled (Nod's Hebrew meaning: "the land of wandering, going nowhere meaningful").

Man has a two-fold nature because the Idea which bears the full panoply of each individual's possible manifestations is not the same as the Idea of Man's material body. The True Idea of the individual Man (again, without concern of gender, race, or even planetary species) is actually that which we call his or her True Soul. The Idea of our Human animal body is generic for our planetary species, although the individual fate of each is tied to that of the Soul.

As a practical matter, we need to regain and then retain a solid connection to our True Soul. This means that we must return the center of gravity of what we experience as ourselves, away from our Human animal bodies, back to our True Soul. A return to being our True Soul, instead of merely remaining in our personality, means that our ultimate Return to "I AM" has now become assured.

Furthermore, because this Return to being our True Soul means bridging the Light Boundary, it therefore also means closing that creative circuit within Existence. Atonement becomes actualized through ourselves, and this sub-luminous Universe no longer lacks significance. God's "Will" will then be done on Earth as in Heaven (as Jesus asked), because True Soul can be an agency of genuine Will. That was always our task to accomplish.

The Multiple Universe Hypothesis

The Multi-Universe Hypothesis has some relevance to religion, because the ultimate basis for this theory is to be found in the notion that Reality (the Biblical Light), as created by God, was not a fixed thing. It was instead, the Transfinite potential for whatever could be Real. And this also applies to anti-being (the Biblical Dark), which is the potential for everything illusory and discontinuous. What this adds up to is that the potential number of forms available within Existence, Real and otherwise, are without limit. And this isn't so difficult to understand. For example, in every sporting event, the possibility is there for either side to win. That's two alternate universes right there. Within each of those alternate realities, just for the outcome of a single game, there are a staggering high number of ways for the team to win: by different scores, by means of different players making the scoring points. Now extend that mental exercise to, say, a war, and see how every divergent possibility is potentially significant enough to need an alternative universe to play out. And those infinite alternative possibilities are just for this one planet.

The theory of multiple Universes is widely debated in scientific circles. But scientists tend to postulate multiple universes—when they consider the idea at all— that abide by the same set of physical laws.

In the religious Cosmology being presented here, there's a qualitative as well as a quantitative component that allows for at least two different *orders* of Existence, and therefore of types of Universes, and quite likely more. But at the higher level of Existence are those Universes which result directly from the Elohim (the Amesha Spenta) themselves. The Amesha Spenta are minds, and the various and differing baseline values can be thought of as the result of those minds focusing their thoughts at different ranges along different spectra. For example, in Physics, these thoughts would refer to what are called Constants, like those for velocity of light, the gravitational constant, for electric charge, the mass of various particles, and so forth. With these constants set at different values, entirely different types of universes would be the result, which might or might not generate a universe in which material life is possible. In this manner, an infinite range of differing types of universes are possible simultaneously, all co-existing.

I would also speculate that when Jesus of Nazareth said, "In my Father's House are many mansions," he may have been referring to different universes created by the Elohim.

There are many religious jokes which describe how different religions, and disagreeing sects within religions, imagine Heaven. Here's one of my favorites:

A man dies and goes to Heaven, and is welcomed at the Gate by Saint Peter.

"We have your reward waiting for you," Saint Peter tells the man, "and your family and friends who died before you are looking forward to welcoming you."

"That's wonderful," says the man. "I'm looking forward to seeing them again. But first, could someone show me around?"

"Of course," says Saint Peter, and he calls over an angel to give the man a tour of Heaven.

They pass a beautiful temple, open to the sky, green with vines and bright with flowers. Inside, people are dancing and singing.

"Who are those?" asks the man.

"Oh, those are wiccans," answers the angel.

Next they come to a magnificent church, where bells are ringing and beautiful stained glass windows are glowing in hundreds of colors.

"Who comes here?" asks the man.

"Here is where the Catholics and Anglicans assemble, now that they've stopped arguing about popes. Lots of incense and choral music."

"I'm amazed," says the man. "This truly is Heaven!"

RELIGION REINTERPRETED

Next the angel shows the man a wooded area with streams, hills, and small temples, where followers of Zen Buddhism and the Shinto tradition tend to settle.

Then they come to a set of huge buildings. One has a gold roof with a cross on top; one has a silver roof with a crescent moon; and there are others with different decorations. But not one of the buildings has so much as a single window.

Puzzled, the man asks, "Who comes here?"

"Shhh," says the angel. "We make an effort to go very quietly when we pass these buildings. Here is where all the different Fundamentalists come. They insist they are the only one's here."

Infinite Presence (Dark Matter)

Matter having reached light speed would become infinite mass in only two dimensions. Whatever such material might prove to be, it wouldn't be ordinary matter. Likewise with Black Holes. A Black Hole is the result of a sufficient amount of mass compressed into a small enough volume of space for its gravity to crush itself out of our Actuality, but not out of Existence. For example, the entire mass of the Earth would need to be crushed into the volume of an ordinary marble to become a Black Hole.

To be crushed out of our Actuality would mean that there was no longer any matter as we understand the word. This much I figured out a while back. However, it was only on 08/24/11 that I found a way to picture what this meant. My thanks go out to Dr. Brian Cox, his TV show *Wonders of the Universe*—once again on the Science Channel—and his episode about Gravity. The trigger for my insight came to me simply because he spoke first about neutron stars before he spoke about Black Holes.

To explain: atoms are mostly empty space. There's a tiny nucleus, surrounded at distance by an electron cloud. This cloud, and its resistance to the electron clouds of other atoms (such as the atoms of your hand and fingers), is what you experience as solidity when you touch something. We think of something we touch as being solid, but the resistance you encounter is really more akin to the resistance between two magnets when like poles are forced together. Now, a neutron star is a result of the space within its constituent atoms (that internal space between each atom's electron cloud and its nucleus), having been forced out by gravitational collapse. As a consequence, the electrons that surround the nucleus have been forced to fuse with the protons of that nucleus. Each "electron + proton" fusion essentially becomes another neutron. The result is that a neutron star is composed of nothing but contiguous neutrons. Were this to happen to our Sun, it would have to collapse into a sphere about 12 miles in diameter, while retaining all of its present mass.

My new insight on listening to the show was understanding that space is a manifestation of anti-being. At the same time, gravity is ultimately a manifestation of the Primordial Holy Reconciling (Impartial Divine Love), at the hierarchical level of Inertia. And this made sense because the only Space left within a Neutron Star is that space which allows its neutrons to remain 3-dimensional. Losing that very last bit of dimensional space means that there's no longer anything physically there. In becoming a Black Hole, that former neutron star has become Infinite Presence (aka Dark Matter). More than that, it's become a localized hole in the Light Boundary.

<u>Ordinary matter, the "contrails" of Lower Dimensional Existence?</u>

Ordinary sub-luminous matter is itself a condensation of energy, of quantifiable potential. Might it be the case that this condensation takes place in a manner analogous to the way that contrails form at the wingtips of high flying airplanes? Contrails are essentially linear clouds which form because the passage through air of those wingtips locally drops the air pressure, which makes it possible for the water dissolved in that air (aka humidity) to precipitate out, becoming that suspension we call a cloud. In the case of ordinary matter, the precipitating factor would be an analogous drop in the number of dimensions in worlds below the Light Boundary. Again, this is only a speculation, a mental groping to envision and understand something.

The Mandelbrot Set as a map of this Cosmology

This is primarily for readers who've not only heard of and seen this wondrous example of computer aided Mathematics, but also who basically understand its significance, and even have some practical understanding of how this form is generated. At the same time, nothing of critical importance to the purpose of this book will be missed by those who are unable to understand this short subsection. I myself barely understand the deeper significance of these forms (Julia and Fatou sets). What I can say, however, is that these functions are the result of iterating a non-linear algebraic function on a complex graph, a graph where the X-axis represents real numbers, and the Y-axis represents the imaginary numbers.

Definition #1: Iteration

A procedure where an equation is solved for a given point on a graph, the answer to which is then fed back into that same equation, again and again. On a complex graph, and given a sufficient number of iterations, that original point in question will eventually reveal itself to be attracted either to the Origin of that graph (the center, coordinates '0,0'), or to infinity. It's important here to remember that Zero and infinity are reciprocal to each other.

Definition #2: Imaginary numbers

These are numbers which violate the mathematical rule that multiplying together two negative numbers must result in a positive number. All imaginary numbers are the result of a number which, when squared, results in a negative number. Imaginary numbers can be written as real numbers multiplied by the square root of negative one, which is expressed as -i (small case I, usually in italics, standing for *imaginary*).

There are certain equations, starting with quadratics, for which these imaginary numbers are necessary. But they aren't "real" in the sense that they can't represent a quantity.

I simply must report my initial emotional reaction to seeing the Mandelbrot Set for the very first Time. It was unexpected, and I had yet to learn how it was generated. And yet, I reacted as I would were I actually looking at a picture of God. Of course, my understanding has since changed, and it would be more accurate to say that the Mandelbrot Set seems to demonstrate how the Primordial Chaos reorganized itself into the Created world. And again, there's no way to represent Will, except only by its results.

Recollect that, according to this Cosmology, Primordial Chaos (aka the Primordial Void, aka Zero), essentially pulled Itself up by Its own bootstraps into a state of genuine Being. This concept is consistent with the name given by the ancient Kurds (Medes), to the Universal Spirit: "Xwede", a name which meant "He Who Created Himself." It's as if the Primordial Chaos were a Dream, because dreams "both are, and yet, are not" (just like the number

Zero is, in its role as the implicit something). This Dream eventually awoke to the fact that it was a dream, following which, It must have chosen to become fully awake. That new state of being fully awake was what we now call Reality, or, BEING. Whereas the status and presence of the Primordial Void was always non-objective and therefore invariably an uncertainty, this new state of being Real was the opposite. This new status of having become fully awake was in fact Creation Itself.

The Creation Itself was the result of designating (separating) the two "attractors": Zero (the Graph's origin at coordinates (0,0) and Infinity. Zero and Infinity are reciprocal to each other (the "Inverse Twins"). On this graph, these two different Attractors represent the Biblical Light and Dark; respectively BEING and anti-being; Absolute Reality and the illusion of discontinuity.

The entire radius-two circle which surrounds the Mandelbrot Set proper, excepting only the Central Singular point, which is the graph's center of origin, represents Existence. Everything beyond this circle is the negative chaos that is anti-being, where every point will reveal that it belongs to this Attractor or Infinity after only one iteration.

The Mandelbrot set itself represents Hyper-luminous Existence. Every point therein represents an internally contiguous Julia Set, and therefore represents an Idea, aka an Ideal Being.

The asymptotic boundary between those points which are part of the Mandelbrot set and those outside of the Mandelbrot set yet still within the radius-two circle, is the Light Boundary.

All points outside of the Mandelbrot set, yet within the radius-two circle, represent sets of "Fatou dust", which is to say that they represent composite material Beings. Therefore, that area within the radius-two circle, yet outside of the Mandelbrot set proper, represents Sub-luminous Existence, with the Fatou Dust representing the Quantum Nature of the finite material world.

The closer an outside point is to the Mandelbrot set proper, the more iterations will be needed to determine whether that point actually belongs to the Mandelbrot set or not. This is actually an analogous equivalent to the increasing energy needed to continue to accelerate towards the velocity of light, in other words, that which happens when one continues to approach any asymptote. But the Light Boundary is an asymptote, and is therefore unreachable, regardless of the number of iterations.

Aleph-Null Ideas: The scaffold of Sub-Luminous Existence

There is a dawning realization in cosmology that this entire universe has an underlying scaffold, a skeleton of sorts. I would propose that this scaffolding is something like a shadow of the hyper-luminous Matrix of Ideas, projected onto the Light Boundary. This would be consistent with Dr. Susskind's Holographic Cosmological Theory. And this scaffolding would account for the filamentous distribution of galaxies in the observable Universe. They would represent the increased density of Julia sets as they cluster on the border of the Mandelbrot Set, that density represented by the increasing number of iterations needed to demonstrate that a given point is indeed a true member of that set. I'm hoping that someone other than myself can express all of this to the scientific community better than I can.

CHAPTER XV

WHAT IS RELIGION FOR?

WHO?; the question of why?; independent Will and Religion's function; dogma antithetical to independent Will and even Faith; evil defined; the logoi of the Biblical Dark; knowledge of "good" and "evil"; animals and angels; The Great Gamble; hamartia; a different account of original sin; ADAM and Adam; is it necessary to believe in a God?; several religions; attribution; worldly mind; feelings and emotions; nervous systems; interpretation and appreciation; conscience; love; personality; New Mind; a simile; essence; the Double; prayer; inner silence

<u>A critical matter of both Orthography and Nomenclature:</u> "WHO"

In this book, the word "WHO" in full capitals is never to be confused with the standard word "who", which is used in the usual everyday sense. In short, "WHO" never refers to your ordinary self, nor to anyone else's ordinary self. It refers instead, and alone, to God as "I AM".

God as "I AM" by our standards is Zero, which is to say, nothing at all. In other words, God, while being the very Source of everything, is yet nothing objective that we can point to or prove to be. This is why the Holy of Holies, the Ark of the Covenant, was empty inside. The "-AM" part of "I AM" is the Creation itself (BEING), and because it is and remains a Singularity, it's but a dimensionless point. The very same holds for the "I AM" we each of us bear within as WHO we are. The "ME" that is each of us, the composite totality of our opinions, our likes and dislikes, are the "riches" that disqualify us from passing through "the eye of the needle". and gaining access to that Heaven which is God as "I AM".

This distinction between "WHO" you are, as opposed to "who and what you are", will be critical in discussing Man and the goal of Religion. For example, it was partly the confusion of those two questions of "who" which led to the belief that Jesus of Nazareth was a deity. Again, no Man is a god. Instead, each and every Man bears "I AM" as WHO she or he is, but never as who or what he or she is.

Another contributing factor to that belief was the deliberate conflation of Jesus of Nazareth with various sons of Zeus/Jupiter— ie, "sons of God"— in the religion of Greco-Roman civilizations. It was easier to convert pagans to Christianity if the God you are introducing has a lot in common with the heroes and gods they already worship. The *real* trouble came about when translations of Holy writ began confusing the Greek article, which is neither indefinite like the English "a" nor definite like the English "the", with the definite article. And so "*a* son of God" became "THE son of God", and we were off and rolling for millennia of dogma-based prejudice, wars, inquisitions and other acts of cruelty that have literally nothing in common with Jesus's commandment that we love our neighbors as ourselves.

<u>A curious question.</u>

The question of what Religion is for, was asked in the Introduction. For a person brought up in one of the West Asian traditions, Judaism, Christianity, or Islam, the answer would likely be something like "Religion's purpose is to teach us to live as God wants us to." And that might be sufficient for most of us, but human beings really need to understand not only *what* they are supposed to do, and *how*, but also *why*. As stated before, your pet dog will never be able to understand why it's not allowed to crap in your living room when it feels the need to relieve itself. It need only understand that it's a really bad idea, one that will lead to considerable discomfort when their unwelcome deposit is discovered. It can and should be different for Man, and it's therefore unfortunate that most followers of the three Abrahamic religions only rarely understand their religion beyond the limited degree of "believe what you are told to believe and do what you are told to do" with the explicit threat of an eternal beat-down for failure. But Religion—*real* religion— aims for something beyond mere behavioral control. Behavioral control is what bad social engineers are after.

To really answer the question of what Religion is for, we must first answer the question of just what is our purpose as Man, which is actually the very same question as asking why we, as Man, were created. The notion that we were created simply to be some exotic flower in God's garden (a flower whose "flower-behavior" is faulty), doesn't make sense.

This World we find ourselves in is irreconcilable with the picture of a benevolent and all-powerful God that can snap its fingers and make every problem disappear. This Cosmology has attempted to demonstrate that to bring forth Something from the Nothing that was Itself did not come free of charge for our Absolute Creator, God as "I". There was a price to pay for separating the Biblical light from the Biblical Dark, if that Light which was brought forth was to persist as something stable, self-consistent, and relatively permanent. The initial (but not final) price for achieving that stability and firmness was what I am calling The Great Sacrifice, where God as "I", God as Primordial Will, voluntarily disengaged Itself from a major part of Its capacity to act because of the incompatibility of those rejected options/logoi (the Biblical Dark) with Its Creation (the Biblical Light). The result of this Sacrifice was that this same God, now as "I AM", would have to achieve its goals indirectly and strategically. Initially, this meant both bringing forth that secondary construct, Existence (the Biblical Firmament in Genesis 1:7). Next, it meant creating a surrogate which could operate as the independent Holy Reconciliation within that Existence: Man.

Existence, as an intervening boundary phenomenon between the Creation (the Light) and the threat (the Dark), was designed to be a living, self-compensating and self-regulating organism in its own right, one governed by the Elohim (essentially acting as the brain and overall nervous system for "I AM").

And here is where Man, and therefore Religion, entered the picture. Man was the means of introducing Independent (God-like) Will into Existence as the Holy Reconciling between the Holy Affirming of God as "I AM" and the Holy Denying of the illusion of Discontinuity. Religion was intended to instruct us in *why* we as Man were given this gift of Will, along with *how* we were meant to accomplish our intended purpose. Having been given a potentially Independent Will means that we weren't put here to simply be predictable.

As for explaining Religion, we can now return to the meaning of the word "Religion" itself. In many languages, the word for Religion directly translates into the English words "belief" or "creed." But can that be all there is to Religion? Only what I should believe, think, do? But the English word "religion", which was derived from Latin, is a much more insightful proposition than the word "belief." It refers to the need to re-bind together something which has been sundered.

But this definition only points us in the direction we need to move. *Understanding* all that this means also includes learning *how* to accomplish this goal, and this is something else entirely. Simply "believing" is nowhere close to what is needed, because only a very rare few of us reach adulthood with an innocent and sincere faith which can genuinely be open to something higher. Regaining such inner openness (which is almost always lost by our contact with the world), is a big part of what Jesus meant by informing us that we had to return to being as little children. He meant returning to that inner openness we were all born with, but which is so often sealed off by the time of puberty, because of delusions and wounds acquired while growing up.

Many Christians would insist that being saved is the point to Religion. But what does that really mean? What must be saved, and from what must it be saved? This Cosmology has taken great pains to de-throne evil as the central problem in Creation. Evil is certainly a very big problem in our immediate human world, but it's difficult to see how evil afflicts this stupendous Universe. And besides, evil only makes sense in the context of Will, and other than God, only Man has the kind of Will, different from resolve, to choose from amongst light and dark/heavy options. Stars and galaxies cannot choose and cannot be judged as bad/evil, and neither can animals, plants, or rocks. Therefore, while this Cosmology accepts that evil is certainly an actuality here in our Flatland Human world, it simply cannot be the central issue for this Universe. Evil cannot even be real unless God created it, and to believe that a Good and all-powerful God deliberately created evil to give Creation a hard time makes no sense whatsoever. THIS is precisely where so many people who become atheists lose their faith, all because too many people who claim to be religious— this happens whenever and wherever religions are reduced to dogma— focus on evil and trying to scare their children and their neighbors into "good behavior" with threats of what their Good and Powerful God will do to anyone who disagrees with them. Which is ironic when you think about it; they are trying to take away their neighbors' free will, which God gave to all of us, for us to exercise.

Neither can there be an independently evil Will, because Monotheism, One God, means One Will, one which actually includes our own Human Will. Our Will is only independent of God in the sense that we have been given the freedom to act on our own initiative, and also in that we are free to make mistakes (the true definition of "sin"). That much latitude was unavoidable if our Will is to be free enough to enable us to play our designated role as the independent "third force" of Holy Reconciling.

In this Cosmology, evil is essentially defined as the intent to work for the Part at the expense of the Whole. Evil is a sin in that it's a mistake. But a mistake can be made out of sheer ignorance without any intent of doing harm, or to profit from it. As Jesus pointed out, it's the mistakes you knowingly make that cause real harm. Expressed differently, Evil is lending your Will to that from which God Himself withdrew— the Biblical Dark, the logoi which were incompatible with the Creation God had in Mind.

The expelled logoi would cancel out this Creation if they came in direct contact with their opposite numbers. This doesn't mean that they cannot serve as a basis for a different Creation; they are simply incompatible with this one. This essential incompatibility *at the level of Existence* is why there needs to be a Firmament separating "the waters above" and "the waters below". God as Zero contains all opposites and all mutually exclusives, the original Chaos.

One representation of the nature of this separation was actually in the movie *The One*. At the end of the movie, the protagonist is living in a reality that includes clean air, solar cars and good working conditions for everyone. This is what our world would be like if more of us understood and practiced the Golden Rule, which, after all, is just another version of the commandment to love our neighbors as ourselves. Simultaneously, the anti-protagonist is transported to an alternate reality where the prevailing logoi are "every man for himself", "might is right", and so on. And he is *perfectly happy* here. He immediately starts fighting.

So again, the Biblical Dark is not itself evil. It only lends itself to such because it is the polar opposite to the original Creation. This far from the light boundary, the logoi of the Biblical Dark are readily accessible to us. And in this context, the meaning of the word "Religion", to "*bind back together something which has been ruptured or torn apart*", begins to make sense. The tension between Creation and what is excluded from Creation, especially this far from the Light Boundary, where matter is slower and denser, generates a sort of sheering effect that pulls us apart from our awareness of our own WHO we are. It is our sense of self that has become sundered.

This sundering is an echo or shadow or reflection of the Great Sacrifice. It is the inevitable consequence of ADAM volunteering, choosing to have knowledge of "good" *and* "evil", not just of Good alone. This knowledge of good and evil makes it possible, or inevitable, your choice, for ADAM to be the interface between God as "I AM" and the Biblical Dark. Without some sort of interface, the original separation would be irrevocable, and there could never be a return to wholeness for the 1 that is Creation and the -1 (minus one) that is Anti-Being.

Animals are more like angels than we are, because they do not contain this sundering in their nature. This is exactly why so many First Peoples and aboriginals take animals as totems. This should not be mistaken for or judged as the worship of idols; seeing angelic (messenger, re-Minder) natures in animals is one way the Mind of Man remembers the purpose of our existence here. It is no more idolatry to have a totem animal or animals than it is to pray to saints for intervention and help.

At the same time, remember that a genuinely independent Will had to include the freedom to make mistakes, even stupid or vicious ones, if it is to be genuinely free. At this level, The Great Sacrifice is more like The Great Gamble. Will we pull ourselves together? Will we wake up and live like sons of God, treating our neighbors— which includes every human, *and all of creation*, not just the people we go to church with— as ourselves?

So just what are we supposed to be saved from? Standard Christianity postulates that we need to be saved from the consequences of sin. That Greek word, "hamartia", was originally used in target practice, and it meant to "miss the mark" (to miss the bull's eye). The origin of the English word "sin" is less obvious, but it seems to have been derived from an older English word which meant "excess"—which sounds like our forebears understood the Deadly Sins to be one form or another of excess: excessive anger, excessive pride, excessive appetite, etc. However, in the standard Abrahamic religions, sin is usually believed to mean far more than a mere mistake. It tends to mean offending God.

RELIGION REINTERPRETED

<u>A tale of original sin</u>

Here I would like to pass along a very different account of the beginning of original sin than what I was told growing up and going to church. I came across it in the Introduction to a book written by P.D. Ouspensky entitled *Talks With a Devil*, a book similar to C.S. Lewis's *The Screwtape Letters* in that it offers a "diabolic" perspective of the Human condition. According to the Introduction, this story was part of a rich oral tradition in Russia that was all but extinguished during the wars of the 20th century.

In this account, God tells Adam and Eve to have twelve children to help them take care of the Garden of Eden. Adam and Eve enjoy the process so much that they go on and have twelve more children. Then they dread that God will not approve.

In this story, *dis-obedience,* which has more to do with not hearing, not heeding, than the actions which follow, is the original sin; *becoming fearful* is the second sin. Which perhaps sheds light on why there are so many admonitions against fear in the Bible.

Here is what happens next:

*God tells Adam and Eve to prepare to present their children to be blessed. (*Notice that God does not specify a number of children to present.*) But Adam and Eve tell their second set of twelve children to hide behind some bushes— in the dark—and not come forth until God is gone,* **no matter what***.*

When God appears, God blesses the twelve children presented by Adam and Eve. Then God asks, "Are there any more children?" And here comes sin number three: Adam and Eve bear false witness— against themselves and against their children. "Oh, no," they say, "we did just what you told us to do and only had twelve children."

God calls out, "Are there any more children to be blessed?" But the twelve children hiding in the dark obey their parents and ignore God. They stay in the dark. (Think of all the children who grow up exactly as their parents and the immediate community render them.)

Before God departs, God calls out again and says, "Any child who wishes to be blessed, need only call to Me at any time; I will hear, and I will bless them."

After that, according to the tale, all the human beings who cause pain and horror and trouble are descended from the children who went unblessed. The sins of the fathers, indeed. However, the Introduction goes on to state an addendum which perhaps I had better leave for adventuresome readers to discover on their own.

ADAM and Adam

All three Abrahamic Religions agree that Man was created to be God's viceroy within Existence. But in order to serve as such, the whole of what Existence is has to be included as part of what Man is. In this Cosmology, ADAM is considered to be a purely Ideal Being, the entire Idea of Man. What comes next is very important.

ADAM alone can have no sub-luminous component, because ADAM as one of the Amesha Spenta is a hyper-luminous being. So in order for ADAM to live and function at the cutting edge of Creation, a sub-luminous component had to be added: the Human animal body. This Cosmology does not consider the expulsion of ADAM from the garden of Eden to be a punishment for sin, because it was actually necessary for ADAM (female and male together), to become sub-luminously embodied in order to become Man. This Cosmology therefore assumes that our insertion (incarnation) into these Human animal bodies to have been intended from the beginning. The reason why this was necessary is explained below.

Note: If I am correct, Islam reports that we were tricked into this state. I found this of interest because I had already come to believe that our so-called "Fall" was a set-up. You simply don't point out a fruit tree to a monkey (or a child, if you prefer that analogy) and then tell it not to go there and eat the fruit. Besides, God being all knowing means that God would have had to know in advance what would happen. Therefore, our insertion into our Human animal bodies (the so-called "Fall"), makes more sense to have been intentional, unless you want to believe we were created to be evil, or created to be punished. Besides, there's a good reason for why we had to be locked into these sub-luminous bodies, where recognizing what's real, true, and good is so difficult.

Addendum: In spite of the above, it's still true that we Human Beings have fallen further (into error and illusion) than was either intended or needed.

Above the Light Boundary where Reality prevails, it's impossible to make mistakes because there knowing is direct, without any need for interpretation. There one can't avoid seeing what's Real and what isn't. Below that Light Boundary, where illusion has priority or "dominance", mistakes are quite easy to make. Still, we were intentionally drawn into this sub-luminous Realm and given these animal bodies, these "skins" to wear (Genesis 3:21), which pinned us down here. In this Cosmology, our Human animal bodies are not considered to be bad, but they are extremely limited and extremely limiting, even as they make our Existence where we need to be possible, and have some built in reminders. Here, as God's appointed Holy Reconciliation, we must work to find and recognize the Reality that is our true center (that Pearl of Great Price) before our choices can be meaningful.

It's actually Man's task to fulfill the request made in the Lord's Prayer that God's Will be done, on earth as it is in heaven. This means that as Mankind begins to achieve our Atonement, sub-luminous Existence ("earth") and hyper-luminous Existence ("heaven") cease to be separated states of our Being because we become a bridge that spans the light boundary.

<u>So then, is it absolutely necessary to believe in a God?</u>
This is a curious question, especially given that this Cosmology is explicitly a religious Cosmology, with God (in some sense) being its most fundamental assumption. But that's not really the question being asked here. The question is closer to whether or not a belief in God is absolutely essential to make a real start in one's process of return. Before I offer an answer, we might first look to the major world religions to see how they address this question of the existence of God. In doing so, we will work from East to West along the Eurasian land mass.

<u>Taoism</u>: No attributes can really be assigned to Tao, not even that of being Real or Alive. The Tao does nothing, it simply is, and whatever "gods" there might be in Taoism are at best secondary and responsible only for the specific workings of Existence (much like the Elohim in Judaism, or the Kurdish Cult of Angels). I would personally equate the Tao to God as "I" or the Zero that precedes and includes Creation; the Tao is not God as some personality.

<u>Buddhism</u>: Buddhism does acknowledge the existence of gods, but they are considered to be somewhat beside the point. One must

focus one's own effort to liberate one's true nature by getting free of certain illusions.

Hinduism: At first glance, Hinduism has a surplus of gods (a major problem for neighboring Islam). However, it's possible to distill something central from this extensive collection of deities by recognizing what seems to be the central goal of Hinduism: the discovery in experiential truth that one's own central-most Reality, called the Atman, is one and the same with the central-most Reality of this entire Creation, called Brahman. This is true, but the Buddhist way of handling this notion seems to me to be the safer path, as will be discussed later.

Zoroastrianism: Here we encounter something more recognizable as a single God of Creation: Ahura Mazda. However, in the orthodox religion Ahura Mazda was only half of the equation, with Ahriman as an "inverse twin".

Judaism and Islam: Here we have God in the full sense of the word as the Autocratic Creator and Ruler of this, His Creation. The corners on this picture of God have softened somewhat over the centuries, with an emphasis on God's mercy. But this velvet glove is still understood to cover an iron (absolute) fist.

Christianity: By all rights, Christianity should be included with Judaism and Islam. However, with the exception of its fire and brimstone fundamentalist versions, Christianity has gone farther than the other two in explicitly emphasizing God's Love and Mercy. Yet it compromised that message brought to us by its founding prophet, Jesus of Nazareth, by elevating Him alone and exclusively to the status of God (something which I personally believe both

Judaism and Islam rightly condemn as Idolatry, St. Athanasius notwithstanding).

The answer to the question

Now to answer the original question of whether a belief in God is absolutely necessary. While for me God is the unquestionable starting point for this Cosmology, the need for a belief in God isn't necessarily so. This is because the answer to this question takes into account two additional issues.

For one Single God to be the whole of everything means that there is One Single Will in the whole of everything, in spite of the appearance of extensive differences among willful human beings. No Man is a god, yet whatever created this stupendous Universe is here as the ultimate center of both your total presence and of mine. Therefore, the question of how to understand this central truth of oneself is actually *equivalent* to the question of how to understand God, because what we believe about the "I AM" that is "I" in myself will have direct bearing on what we believe about God. And here we have a big potential problem: the problem of attribution. This is issue number one, because most of us imagine God as being this or that; as wanting this or that; and as hating this or that. That's what is meant by attribution, and countering this tendency is the real point to the firm prohibitions against Idolatry in the Abrahamic religions.

Attribution is the mistake of assigning definitions, qualities, purposes to that which is beyond whatever we can imagine. Therefore, thinking that God is this or that, that God wants this or that, that God hates this or that, and that God intends to do this or that, is essentially to fix and thereby limit God in your mind. And those sort of thoughts are as much an Idol (a dead Idea) as anything externally fixed in stone or ceramics. If one needs some recognizable and understandable purpose for God, let it be to preserve Its Creation, which includes Their True One Son (Man), sent here to help in that regard. Everything else is thin ice, because an attribute is a limit, whereas God is, "by definition", beyond all definition. This is why the Persian attributive names for God are words that point to something indescribably beyond all words: "The Ineffable", "The Inexorable", and such like. The best description for God I ever came across was written by C.S. Lewis when he described true prayer as something addressed "not to that which I think Thou art, but to what Thou knowest Thyself to be."

Attribution can go so far that when one group (A) believes another group (B) is doing something that group (A) believes God to hate, they then feel that they have the right, and even the obligation, to force group (B) to do or believe otherwise. Hence the Sunni versus Shia conflict in Islam, or the violent Catholic versus Protestant conflict in Christendom. And the Holocaust. This supposed "obligation to correct others" extends to group (A) feeling justified in exterminating group (B)… all in the "name of God", even though such behavior is in utter violation of the Commandments. This is unjustifiable madness regardless of whoever does it to whom. Such conflicts have produced an inconceivable amount of carnage and suffering to every aspect of Creation.

In light of this problem of attribution, the reasonable answer to the question of whether one needs to start by believing in God is probably best an emphatic if temporary "NO!" The issue of God is best left alone until one is no longer inclined to think in terms like "What does God demand that I think or do?" Why this might be best will become much clearer as we discuss the "worldly mind." But for the moment, this is why Buddhism simply avoids addressing the issue of a God. Likewise, it's why Judaism and Islam both insist that no graven images be made of God.

The fundamental problem here is that the ordinary, everyday worldly (material) mind and its attending ego cannot allow for God. By itself, our worldly mind will unavoidably make a hash of Religion by assuming that God is like itself. Everything genuinely helpful about religion ends up in the trash heap or perverted into some worldly agenda.

Understand that all of the received proscriptions of any religion can actually be boiled down to something very simple: Do no willful harm to yourself, nor to each other, nor to this larger world. And do nothing that will compromise or interfere with your ability, or that of others, to find and bring forth that central-most "I AM" that is WHO you most genuinely are.

<u>Critical addendum</u>: Seeking one's own inner Reality can and must be a voluntary choice made by each and every individual. Punishing someone for being a "disbeliever", simply because they haven't yet awakened sufficiently to confront the need to make this choice is directly contrary to the reasons for which we were given a free Will.

At first, it's usually best to treat the "I AM" we each of us bear within as emptiness. In the early stages of one's efforts to Return to God, all speculation about what God is and about what God wants can only be in vain (delusional), so it's best to just leave all of that alone, and focus only on learning just what the above commandments actually mean in practice, and work at maintaining, or acquiring, the necessary *inner silence* to hear the "still, small voice" when it does speak. That's what Religion is really all about.

And it is precisely here that we find the two-part answer to our question of what religion is for. The first part concerns all Mankind, all societies, all communities. It has to do with how we think about and treat each other, because without recognizing and respecting our common Sonship in everyone, no genuine growth towards fulfilling our purpose as Man is possible. But at the same time, a religion must have provisions for enabling the accelerated growth of those individuals who've consciously made their choice that Returning back to God be their given task, a task second to no other. Gurdjieff used to refer to such people as "those who wish to reach Heaven in this lifetime." This book is an attempt to address both aspects of Religion.

All genuine Religion, beyond simply behaving decently towards others, starts with the effort to awaken and substantiate this New Mind and corresponding Being in ourselves.

So what is this "worldly mind"?

Man has one mind made of and for this material sub-luminous world, and a potential New Mind which, while also material, has a different function. It is designed to be a bridge to that very much higher mind and Being which has different names in different religions. This New Mind is no longer widely known about in today's world, and yet without it, little that is meaningful about Religion can be understood. Nor can anyone make any meaningful progress in one's effort to Return to God, without first acquiring this corresponding New Mind.

Denying or punishing the material body or brain for their natural focus on what is materially needful for our lives is not the way one finds the doorway to the path of Return, as even the Buddha himself learned when he finally rejected the extreme asceticism that almost killed him. And while it's true that we must escape from this labyrinth of illusion, such a withdrawal is done inwardly. Buddhism uses the image of the lotus which has its roots deep in the mud yet flowers above the water. It's the very same notion as "being in the world, but not of it."

Our brains recapitulate layer by layer, the entire evolutionary history that led to our Human animal body. There is the medullary brain stem, which keeps us physically alive: heartbeat, breathing, digestion, etc. The cerebellum's domain includes movement in space and time, our own and other objects, and it is capable of rapid, accurate calculus. There is the mid-brain, which developed in ancient mammals and includes the limbic system. It has a great deal to do with registering and responding to environmental factors, including interactions with other life forms. Then there is the cerebral cortex, a vast, interactive processing and storage centre, which developed much more recently. Dogs and other animals with a highly developed, intelligent sense of smell use their cerebral cortex to process the information that comes to them through their noses; humans use their much larger cortex to correlate all sorts of information in many ways, including language, musicality, mathematics, and sensory impressions.

Our brain-based worldly mind is roughly tripartite in its functions. The most fundamental function is to process and manage sensations, which includes more than just the standard five functions of sight, hearing, taste, smell, and touch. Touch alone includes several different types of sensors: pressure, pain, and temperature. Add to these that sense called proprioception, which includes the sense of gravity and of the relative positioning of one's skeletal joints, all of which control posture. There's also the inertial guidance sense in our inner ear. And finally, moods are a kind of visceral sensory function, but we'll speak of these along with the other "feeling" functions. Overall, sensations mostly orient our bodies in space.

The ordinary intellect is another broad function. Its primary function seems to be its ability to abstract a generalized pattern from what is encountered and experienced in life. The word "abstract" means to "pull something out of or away from" something else ("ab—" = "away from", "tract" as in "traction"). For example, circles are a spatial abstraction derived from many material structures. The invention of wheels was one consequence of this ability to abstract. We extend this generalized spatial pattern to analogous temporal patterns, such as cycles (circles) in time: day and night, the seasons, which are not visible to the eye in a single instant.

Feelings

There are several functions which in English are called feelings. If I were to generalize their mode of orientation, analogous to the spacial orientation of sensations and to the pattern and temporal orientations of the intellect, I would say feelings are eternity oriented. By this I mean that feelings orient us to the meaning, the significance, the value or quality of something.

Moods are actually the sensation of the state of health and the state of readiness of the body's structures and functions, both visceral (the internal organs) and somatic (muscle-skeletal) in the context of the environment. Moods could well be thought of as "body climate" and/or "body weather". Moods are strongly affected by situations external to the body, such as by the loss of someone significant in one's life, or by ones' anticipation of something good. This is originally a brain dependent sensory function, but it's extensively modified by our socially acquired *interpretations* of those sensations, which is why they are experienced more as feelings than as sensations.

Emotions

There's a very good reason why the word "feelings" not "emotions" was chosen to designate this general category of brain functioning. The reason starts with the word "emotion" itself. This is the English version of the Latin "ex-motivare", which means "to get something started, or get something to move out of its previous state." In other words, true emotions are the psycho-physiological equivalent to Acceleration in physics, in that they are the material mind's means of altering the body's inertial state. Emotions are the brain's way to give priority to the body's somatic, musculoskeletal functions, thereby moving you to do something. This system also de-accelerates the body, thereby giving priority to the viscera by slowing down one's activity to allow the parasympathetic functions like digestion and sleep to take over. This works via a dual nervous system with hormonal back-up. The Autonomic Nervous System consists of two branches. The sympathetic system gives priority to the somatic portion of the body—the musculoskeletal—for movement in space, the "animal" functions. The aforementioned parasympathetic system gives priority to the viscera—the body's organs—the "vegetative" functions of maintenance, repair, and growth.

The Sympathetic Nervous System

This part of the Autonomic Nervous system is responsible for acceleration of the body, making one more physically active. In extreme circumstances it's responsible for the well-known "fight, flight, or freeze" response, giving priority of blood supply to the muscles of the body for any potential effort or struggle. This diversion of blood away from the viscera is why such stress is so often followed by nausea. Whatever food is in your stomach during the stress has to sit there for the duration of your efforts to cope with the stress; it doesn't get properly digested.

Here we can most easily see how socially acquired interpretations modify our experiences. Here is an example. From a physiological standpoint, there's almost no difference in your body between anger and fear. (This is why animals are much more likely to attack someone who is afraid, or angry. A fearful person smells aggressive to most animal sensory arrays, so the animal attacks in self-defense.) Both fear and anger are states of arousal, the result of adrenal reinforcement of our sympathetic nervous system's response to a situation. The primary difference between anger and fear lies in your interpretation of the situation and your expectation of what's likely to happen. If you believe you can win a potential conflict, you will interpret your hyped up emotional state as anger. Or if you're too angry to give a damn about being injured, you won't be afraid to lose. Whereas if you don't believe you can win, it's more likely you'll interpret your sensations as fear. People who are good at taking tests usually interpret their sensations simply as excitement, as a state of heightened awareness which improves their abilities. And if you think about what's been said here, you can see how the state of sexual arousal, which is also a response/interpretation of a situation, can arise from or be strongly colored by anger, fear, or exhilaration.

The Parasympathetic Nervous System:

This system is responsible for de-acceleration, of slowing the body down. Its anatomical taproot is the vagus nerve, and its primary function is to shift the body's blood supply to the viscera, primarily to the digestive system after a meal, or to allow your body to sleep and/or heal. This is why it's so easy to go to sleep after eating, and so hard to focus on work that requires active cogitation when you are stuffed. It's also why it is dangerous to go swimming too soon after a big meal; muscles are likely to cramp up when you give your body conflicting "orders": digest this food AND quickly move all these muscles. (The sympathetic and parasympathetic systems don't fully separate out, don't "specialize" in humans until around age seven. This explains how it is that small children can run around right after eating without getting sick, whereas an older person who tries that is probably going to feel very uncomfortable, or even throw up.)

Looking back: Catching the Flu is a well-known month long misery. However, the first hour or so before that long period of being unable to find any physical posture of comfort sets in, is one I found to be quite peaceful. Everything within would quiet down, as my body shut down all unnecessary functioning and tension (physical, emotional, and mental), in its effort to conserve energy for the coming fight against the virus. For myself, there was no wish to move or think, only the peace of a profound inner quiet was left. That short interval of peace was a faint hint of what is called the "Peace of God", because the various parts and functions of my body basically left each other in peace and stopped trying to impress each other to satisfy their diverse desires.

The *interpretations* of our experiences represent an entire class of acquired feelings that are a composite of sensations, limbic system feelings, and cortex-based generalizations. They are strongly influenced by what we are told and the behaviors we witness, and they belong entirely to the worldly mind. When, as so often happens, such feelings are based on misinformation or misinterpretations, they have a counterfeit quality to them. They do not ring true; they have a false edge.

To give a quick example of what I mean, guilt is basically a counterfeit feeling. It's the fear of the consequences of how other people will react to something one has done. Its legitimate counterpart is remorse, which is the sorrow that comes from honestly seeing that one has done harm to someone or something. Fear of being punished, whether physically or socially, is not the concern here. One is too conscience-stricken to rationalize what one has done and make up excuses, and usually one searches for some way to repair the damage.

Appreciation:

Not many people recognize appreciation as an explicit category of feelings. This one also has its roots in a sensory function, that of pleasure versus pain. However, as this function ascends in abstractness, it transitions into like versus dislike, which is not very different from pleasure versus pain. The more abstract this function becomes, the more it becomes the recognition of affinities.

The word "appreciate" literally means "to assign to or to recognize the price or value of" something.

Genuine Conscience:

At the highest level, appreciation is no longer a function of the worldly mind because it no longer relies on socially acquired interpretation. It can actually transcend the brain. The best name for this level of appreciative feeling would be Conscience, even though this title has been badly compromised by its long-term conflation with the bogus feeling of guilt. "Con-science" means "shared knowing by way of one's feelings." A good definition would be "to consciously appreciate with one's feelings."

When feelings and emotions are dismissed as invalid, they are called "irrational". However, that irrationality can be understood in two ways. Worldly mind feelings/emotions are indeed for the most part irrational in the ordinary sense, because they are so often warped by fears or judgements. Even when they are honest feelings, based on accurate readings of our inner state and our situation, we have no suitable language to express them. Our feelings are like unattended gardens which accumulate innumerable weeds, thorns, and parasitic vines, all of which tend to choke out the flowers, fruit, and vegetables which should grow there, as per the "Parable of the Weeds", Matthew 13: 24-43. This parable should be given far more attention than it gets.

But there's another type of irrationality. Intellect and sensation are both rational functions: they function by comparison and analysis, as the root word *ratio* indicates. You simply can't notice a white dot on an equally white wall, unless its texture is sufficiently different. But the "irrational" feelings, which we sometimes call intuition, are a *direct* evaluation or appreciation of something, not based on any comparison (ratio). They are only irrational in the same way that the diagonal of a square is irrational relative to its side, because you can't describe it by forming a ratio. You cannot measure the diagonal's length with the same units of measurement you use to measure the length of the side. But the diagonal is just as real as the side. Genuine Conscience is a very accurate evaluation or appreciation of the validity, worth, meaning or significance of something. Unfortunately, this function remains largely unrecognized for what it is.

This function of Conscience is properly a woman's natural strong suit, assuming it's been allowed to mature and not been diverted into self-absorption or superficialities, which present day culture encourages. The reason for this is because females more than males tend to see what is actually there, which is why women so often seem to be more realistic and practical about things than men, especially with what matters most about life. In contrast, males tend more to see what is potentially there, and so they want to make things, shape things, invent things. This "hard wired" difference is why, in ancient times, seers were so often female—and later on, so often branded as "witches"—a word which has its source in an old English word which meant "holy". Nowadays, this natural gift is typically drowned out in girls because they're mostly taught that looking desirable to men and being frivolous are the way for a woman to go in life. The "irrationality" of women which men so often bemoan is actually a consequence of this natural gift having been squashed and never allowed or encouraged to flower. Listening to a woman who can speak quietly from her own true center is invariably the wisest course to follow. I myself quickly learned this by listening carefully to the nurses I worked with, instead of posturing simply because I was an M.D.

After I wrote the above, I showed it to a number of my women friends to check if they approved it, and several of them contributed to its refinement. One young lady went quiet for a while, then said, "I see a shift happening at a very deep level, which a lot of people are feeling instinctively, intuitively. Remember the eighties, when so many young people became androgynous? The way I see it, they were feeling a wish to be whole, to be male *and* female, female *and* male, no arbitrary limitations or assignments. In other people it's more like a pendulum swing: women becoming aggressive, men preferring to be at home."

Love:

Conspicuously, "love" was not included in the discussion of feelings and emotions. Love is almost always conflated with sexual attraction, or equated with family affiliation. I still think the best description of different kinds of love is *The Four Loves;* once again, C.S. Lewis. And it seems to me that, once one swims beyond the pull and tug of attraction and revulsion, Love is essentially an act of Will, not a mere feeling. It stems from the recognition of the fundamental Oneness of everything Real. The resulting disposition is simultaneously a feeling *and* a way of seeing, a disposition of good will towards all.

What is the Personality?

Personality is a direct outgrowth of the worldly mind. It's a constellation of the combined "software" of acquired learning that has accumulated since one was born, the lights of which are refracted though the prism of our essential nature. This includes one's acquired, habitual interpretations of one's surroundings, of other people, and of one's own sensations, ideas, and especially feelings. Personality includes one's acquired motor function habits of posture, behavior, and self-expression. Personality is also colored to some extent by the potential New Mind, about which we will next speak. Personality is inevitable and absolutely necessary, yet it is an artificial self, a "per-sona" (a mask).

It's unusual for most of us to even begin to realize the extent to which our attitudes and motivations have been intentionally cultivated.

Personality includes the consequences of the myriad forms of child abuse which can leave a person crippled, with a stunted personality, all the while never suspecting that what was wrongly learned early in life can usually be undone, at least partly. Rectification is possible because, properly speaking, the personality is never "WHO" you really are. It is only ever part of "what" you've become.

RELIGION REINTERPRETED

As reported elsewhere in this book, for the religions of Eastern Asia, the everyday worldly mind, along with its "puppet self", the personality, are simply considered to be inert things, like a computer's calculations. This perspective was originally part of Christianity, but it became obscured by a fixation on and obsession with sin.

This worldly mind, which we all have, is not intrinsically bad, wrong, or sinful. At its most basic, it is an animal mind amplified by an ability to abstract things. Consider that money is an abstract substitute for material wealth. The widespread pursuit of money by the worldly mind means that it is seeking what animals seek: material resources like food and shelter and mating partners. That isn't intrinsically wrong, and it only becomes "sinful" when it overrides every other consideration. Because this mind is a function of the Human animal body, nothing that is primarily spiritual can have any genuine meaning for it. It was never designed to be an organ of higher perception or knowledge.

Jesus actually spent most of his time speaking about the need for us to acquire a New Mind, a mind which transcended the worldly mind.

<u>What then is this "New Mind"?</u>

A word used in the Gospels was the Greek word "metanoia", and it is very important to recognize that metanoia does *not* mean repentance. You need only consider that the "-pen-" of the word "repent" comes from the same Greek and Latin words which gave English the words "pain" and "punishment." When preachers say that Christ told sinners to repent, whether they know it or not, they are misrepresenting the actual message. They are, in a word, violating the commandment against bearing false witness. But you probably won't make any friends if you point this out to anyone who gets their strokes from holding a position of authority in church.

In contrast, the first part of the word metanoia is "meta-", which means "across", or "beyond", much like the Latin element "trans-". We see it in the word metaphor. There are also words like metamorphosis, which literally means a transformation, a change in form, and metaphysics, which is the study of a reality beyond physical reality.

The second half of metanoia comes from the Greek word "nous" which means "mind"—not the physical brain, but the intellect, the ability to "read between the lines".

Accordingly, meta-noia means a transformation of mind, or, the transcendence from one's old mind to a New Mind. And this New Mind has the capacity to serve as a bridge to a way of perceiving and understanding actual Reality, distinct from the labyrinth of illusions and delusions to which the worldly mind is susceptible. When the fire and brimstone crowd insist that metanoia means the same thing as repent, which literally means to "suffer pain again", I shake my head. The "New Mind" they seem to want followers to have is not a mind capable of independent thought and free will, but a programming.

So just what is the New Mind Jesus of Nazareth spoke of, and where does it fit into this overall picture of Man? This New Mind is intrinsically more awake than is possible for our ordinary worldly mind. Where the worldly mind deals with comparisons and categories, the New Mind is capable of perceiving ideas and the power of ideas. The feelings associated with the New Mind are appreciation and excitement, which, if you remember, is a clearer version of physical arousal than fear or anger, and even delight. The brain-based interface between this New Mind and our worldly mind seems to involve the temporal lobes of our brain.

RELIGION REINTERPRETED

A simile

In the previous description of Personality as "software", mention was made of one's essential nature, and it's time to take up that thread again. In fact, I'll start with a simile from weaving.

When a weaver sets out to make cloth, the loom is strung with many parallel, longitudinal, up and down threads that are called the *warp*. The more numerous the warp threads are, the wider the final weaving will be, and the length of the warp determines how long it can be. The threads which get shuttled over one warp thread and below the next, over and under, are called the *weft*. In a simple weaving, the weft may be all one color. But weavers come up with complex designs and use patterns and colors to vary the weft threads. If you've never watched a weaver at work, I recommend you do so; it's quite a lesson. So Personality is like the weft. Depending on what colors and patterns are made available to you, (or inflicted upon you) by parents, family, friends, enemies, teachers, classmates, etc., your personality may become highly variegated, or it may be a few colors in a steady pattern. The warp threads get *warped* (the same word we use for wood that gets bent out of shape), pulled out of their original alignment by the passage of all those weft threads. But that is what they are there for, to provide the essential structure for the project in hand. You simply couldn't have cloth or a carpet without both warp and weft.

We are fashioned along the same lines. Our essential natures, which are shaped by and consist of many factors, are the foundation for our lives and set certain kinds of limits on what is possible for us, the same way that the number, length, and strength of warp threads set soft limits on what can be woven across them. A skillful weaver can play with the warp threads to adjust those limits. A weaver also needs to be attentive to how the weft threads constrain the warp, or the result will be misshapen. If we are fortunate enough to have good parents, families, friends and neighbors, if we have good instructors and like to learn, we do not get harshly "warped out of shape" as we grow up. With the "weft" they provide, we develop bright, vibrant, interesting patterns as our personalities.

Here's a question: if our essential nature corresponds to the warp, and our personalities correspond to the weft, what, if anything, in us corresponds to a weaver? And what manner of weaver?

I am reasonably sure that there is a material nature to Essence, even if it presently eludes our capabilities to detect, measure, quantify and qualify by means of mechanical instruments. But I'm willing to bet that almost any reader knows, from their own experiences, how possible it is to get a read off another person and know, without ever being told, something about their essential nature. The classic description of four Humors—melancholy, sanguine, choleric and phlegmatic—was a qualitative assessment of types of essential nature. It has been said that the twelve disciples were chosen by Jesus of Nazareth because they each embodied distinct essential natures.

As for what physical material this Essence might be composed of, I can only offer a supposition. My guess is that it be a low temperature, low density plasma, that fourth state of matter, beyond that of ordinary gas. Plasma is ionized gas, something you see every time you look at the sun, or turn on a fluorescent lamp. Even an ordinary flame is mostly plasma.

I make this speculation because our "Essence" must of necessity function as the medium between the "Sentient Light" which is our True Soul, and the electro-chemical circuitry by which our brains operate. Without this intermediate stuff as a channel, there would be no way for our Will to manifest through our worldly minds.

<u>An aside</u>: Any substantive material basis there might be to such things as halos and auras would be found to be just such a plasma. This same stuff would also explain the appearances of Angels when they become visible to ordinary mortals in this material world, such Angels as the burning bush which spoke to Moses, Gabriel who appeared to Mary and who later recited the original portions of the Quran to Mohammad, the angels who addressed the shepherds of Bethlehem, and the Angel with the flaming sword who guards against any premature return to Paradise (hyper-luminous Existence).

Man was originally meant to start his&her Return after reaching maturity, when a healthy personality was in the service of a healthy essence. This was what used to be called Natural Man. Unfortunately, what should be the ground floor level for us is instead something we have to work for, if our earlier life experiences left us "buried alive" in familial and/or societal rubble. This is why we've been sent so many Prophets to help us climb out of the pits so many of us find ourselves in. Living a life of Return gradually builds up something new on the foundation of natural essence and healthy personality. (The absence or lack of this "something", which is the result of a robust essence and well developed personality focused on Return, is why boys and even young men used to be called "soulless young devils" in several cultures.)

This "something", this "second body", has many labels. Some call it the astral body. Gurdjieff called it the kesdjan body. J.G. Bennett reported that this word "Kesdjan" was Persian, and that it meant "the Vessel of the Soul." Gurdjieff emphasized that one isn't automatically born with this body. Instead, it has to be intentionally allowed to gestate in each of us, similar to how a caterpillar, after spending its immature stage eating vast quantities of leaves, arranges itself to allow for a profound transformation. It is precisely because the ancient Greeks recognized the stage of being a "soulless young devil" that they chose the word *psyche* to represent the soul which a person can cultivate, for the word "psyche" literally means "butterfly". In the same way that butterflies do not hatch from eggs, the kesdjan soul is not evident at a baby's birth— with certain exceptions— but the essence that babies are born with often has a quality of inherent soulfulness. The poet William Wordsworth remembered this and wrote "Ode on Intimations of Immortality from Recollections of Early Childhood".

I tend to call the second body the Double, from reading Carlos Castaneda. The effort to intentionally mature this aspect of oneself was the main point to the practices Castaneda undertook to describe in his books. It's my supposition that this second body, when matured and firmly established in its connection to our True Soul, is what Castaneda's Don Juan called the Nagual. It becomes the means by which our True Soul can manifest directly into this subluminous world. I also believe it's possible that the Egyptians called it the Ka. And I'm quite certain that the maturation of this inner Being is what the ancient Indo-Iranians meant by referring to themselves the Dva-ji, the "Twice Born".

This body is known in Catholicism as the Resurrection Body. The fact that this name exists demonstrates that at one time the Catholic Church understood that whatever walked out of that tomb, three days after the crucifixion, was not the Human animal body of Jesus. It's quite transparent in the Gospels that Jesus did most of his teaching while in this second body. What eventually clued me onto this was Luke 4: 24-30, where Jesus simply walked through, and away from an angry crowd which wanted to kill him. And walking on water would be no big deal to a Resurrection body. And during the period of very recent separation from his organic, Human animal body, Jesus forbade Mary Magdalena to embrace him, most likely because his newly separated second body had yet to completely adjust to no longer having his Human animal body to depend on. Later, he was able to appear inside rooms to which the doors were locked, and yet be physically substantial to the touch of Thomas (solidity being but the experience of electric repulsion).

Jesus is described as finally leaving by ascending. What place could be "up" from the surface of this planet, and also be a "place" suitable for a sub-luminous Being composed of a low temperature and low density plasma?

There's a persistent element in both literature and in near death reports, of some intermediate place, one pristine and full of light, and yet still earth-like in appearance. C.S. Lewis (who nearly died when a bombed trench collapsed on him during World War I) describes this intermediate place both in *The Last Battle* and *The Great Divorce*; so does Richard Bach in *Jonathan Livingston Seagull*, when the two silver seagulls take Jonathan after he realizes that his time on earth is over. J. Seagull eventually realizes that this new place isn't really heaven, just a more perfect replica of Earth, where an easier and more comprehensive effort to Return is possible.

However, my favorite description of this place comes from *The Lord of the Rings*, where Gandalf is speaking to Merry Pippin, just when the attack on Minas Tirith seems about to succeed:

HALE MICHAEL SMITH, M.D.

Pippin: I didn't think it would end this way.

Gandalf: End? No, the journey doesn't end here. Death is just another path... One that we all must take. The grey rain-curtain of this world rolls back, and all turns to silver glass... And then you see it.

Pippin:What? Gandalf?... See what?

Gandalf: White shores... and beyond, a far green country under a swift sunrise.

Pippin:[smiling] Well, that isn't so bad.

Gandalf: [softly] No... No it isn't.

Such descriptions are quite common in reports of near death experiences. I'm not ready to dismiss them out of hand. Awareness trumps physicality in this Religious Cosmology, but awareness usually has a corresponding physical locus, as we see in localizations for specific brain functions which we experience as different kinds of awareness. As a consequence, I will risk speculating that the Van Allen belts which surround this planet serve as this temporary home for our Double soul-selves, because it too is sub-luminous, a world of plasma, where our Double could continue to work towards our ultimate Return to God.

This doubled arrangement enables us to make our effort to Return in stages, much like a rocket being launched into space. The first stage of our ascent would be acquiring our New Mind, which is the "hand" reaching up from below to take hold of that "hand" which has always been waiting there, reaching down from above. Apparently, this Noticing (reaching) which the New Mind is capable of and the worldly mind is not, must accumulate sufficiently, then be allowed or enabled to set properly with the developing second body into something more substantial than mere fantasy. And it's in these two prerequisites, both the need for sufficient accumulation, and the need to properly set, that we begin to find the fundamental rationale behind so many well-known religious practices and prohibitions. Perhaps the first and most fundamental of these is Prayer.

<u>Prayer</u>

Although the word itself comes from older words which meant "to petition, to ask for", the primary purpose of prayer cannot be to always be asking God for this or that, because God doesn't communicate in words. Verbal language is a function of the brain based (worldly) mind. In contrast, messages from, and our prayers to the Above/Within, are communicated directly via meaning. This is another example of how the Light Boundary is a prism that diffracts form from substance. Words are forms intended to encapsulate meaning. These forms are arbitrary in that any specific collection of sounds can be assigned to indicate any meaning. This is why we have different languages. Each language only needs a common agreement among its speakers about which verbal form is to be assigned to which meaning, and then, after an extended period of learning, the brain will usually do the matching of form with meaning automatically. At the Pentecost miracle in Acts, everyone was able to "hear" God's voice as if spoken in their own language because each received the message directly as meaning, and their brain translated the meaning into words.

As for asking, we have each of us already been given God's very own Will and Name ("I") to share as our own. What that actually means is that God has already given each and every one of us everything there ever was to give. Our problem is not one of whether or not we actually have this bounty, but whether we can become genuinely aware of that bounty which is already ours. Such awareness is simply not possible for the worldly mind. That mind only understands scarcity. As Jesus is reported to have said in the last three lines of logia 3# in the Gospel of Thomas:

xiii) "But if you do not know yourselves
xiv) then you are in poverty,
xv) and you are that poverty."

<u>Learning to "shut up" before you die</u>

By the time we become adults, the incessant churning of words in our head is habitual, entrenched as part of who and what we believe ourselves to be. It can takes years of determined effort to recover that quiet inner closet we were born with, the one which Jesus told us to enter when we pray. Real Prayer starts with re-learning to be inwardly quiet as a permanent back-drop of living. Constant Prayer, like the Orthodox prayer "Lord Jesus Christ have Mercy upon me", is aimed at maintaining inner silence in the midst of being engaged in whatever happens in one's everyday life, by giving the mind a single point to focus on. Constant prayer can eventually proceed in oneself without the use of its words.

The title of this section has a special significance for me. I knew someone for many years who was an incessant talker. It was as if this person were afraid of silence. Late in life, a stroke imposed involuntary silence. Over many months, I beheld a gradual change in this person's eyes, from terror to bewilderment, to a kind of searching.

CHAPTER XVI

COMMENTS ON GENESIS

The limits of literal interpretation; a teaching story; the two timelines of Genesis One and Two; ADAM; Eden; the tree of knowledge; naming the animals; the Helpmate; a joke; ADAM asleep; alone with the serpent; nakedness; Eve; skins to wear; the generations of Man; logarithmic aging; the nephilim; the Flood; the Ark; the Golden Mean; the crucial joke; the Tower of Babel; grammar as a sacred construct.

I once watched a man on TV explain why he believed a literal interpretation of the Bible was the correct one. His reasoning boiled down to "Why would God complicate something that He wanted us to know?" This was actually better than many answers to that question. However, it overlooked the fact that the most important things usually can't simply be put into words. There's this persistent belief that everything which needs to be learned or conveyed can be expressed in words, but that is flat-out untrue about most of the important things in life, including religion. Simply look at the many points in your life you wish you'd been told about but had to learn the hard way, and you'll understand why this is true. I'm reminded of an old Jewish teaching story.

*A Rabbi is speaking to a class of young pupils. As he speaks, they diligently write down his words. When he has finished speaking and they have finished writing, the Rabbi tells them that they must take the teachings he's giving them and place them on their hearts. After the class, a pupil asked him "Why should we place these teachings **on** our hearts, not **in** our hearts?" The Rabbi's reply is, "We are unable to do that. The most we can do is place God's teaching on our hearts so that when our hearts break, the teaching can then drop inside."*

Understanding comes from experience. Without experience and understanding, God Himself could literally tell you everything directly, and it would still change nothing within you.

The worldly (material) mind by itself can only understand knowledge in terms of information. That is its major limitation. Information can be stored in computer bits or in neurological circuits, but religious "knowledge" (read: understanding) can only truly be known in the heart and gut. Our TV friend believed that God would speak to us directly in a way no one could possibly mis-understand; but then why did Jesus speak in parables, and why did he repeatedly state that most people—"those without ears"—would miss his true message? Why did he say that many who thought they knew the way to his good side would end up in the place of darkness and gnashing of teeth? And sadly, a literal interpretation of the Bible does not preclude misunderstanding, argument, and divisiveness, so the claim is disproved right there.

The opposing timelines of Genesis One and Genesis Two

In Chapter One, material life is brought forth and elaborated by the Elohim, whereas in Chapter Two, ADAM is created directly by God as "I AM". The Elohim are mistakenly assumed to be identical to "I AM" (YHWH), even though the word for Elohim is a plural name in Hebrew and means "gods", not "God".

In contrast, in Chapter One, both genders of Man are said to appear simultaneously. In Chapter Two, ADAM appears even before any vegetable life. Furthermore, the "Woman" (not Eve), is not created, but derived from ADAM at the end of this sequence, *after the animals.*

The seeming discrepancy between Chapter One and Chapter Two is the difference between how things appear to come about in the higher Realm of Intention & Mind (for Genesis, Chapter Two), in contrast to how things appear to come about in the lower Realm of Time & Space (for Genesis, Chapter One).

If you wish to build something, whether a physical structure like a house or an abstract structure like a corporation, the very first step you take is to visualize what you want, what you intend to build. From that first overall vision, you then progressively work out the details. Eventually however, as you begin to actualize that vision concretely, you must then begin to work in the opposite direction, from the details up to the finished project.

As it concerns the appearance of life and of Man on this planet, the first Ideal half of this process was spoken of in Chapter Two, whereas the secondary, concrete process was presented in Chapter One. The evolution of life on this planet took place in Time & Space (as the term "days" implies). The Bible doesn't tell us that God simply snapped fingers and brought forth everything fully formed; it was a labor, from which it was necessary to rest.

Everything in this material world came about as the result of a process (one designed and guided by the Elohim, aka Natural Law). In the same way, no child has ever popped out of their mother's womb fully formed and matured. It's the same for all the vegetable and animal life of this planet, and for the planet itself.

God as "I" also created every Real possibility as a Singular act, one which included the Elohim and ADAM; "I AM"'s agents, the Elohim, created the process to actualize in material form their "brother" ADAM.

ADAM (Genesis 2: 7)

The crucial understanding is that the Human animal body was created (evolved) separately from the Idea (the "spirit") of Man, called ADAM, which is precisely what the first two Chapters of Genesis literally say. The form of ADAM (the name refers to red clay), was "moulded" out of the particulate "reality" called Existence, and was then directly animated by God's own "breath". Bear in mind, the word for Breath was also the word for Spirit.

This "breath" God gave to ADAM (and thereby to all Mankind regardless of gender, race, or even planetary species), was our "free and independent" Will, along with God's very own name ("I AM") to share as our own.

To borrow a term from the mining industry, what Jesus did was to strip away the overburden that was his self as an existing individual, which then revealed the hidden Divinity for what it is. He himself referred to that process of stripping away the overburden of self as "selling off all that one owns" in order to make possible the acquiring of "the pearl of great price". Just as the Buddha did 500 years earlier, that's what Jesus came to teach us to do. And although the modern message is that Grace should be an instantaneous (and permanent) change of state, so that one never has to suffer or struggle ever again, the original image of a pearl carries a different message. A pearl, after all, is the result of years of enduring irritation in a way that transforms suffering into smooth, shining beauty. Maybe the purchase price that leads to having the pearl is to become something like an oyster oneself.

Eden: (Genesis 2: 8-15)

"Eden" is the garden also called Paradise (the word "paradise" is Persian, which means a "walled garden"). In keeping with the assumption that everything in the Bible refers to concrete historical facts, most of the deduced locations for this garden place it at the lower confluence of the Tigris and Euphrates rivers, now drowned by the Persian Gulf. However, a convincing argument was also made in the work done by the British Archeologist David Rohl, who placed this "garden" in the Adji Chay valley in Northern Iran. The mountains (walls) surrounding this valley are where one finds not only the headwaters of the Tigris and Euphrates, but also of two other rivers, the Araxes and the Uizhon. As Dr. Rohl believed, the latter was likely to be the Pishon, after linguistic adjustments were made to its present day name as compensation for the passage of several thousand years. And most scientific research places the origin of Man's Human animal body in eastern Africa.

However, this Cosmology specifies that this valley was likely used as a *metaphor* in order to establish Eden as a "walled garden." Genesis Chapter Two does not speak of Man, male and female together, as being created in some garden on the sixth "day." Gender differences only refer to material bodies, and not to Ideal Beings. This discrepancy is consistent with the idea that our "walled garden" was something other than some literal "place on the surface of this planet". This Cosmology equates this garden to hyper-luminous Existence, the place of dwelling for Ideas. ADAM's embodiment was necessary, "clay" and "spirit/breath" conjoined.

Where arguments erupt in a fractal pattern all their own is over the issue of whether ADAM's "Fall" (and banishment from Eden) was equally necessary and planned, or was an error. Here again, if two conflated things are teased apart, there is no argument left. If

ADAM could have done all that was appointed without knowledge of Good *and* Evil, with knowledge of goodness alone, then the Fall is a consequence of error, of dis-obedience, of not hearing/seeing aright; in short, of mistaking the illusory for the real, of making false realities, of saying "I AM" to what God as "I AM" does not say "BE!" But if ADAM needs to be deluded in order to win/find/fight/suffer his way back as a process of redemption, in which ADAM's efforts actually safeguard the boundary between Existence and Non-Existence, and/or redeem the banished Elohim, then the "Fall" was more of a Leap. And because paradoxes are where we know we are approaching the Light Boundary, maybe both are true at the same time, depending on who you are.

The Tree of the Knowledge of Good and Evil (Genesis 2: 17)
Evil cannot be Real, simply because God did not create It. Instead, God as "I", it is believed by this author, voluntarily disavowed any access to those logoi which were antithetical to the new Creation. Those anti-real logoi still remain, and Man's Will has access to them (simply witness our history); when Man's Will and choices mirror God's own, when "As above, so below" is realized, then the antithetical logoi are denied mastery over life on earth. But the actions and consequences of resorting to these "out-of-bounds" logoi only have actuality in this sub-luminous portion of Existence, (called "Earth" in the Bible). In other words, those actions and results are illusions to God, and have no genuine effect whatsoever on anything which God directly created as Real... including our own true selves. This is why people sometimes have an experience of renewal, of realizing that they are not wholly defined by what happens to them. The danger here is to assume that what you do doesn't matter either, that nothing you do is "real". Jesus was quite specific when he warned there was a category of sin that

was unforgivable, that had, in other words, real non-illusory consequences. The "sin against the holy spirit" can be understood in more than one way, depending on where one is at with respect to understanding and nature; certainly, a person sins against the spirit within when he or she abuses Will. And it seems to me that all we need to avoid sinning against the holy spirit in others is to heed the promptings of conscience.

Why should simply knowing that there is such a thing as evil be a problem? Choosing to know that there is such a thing as evil, that there is an alternative to Reality (and therefore to God), means that Illusion has thereby become "real" to your mind. One is therefore now afflicted by the need to learn to recognize the difference between what is genuinely Real, and what is not. This is to say that one must now deal with problems which are actual, yet nevertheless simply can't be Real as God defines that term. One must now learn to deal with limits, scarcity, losses, and troubles, which range from junk mail to identity theft, murder, and planetary mass extinctions. Because illusion now has equal status with Reality in the afflicted mind, by necessity, that mind can no longer function at that level of Existence where illusion is sub-ordinate to Reality. In other words, one will no longer be able to remain in the hyper-luminous realm called heaven in the Bible. Such a truncated and hobbled awareness is only able to function sub-luminously, hence, the Fall.

What isn't typically recognized is that God as "I AM" is not as functionally Absolute as was God as "I". Once the "game" of creation was afoot, then the need for boundaries, separation, and compromise to protect Creation from the antithetical elements left over from Chaos became a condition that reiterates throughout Existence. Without Creation, without God as "I" restricting itself to God as "I AM", there would be no need for something like Man to play the role of the Independent Will, of Holy Reconciling. But because Creation necessitates Agency that is NOT mechanical, ADAM was given our unique and anomalous gift of an independent Will to choose between Reality and illusion. And that independence of Will only became meaningful when we lost the ability to easily distinguish between the two. To me, this suggests that Man's so-called "Fall" into sub-luminous Actuality was of necessity, intentional. That supposed "Tree" was placed in Eden precisely to have the effect it did. However, as regards Humanity, the species of ADAM endemic to this specific planet, things went further downhill than they actually needed to.

Naming the Animals (Genesis 2: 20)

The animals were co-created by both "I AM" and ADAM insofar as ADAM was given the task of naming them. This was not merely "naming" creatures in some Human verbal language like Hebrew, English, or Chinese. Rather, ADAM, a genuine member of the Elohim, was given the opportunity to name their logoi, thereby making classes of animate Beings with specific characteristics a concrete possibility. (Given that the Human animal body would be derived from preceding animal formations, this was an important undertaking.) Other than God as "I AM", only Man is able to bring something brand new into Existence by "naming". We accomplish "naming" pretty much as did "I AM", by circumscribing a select constellation of logoi. We even call our ability to bring new Ideas into our Human world "creativity".

What else do we name?

The downside of this ability is how we also can "name" ourselves and others with labels, pigeonholes, stereotypes— all the variations of expectations and impositions.

The Helpmate, "the Woman", the Soul (Genesis 2: 18-19)

This is intentionally out of sequence because it made more sense to get the animals out of the way before speaking specifically about the "helpmate." If God's purpose was to have a conjugal companion (a wife) for a male ADAM, why not make one from scratch in the first place, just as it seems to say in Genesis, Chapter One? At any rate, it seems odd that God would look among the animals for a "helpmate" for ADAM, if that "helpmate" was intended to be a conjugal companion (a wife) for a material ADAM. If, however, a helpmate is understood as something that helps ADAM remember and achieve the purpose of incarnation, of being God's Agency in the world, then the fact that God considered the animals explains the experience that many of us have had, that animals can comfort us, instruct us, serve as totems and teachers and spirit guides and companions. Since I don't believe that God actually had sodomy in mind, and I doubt that God was looking for a literal "wife" for our already androgynous ADAM, it makes more sense that ADAM as an Idea needed something subordinate, a more concrete version of Itself to serve as an intermediary between Itself and Its intended sub-luminous embodied manifestation. Witness the appearance of the Soul of Mankind and of all Men, as a universal class of Being. And because this story was written in the Middle East, well after the matriarchal civilizations (which were previously predominant there) had been replaced by patriarchal cultures, this subordinate class of Being derived from ADAM was called "the Woman".

In Greek, the word for soul is the feminine-case word "Psyche"; in Latin, the word for soul is also feminine: "Anima"; it specifically means the spirit which "animates" flesh-and-bone bodies. According to Genesis, this helpmate is subordinate to the ultimate Idea ("spirit") of ADAM. In a patriarchal world view, the helpmate helps anchor ADAM in Creation and remember its purpose—the function of the True Soul. A matriarchal version of Genesis might have called the helpmate "the Man" and emphasized the helper aspect as being good at coping with the physical world, making more diversity possible, and being inventive. Biologically speaking, that would be the more accurate version. At the chromosomal level, Y chromosomes are essentially truncated X chromosomes; they are less, not more. And XY embryos do not develop male features for several weeks. And there are species that are able to reproduce through the process called Parthenogenesis (literally "birth by a virgin") whereby females produce viable clones of themselves. This is why we speak of "mother" cells, never of "father" cells. And notice that most species are named for the female. We say "chickens" not "roosters", "ducks" not "drakes", "cows" not "bulls", "geese" not "ganders", and so on. And here's another joke.

One day Eve said, "God, it's a beautiful garden, and the animals are wonderful, but I'm lonely, and I'm sick of eating apples."

"Well," says God, "I can create a Man for you."

"What's a Man?" asked Eve.

God replies, "He is a creature with aggressive tendencies who doesn't listen and gets lost easily, but he's strong and can open jars and he's fun in bed."

"Sounds great!" said Eve.

"There's just one more thing," warns God. "He's going to want to believe that I made him first."

All joking aside, it is important to understand that this helpmate, like ADAM, had to have been androgynous, so that it too was equally male and female. (Carl Jung was quite specific that there is an *animus* as well as an *anima* among the archetypes.)

Bone is an odd substance to use as a metaphor for creating a helpmate. This is not to say that women aren't sturdy creatures, quite the contrary. On the one hand, being as equally Man as the male, females too must be able to live in the world. On the other hand, in the lives of most women, fending for themselves becomes unavoidable for any number of reasons. The female of our species was originally recognized as the guardian of our inner lives, of what's most important about being Human, just as the male was originally viewed as properly the guardian of our external lives. For that reason, and also because it is literally true that whatever happens to a girl or woman happens to all her future children and all her female descendants for untold generations—because of the way gametes are formed—it's important for women to be shielded to some degree from the harsher aspects of life. But this is not an absolute because, as was said just above, women too must live in this material world.

Presenting the True Soul as a "Woman" occurs elsewhere in the Bible. Jesus met a "Woman" at the well in Samaria. Recognizing this "Woman" to be one's True Soul makes it impossible to be mistaken about the nature of what those "five husbands" represented—our five senses. And as for the sixth husband? It was none other than our worldly mind.

An example in mythology of True Soul appears in Greek mythology as both Theseus and Ariadne, who together must enter the Labyrinth in order to undo the dominance of a monstrous anomaly, the result of a previous generation's errors, the Minotaur. Remember, our True Soul is androgynous. Theseus as the male aspect goes on the quest, while the female aspect holds on to the (internal) thread which leads back out of the Labyrinth. Being hyper-luminous, the True Soul should be actively and directly in charge of our lives, not wasting Itself away imitating Narcissus by dreamily staring at reflections.

Why was ADAM put to sleep? (Genesis 2: 21)

The answer to this question only becomes apparent further along in the story. The important detail is that, strangely enough, after the "rib" was removed and the "Woman" was completed, ADAM wasn't re-awakened by God. *Adam is never described as waking up,* even though ADAM then speaks about the connection between this new Woman and Itself. (This lack of awakening is explicitly pointed out as significant in *The Course of Miracles*.)

It seems to me that ADAM was left asleep because it was intended that the "Woman" be alone when the serpent presents itself. ADAM, whether understood as presented in this Cosmology, or taken as the ur-male, should have been the one of that pair dealing with the temptation the serpent represented. Had ADAM been awake, he would have been expected to intervene, or at the very least refuse to eat the fruit when it was offered. Then, no matter how much the True Soul became aware of the antitheticals, our Spirit would still clearly know what was Real and Good in each situation, instead of getting fooled.

Alone with the Serpent (Genesis 3: 1-5)

Because ADAM was still asleep, the "Woman" was alone when it faced the serpent. The True Soul is here shown as the susceptible thing it is. Remember, the True Soul is as androgynous as ADAM, and just as ADAM is refracted into billions of people, the True Soul is refracted into the myriad of archetypes, which give rise to many stories about susceptibility. The Greek Myths and the Arabian Nights are full of accounts of people being persuaded to foolishness or downright evil. But you don't have to look beyond your own doorstep to find susceptibility. Look at how vulnerable children are to whatever adults tell them. Look at how easily people are persuaded to believe the worst about themselves, and others. Look at how susceptible some people are to being deceived and manipulated. Look at how fascinated we are by horror and bad news.

Typically, no explanation is given for the presence of the Serpent, or the existence of evil at all. Furthermore, how can someone just fashioned out of a piece of bone be expected to understand consequences? Besides, if you point a fruit tree out to a monkey, the only prediction you can make with any certainty is that the monkey will go for that fruit as soon as possible. And finally, this supposed "Woman" was by Itself, without guidance from God or from its supposedly male counterpart, who had been intentionally left asleep. So any way you look at it, this "Woman" was set up for "failure." Nice guy this "God" of the traditional interpretation.

According to this Cosmology, the Serpent represents the negative space or echo or shadow of the antithetical logoi. It's almost as if they want to be known and included in Creation, or at least be allowed in to influence sub-luminous Existence directly. The True Soul, being perceptive, trusting, susceptible, impressionable, and ALONE, hears the Serpent, and follows its advice like a child going off with a stranger who offers candy. Now, as has been discussed elsewhere, one way or another some susceptibility to the antithetical logoi was necessary/inevitable, at the very least the ability to detect the boundary between Creation and Unreality, maybe even the ability to hear their voices, in order to behave like clever Odysseus with the sirens, or like the wise sister in the Tale of the Talking Bird, the Singing Tree and the Golden Water. Even so, it seems to me that most translations of Genesis have been written in a way that, sadly, perpetuates a tradition of setting women up to take the blame for all of mankind's failures.

In spite of all that's been said about necessity and inevitability, there's still an element of genuine "mistake" in the human condition, that is our persistent inclination to look everywhere outside of ourselves, instead of looking inwardly to God as "I AM", for what is Real, True, and Good. "I AM" is the only Source for all three. But we continue to look elsewhere, and so we barter away our birthright. When that happens, we only see the world through our worldly eyes instead of our heavenly eyes, and we judge everything and everybody only according to our worldly minds. As for blaming women (or men) for all the world's problems, all that accomplishes is to place our children in greater jeopardy, and to make our own spiritual development impossible.

Let Man's schizophrenia begin! (Genesis 3: 6-19)
The reader will hopefully remember what was said about Schizophrenia in Chapter XII. Well, eating the "forbidden Fruit" set off a new cycle of schizophrenia, this time in ADAM, the progressive contraction in our awareness of Self, with corresponding dimensional losses. This started with the "recognition" of separate genders. This was expressed as the onset of recognition of mutual nakedness.

Note: Most traditional people spend their entire lives naked where climate allows, and have no problem with this lack of clothes. It simply isn't an issue, and it's most certainly not a moral one. Therefore, mere nakedness of the body simply could not have been the nakedness referred to in these passages.

Clothes mostly became important as Human migration moved up the Indus valley, north into the much colder areas of Central

Asia. Even then, very young children everywhere were allowed (weather permitting) to go around wearing little to nothing without suffering harm. Children actually start out as Natural Men, but lose that status as they encounter adults who have forgotten themselves in the world.

But the worst schizophrenia was the divide whereby God was now experienced as something external to ourselves, distant—and punitive. As we progress, an attempt will be made to underscore the notion that free Will is impossible without the freedom to make mistakes. In no way is this a license to do just anything, and harming others is especially dangerous. But even that possibility must be left open if Man's Will is to be genuinely free. The single compensation for the unavoidable difficulty this allows is that nothing Real is ever truly lost. What can be lost, however, is our potential to act as God's agency.

<u>And finally, Eve (Genesis 3: 20)</u>
Only after the "Fall" does Eve actually appear. Unfortunately, I've seen several Bible translations, including one which I still have from my own early childhood: *The Bible Story, Volume One* by Arthur S. Maxwell, copyright 1953, where the "Woman" derived from the rib is assumed to be and is explicitly referred to as "Eve" from her very beginning. This is blatantly not what the Torah actually says. Instead, this is an example of what might be called ossification, where pre-established interpretation dictates word choices, diverging further and further away from an accurate translation of "the word of God".

Physical gender distinctions only became differentiated with the Human animal bodies. Once Spirit and Soul were embodied, physical childbearing became inevitable, hence the name "Eve".

The specifically female body was honored for its ability to bear and bring forth life.

Given Skins to Wear (Genesis 3:21)

Gender distinctions only became differentiated because of the Human animal bodies which we were given to wear—the "skins" that sub-luminous ADAM and the True Soul put on to "hide their shame".

I did not make up this interpretation. A long time ago, while an undergraduate, I read somewhere that Jewish religious scholars had traditionally held that this verse was the moment when Adam and Eve took on their corresponding material bodies. I no longer have any memory of where I read that, but I'm certain of that memory because it made a very deep and lasting impression on me. Besides, explaining that our animal bodies and our "spirit/soul" were created separately and then later joined is the only way to explain and reconcile the differences between Genesis Chapter One with Genesis Chapter Two.

This verse actually addressed something quite important in human history, because it's well known that something unprecedented happened which distinguished Homo Sapiens Sapiens from other hominids, somewhere between 100,000 and 40,000 years ago. Things started to change: hominid tools began to change from Paleolithic to Neolithic; art appeared; verbal language developed; and we started to migrate on a scale well beyond anything attempted previously by our earlier hominids. Our Neanderthal cousins had already been around for at least 300,000 years and were still using much the same tools and still living much the same life.

Since the change, we've not only overrun this entire planet, we've touched down on the moon. And I don't for one second believe that it was simple brain capacity alone that accomplished this.

RELIGION REINTERPRETED

There has long been this deep seated restlessness among us Human Beings that made changes inevitable, some overriding, subliminal need to find something greater than ourselves within ourselves, and to express it in the world.

Paradise Lost (Genesis 3: 22-24)

Incarnation meant that ADAM and the 'Woman" (True Soul) were now partly incarcerated below the Light Boundary. This boundary was the Cherub with the flaming sword meant to bar any easy passage back to where we came from—remember, an asymptote is the border of infinity when approached from the side of the finite. Now living in Flatland, we find ourselves very small, very vulnerable, and very mortal. The stage is set for our effort to Return to God.

The Book of Generations (Genesis Chapter 5)

A claim has made elsewhere that the long life-spans of the Patriarchs in Genesis corresponded in some manner to the length of life proper to Natural Man.

An extended aside: There's more here than might meet the eye, depending on how one calculates a Lunar Month. This is something I learned about in a book about Astrology which I long ago possessed but now longer have, and therefore cannot properly credit its author. The author explained that a Solar month, from new moon to new moon, is roughly 29.5 to 30.0 days, the time it takes for the moon to return in its orbit to a position directly between the Earth and the Sun. In contrast, a Lunar month is actually a Sidereal month, which means that its reference is not our sun, but any given distant star. This means that a Sidereal month is the time it takes for the Moon to return to a position between the Earth and whatever distant star one has chosen to serve as one's reference point. A Sidereal month is closer to 28 days instead of to 29.5 days.

In both cases, whether a Solar month or a Sidereal month, the Moon will have made one complete circle. The reason why the Solar month is almost two days longer is because from a solar new moon to the next solar new moon, the Earth will have moved an additional 30 degrees in its own orbit around the Sun, and therefore, the Moon will have to travel (roughly) an additional 1.5 days in its own orbit around the Earth to catch up to where the Sun now appears in the sky against the backdrop of stars. Why bring this up here? Well, it just so happens that there's a logarithmic progression in life-spans.

1 lunar month = Ovulation.
10 lunar months = Pregnancy
100 lunar months = 7.67 years of age = transition from Infancy to childhood
1000 lunar months = 76.7 years of age = a median Human life span (for the Human animal body).
10,000 lunar months = 767 years of age = the median age of the Patriarchs.

Very curious. And one place where this progression might have some obvious bearing on our own lives would be our experience of the passage of time. If you take this logarithmic progression literally, it's saying that the very long year between two Christmases we experience as 4-year-old children corresponds to how we experience a decade when we are in our forties. Disturbingly, this also means that by the time we hit puberty, we've already experienced more than half of our lives, in terms of the subjective experience of the passage of time.

But the important thing here is the amount of Time represented by 10,000 Lunar months. In other words, it roughly adds up to the life-span of the Patriarchs, which is also to say that this was possibly the natural life-time of Man expressed in years. Draw your own conclusions.

The Nephilim, and the Flood. (Genesis Chapter 6)

The "Nephilim" refer to the offspring of the "sons of God" who joined with the daughters of men. Those "sons of God" might well refer to sons of ADAM who had succeeded in recovering that "Pearl of Great Price" at their core, thereby acquiring that air of divinity which Buddha and Jesus later acquired. Either way, something aided us by accelerating our biological and cultural progress. (I don't believe it was men from outer space.)

The description of the Flood may refer to the thaw this planet underwent when the last Ice Age (the last glacial maximum) ended. In fairly quick order, sea levels rose 300 feet, cutting England off from the continent, separating Alaska from Siberia, flooding the Black Sea and its inhabited surrounding coast line, transforming Southeast Asia into the archipelago we now call Indonesia, and drowning all coastal evidence of Man's coastal treks from Africa to Australia, from eastern Asia down the American Pacific coast to Monte Verde in present day Chili. As is the case nowadays, people back then preferred to live near water, so it makes sense that the entire world seemed to be flooded. Unfortunately, we're about to have a repeat of that experience with another sea level rise.

About the metaphorical meaning of the Ark: Man has a good number of natural tendencies and impulses that are an entirely proper part of our Human animal portion, and some tendencies that aren't always as helpful. These tendencies and impulses can be represented as animals, as in Aesop's Fables or the Jataka Tales of Buddhism. What the Noah's ark seems to be telling us is that while we remain physically alive, these natural tendencies and impulses ought to be mindfully conserved and respected, given their due. This does not mean a license to indulge them, but nor does it mean that one should ignore or abuse them. The Buddha discovered that much when he finally disavowed extreme asceticism as a proper path to enlightenment. It's true that we must inwardly detach ourselves from the dominance that our animal portion can exert over us, but this ought to be accomplished without abusing the body. In other words, enjoying good food, good music, good company, dancing, and appropriate sex are not in themselves to be adamantly avoided. We are meant to find the Golden Mean in everything about our material life, between the extremes of too much and not enough.

A young monk arrives at a monastery.

He's assigned to help the other monks in copying old canons and laws of the Church by hand.

He notices that all of the monks are copying from copies, not from original manuscripts.

So the new monk goes to the head abbot to question this, pointing out that if someone made even a small error in the first copy, it would never be picked up! Any error would be perpetuated in all of the subsequent copies.

The head abbot says, "We have been copying from copies for centuries, but you make a good point, my son.

The head abbot then goes down into the dark caves underneath the monastery where the original manuscripts are held in a locked vault that hasn't been opened for hundreds of years.

Hours go by, and nobody sees the old abbot.

Eventually, the young monk gets worried and goes down to look for the abbot.

He sees the abbot banging his head against the wall and wailing: "We missed the R! We missed the R! WE MISSED THE R!"

His forehead is all bloodied and bruised and he is crying uncontrollably.

The young monk asks the old abbot, "What's wrong, Father?"

With a choking voice, the old abbot replies, "The original word was...CELEBRATE!

The Tower of Babel (Genesis Chapter 11)

Gurdjieff used to speak of something which he called the "formatory apparatus." It's a part of our brain which automatically gives verbal form to the meanings we wish to express. This mechanism matches words (verbal forms) to the meanings which come to us. Anatomically, this "formatory apparatus" would seem to be distributed between the parietal and frontal lobes of the brain, Broca's area #44 being the frontal lobe component, primarily responsible for translating words into the necessary muscular vocal movements needed to speak. The unbridled and incessant activity of this brain function eats up (or expends) so much nervous energy, and interferes so much with our ability to be aware of ourselves and of the world around us, that every religion tells us we need to be able to quiet it.

Hominids developed primitive languages. The linguistic clicks in the documented oldest distinct tribes of Humanity, the San and the related Hadza peoples, respectively in Southern and Eastern Africa, would be much less likely to reveal human presence to animals than more vocalized sounds, yet would carry clearly over relatively large distances. The original language of the ADAM in each of us was naturally one of Meaning. And this language is still latent in us. We all still recognize the presence of need in each other, and the importance of things like Family, even when we don't share a common verbal language, even when we choose to act in disregard of our recognition.

Elaborate verbal languages for the conveyance of specifics became necessary as our expanded awareness of this material world demanded the ability to share information, as well as meaning. What the Tower story tells us is that somewhere along the line, we generally lost our primary ability to directly convey and perceive meaning, and had to rely increasingly on verbal languages which are susceptible to changes due to distance, accident, and fashion. The result was the diversification of Human languages as we spread over the face of this planet. Art forms like poetry arose as an attempt to circumvent the limits of verbal language's inability to convey subtleties.

Sacred Constructs

There's something important to add here, which is that verbal languages, now the primary form of Human communication, were intentionally modified to be "Sacred Constructs". Modern Scientific Language studies will disavow this, so I can only present this example as my own insight.

There seem to be twelve basic language families (along with a very few language isolates which cannot easily be placed, the best known one being the Basque language of the southern Pyrenees, Northern Spain). What characterizes each of these families is a fundamental type of grammar which tends to organize the surrounding world in its own idiosyncratic way. Before saying anything more, I can already hear the groans of modern linguists who object to any mention of the name Benjamin Whorf, the amateur American linguist who was analyzing American Indian languages in the 1930s (by trade he was a fire insurance assessor). But it was reading his papers which drew my attention to this direction of thought, and after reading his works I began to see how grammar was actually a sophisticated analysis of Actuality.

For the crudest example of this, the Indo-European languages (which include most of the languages of Europe, Iran, and Northern India) resolve the world around us with a type of "noun vs verb" (thing vs action) system of perception and description. Most other language families (though not all) have something similar, but differ with respect to where the lines are drawn between what is a thing and what is an action. Then there's the Afro-Asiatic family (which includes the Semitic languages like Arabic and Hebrew), where the fundamental element of meaning is a triad of consonants. The subsequent placement of vowels within and around those three consonants will indicate that triad's more specific meaning, as well as its grammatical function. This is why in Arabic, the words for "peace" and "submission" are based on the Triad SLM, which is also used for the name of the Religion brought to us by the Prophet Muhammad, and the title for one who practices that religion: respectively, Salam, Islam, and Muslim. The equivalent in the closely related Hebrew language is ShLM, as in "Shalom", which also means "peace". You see this same root in the name "Jerusalem."

I therefore believe that originally, there were at least twelve primary schools, each of which provided a basis for a distinct way to analyze and understand this actual world. The rebuttal to my belief will be the standard reductionist assumption that everything is "built from the ground up" without conscious intention. But my belief is that a few very Conscious people, perhaps the Nephilim or the Patriarchs, gave Humanity a big boost by means of deliberate linguistics. I don't believe these differing grammars came about by accident. And to give you an example of why I take this notion seriously, I present the original system of declensions of Indo-European nouns, and how they correspond to the seven-day week:

Nominative—Sentence Subject—corresponds to SUNDAY (Sun)

Accusative—Direct Object—MONDAY (Moon = receiver of action)

Instrumental—"by means of"—TUESDAY (Mars = the means of action)

Dative—Indirect object—WEDNESDAY (Mercury = the postman of the gods)

Ablative—"source of"—THURSDAY (Jupiter = expansion)

Genitive—Belonging, relationship—FRIDAY (Venus = connection, relatedness)

Locative—Location—SATURDAY (Saturn = location, limits, form)

Vocative—Direct Address—return to Sunday

I also saw that this declensional system was likely to be an Octave when I was 16, simply because I had grown up in the house of a composer and had some training in Music theory. I never became a musician, but I could certainly recognize a possible Octave when I saw one. What clued me here was that there were the first seven cases, and then there was the eighth, the Vocative case, which was functionally a repeat of the Nominative. However, at that time I just didn't know what each note might represent, although I did recognize that the Sun would be the only candidate for the Nominative case, and the Moon would be a good candidate for the accusative case (as the direct object of sunlight).

RELIGION REINTERPRETED

That was about 1965. I knew absolutely nothing about Astrology until November 1970 while I was in college, when a fellow student loaned me his Astrology textbook, and it was two years after that when I stumbled on the clue that led to the above diagram. I was failing my class in Sanskrit, and therefore I was home alone studying one Friday night when everyone else was out having fun. I was reading my second edition copy of Whitney's Sanskrit Grammar (12th issue, 1971, Harvard Press), when I chanced upon a stray comment that Sanskrit grammarians had listed their declensional cases in this specific sequence for hundreds years before the birth of Jesus. When I saw this statement about the ancient grammarians, I almost fell out of my chair, because I immediately realized that I was looking at the days of the week!

It was only now that Astrology entered the picture, because there had to be some correspondence between those days, which after all were named after planets (as the gods of the Ancients), and the meaning of the declension cases, if there were to be a reason for this order of listing those cases. The traditional astrological meanings of the planets in question made the most sense. *This had absolutely nothing to do with any validity that Astrology might otherwise have or not have.* The Sun as the central most important element among the planets was the basic or root form of a noun (the Nominative). We've already mentioned the moon which receives its light from the Sun (the Accusative). Mars (the Germanic god of war, Tiu, hence "Tiu's day"), here represented instrumentality as in "writing with a pencil" or "going to work by bus" (the Instrumental). Mercury (the Germanic Woden or Odin, hence "Woden's day") presides over the indirect object case (the Dative). Jupiter (the Germanic Thor, hence "Thor's day"), represents "growth, expansion" in Astrology: being the *source* of something, as in: "this letter is from Sally" or "this table is made out of wood" (the Ablative). Venus (the Germanic god and goddess Frey and Freya, hence "Frey[a]'s day") represented belonging (the Genitive case), which has been debased to the Possessive: "the son of the father" rendered as "the father's son". And Saturn (which represents limits in Astrology, hence "Saturn's day"), indicates location in space or time: "he's in his house by his window, but he'll be here at 6 PM"—three instances of Locative case.

Not everything here is exact (precise), but most of it is pretty damn close (accurate). And such correlations are to be found in the grammars of other language families.

CHAPTER XVII

TWO BROTHERS

Composite being; a joke; the motif of two brothers: material mind and material soul; a joke; Cain and Abel; Ishmael and Isaac; Esau and Jacob; Jacob's sons; the twins; Pharaoh, Aaron, and Moses; John and Jesus; Peter and Mary Magdalene

This is another study where Psychology has primacy over History in the interpretation of Biblical scripture. The question of whether or not the people and events described were factual history is a side issue. From the perspective of this Cosmology, what's most important about religious scripture are the instructions they give us about how to Return to God, and if historical events and peoples convey that information, they are recorded. It's also irrelevant what you call God or the goal of Returning. We all eventually aim to Return home.

The specific point of this Chapter is to demonstrate how a certain class of Biblical stories is aimed at clarifying the nature of our connection to what is higher in ourselves. And that connection has to be properly established before any genuine efforts to Return can even begin.

As a young child I well understood the lesson drilled into us that if my behavior fell short of what my Church taught, my Soul would burn in hell. The problem I had with this was, what was my soul? How could my Soul simultaneously be responsible for misdeeds which involved willfulness and being involuntarily angry or scared, hungry, or simply mistaken? Why would my Soul have to pay for something it wasn't directly responsible for? How did I even know I had a Soul? And how was a Soul different from so-called "spirit?"

Directly below is a fourfold diagram of Man's Composite Being. ADAM is our common spirit, the full Idea of Man. Our individuality as separate people, male or female, is meaningless at this highest level. If ADAM is the entire alphabet of Man, our specific names as genuine individuals are our pattern of emphasized qualities. It's like Chemistry: if ADAM is the Periodic Table, you as an individual are like the molecular spelling (formula) of some complex protein.

The four level Pyramid of Man's Composite Being:

Fire—Spirit ... ADAM
Air—True Soul ... The "Woman"
================ The Light Boundary
Water—Material Soul ... one's Essence
Earth—Physical Body ... the Human animal

When Jesus spoke to Nicodemus about rebirth, Nicodemus, himself a Pharisee and teacher of the faithful, didn't understand what Jesus was speaking about.

Jesus then told Nicodemus that in order to find the "Kingdom of Heaven" (the one that was at hand), one had to be reborn in water, and in spirit, in that order. What Jesus was telling Nicodemus was in order for God to become a Reality for you, you must reconnect to that which is ADAM (Fire) within you by first reconnecting to one's True Soul, because your True Soul is already directly connected to your spirit. But you aren't yet reliably connected to your own True Soul if you are disconnected from any reality other than your body. We are all essentially bottom feeders, fighting each other for scraps that sink down from above to the deepest and darkest depths.

However, we are each of us born with this other, higher, potential Being within. It's usually very much alive and active in children, but little to nothing in our present day culture genuinely nourishes it, or even tolerates it. And so it weakens as the years pass, becoming moribund by the time we reach puberty, with something only barely alive in later years. Some of us figure out how to sustain or recover a connection. When sufficiently substantiated, such people eventually discover that they can walk on water... when this second self can safely separate and return to its home.

This was the message that Jesus brought us. Unfortunately, this message became obscured. This is not a condemnation of present day Catholicism; this mishap, profound and intentional as it was, occurred when the organization of religion became more important than the message. When the Gospels, originally written in Greek, were translated into Latin, errors were knowingly, deliberately introduced and perpetrated. Remember, Constantine's aim at Nicea in 325 A.D. was to reign in the Roman Empire, and he saw Christianity, suitably "reformatted", as a means to consolidating power.

A modern parallel is the formation in the late 1970s and early 1980s of HMOs. At first, these were groups of young, new doctors who wanted to earn a living while offering affordable health care to anyone who needed to be seen by a doctor. (A visit and treatment might cost a five dollar copay above an annual fee of about two hundred dollars, and visits could typically be scheduled within three days.) Offering accessible, affordable health care to all was the original "message". But tending to patients, which is a doctor's real work, is antithetical to financial book-keeping, so the young doctors hired accountants to manage the money side. You can see where this is going. The accountants decided to pay themselves higher and higher salaries. Also, the doctors began raising families and needed more money themselves, so prices went up and up. Then insurance companies got involved, and pharmaceutical companies, and in less than two decades the original message was entirely lost in the noise.

The Latin translations emphasize the need for "repentance" as preached by John and Paul, as has been described earlier. In contrast, the Greek word used to convey Jesus' original message was *metanoia*; "meta-" means "beyond", and "noia" means "mind" (*nous*). Jesus was telling us again and again that we needed to find that Mind which sees Beyond in ourselves, if our efforts to Return Back to God are to amount to anything. Attempting to understand Religion with our everyday worldly mind can only ever add up to casting pearls before swine. Our worldly mind is not necessarily bad or bent on evil, it simply is not suited for desiring or even comprehending anything that isn't mundane. That this mind is our primary functioning mind is a symptom of our larger problem, that we live in the basement of ourselves, in the animal portion of our total Being. This entrenchment goes so far that many people believe that the final resurrection will involve returning these animal bodies back to us intact from the grave. They choose the extreme finitude of these bodies over a life of Spirit, over God as "I AM".

And it's time for another joke.

RELIGION REINTERPRETED

An Angel came down from heaven and spoke to a Pig.
"Why not come with me to heaven? The Angel asked.
"Why should I do that?" The Pig replied.
"In Heaven, you will live forever, and it is splendid there."
"Hmm," said the Pig, thinking about everything it liked best. "Is there mud in Heaven?"
"No, not mud as such, but there is music," replied the Angel.
"Are there heaps of straw in Heaven to burrow in?" asked the Pig.
"No, there is bright radiance," replied the Angel.
"Hmm," said the Pig, then it asked the most important question. "Are there... slops in heaven?"
"No, there aren't slops in Heaven," admitted the Angel.
"Hmm, well, if there aren't any slops, I don't want to go," said the Pig with finality.

At death, your Human animal body is simply plowed back into the ground, and the worldly, brain-based mind dissipates. The material Soul is not your True Soul, but it's your essential connection to that Soul while you inhabit this animal body, and failing to establish anything substantial at this ground level of yourself while you're alive means starting from scratch once again your next time around.

The notion that we only have one chance at life is not Christian; ironically, it is derived from a pagan idea of life and afterlife. Jesus, growing up in the Jewish faith, would have been raised in the prevalent belief in reincarnation that was an essential component of Judaism, just as it was in the religions of India. This is why so many people expected Elijah to return, and why Jesus was asked if he was the return of Elijah.

HALE MICHAEL SMITH, M.D.

<u>The Two Brothers</u>

This motif is a generalization. Sometimes it's two brothers, as with Cain and Abel, Esau and Jacob; other times it is two groups of siblings, as with Joseph and Benjamin and their ten older brothers; in other stories it might be cousins. Sometimes it is sisters, as with Leah and Rachel. And the basic premise underlying these stories is not limited to the Bible. The very same underlying theme is present in myths and fairy-tales, especially where an evil relative or servant has wrongly stolen something important from a younger relative or child, the one for whom a special something was intended. Examples of such stories abound, and include *The Mahabharata* of India (which includes the *Bhagavad Gita* as one of its parts), the Greek myth about the Golden Fleece, and fairy tales like "The Goose Girl".

The central theme of these stories is the relationship between what in us is closer to God and Paradise and what in us is closer to illusion. There is almost always an element of confusion: babies switched at birth, or usurpation, or a lie being told, as in "your son, our brother, is dead." In many of these stories, the younger brother or sister is the rightful heir because of ability, despite expectations or customs of primogeniture. These stories acknowledge that what is "older" in us, *and which expects and wants to be in control*, in other words, our material mind, is usurping an authority which does not rightfully belong to it. People with a healthy material soul oriented towards Heaven are already at the point where these stories conclude, with the establishment of good order and contentment. For the rest of us, our "next right thing" is to give precedence to a New Mind which will prepare a way for Soul to develop. Almost invariably, we need outside help with this process, and finding real help is a sort of test, because there are charlatans out there who are intent on fleecing the sheep. Something real in us has to be able to discern what is really good out there from what is a trick or a trap.

In John 3: 3-6, Jesus tells Nicodemus that one cannot see the Kingdom of God unless he be born anew. And when Nicodemus asks what must be done in order to accomplish this, Jesus tells him that he must be reborn in both Water and Fire, in that specific temporal order. Refer to the above diagram to interpret the fire and the water. And Jesus had to work just as hard as every one else to accomplish these inner transformations. I personally suspect that the Descent of the Dove marked the occasion of the rebirth in water, because Jesus was symbolically in the water at that time, and because he still had yet to clean up certain issues concerning his own worldly mind and personality—specifically, the temptations he faced next in the Wilderness. And by the way, these Temptations are themselves proof that Jesus was as human as you or I.

Jesus did most of his teaching in his second body. I only understood this after reading Luke 4: 30, where a crowd was ready to toss him over a cliff, and he simply turns around and walks away. This was possible because a firmly developed second body has a measure of authority over material bodies. This is precisely how it was that people encountering Jesus for the first time recognized that he had "authority". The Greek word does not mean the pseudo authority of a manager who gets a position through contrivance; the Greek word is very specific: "ex-ousia" literally means "from being".

In Western civilization, this notion of a Material Soul began to fall off the map of what a total Human Being is composed of millennia ago, and for a simple reason: it cannot be seen by the material mind, the material eyes. But it was real enough to most human beings for most of humanity's history. I suspect that until fairly recently, most human beings *could* see it, and many children still can. The depictions of haloes in paintings are there to show the Soul of a holy person. Even crowns for rulers are an attempt to indicate, or, sadly, substitute for, the luminescence of Soul that a proper ruler can manifest.

The sub-luminous Material Soul is what can connect us to Heaven. We are born with it in a diffuse way, which is why children can ask such penetrating questions. It's why some children can see and sense what is more or less real about adults and animals; it's why some children have psychic abilities. Without that something there, one has no direct and immediate connection with one's own True Soul. And that Soul, because it is hyper-luminous, can genuinely glimpse Reality. But without intentional cultivation, a Material Soul can only slowly attenuate and evaporate away, all too often by the time puberty is reached.

As it concerns these stories in the Bible, a New Mind, and the Being it corresponds to, are the second or younger brother, the one for whom the Birthright is intended. A cultivated second body is not nearly as limited by Time and Space as is our Human animal body. Such a Being&mind can be wherever it envisions itself to be. Sub-luminous distance is but an illusion anyway, so that this ability should be no surprise. We see an example of this of Peter in Acts 8:26-40. All religious traditions have accounts of men and women who transcend time and space.

In contrast to this animal level existence, our true destiny is to Return to that Absolute Freedom which can only be God as "I AM". That "Pearl of Great Price" is the very same "I AM" that is the touch of God within us, and the truth is, it never ever actually left home. Our task has always been to find it within ourselves, and to purchase it by selling "all we have". That phrase is important in several ways. Jesus tells one questioner to "give away all his wealth", but in this parable he says to "sell". In other words, sometimes it is appropriate to re-assess all your "worldly wealth", which means the stuff our worldly mind holds dear: our opinions, our certainties, even some of our habits and favorite activities. And why does this Pearl come at such a seemingly high price? It's because individual personality only has meaning in the context of Existence. The sense of being distinct from each other is incompatible with the Transfinite Singularity which God as "I AM" represents. Buddhism calls the freedom Nirvana; Sufic Islam calls it Fana. Jesus referred to the process of attaining this state as going through the eye of a needle.

That journey starts with our "rebirth in water", with a New Mind and the recovering or restoring to life our Material Soul and its connection to True Soul which is the Birthright intended for us, because only this Second born in ourselves leads to any future beyond the grave. We must thereby become what we were intended to be at the beginning: a Natural Man, one for whom our True Soul is an immediate concrete Reality, not an abstraction or fantasy. Our worldly mind and Human animal Being/self were only ever intended to be a good servant, and never to be our master (or our own personal Minotaur).

Seven Biblical stories of this relationship will be presented here, starting with Cain and Abel. There are many others, as for example that of David's conflict with King Saul. But the following seven will present sufficient material to get the point across.

1) Cain and Abel

This story itself seems pretty straightforward, with Cain obviously being the older brother, Abel the younger, and a story about moral prohibition against murder. But there are any number of problems with this story.

The first of these is the question of why the offering of Cain was not "regarded" (accepted) by God. Many commentators have offered explanations, but focusing on *what* was offered is entirely beside the point. What matters is *who* gave the offering, and *how*. The expanded oral tradition of the Torah makes this quite clear. Abel makes his sacrifice carefully and attentively, with heartfelt prayers. Cain merely goes through the motions. He wants rewards, not the relationship with God that Abel cultivates, which is exactly how the material mind operates, as opposed to the Soul.

Remember, the "older brother" represents what came first chronologically in terms of evolution: the body and the material mind. The "younger brother" represents the incarnated Idea of Mankind as God's agency on Earth. As has been said elsewhere, this Idea has its reality beyond the dimensions of time and space, but it only came into a state of Being, it only manifested *after* the material body had already been formed and established in existence.

The next issue of concern is the murder of Abel. This refers to the usurpation of potential by the worldly mind, hence the ubiquitous stories about the older and/or "evil" relative, or servant, or advisor, or companion, who steals the throne from a younger prince. In fact, this could be called our "second fall", the unnecessary further loss of ground to the point where, nowadays, only the material mind and animal self is usually active in us. The worldly mind's usurpation of the Soul's prerogative really does feel like murder when it happens to us. It is why so many people experience a feeling of being dead inside; it's part of the reason why so many young people are willing to commit suicide when they realize that many adults only want them to function like automatons, to do what is expected of them. They would rather die than live a soulless existence.

The second big aspect of this story that theologians struggle with is, why is Cain seemingly let off the hook? For mercy? Consider that Cain's parents have recently been stripped of almost everything and condemned to lives of pain and suffering, which, even worse, will be inflicted on all their descendants, and all for an illicit bite of fruit. Cain murders his very own brother out of jealousy, and yet, he's immediately put into protective custody and sent into hiding. Within the traditional framework of Old Testament Bible interpretation (an eye for an eye), this simply doesn't add up.

However, it does make sense if you see Cain as metaphorically standing in for the worldly mind. This mind is absolutely necessary to maintain life on the surface of this planet, because you simply can't live here without it. So this is why Cain was sent to the Land of Nod, which in Hebrew literally means the "Place of Wandering". (I would express it as the "Land of wandering blindly".) Unfortunately, this same worldly mind is entirely unsuited and unable to lead one to fulfilling the purpose which is our very *raison d'être* as Man. This is why Humanity, where the blind almost invariably lead the blind, long ago fell into a deeper pit.

The last "troubling" aspect of this story about Cain and Abel is the question of where in hell did Cain's new wife suddenly come from? In any literal understanding of that story as factual history, their marriage could only have been a case of incest, unless there were other Adams and Eves in adjacent counties. Once more, a literal interpretation of this story leads one into theological traps that don't stand up to scrutiny. No wonder so many people would rather be atheists than believe in, let alone worship, a God who protects murderers and promotes incest. But I can think of two different ways to understand this unaccountable appearance of a wife for Cain, and they are not mutually exclusive.

The first stands on the fact that as the first two Chapters of Genesis report, ADAM was created separately from the Human animal bodies we now wear here on the surface of this planet. (These Human animal bodies can actually be thought of as "environmental suits" for our sub-luminous existence.) ADAM was only inserted into these bodies after they had evolved to a certain degree. And it's a historical certainty that by the time this happened, there were far more than just two of those Human animal bodies walking around. The initial number of "insertions" might have been numerous, accounting for Human origins in multiple locations, or it could have been very few, perhaps even only two. Either way, there would have been many male and female hominids wandering around, and many of them might have been inclined to kill Cain on sight as an Outsider.

The other, alternative way to understand the appearance of this woman (Cain's wife), is to see Cain as being the "sixth husband" of that very same Woman which later spoke with Jesus at the well in Samaria. In other words, in this alternative interpretation of this story, Cain's "wife" would now be seen as the True Soul of Man, now trapped in a problematic "marriage" to the worldly mind and the five senses. So keep both explanations in mind. They can both teach you something.

Something similar to the murder of Abel by Cain is conveyed in Castaneda's book, *The Power of Silence,* in the fourth chapter, "The Descent of the Spirit". Just after a disturbing part of that chapter, Castaneda begins to become aware of a duality in himself. Don Juan gives form and meaning to that sense of duality by describing the two minds involved. He described one mind as lacking the capacity to connect with anything but itself, because it is superficial. He describes this mind as new, light, and fluffy, which at first glance might seem to be a description of the New Mind or even the Soul, until you take context and speaker into consideration. Western minds tend to associate lightness and fluffiness with spirituality, whereas Don Juan is speaking from a tradition that associates spirituality with being grounded and connected to ancient ways. He's actually calling this mind ephemeral, vain, and trivial. Don Juan then characterizes the other mind as being very ancient, and connected to what he calls the "Dark Lake of Silent Knowledge".

> "Silent Knowledge is something all of us have," he went on. "[It's] Something that has complete mastery, complete Knowledge of everything. But it cannot ... speak of what it knows.... Man's error was to want to know it directly, the way he knew everyday life. The more he wanted, the more ephemeral it became."
>
> "But what does that mean in plain words, don Juan?" I [Castaneda] asked.
>
> "It means that man gave up Silent Knowledge for the world of reason," he replied. "The more he clings to the world of reason, the more ephemeral Intent becomes."

Why do these stories of two brothers start with a story of murder, the worst possible interaction? *Because this is the starting place for most adults, this is where we live, with the Cain in us murdering our inner Abel every day*, usually by the time we get out of bed. The series of tales of two brothers (and their variants) shows a progression of gradually improving interactions between these inner natures, showing all the while the differences between them.

It also seems to me that these stories are also a sort of litmus test, so a reader or listener can recognize where they are. Children often "tune out" the story of Cain and Abel because it is not appropriate for them, that's not "where they live"; a child may "resonate" to the story of Jacob, or Joseph, or Moses, or Rachel because that story is closer to their inner reality. But most adults are already living in the land of Nod.

2) Ishmael and Isaac

This is an account in which the "second son" is born by the more beloved of several wives. In this case, the older son Ishmael was born to the maid Hagar (an Egyptian), while the younger son Isaac was born to Abraham's "true" wife and love, Sarah. Oddly enough, these beloved wives also always seem to have problems conceiving and bearing their sons, and I cannot at the moment explain what the significance of this might be. It does seem to underscore the consequences of wanting sons so much you'll connive at anything to have them, with or without the Soul's blessing and participation. But it also shows that gestating and giving birth to BeingMind in ourselves is no easy matter.

At any rate, Ishmael was born because Abram wanted a son, and Sarai had been barren. Later on, Isaac only became possible because both his parents were "rejuvenated". This was represented in the Biblical story by the addition of an 'H' to each name, Abram thereby becoming Abraham, and Sarai becoming Sarah. The addition of this letter 'H', "Hai", which in Hebrew means "life", to each name means that they were given extra life.

There may be a very specific reason why Sarai was barren for so long, and it has to do with why Isaac had to be sacrificed—literally, to be sanctified. This again I learned from the oral traditions that elaborate the "bare bones" transmission of what is written in the Torah. Isaac's birth is a reiteration of the Second Day of Creation, when that firmament divides the "waters above" from the "waters below", which, in accurate and careful translations, *is the only Day which is not called Blessed.* So Isaac, like the firmament, is necessary but not inherently good. But he is also a "descendant" ADAM, and the only way for him to become sanctified is by his willing, voluntary acceptance of his role. In the oral tradition, there is an entire account of how Abraham and Isaac only go forward and climb the mountain when they reach a place that *only they can see, and none of the servants.* Abraham cannot sacrifice Isaac without Isaac understanding what is at stake.

Insofar as Isaac represents the Material Soul, this is a choice available to it that is simply not available to the material mind. It also demonstrates that even the Material Soul may not always be in alignment with the True Soul. Nevertheless, it is unjust to equate Ishmael with the material mind, because as a son of Abraham, no matter how conceived, he has a potential to behave as a true son of ADAM. (Remember the story related earlier, about the two sets of children born to Adam and Eve.)

But even after Isaac participates in the act of sacrifice (which represents the potential redemption of all sub-luminous Creation susceptible to the antithetical logoi), he still isn't the brightest bulb. Nothing about his life as reported in the Bible strikes me as particularly noteworthy or admirable. He even goes "blind" with respect to his two sons. Perhaps this is an indication that the Material Soul continues to be susceptible to entrapment in the world, to what Buddhists call personal attachment.

3) Esau and Jacob (Israel)

This story is perhaps the most archetypical of them all. Here, the older brother is favored by their father, even though it is Jacob who has the potential to have dreams of Heaven and wrestle with an Angel. Esau tries to murder Jacob over a birthright and a blessing, and Jacob has to flee. And just what was this all important birthright? In a nut shell, it was the right to be the primary or authoritative mind in oneself, the one which had a right to say "I AM".

By this it should be obvious that the birthright was never intended for the "older brother". But Jacob had to leave home in order to avoid becoming another Abel. It is on his journey to his Uncle Laban that he has the dream of a ladder descending from Heaven to Earth, with the angels going up and down.

The meaning of a "blessing" isn't well understood in today's world. Usually it's understood to mean that which is conveyed by the Latin word "benediction", which means "well spoken" or "spoken goodness". However, the English word "bless" literally means to "consecrate with blood". This is usually interpreted to refer the making of blood sacrifices, the literal shedding of blood —usually not one's own, although the aborigines of Australia retained an understanding that one only has the right to shed one's own blood in sacrifice, not anyone or anything else's. The significance of blood will become apparent later. For now, I'll simply point out that in Eastern traditions, including traditional Chinese medicine, and also in Judaism, great significance and power is recognized in the properties of blood.

In this regard, Gurdjieff used to speak of something he called "Hanbledzoin", another of his invented words derived from any number of languages. I can only confirm the "-bled-" part, which came from the English word "blood", and the "-zoin" part, which comes from the Greek "-zoin" meaning life (zoe). I have no certain notion of where the initial syllable "han-" comes from, or what it might mean. However, this "hanbledzoin" was explicitly defined by Gurdjieff as the "blood" of the Kesdjan Body (of the second body, of one's matured Essence).

In the context of this story, the Blessing was powerful enough to give the slight and refined Jacob the force he needed to survive long enough to become Israel, "He who struggles with God".

4) Jacob's First Ten Sons, and the Last Two Sons

Once again, we have the same basic story, although with additional twists. Joseph, the elder of the two sons born to Jacob's beloved Rachel, was obviously by Jacob. This engendered jealousy from Jacob's ten older siblings. What set them off was Jacob's gift to Joseph of a coat of many colors. The coat was the paternal blessing from Jacob. Joseph represents the potential Natural Man, one in whom the second body or Double is becoming active; that is why he is able to interpret dreams. Then he goes and tells his dream wherein his eleven brothers bow down to him. Joseph's older brothers sell him into slavery, exiled like his father Jacob had been. He became a high official in Egypt, eventually rising above all of his brothers. And there is historical evidence that this transpired during the rule of the Hyksos in Egypt. But evidence of historical fact is not always the main import of a spiritual document.

As for Benjamin, he too was born of Jacob's beloved Rachel. For some reason, I've always equated Benjamin with innocence. Of additional significance, Mary Magdalene was descended from the tribe of Benjamin.

5) The Twins of Judah and Tamar (Genesis 38)

Tamar's first husband, the eldest son of Judah, died. Her next husband was Judah's second son, who then also died. After that, Tamar had to return to her birth family to wait for the third son to become old enough to marry her. However, Tamar heard that Judah was coming to town, and after disguising herself, she intercepted and seduced her father-in-law, and became pregnant by him. After saving her own life from a charge of adultery by proving that Judah was the father, she went on to bear twins.

Here's where things get even more weird. The first child was in the process of being born, and he extended his arm to the outside of the birth canal of his mother. The midwives promptly tied a ribbon around its arm for proof of that this son was the first born. However, instead of finishing the process of birthing, this child with the ribbon withdrew its arm back into the womb, and then its twin was born first. Our ribbon tie-dyed child was born second. Why would such a story even be recorded? The very improbability of it reinforces that this motif of "the first shall serve the second mind" is the real concern here.

6) Pharaoh, Aaron, and Moses

The historical existence of Moses is well established, but again, apart from any and all historical significance, the stories are lessons, blueprints or maps for our inner lives.

Moses has two older brothers. His brother the Egyptian Pharaoh represents the worldly mind in its defiant mode. This aspect of ourselves will fight tooth and nail to avoid being demoted to the secondary status of subordinate executor for our New Mind, just like Cain, Esau, and the older brothers of Joseph did.

Aaron, on the other hand, is this same worldly mind when it has accepted its place as the subordinate executor for Moses. But there's more to the story of Aaron, because he repeatedly made the mistake of wrongly taking the initiative during the times when the true "head of state" (now represented by Moses) was absent. Most egregiously, Aaron sanctioned the worship of the golden calf while Moses was off consulting "I AM". And just like Cain, Aaron was not killed for this transgression. Again, the worldly mind remains necessary as long as we remain physically alive.

As for Moses, it's odd that he was not allowed to enter the Promised Land. This actually has direct bearing on the meaning of the verse Matthew 11:11 in the New Testament Gospels, which will be addressed when discussing the last pair of "brothers." The basic issue here is that even one's New Mind and Self are still sub-luminous. The "Promised Land", the place of Approximation (Note SOL) on the Enneagram, is but a Rest Stop, and that Rest Stop in this case is our True Soul, which resides as part of the Light Boundary, literally the gateway to Reality (to God as "I AM"). Our New Mind and Self are bridges to our True Soul, but have no direct presence within hyper-luminous Existence. The Natural Man and its corresponding mind is a sub-luminous affair for which the Light Boundary (let alone heaven, aka hyper-luminous Existence) is out of reach. The real, historical Moses may have Returned back to God, but the Moses as written up in Exodus is described as he is to serve another purpose.

7) John the Baptist and Jesus

Now for what Jesus meant by saying what he did about John the Baptist, in Matthew 11:11:

> *"Truly I say to you, among those born of woman there has risen no one greater than John the Baptist; yet he who is least in the Kingdom of Heaven is greater than he."*

This verse has long been my favorite Biblical verse for confronting someone who insists on a literal interpretation of the Bible, because I have yet to encounter such a person who will accept that this verse means what it literally says. However, this statement can't simply be dismissed. Instead, one must make every effort to understand why it means what it says. If even the least in the "Kingdom of Heaven" is greater than John the Baptist, then John simply can't be in the "Kingdom of Heaven."

John represents the externally oriented, worldly mind in these Gospels, in contrast to his younger cousin Jesus who here represents the New Mind and Self. John preached repentance, whereas Jesus told teaching parables.

<u>An aside</u>: There is a present day echo of historical discord between John and his cousin Jesus. A group of Hebrew transplants long ago moved to present day Southern Iraq, and are known as the Mandeans. They are followers of John the Baptist, and actually condemn Jesus as a false prophet who supposedly misused the "true" teachings of John. It's possible that both John and Jesus were once connected with the Essenes. For the Essenes, recovering the prominence and independence of Israel was their primary religious concern. In contrast, Jesus opened his message for all of Humanity, even the Romans.

<u>An addendum</u>:

The argument between Mary Magdalene and the disciple Peter, as recorded in the *Gospel of Mary Magdalene* depicts Mary as the New Mind and Peter as the worldly mind that is unable to accept that Jesus would "stoop" to sharing more with Mary than with the male disciples.

CHAPTER XVIII

HOW CHRISTIANITY BECAME "CHRISTIANITY" WITH QUOTATION MARKS

Missing the mark; the unforced error; the error of the possessive pronoun; historical context; Christianity and the Age of Pisces; the error of the definite article; Christianity and the consolidation of Roman rule

These next few Chapters, probably more than any others, are almost guaranteed to be problematic for many readers. Giving offense is not the intention here, but people tend to take offense, whether it is intended or not, when any suggestion is made that something they hold dear "misses the mark". The modern interpretations of the original messages brought to us by Jesus were and continue to be based on blatantly erroneous translations from the Greek and Aramaic into Latin and English. Unfortunately, for two thousand years erroneous translations have eroded the genuine understanding of the real message that Jesus brought. This reinterpretation is primarily a redistribution of emphasis among already well-known subjects raised by the Prophet Jesus of Nazareth.

But anything to be written here can only go so far. The "Good News" brought to us two millennia ago was intended to transform our inner nature as Man, back to what it had always been intended to be. We've forgotten something of critical importance, and that is that Knowledge and Being must correspond to each other in degree of advancement. Without the ability to understand something in one's Being, Knowledge can only remain as mere information, and as such it's largely useless, often to the point of being counterproductive or even dangerous. I will emphasize the point being made here by quoting a passage from Ouspensky:

> *"We all understand that to operate some complicated piece of machinery, one must spend considerable time in learning how to operate it safely. Likewise, when learning medicine, architecture, music, and like professions, a person must spend years in learning, if one is to do more good than harm. However, at the very same time, people also believe that any old person can pick up and read some piece of sacred scripture, and expect to know what it means without doing any harm to that message, and to themselves and others!"*

Our most fundamental problem in this regard is that our everyday worldly (material) mind has absolutely no business being anywhere near anything to do with religion, because it can only distort such knowledge into something which it thinks it can "understand" ("pearls cast before to swine"). Invariably, what is intended for one's inner transformation becomes something attributed to the outside world as some "commandment", and ultimately as a weapon, as happened when the Puritans did away with music, and also did away with the celebrations of the 12 Days of Christmas. There were self-styled "Christians" who burned the libraries of First Peoples in the Americas. We also see the weaponizing of religion in the way Islamic extremists murder girls who wish to learn to how to read, or blow up irreplaceable cultural artifacts on the false charges that they are "idolatrous".

Anyone who cannot perceive the irony and hypocrisy of using a crucifix as a focus for prayer—seemingly, praying TO the crucifix—and then accusing others of idolatry (if they use a spiritually significant carving or object as a focus of prayer) is running a risk of committing the sin against the Holy Spirit. They are almost certainly in violation of Jesus' commandment to "Judge not". And all of this happens when our so-called religious leaders fail to understand that our very necessary inner transformation cannot be imposed from the outside through rigid restrictions on behavior, but must instead originate from within. Everything about our Return to God has to be voluntary, which means that we must be allowed to made mistakes, otherwise why would we have been given a Free Will? There must be some allowances made so a person can learn to act from one's understanding of inner meaning.

The unforced error

It is a fundamental axiom of this reinterpretation of Religion that Reality, Truth, and Meaning are beyond Form. This means that they are hyper-luminous, whereas Form is a sub-luminous actuality, one which only allows for an approximation of the above three (again, the discrepancy between accuracy and precision). Unlike those above three, form is conditional, which is to say that form is always highly dependent on conditions external to itself. This is why material life on this planet, whether organic or cultural, has taken so many different forms, and why we Human Beings have so many distinct features, languages and religions. That being the case, it then follows that any guidance (Religion) given to us from above, such guidance as is needed by us to find our way to Return to our Source, is very likely to have more than one specific form.

This does not mean that anything goes, because the form has to correspond to actual inner content. But it does mean that any guidance intentionally provided from above will have been "packaged" in a form suitable for those who locally received it directly. By extension, this means that it's asinine to believe that God would ever play favorites with the form in which such guidance is provided to any one particular group of people. Any time a person or group of people starts playing the hard game of "My God/ Prophet/ Message is better than your God/ Prophet/ Message", it's a surefire indication that their primary concern is *not* religion, it's power.

Actually, it's likely that a single message was originally given to Humanity at the "Time of our Insertion" (Genesis 3: 21), but the "packaging" of that message began to change with the passage of time, especially with the dispersal of humanity across the face of this Earth.

In earlier times, gods were compared, swapped and shared when cultures encountered each other. Worshipers would practice the forms of their faiths side by side, and borrow practices and words from each other. But later on, a dogmatic interpretation of Monotheism made this difficult, even impossible. The new incompatibility of pantheism and monotheism eventually reached its height with the "transformation" of Jesus of Nazareth from Rabbi and Prophet into "The One True God"— a claim Jesus did NOT make for himself in the Aramaic language, nor was it perpetrated in the Greek translation. And how does anyone compete with a claim that one's prophet is also God Himself? Historically, the most effective way to compete with that claim is to say that *your* prophet or message is the newest, latest, greatest, God-approved model.

If religion were the game of American Baseball, that assignment of "divinity" to Jesus would have to be called an "unforced error." This error was unforced because there has always been another way to understand Jesus and his message, one which would keep the message he brought to us intact, without the need to bestow divinity on him personally. As was pointed out earlier, what Jesus did say proves he did not claim to be the only Son of God, for he clearly, unequivocally states that those who follow his guidance shall become as him, and more so. And yet, an unspeakable number of murders have been committed over two millennia in an attempt to force people to accept the error of the exclusive divinity of Christ. Some of the mass murders include the Crusades, the Inquisition, the forced conversion of native peoples during colonialism, and the Holocaust.

Both Judaism and Islam are correct in calling this supposed divinity of Jesus an Idolatry. It takes the focus away from how we Return to God and how we are to treat each other with kindness. And yet, even today after so any centuries, the vehemence of insistence that this most fundamental error be taken as truth is unmitigated. The Teachings of Jesus are rarely allowed to stand on their own merits, without implied and actual violence enforcing "You must believe, or else!"

One major demonstration that this is an error is that, in spite of the teachings of Jesus, most "Christians" look outside of themselves to find Salvation. They look to an external God, and to an external Jesus representing that God. There is the expectation that the Messiah will return and resort to force to alter the trajectory of Human history. They forget or ignore that in the Wilderness, Jesus intentionally rejected temporal power. In other words, Jesus rejected the use of political and social force to change Human behavior. To do so would actually run counter to the very reason for which Man was given an independent Will in the first place.

HALE MICHAEL SMITH, M.D.

<u>The origins of this error</u>

It's certain that there are many scholars far more capable than this author, when it comes to tracing the notion of the supposed "unique divinity" of Jesus. However, having made this claim of error, the onus is on me to explain why I believe this to be so.

This author believes that a notion of Man's universal status of Sonship was once common knowledge and understanding, from our early years after our Insertion (Genesis 3: 21) at least up to the time of onset of the Great Dispersion which the Tower of Babel story alludes to. After an extended period during which Humanity consisted of small groups or tribes, there began a period of increasing specialization in occupation within many of the larger groups, something which likely coincided with the development of Agriculture, which allowed some groups to settle permanently. This resulted in the local transformation of Shamanism (which was sufficient for small groups), into specialized Priest castes who were responsible for prayers of intercession via ritual. The pendulum finally began to swing back to the original notion of Man's Common Sonship with the onset of what was called the Axial Age by the German philosopher Karl Jaspers.

This title, Axial Age, refers to the period roughly between 600 to 300 BCE, which marks the onset of most of the world's present day major religions—Christianity and Islam being relative latecomers. Essentially, this was a movement away from the priest driven religions of ritual, towards the (I presume original) notion that the destiny of each individual Human Being was important, that not only is direct contact and communication with higher powers possible, it is what we are here to cultivate. This period also saw the rise of many early philosophical and legal systems, which appeared across Eurasia, a widespread process which to some degree is ongoing today, as for example with the American experiment in self-governing.

As for the notion of a Man-god who would save the world—a Messiah—I could be wrong, but I believe that it entered Judaism as a result of post-Babylonian interaction with Zoroastrianism. The anticipation of such an event was intensified after the overthrow and replacement of Persia by the establishment of the Seleucid Empire, which was itself eventually overthrown in Israel by the Maccabees. Unfortunately, that short-lived independence was soon followed by Roman enslavement. The Messiah was subsequently expected to assume temporal power, thereby restoring Israel to independence and prominence.

The Crucifixion left many of the apologists for a "Jesus as Messiah" awkwardly scrambling to explain why their supposed Messiah from God had been stopped by Rome. They began to compulsively search Jewish Scripture for "proof" that Jesus was in fact the Messiah whom the Jews had long been expecting. They insisted—and here is that fundamental error again, expecting what are supposed to be inner experiences to be external events—that the Coming of the Messiah had to be a literal event "in their day". The fact that Jesus had renounced temporal power in the Wilderness was overlooked.

Paul of Tarsus further aggravated this error about Jesus being a messianic "Man-god." He explained the murder of Jesus by Roman officials—who had a long and bloody history of putting to death any perceived threat to Roman supremacy by local demagogues or military leaders—calling it a "sacrifice" made for Human sin. Jesus was after all, killed during the time of Passover. It's important to know that the Hebrew Church, led by the brother of Jesus, James, after the crucifixion, never bought into this fiction. But St.

Paul's goal was to universalize the Christian message, and the image of Jesus as a Jewish "Passover Sacrifice of God's Lamb" was one that would appeal to the Greeks, especially because of the timing of Earth's precessional orbit. Explaining this demands a short digression.

"Death of the Lamb of God", Astrology, and the precession of Earth's axis

Few people know this, but there are actually two Zodiacs used in Astrology: the Sidereal ("star" or "constellational") Zodiac, and the Tropical (seasonal) Zodiac. The difference between them is due to the backwards "precession" of the Spring Equinox. Both Zodiacs were organized exactly the same, with 12 divisions of 30 degrees each, each 30 degrees of which is given a sign name, in a specific sequence.

The Sidereal Zodiac, which is still in general use in India, refers directly to the background of stars, to the actual constellations themselves, with the Astronomical 1st Point of Celestial Longitude starting at the very beginning of the constellation of Aries. And that point in the sky would also be the beginning point of the Tropical Zodiac, if only the Earth didn't wobble on its axis. Today, the star Polaris (the tail-end star of the constellation Ursa minor, also known as The Little Dipper), is the star most directly above our planet's North pole. However, in the year 12,000 B.C.E., that honor was held by the star Vega in the constellation of Lyra. And Vega will be so again in the year 13,727 A.D.. The reason for this is that our planet Earth wobbles like a top as it spins daily, taking approximately 25,920 years to return to any given North Star. This full 25,920 years cycle of an axial wobble is known in Astronomy as a Precessional Year.

Now, the Tropical Zodiac (the one most used for Astrology in the West), differs from the Sidereal Zodiac in that it is based on the yearly Solar Cycle of Spring-Summer-Autumn-Winter-Spring in the Northern Hemisphere, and not on the actual Constellations. Unlike the first degree of the actual constellation of Aries, which is the starting point of measure for both the Sidereal Zodiac and for Astronomical longitude, the starting point of measure for the Tropical Zodiac is that point in the sky where the Sun rises at the first moment of Spring, that first moment when the equator of the Sun climbs north of the Earth's ecliptical (orbital) plane (presently some time during March 20th). That point and time, the very first moment of Spring in the Northern hemisphere, is the beginning of the Tropical sign of Aries. In other words, the Tropical Zodiac refers to the seasons of the year, unlike the Sidereal Zodiac which refers to the actual constellations.

The point where each Zodiac begins its cycle of 30 degree measurements is called the "First Point of Aries". But because of the Earth's backward precession, this first moment of Spring (of Solar ascendency) in the Tropical Zodiac yearly slips backwards against the background of constellations (of the Sidereal Zodiac). This means that the point of ascension of each successive Spring will spend approximately 2160 years rising in each constellation of the Sidereal Zodiac (it takes 72 years for this first point of Spring to move a full degree backwards against the background stars).

This backwards movement of the Solar ascendency is the source of the so-called Astrological "Ages", and why we have been in the "Age of Pisces", but are transitioning into the "Age of Aquarius". Much history is associated with these ages. For example, the "Golden Age" was the period of time when the first moment of Spring arose in the constellation of Leo, the sign ruled by the Sun. The Sphinx was likely built during that period. The subsequent "Silver Age" was when the first point of Spring was in Cancer (ruled by the Moon = silver), followed next by the "Bronze Age" of Gemini, likely named for the "Twins" of Tin plus Copper, which together make Bronze. Following that was the Age of Taurus, when the Golden Calf was worshipped in Egypt, when bull-leaping became the rage in Crete, when bull-fighting became a ritual sacrifice in Iberia (present day Spain), and when cows became sacred in India. This was during the period from 4320 TO 2160 B.C.E. prior the birth of Jesus. In the next Age, myths like the Golden Fleece and the use of sheep and lambs for sacrifice became important as representing the Age of Aries (the Ram, and therefore the Lamb). A Ram's horn is still used to call the faithful to Synagogue in Judaism, for the advent of this Age corresponded with the leadership of Moses.

Jesus was born, lived, and died during a time when these two Zodiacs actually aligned perfectly. In other words, that specific period of time was the first time in Humanity's "civilized" history, that the First Point of Aries in the Tropical Zodiac was in conjunction (in the very same place in the sky), with the First point of Aries of the Sidereal Zodiac, thereby perfectly aligning (overlapping) the two Zodiacs. (The previous coincidence of the two Zodiacs had occurred 25,920 years prior, well before large scale civilized history began).

I must acknowledge here that there is uncertainty as to exactly where the precessional transition from Aries to Pisces actually took place. I've seen calculations which placed it as early as 66 B.C.E.. However, I don't think this uncertainty invalidates my basic argument.

However, that First point of Aries in the Tropical Zodiac continued to move backwards, soon completely out of the Sidereal constellation of Aries, backwards into the Sidereal constellation of

Pisces where it still is today, some 2000 years later. The result of this was the symbolism of the "Death of the Lamb of God" (Aries), was replaced by the Ascendancy of the Fish (Pisces). Hence, the Fish, (not the Cross) was the original symbol of Christianity, as it is still represented today in the shape of a Bishop's mitre. The canonical Gospels made a point of emphasizing this connection to fish in that many of the disciples were themselves fishermen, and also with the feeding of the 2000. This can hardly be a mere coincidence, in spite of modern insistence that Astrology has no bearing on the "Christian" message.

Regarding another example of Christianity and Astrology, please reference Luke 22:10 about encountering a "man carrying a water jar" (the symbol of the sign Aquarius), who would lead the disciples to a upper room wherein to hold their Passover ceremony—in other words, to that quiet, inner closet of higher consciousness wherein to pray, the silence needed to connect with that which is higher in oneself.

This symbolism derived from the precessional retrogression from Aries to Pisces had to have been a big help in selling Christianity to pagan Europe, by establishing the notion of the "Sacrifice of God's Lamb", as being the reason for the death of Jesus. The murder of a genuine Messenger/Prophet was "transformed" into the "beneficent" Sacrifice made by God of his supposedly "unique Son" for the sake of Humanity. And this sort of symbolism would have made sense to the Greeks, and later to the Romans, given that several of their religions already featured sacrificial man-gods like Mithras and Osiris, and sons-of-god like Perseus, Heracles, Apollo, and Dionysus. And so, St. Paul's popular—and patriarchal—Christianity won out over the original Hebrew Church, which, among other differences, allowed women equal status with men. The original Hebrew Church was all but annihilated during the Roman crackdown in reaction to the Jewish revolt of 70 A.D. Meanwhile, with Paul converting the Greeks, an unfortunate linguistic basis for error was entering the picture.

The crucial difference between "the" and "a"— the definite and indefinite articles

The Greeks did not use the possessive case, they used the Genitive. Their language was not designed to say "my house", "my slave" or "my god". Nor was it designed to differentiate between "*a* son of God" and "*the* son of God", because while the Greek articles indicated masculine, feminine, or neuter case and also number, they did not emphasize the difference between "a" and "the". So calling Jesus "a son of god" looked identical to calling Jesus "the son of God".

Cementing the error

The error that Jesus was a "man-god" was cemented in place by Constantine. Constantine was no Christian; he was a Roman Emperor, on average no better, but little worse than most others. Constantine did largely stop the persecutions of Christians, but he was quite devious in how he did so. Christians had largely been crucified because they refused to bow to the "divinity" of the Roman emperors. So Constantine simply substituted Jesus Christ as the "divine" emperor, the unique Son/Sun-emperor appointed by God Himself. This satisfied the crowd, and largely destroyed whatever humanity remained in the understanding of Jesus.

The problem with this error is that it takes the need for effort to Return completely out of Human hands. While it's true that we cannot accomplish our Return by ourselves, God will not do it all for us. Rather, for the most part, God will only cover our shortfall in our own efforts (when they are honest efforts). Knowing that an ordinary mortal can make this effort because Jesus showed us the way is very different from being confronted with an effort that a god made. By this conflation of Jesus the rabbi with a pagan style man-god, the Christian population of Europe was, as intended, reduced to absolute dependency on God for forgiveness, and on the Church to negotiate our "salvation." And Constantine saw to it that the Church priests were firmly in his pocket.

Constantine himself was a devoted religious follower of the god Sol Invictus (the Invincible Sun or the Unconquered Sun). This is why the birthday of Jesus was set on the date of the Winter Solstice (December 21st today, but December 25th in the old Julian calendar), when the Sun is "reborn". (Actually, the solstice is properly the Sun's conception. The following three months of winter are its period of hidden gestation, after which the Sun is reborn on the first day of Spring). This is also why Sunday (the day of the Sun) became the Christian holy day, moving it away from the Saturday Sabbath of Jews. And finally, Constantine was only baptized a "Christian" on his death bed, and that was done primarily as a precaution, an attempt to prevent the Christian population from falling away from compliance with Rome.

Another aside: I simply cannot accept that the genuine Jesus would appear to Constantine with the message "conquer in my name", when "conquering" meant killing so many other human beings at the Milvian bridge. It is well documented that rulers have deliberately faked religious "messages" in order to sway popular opinion.

Fundamentally, Constantine's real purpose for setting up Christianity as the religion of Rome was to consolidate his power over a crumbling Roman Empire. I'm quite certain that a God capable of creating this stupendous Universe doesn't give much of a damn about which day out of a year we human beings choose to celebrate the accomplishments of one of God's several genuine Prophets. But this need of Constantine to centralize power had less than fortunate ramifications.

The term "Western Church" is a term intentionally used in this book to diffuse any appearance of being specifically anti-Catholic, which in fact I'm not. Rather, I believe that "Christianity" overall has run off the rails, in spite of the considerable good which still remains therein. The Eastern Church does seem to me to have remained somewhat closer to the original message, but it too has its short comings.

Whatever core mistakes were made by the Church in Rome were later passed onto and accepted almost wholesale by Protestantism, which is why I include Protestantism as being part of the "Western Church". Finally, the primary problem I see with the Western Church was and still is its over-zealous focus on "sin" and reliance on fear. This is not to say that our behaviors towards each other are of no consequence, but to threaten damnation and hellfire??? And to burn people alive at the stake???

Setting aside for now that many of the early Popes wouldn't come close in measuring up in decency to our present Pope Francis, there was still some justification for the position taken by the early Western Church. Rome had fallen, and Europe had descended into "winner-takes-all" warfare by those who had little respect for our common humanity. Control by the fear of one's eventual eternal condemnation was pretty much the only brake there was available to curb such behavior. But the Western Church's desire to keep centralized control resulted in the Church becoming a temporal power, the very same power that Jesus had rejected in the

RELIGION REINTERPRETED

Wilderness. And to keep this power, it used methods similar to those of its parent organization, the Roman Empire.

The Cathars chose to demonstrate their genuine faith by voluntarily entering the bonfires set by the Roman Church, after they were defeated at the Siege of Montsegur (the Albigensian Crusade). Later on, Galileo had to choke down his own words about his discoveries just to stay alive, in spite of the telescopes available which proved his claim. And the "Christian love" that was shown to the original inhabitants of these Americas, and to those forcibly imported here from the slave markets of Africa for hard labor, are thinly disguised abuses of power very much in the Roman style.

CHAPTER XIX

CHRISTIANITY WITHOUT QUOTATION MARKS
An apology; 4 Tenets; morality; "One True Son"; morality; the view from Flatland; Buddha Nature; A difficult passage; feeding time for a snake; being subject to the Law of Accident; an analogy; withdrawal from life; the Peace of God; hesychia; apatheia; passions start out as thoughts; two birds

<u>Apology</u>

It must first be acknowledged before anything else that the mere suggestion that there's another way to understand Christianity which is more likely closer to the original teaching can only sound like the height of arrogance. Once again I can only apologize to the reader for this, but what will be written here is the result of 60 years of pondering these matters. It will unfortunately and unavoidably anger some, but I also suspect that there will be some who see that there's merit in what's to be presented here. However, there's no pretense that anything written here can be the final truth because that belongs alone to God, and such truths cannot be fully expressed in Human language. Human interpretations can only aid by pointing the way, and that way intrinsically requires a subsequent upgrade in one's Being, an upgrade up to that level where interpretation is less needed. Without such an upgrade, error always remains possible, and I too am far from the needed degree of upgrade. So please understand, the problem does not lie in whatever scripture one believes in, but instead, in our limited ability to understand whichever scripture is part of our heritage. If our understanding were better, there would never be any (so very mistaken) rationale for the members of any one religion to ever condemn those of another religion as infidels.

Without any further beating around the bush, here are the four most fundamental imperatives of Christianity without quotation marks:

Four Tenets

I) Each and every individual Man, regardless of gender, race, or even planetary species, is the *Same One Son of God as you are, and as was Jesus*, intentionally created to bear The Will that is God into this sub-luminous world, for without Mankind as God's agency, there is no way for "thy Will be done".

II) We are each of us meant to find that *pearl of great price* which we each bear within as the real "WHO" we each are. This is how we fulfill the purpose for which we as Man were created: to do what "all of the King's horses and all of the King's men" could not (putting Humpty Dumpty back together again, aka, restoring the awareness of Oneness). At-one-ment is how we accomplish our destiny of being the Holy Reconciliation between The Biblical Light and the Biblical Dark and how we as the Prodigal Son Return (ourselves) Back Home to God.

Finding this "Pearl", this spark of unadulterated Reality we each bear within, is the Real meaning behind the notion of "Salvation." God only ever seeks your Salvation and your Return (your recovery from "banishment" in Flatland), and never your punishment or destruction.

III) Learning to avoid doing, thinking, or believing anything which will compromise one's ability to fulfill the first two Tenets is how we start to "pay for" the *pearl of great price*.

IV) This effort to Return to complete Oneness with God (Atonement), *only genuinely begins with Metanoia,* with the effort to recover one's New Mind, and not with public claims of "repenting for one's sins." There will be more than enough unavoidable humbling sorrow when you've grow enough to be able to see your past behavior without rationalization. At that point, however, your mistaken behavior will be seen for what it actually was: mistaken behavior.

I would go so far as to say that any Man for whom these four tenets hold as the laws for his or her inner life is as much a Christian as Jesus of Nazareth could have hoped for, regardless of whatever name they give to their practice.

<u>A bit more about</u> *There is but One Son of God: MAN*

This is only a more emphatic version of saying that *we are each of us made in the Image of God.* This tenet is the basis for all genuine morality (how we treat each other). This is also the basis for Jesus's injunction to have charity and bear good will towards each other (usually translated as "love one another"), because without recognizing in every Man you meet their equal status as bearing the identical spark of divine Will as you do, you remain unable to recognize your own status as an aspect of God's One Son. The widespread lack of this awareness is all that's needed to explain the horrific behaviors that are evident in so much of history and the news and, sadly, our daily lives.

Definition: "Morality"
This word is derived from the Latin "mos" / "mor." It refers to a customary way of behaving, and as such, morality can be either rigid habits of thought and behavior that are actually divorced from any sense of conscience, or sound practices accumulated by people over centuries of co-existence. For example, the Western practice of having both genders together in classrooms and places of worship is seen as immoral through the lenses of several religions. Whereas, Westerners have a problem with the mandatory public veiling of women in conservative Islamic societies.

Morality tends to be stupid, insofar as it is based on habits or precedent instead of on what is kind and appropriate under the circumstances. But a considered morality is like having strong bones; it helps you make your way through life. The old moral codes of hospitality, of guest-host obligations of courtesy, literally made civilization possible.

As for why it's emphasized here that the whole of Mankind is God's True One Son (ADAM), remember that from our standpoint in sub-luminous Actuality (Flatland), we see things inverted. Because illusion has primacy here, we see the discontinuous nature of Existence, the distinction and separation of everything from everything else, as being more "real" than the underlying Oneness that is God. This "I versus You, Us versus Them" is not how God as "I AM" sees Its Creation. Nor can it be how "I AM" sees Its Son. The spark of divine Will borne by each individual Man is part of the very same Singular Will which is God Itself. The apparent rivalry of Will among Men indicates that we are susceptible to the illusions of oppositions and conflicts.

There may be readers who would prefer to reserve the title of being the "One Son of God" for Jesus alone, which would allow Jesus to remain a special divinity. My reason for referring to each Man, female or male, as God's (One) Son, and not as "children of God" or "Sons of Adam and Daughters of Eve", is to place the emphasis on our Authority and Inheritance. In patriarchal cultures, the son is typically the one who inherits the property and the authority of the father. However, gender is nothing more than a function of our Human animal bodies which makes diversity possible, whereas a Man's spirit is without gender, as is that particle or spark of "I AM" which defines us as Man. That particle of Will is equal in each of us, regardless of any local social customs, or the formal demands of any given religion in any locality. A female's task in this life is no different from that of a male; every female is equally God's One Son, as is every male. So therefore, every female has the same responsibility in life, and the same authority over herself, as does every male.

Imagine that a person dips their fingers straight down into a bow of water, with the palm remaining outside in the air. Now, imagine that you are a microbe which lives upon the surface of that water. If you happen to drift into contact with those fingers, you can only be aware of four or five separate and roughly circular structures (the fingers in cross-section). You have no means of being directly aware that all four or five of those things are not only structurally connected, but that they share a single life. The flatness of your world-awareness does not allow you perceive those "higher" connections. This example is why this book so often refers to our Human world as Flatland. The only awareness typically available to our Human (animal) brain, our worldly mind, can have no awareness of the inner, vertical dimensions. It can never genuinely know anything about God, nor about our purpose for having been created, in spite of all the emotional outcries of belief which insist otherwise, but which are really about social status and playing a role to be accepted and admired, followed and envied.

Instead of seeing One Man, the One Son of God in the face of everyone we encounter, we only "see" individuals and "others", with claims and needs in competition with (or in opposition to) our own. We feel compelled to believe that another's gain can only come from our loss, and thus we tell ourselves, and others, that we are justified in securing what we think of as "our own", regardless of whether or not that leaves enough for the needs of others.

The only difference between Jesus (and all other genuine prophets) and the vast majority of us ordinary people is that he progressed in his inner life enough to directly know that he was a Son of Man (of ADAM), one just like everyone else. The vast majority of us still have yet to learn this about ourselves, and this is what Jesus actually came to teach us. All of us are only One Man in the mind of God. A mutual acceptance of a shared Sonship that excludes no-one is not a sentimental notion about "being nice" to each other. Instead, it's a frame of mind which, when cultivated, makes it possible for us to progress in a spiritual evolution. This is why Jesus informed us that whatever we did to one another, we also did to him (Jesus; Matthew 25: 40). By denying that common inner Reality, that Name ("I AM") which you share with every Human Being you'll ever encounter or even think about, you do more than just deny yourself. *You also deny God!* You deny yourself the possibility of any genuine awareness of God, because God is that same "I AM" you are denying in others. There is simply no way to escape or circumvent the logic of this Law.

The consequence of such a denial is that it condemns you by restricting your own self-awareness. God doesn't condemn or punish you for reducing yourself to such poverty; God doesn't have to. You punish yourself, reducing yourself to a shadow of your actual nature. If there is a true hell, then this is it. To again quote *The Course of Miracles*:

> *When you meet anyone, remember it is a Holy encounter. As you see him you will see yourself. As you treat him you will treat yourself. As you think of him you will think of yourself. Never forget this, for in him you will find yourself or lose yourself. Whenever two Sons of God meet, they are given another chance at Salvation. Do not leave anyone without giving Salvation and receiving it yourself. "For I am always there with you, in remembrance of you."*

If I understand this correctly, the salvation both given and received refers, at least in part, to the inward acknowledgement that each are equally Sons of God. In the far East, this common Sonship is known as a person's Buddha Nature. It's to this Buddha Nature that Asians typically bow when meeting and greeting one another. The greeting "Namaste" means, "The divine nature in me salutes the divine nature in you."

A difficult passage

I refer to the story of the Collapse of the Tower of Siloam, Luke 13: 1-5, which I will first quote in full. But first I wish to remind readers that the word "repent", which literally means "to think again", is badly misunderstood when it is taken to mean "to feel awful about one's past behaviors". The word "metanoia" means "to think in a new way, from a higher order of understanding." And that higher order of understanding is the essential part. That isn't something you memorize by rote and pay lip service to; it is something you have to discover in yourself, for yourself. And here is the litmus test: if the new way of thinking helps you see others with a kinder eye, you are on the right track. If it is merely another set of categories for judging others, it is not the New Mind, it's the "old wine" (the old whine) with a new set of labels/libels. Now on to the warning Jesus issued:

> *There were some present at that very time who told Him of the Galileans whose blood Pilate had mingled with their sacrifices. And He answered them, "Do you think that these Galileans were worse sinners than all the other Galileans, because they suffered thus?*
> *"I tell you No; but unless you repent you will likewise perish. Or those eighteen upon whom the Tower of Siloam fell and killed them, do you think that they were worse offenders than all the others who dwelt in Jerusalem? I tell you No; but unless you repent you will all likewise perish."*

This story addresses that age old question of "Why do bad things happen to good people?" And there's a harsh point being made here by Jesus. He is saying that bad things *do* happen to people who didn't do anything to deserve them, that it is the omission of "repentance" (metanoia) that renders people susceptible to both random and intended violence.

Again, wiser writers than I have commented on this passage, and I do not claim to offer a complete explanation. But I do have an insight based on actual observation, something I first encountered as a ten year old, something I only began to understand much later in my life.

I spent my first 12 years growing up on the East side of Cleveland, Ohio. On Central Avenue there used to be a store like a Wolworth's. I was visiting that store one day, and it just happened to be feeding time for the snakes. I chanced upon this small yellow boa constrictor snake in a glass terrarium, into which had just been dropped a live mouse for the boa constrictor's dinner. That mouse just sat there in a corner of the snake's tank, frozen in terror. And I saw something at that moment, something that quietly but firmly "stopped" me so completely that I can still see that mouse today. I suddenly realized that this mouse actually knew why it was trapped in that cage and what its fate would be. That mouse had suddenly realized that *its time on this earth was over*.

I have seen this sudden stark realization and awareness of impending death in animals many times since then, and it's always been very unsettling. I've also listened to similar impressions from people who worked in stockyards where animals were being slaughtered. Wildlife observers have noted that often animals caught by predators stop struggling and simply allow themselves to be eaten alive. It seems that if no escape seems possible, many animals will simply accept the inevitable by becoming calm.

Again, it was Gurdjieff who finalized my present understanding about this, when he explained that a man's level of Being decides what he becomes food for. Remember, the once widespread practice of animal sacrifices often included human sacrifices, whose deaths and blood were literally intended to feed the gods.

Human beings are supposed to generate qualities of energy intentionally, free of any taint of violence, and *mostly for our own use*. These energies also feed the universe. Some of this energy is comparable to what most vertebrates only release when they "wake up", as when they realize the immanence of their death. Unfortunately, when we do not live even with the level of Being of Natural Man, we feed the universe as if we were nothing more than any other class of Vertebrates. And we aggravate the problem by destroying and/or crowding out those very same animals whose existence is needed for the local ecology of this Earth. Guess who then has the "honor" of making up the shortfall? This isn't going to be at all pleasant to hear, but in that story of Luke 13, Jesus is warning us that *the local ecology of this Planet (aka Mother Nature), can't differentiate human beings from any other animal when humans do not live with sufficient self-awareness. Nature will then squeeze the additional "blood" it needs out of the only "stones" left available to itself: human beings. And this unworthy fate will be indiscriminate with regards to who suffers it.*

Some accidents are no accidents. The tower collapse in Siloam and the attack on 9/11 were results of human carelessness and human malice. But being caught up in such events is part of what being under the "Law of Accident" means. And yet, here is something to consider: an unusually large number people called in sick, took personal days, or decided to go in late that morning of September 11th. Like Miss Clavel, they sensed that "Something was not right." They heeded (obeyed) their intuition, and attentiveness shifted them out of the way of that day's calamity.

The one mercy for us, even in the face of so much useless pain and tragedy in this world, is that nothing Real is ever truly lost at the hyper-luminous levels, but that is cold comfort while we are here in Flatland. I do not ever recommend preaching platitudinous "comfort" to anyone who has suffered a loss. Being stuck in Flatland is bad enough alone in itself, and sufficient reason to wish to search for a better place to live, a better way to be.

Let's pretend that human situation and the effort to awaken to this New Mind in oneself is analogous to deciding whether or not to make the effort to learn to read. Now maybe you have chosen not to bother to do so, deeming it unnecessary, or more likely, you were simply never taught about the importance of being able to read. Let's next say that you are looking around for a new piece of land to live on, and that you eventually find a plot of seemingly unblemished and unoccupied land that seems to be very suitable. The only problem is that it's actually an old battlefield, one loaded with unrecovered mines and other explosive ordinance. There are warning signs up everywhere to this effect, but you cannot read them. So you make the arrangements to move onto that piece of land with your family. One day someone, maybe even you, gets killed by stepping on some explosive ordinance. Or you could live there all your life and never have a disaster on that plot of land. That's the Law of Accident in action. The warning given us by Jesus in Luke 13: 1—5 amounts to this: if you never make any genuine effort to wake up, you will be vulnerable to an accidental and meaningless death, one which simply has no bearing on whether you are a morally decent human being or not.

<u>Addendum</u>: Having just such a say over one's own life and death is what Jesus meant when speaking to Pontius Pilate about being able to call on Angels for his protection. It's clear that Jesus wasn't looking forward to what was soon to happen, and he could have avoided it. And yet, he went through with it. The story of the life and death of Jesus was a mystery play, one played out in actual life, and Jesus knew that, as the saying goes, the show (literally) must go on.

The humiliation and murder of Jesus was a genuine sacrifice he intentionally made. I think it was meant to demonstrate that nothing Real can ever be truly lost. True, His earthly body was destroyed, but the Real Jesus Barabbas was not. Unfortunately, the recognition of this point gets lost by the elevation of Jesus to divinity, because for a god, living forever is an automatic given.

In contrast, knowing that every ordinary Man has the potential to cultivate abilities and understanding comparable to Jesus's means everything, because it means that going through the difficulties of this life can serve a real purpose. It's a travesty that so much focus is placed on how Jesus died and on his suffering, and not on his teachings. But there's more to this story, which will soon be presented.

Withdrawal (Apathea, Hesychia, and Mindfulness).

There is more to this process of Metanoia than I am qualified to speak about, even where it concerns the very little which I know from experience. Most people at least understand that beginning one's path of Return involves a withdrawal of some sort from this world. For some, such a withdrawal is literal: entering a monastery or ashram. In contrast, The Course of Miracles is predicated on accomplishing this withdrawal while remaining involved with everyday life. Whatever form one's withdrawal takes, whichever approach one initially adopts, the ability to remain inwardly apart while outwardly involved is something which must be cultivated as a sort of first step. Gurdjieff called following a path of withdrawal while remaining embedded in one's life "The Fourth Way", since it means working on the whole of oneself, instead of focusing on body, feelings, or mind.

Buddhism has this beautiful image of the Lotus flower which dwells in muddy swamps. It can do so because the mud never sticks to the flower or leaves, but is instead always sloughed off.

It's the same notion of "being in the world, while not being of the world."

Reality, as created directly by God, is invulnerable. Therefore whatever is vulnerable, whatever can suffer, be subverted, injured, damaged, made sick, or destroyed is not created by God. The Peace of God, which is the Peace sought by Jews, Buddhists, Christians, and Moslems alike, begins by achieving some significant measure of inner silence, in part so that one can hear the "still, small voice" within when it does speak. The Greek word for this inner silence is "hesychia", and the Hesychast tradition was a very important part of early Christianity, although this word was used in Greece to designate this precondition of any genuine religion long before the arrival of Christianity. *The Philokalia* is primarily the collective writings of the Christian Hesychast tradition.

The silence aimed at here is not that of not talking to other people, even though any unmindful talking does tend to defeat one's purpose here. The real aim is to quiet the non-stop chatter that runs unchecked inside of one's head, that which is euphemistically called the "stream of consciousness." In fact, one cannot be ceaselessly engaged in such inner talking and be conscious of much else. One can only function on automatic when one's talking machine is running amok. Some of us may remember a quality of silence that belonged to us in childhood.

The food which is needed to support the formation of (or access to) one's New Mind, happens to be conscious impressions, which includes being mindful of the sensations of one's body and brain, as well as being mindful of one's feelings and thoughts, along with being mindful of reality. But one's inner talking drowns out everything else.

Another aspect to the question of what must be preserved for the substantiation of one's second Mind & Body concerns what is best called *apatheia*. This word is also Greek, and it means "not to suffer passion." It's the source of the English word "apathy", but the English word means something quite different. *Apatheia* means not to allow oneself to be enslaved by emotions and passions, whereas the present day English word apathy refers to a state of being emotionally dead. Unfortunately, our identification with our emotional reactions are ordinarily considered to be something natural, unavoidable, and right. One is expected (supposed) to get offended when insulted, attacked, or snubbed, and to carry indignation around in one's head and solar-plexus as a constant churning of angry thoughts, emotions, and stomach acid.

In contrast, genuinely conscious feelings are quiet and informative, whether pleasant or otherwise, and one doesn't confuse them with evaluations of oneself. Furthermore, their intensity is not one of amplitude (loudness), but of depth (quietude).

In Jacob Needleman's excellent book *Lost Christianity*, in Part Two (The Lost doctrine of the Soul, Chapter VI), he speaks about the teachings of the early Church Father Evagrius, who pointed out that the "passions" which take such firm hold of our lives and burn up so much of the energy we need to experience life vividly, actually start out as thoughts. They only become emotions—passions—when we identify with them, which is literally to say, when we say "I" to them, confusing those emotions with our sense of self. It's only then that emotions become passions, and from then on they will continue to burn as long as there's emotional fuel available to be consumed. Just think of the last time you were genuinely jealous about losing the affection of someone close to you. Very few of us can put out such a fire once it gets started. It's far better to stop the thought before the match is struck. This is what Jesus was referring to in Matthew 12: 43-45. And he gave the remedy to this problem of passion in Matthew 24: 42-43, where he speaks about remaining awake so that you can avoid having your (inner) household plundered. I myself try to remember to say "Avert!" to certain thoughts, and then put my mind on other things before those negative thoughts can mutate into soul-devouring passions.

Cultivating both Hesychia and Apatheia are part of the path which leads the invulnerability that allows one genuine Peace. Both mean that one is no longer a pawn of the "players" in our world. Furthermore, only this inner silence of thought and emotion will allow one to see and hear what surfaces from our deeper selves, and it's only from there that we ever hear the call to Return home. The image I use for this is that of a deep swimming pool wherein one has lost a pearl. As long as you splash around, you have no chance of finding what you're looking for.

Genuine prayer is akin to inner silence. To understand what this means, first recognize that God does not speak in our Human languages for two closely related reasons. The first is that God does not deal in terms of information, but instead, only with Meaning. Second, there can be no direct, real communication between "I AM" *and anything sub-luminous*. This means that the dramatic, verbose prayers (speeches really), such as those one sees on television and in many church services, don't get off the ground. But they're not even meant to. They are uttered to impress and persuade a human audience. They are street corner prayers, not the sort of prayers made in one's inner "closet" (one's inner Self).

However, something verbal, short and to the point, can still be of genuine help. Even better is an image formed and held in verbal silence. But best of all is no inner talking, nor visualization whatsoever. In giving Man the spirit of "I AM", God has already given each and every one of us everything there ever was to give. Our primary problem has always been the need to become aware of this, because without our awareness of it, that gift might as well not be there. It's like having been left a huge inheritance that one is completely unaware of. Even though you may desperately need food and shelter for yourself and family, you'll end up starving to death because of your ignorance of your un-accessed wealth.

Our ordinary world is seemingly one of scarcity, and it's no easy task to reverse years of being trained to believe that scarcity is the reality. Letting go of the conviction of scarcity is part of "selling off all that we have" in order to purchase the pearl. Here in Flatland, it's genuinely difficult to avoid being mistaken. But we wouldn't have been sent into this "no-man's land" if our potential were not real.

Flatland doesn't follow the laws of Reality, and doesn't follow the Law of God. Jesus indicates this quite clearly in the Lord's Prayer. There would be no need to pray that it be "on Earth as it is in Heaven" if there were no difference between hyper-luminous and sub-luminous existence.

Ultimately, Mindfulness, Hesychia, and Apathea require that something internal remain separate from whatever is noisily occurring within oneself and outside of oneself, even while we remain aware of these things and engage with them. There is an image presented in the Hindu Upanishads which speaks to this necessity. Two birds are depicted as sitting together on a branch, with one leg of each bird tied together by a string. One bird is involved in eating a sweet fruit, while the other simply looks on. This image depicts the relationship that inner detachment (the bird who watches), has with that in us which engages with the world (the bird eating the sweet fruit). It is worth noticing that this image is advocating the cultivation of detachment even from what is pleasurable.

Remember, Zero and Infinity are reciprocals. One day, there will simply be a great "hole" where you used to be. Facing that "hole" will be like standing at the very edge of an infinite Chasm. The best advice I can give is, "get out of your own way."

CHAPTER XX

THE 4 GOSPELS—AND OTHERS

Sacred constructs; The life of Jesus as a mystery play; the name Barabbas; biblical chicanery; gnosticism; Constantine's "Christianity"; the closed mouth; the still, small voice; becoming as little children; the body as a dream avatar; the cross; Mary Magdalene's recognition; the second coming; virgin births in religions; the metaphor's significance; the temptation in the wilderness; temptation / tempering

The Four Canonical Gospels are Sacred Constructs

In the four canonical Gospels, the life and teachings of Jesus of Nazareth was presented as a sort of mystery play, and his death was part of this mystery, a part which Jesus clearly would have preferred to avoid (Matthew 26: 39). Historical details were modified to illustrate points that were deemed more important than accuracy. The four canonical Gospels, those four Gospels chosen for inclusion into the Bible by Constantine and the Council of Nicaea, were much like the first two Chapters of the Torah in that actual history is secondary to psychology—not to spirituality, because Spirit needs no correction or modification. Only our own minds need such.

The name Barabbas

The story goes, a criminal named Barabbas was freed by Pilate, supposedly because of some Passover custom. Supposedly, Barabbas was chosen over Jesus by the crowd, and this little adjustment to the story has been used as an excuse to shift responsibility for the death of Jesus from the Romans to Jews, but was this factually historical? Almost certainly not, and I would venture to say absolutely not.

First of all, there's no historical record of any such Passover custom. The only place where there's any reference this "custom" in any original source material, that is to say, other than in commentaries on this passage, is in the Gospels. And Roman conquerors were not in the habit of honoring religious customs of people they'd conquered. On the other hand, Roman emperors and Roman popes were very much in the habit of editing, altering, deleting and censoring texts, including religious ones, when it suited their political purposes.

Secondly, the name Barabbas, which is Aramaic, literally means "Son of the Father" (Bar—Abbas), and the Western Church committed an intentional Biblical travesty by deleting Barabbas's first name from Matthew 12: 16-17. In presently available, earlier versions of Matthew, that first name is explicitly Jesus. Our "criminal's" full name, as originally presented in the Gospel of Matthew, was therefore "Jesus, Son of the Father." So if Jews were clamoring for the release of a prisoner, they were asking that Jesus be released, and the Roman governor Pontius Pilate pulled a bait and switch by basically asking, "Do you want Jesus, Son of the Father, or Jesus, Son of the Father?" Given Jesus's enormous public following at this point—the entry into Jerusalem had taken place only seven days ago—it is very likely that efforts were made to beg for or bargain for his release.

RELIGION REINTERPRETED

I first learned about this first name and the shady business surrounding its disappearance in my *New Oxford Annotated Bible*, where it appears as a footnote. This knowledge should be circulated in every church, along with admonitions to stop slandering Jews.

Why record this account in the Gospels at all, especially when a non-existent religious custom had to be invented? The obvious reason is that it was a move to reassign the no doubt embarrassing blame for the murder of a subsequent "celebrity" from Rome's shoulders onto the shoulders of a scapegoat. After all, it had to have been hard for Romans to convert people to their Christian church if they had to answer the question, "So, how did this saviour of yours die?" with "Uh, we killed him."

(Another political reason for the Roman church leaders attributing godhood to Jesus: if he was a god he couldn't be killed, so there wasn't really any murder. Sounds like the sort of dodge a lawyer would come up with, doesn't it?)

But there is also a psychological version of this account, in which "Jesus Son of the Father" was freed and "Jesus, Son of the Father" was crucified. And it seems to me quite likely that Gnosticism was involved here. Because of the possibility of cultivating a second body, a "Double" that can live on after the death of the Human animal body, this "second" Jesus (his Resurrection Body) was now independent enough to survive the body's murder on the cross. This Double was called a "criminal" because it, and not the body of Jesus, was the one truly responsible for the teachings which made Jesus seem to be a political opponent of Rome.

<u>An aside</u>: I don't for a minute believe that the Jewish religious authorities were collaborators with Rome (as the Gospels seem to suggest in places), but it does make sense that they would be trying

to avoid trouble with Rome. Being on the receiving end of Rome's military attentions rarely ended well. Look at what happened in 70 A.D.

This explanation is consistent with Gnostic traditions of paradox and metaphor. It also coincides with the assertion made by Islam that Jesus did not die on the cross, because *the Real Jesus did not*, as demonstrated by the resurrection. The possibility of resurrection was the only thing Jesus could salvage from the debacle of his unsought notoriety and subsequent arrest. Remember, for all his teachings and healings, he tried to stay under the radar, requesting that people not gossip about the miracles, and going so far as to leave town when his requests were ignored. He may have accepted his death by torture when it became inevitable, but he did not seek it out.

The second body, the Double, may seem ephemeral, intangible, even invisible to people who lack "eyes to see", who only see what the animal brain can detect, but it is luminous and quite real to people who have spiritual "eyes to see". In fact, the second body is the more real of the two, the one for whom the human Birthright is intended. And it was this second body, this "other" Jesus who eventually walked out of that tomb. But the ability to decipher this outcome is lost when one expects factual history and ordinary morality from a Sacred Construct. Furthermore, the keys, the key words that let a reader decipher the text, are typically left out or altered whenever behavioral control is the primary purpose of a "religion".

Gnosticism

Early Christian texts were discovered in Egypt (Nag Hammadi) in 1945. The Christianity presented in these gnostic texts is very different from the state religion sanctioned by Emperor Constantine and Bishop Athanasius of Alexandria at Nicaea in the year 325, which was "Christianity for the masses". This version of Christianity was focused on history (rewritten to make the Romans look good), common worship, and ritual. In contrast, the Gnostic teachings were Christianity for individuals on the "fast track to Salvation" (on the road of Return). (And as far as I can tell, every one of the world's major religions has exoteric and esoteric versions of its teachings.) A focus on a common worship is not necessarily bad or wrong. People need some sense that they are part of a larger whole, and meaningful rituals can convey genuine teachings without relying on words. But Constantine wanted a uniform "Christianity", primarily to suppress dissent from the many sects of Christianity. Religious freedom is problematic when social control is your intention. "Standardizing" Christianity made it very easy for the emperor and church fathers to say, "You're either with us or against us." And it was no accident that all the Gospels about and by women were excluded. You might also wish to ask yourself why the church fathers decided to include a fever dream "end of days" account called "Revelations", when Jesus specifically said not to make predictions about his return.

Gnostic Christianity was never intended to be a religion of the masses, this is why it was associated with monasteries. Monasteries, at least originally, were structured for those who sought that inner transformation that would make possible an accelerated Return to God, although a formal monastic order, of whatever faith, is not the only way to go about this work. A Sufi sheik's tent community, when genuine, is just as viable. However, the vast majority of people are simply not ready to make this sort of withdrawal from life.

Gnosticism was deemed a threat to "standardized Christianity" because, being aimed at the individual, it ran contrary to the Church's arrogation of being the only means of contact with God and the only means of access to heaven. Therefore, acting as Romans did, church fathers went out of their way to destroy every vestige of Gnosticism.

Likewise, Wahabist (Fundamentalist) Islam is bent on exterminating every vestige of Sufism. Go figure.

In the four canonical Gospels, everything is presented in story book fashion, which is why they lend themselves to being presented as factual history. In contrast, the gnostic texts are more philosophical and abstract, mystical, and often paradoxical in wording, intended to set a person thinking instead of giving a person a story that's easy to remember. The problem here is that ignorant announcers and reporters present this as "secret or magical information", as if Gnosticism were a cult. In today's world, knowledge is equated to information, and the idea that knowledge, coupled with experience, can lead to understanding is all but lost. This confusion of knowledge with information is the basis for the common belief that everything can and should be explained, and if someone doesn't explain what they are doing, they must then be keeping secrets. But the religion of inner transformation is the religion of acquiring experiential knowledge which, by its very nature, cannot be easily expressed or conveyed in words.

Assuming we could travel back in time, how would anyone of us explain to a Roman citizen how chocolate tastes? Or tomato sauce on a pizza for that matter? The experiences which we take for granted were unavailable to any European in that earlier time. The word "mystical" really means "the closed mouth", but that doesn't just mean that one *won't* speak about something. When genuine, it means that one simply *can't* speak about experiences which are not typical of everyday life.

The work of genuine inner transformation (Metanoia) largely takes place in inner silence, as one begins to experience oneself in ways not typical in ordinary life. Think of how "quiet" a caterpillar becomes in its larval state when it "withdraws from life" and spins itself into a cocoon.

The still, small voice

The role of the Holy Spirit is that of Advocate between God and Man, and one way we can become aware of the presence of the Holy Spirit is to hear it as "the still, small Voice within" (in Greek: the "Paraclete"). To quote *The Course of Miracles*: "the function of the 'Holy Spirit' is to mediate between the two worlds. He can do this because while on one hand, He knows the truth that is God, on the other hand, He also acknowledges our illusions, but without believing in them."

In other words, the Holy Spirit is able to be aware of the needs which seem to afflict us as individuals by the overwhelming sway of illusion here in Flatland, and is able to be responsive to those needs, even while always remaining aware of God's Singular Reality, Truth, and Goodness. And just who or what might this advocate, this Paraclete actually be? I would hazard a guess, and it's exactly only that: a guess. And this guess is that it's none other than ADAM, that very same entity created directly by God as "I AM". Who else could simultaneously be in direct contact with God and with every single member of the entire Sonship? There's more to this supposition than immediately meets the eye, because there's only one ADAM, and every individual (female or male) who reaches the penultimate stage of Return called ADAM-hood becomes completely aware of our genuine, real relationship to God as "I AM" and to all of Creation, including each and every fellow human. And importantly, each one of us who attains this level also brings something along with him or herself, something which ADAM, as originally created, couldn't have had: the experience of coming up through the ranks. Sub-luminous Existence is our gymnasium, our "School of Hard Knocks", and the acquisition and accumulation of these experiences, through our efforts to return is what makes ADAM qualified to be each Man's Advocate, very much as our individual True Soul is most directly qualified to be our individual Guardian Angel.

ADAM is the ultimate Bodhisattva, and we are each of us free to think of "Him" as Jesus, Moses, Mary Magdalene, Muhammed, Buddha, Mahavira, Deganawida, or any of the myriad of genuine Saints who have accomplished their Return. Our Returns to being ADAM are the penultimate progression on our way Back to God, just as the spokes of a wheel converge at the hub of a wheel.

<u>Becoming as little children</u>
Here, Jesus is telling us to find and reestablish ourselves as our Essence (as per Gurdjieff), because our innocence resides there, as well as our potential to become our "Double" and develop the second body. In small children, Essence is very much awake and active, not yet moribund, as it too often becomes by the time we reach adulthood, or even puberty. You have to be taught to be cynical about the world, taught to be hateful towards other Human Beings. Such souring usually becomes a hard, suffocating shell, an exoskeleton of sorts which inverts one's innocence and smothers any possibility of inner growth for that given lifetime.

Here is an example of why one should not let one's left hand know what the right is doing, because one must somehow acquire a practical working knowledge of the Human world (Flatland), without allowing it to stunt or kill what is most important within oneself. The capacity to be serious and careful must never replace one's ability to be playful and open-hearted, because like the kernel of a seed, this inner child represents our genuine capacity for real growth, for genuine At-one-ment. Our everyday self (personality) is part of the experience we bring with us on our Return to ADAM-hood, but the true Birthright properly belongs to the child, the younger self, within.

Becoming again as little children is a form of psychological or spiritual Neoteny.

The organic body as a dream

Perhaps more than anything else so far presented in this book, this subject is likely to become a focus for mockery. At the same time, it's pertinent to explaining something about the ability of Jesus to heal, and beyond that, to explain what happened to the organic Human animal body of Jesus during His internment in death before the Resurrection. This discussion starts with the story told in the Preface, where my friend the nurse had that strange, vivid dream that her favorite patient, a former pediatrician, had died overnight, and had left her an Amaryllis as a way of thanking her for the care she had given. On returning to work the next day, my friend did discover that her patient had indeed died, and that the Amaryllis in question had not been removed, as it should have been, by those who had cleaned the room in preparation for some new patient. My friend therefore kept it for herself.

The reason for that story having been made the centerpiece of the preface, lies in the two contrasting explanations for why that Amaryllis was still there when my friend arrived at work the next morning. There was both a sub-luminous explanation, that the cleaning person simply overlooked it or forgot it; but also a hyper-luminous explanation, which affirms that the Amaryllis was intended for my friend, and the inner child of the person who prepared the room for the next patient quietly sensed that intent and left the Amaryllis to be found by the nurse. And this very same dichotomy applies to the explanation for most everything in this Flatland, including our physical, Human animal bodies. The sub-luminous reality about our bodies is that they were generated by the temporal process called evolution, via the origin and diversification of animal life on this planet. This Cosmology interprets the Elohim as being directors of what manifests in Existence as Natural Law; it also recognizes that more than mere accident (random mutation) was involved in producing some of the critical changes that eventually led to our Human animal bodies. Intelligence had something important to add, just as it does with our Human domestication and cultivation of our food plants and animals. That too has been a guided temporal process.

However, from a hyper-luminous perspective, the entire sub-luminous Realm is actually a dream, precisely because illusion outweighs Reality here. And our physical bodies are definitely sub-luminous. To be explicit, this means that our physical bodies are also dreams, even though for ourselves as we usually are, they seem otherwise. But then, for ourselves as we usually are, what this Cosmology calls hyper-luminous Existence seems only a theoretical abstraction.

At our most fundamental, our most basic level, we are nubs of Awareness and Will. Our Being and Mind are manifestations of this most central nub of Awareness. And at this sub-luminous level, our bodies are forms which our awareness has taken, in order to project ourselves into this dream world (like the avatar bodies in the movie *Avatar*). This is the hyper-luminous Truth, and even if it seems irrational, it is not inconsistent with the sub-luminous explanations that our bodies are the results of seven million years of evolution diversifying from our organic cousins, the chimpanzees and the bonobos. The main point to be made here is that both explanations count as true, and they are no more or less inconsistent than the measurements of the side of a square and the same square's diagonal, or the measurement of a circle's diameter and its circumference. In other words, both accounts are correct, even if they are, to use the Euclidean term, incommensurable.

Somewhere along the line, I read something to this effect in the writings of Carlos Castaneda. However, and this will be embarrassing to report, what really triggered my understanding about this was seeing Yoda die in the third movie of the original *Star Wars* Trilogy (#VI). The same thing had happened to Obi Wan Kenobi in the very first movie (now listed as #IV), but I missed the idea at that time. Essentially, what all of this adds up to is that when our Double has fully matured and become fully independent of our organic animal body, the dream of being an animal body simply ends. And it seems that, under extraordinary circumstances, the energy which supported that dream of being a material entity can instead give our Double a "boost" in its independence, and in those instances the animal body itself would simply, "inexplicably" disappear. The release of that energy might very well leave behind a signature expression, as with the Shroud of Turin.

In short, this means that the Human animal body of Jesus simply disappeared, when His dream of ever being such a body, ended.

Last of all, I will only say that understanding this about our bodies is the key to understanding how Jesus (and many others through history), was able to heal the people he helped. Such healing was always a case of assisting someone to awaken from the dream of being sick. A genuine "Blessing" such as defined in this book, is the critical help needed for that awaking to both happen, and for its result to remain in force after the person who was healed returns to their usual state of mind.

The Cross

For a very long time I had a problem with the symbol of the Cross, a problem many people still have. Why would a symbol of torture and murder be chosen as the symbol of a religion supposedly of Peace? It always seemed such an unjustifiable contradiction, and it supported my roughly thirty year disenchantment with Christianity as I heard it preached in most arenas. It was only in my late thirties that I began to see this question from another angle, one which made possible my reconciliation with Christianity.

This reconciliation came from contemplating what Jesus said in Matthew 116: 24, and in Luke 9: 23, where he says, *"if you would come after me, take up your cross and follow me."* It came to me what this "cross" might actually refer to. Martyrdom or self-affliction in any form were completely out of the question for me. Both are literal interpretations made by the worldly mind. On the other hand, our center of gravity as Man is literally *at the crossroad of Existence*. While we remain imbedded in sub-luminous Existence, we ourselves are that intersection, the very fulcrum. Unlike animals or angels, we must somehow find a balance between the immeasurable freedom above, and the near absolute slavery below the intervening Light Boundary—literally, the Cross-bar to the vertical Hierarchy of Existence. Another way of saying this is that we must learn to pay Caesar what we owe Caesar, while at the same time, paying God what we owe to God. Our lives here are meant to be informed by what is true in the upper regions of Existence, while we encounter "harsh necessities" here in Flatland. (Debt to J.G. Bennett.)

<u>Mary Magdalene: disciple, yes, but also wife?</u>
This question came to light in the wake of several books and movies on the subject, much to the horror of those who are invested in, who profit from maintaining the version of "Christianity" that insists on a uniquely divine Jesus. I have no stake in presenting a Jesus who's a celibate divinity. Nor does it make any sense to me that sex is sinful. Why would God first demand that we be fruitful and multiply, and then consider it a sin to follow His command by using the only method He gave us to do so? Irresponsible sex is certainly problematic, but all the error lies in the irresponsibility, not in sexuality itself.

Jesus was a Man who, like every Man, carried Divinity within as WHO he was, not as what he was. In other words, Jesus was not a god, but like every other Human Being, Jesus was a center for I AM and for Will beyond his individual Being.

I first came across the idea of a married Jesus back in the very early 1970s, possibly by the courtesy of Dr. Maurice Nicoll, although I've been unable to find the specific statement. Whichever the source, it was suggested that the marriage at Cana was the actual marriage of Jesus himself. Otherwise, why would both the Mother of Jesus and the Steward of the Feast go to Jesus about the need for more wine, if Jesus Himself weren't the bridegroom and therefore the Master of the Ceremony? That alone raised this question for me decades ago.

However, the primary reason why I now believe Jesus and Mary to have been husband and wife is because Mary was the first to see Jesus arisen, and recognize him for WHO he was. Furthermore, as far as I can tell, and in spite of Leonardo da Vinci's famous mural, Mary Magdalene was not at the Last Supper. This is important, because one of the first things I remember learning from reading *In Search of the Miraculous* while a teenager was that the Last Supper was literally a Blood Brotherhood ceremony. As it was explained, Jesus knew he would soon be taken prisoner by the Romans, and he also knew that he needed more time than he had available to help his disciples. The blood brotherhood ceremony would enable him to directly interact with them even after the death of his human animal body. By incorporating some of the blood of Jesus, they could, for a period of time, interact directly with the second body of Jesus, even after the death of his organic body. The explanation continued that it was the need to complete this ceremony that forced Jesus to buy time by commissioning one of his more advanced disciples, Judas Iscariot, to delay the Romans by cutting a deal with them.

Mary Magdalene wasn't at the Blood Brotherhood ceremony because, being his wife, *she didn't need to be*. The exchange of Noticing Being-Grade hanbledzoin is an inevitable part of having sex. This is why partners can become supernally aware of each other, even before the act of sex is consummated. (It is also why the experience of being raped can be so devastating. The rapist is literally forcing a permanent awareness of himself on the other person.)

This was hardly the first appearance of Jesus as his Double. Much of His ministry was carried out in this state. However, it's only at the resurrection that Jesus as his Double was fully independent of its organic template, the Human animal body. And this is why he didn't let Mary embrace him right away, as described in the Gospel of John. However, once that independent consolidation was complete, Jesus was able to confront Thomas with his "solidity." This explains why Jesus was able to suddenly appear wherever He chose… even inside rooms which were locked. And later on he was able to be seen by many others, as when he ascended. But Mary both saw and recognized him first. It took much longer for the other disciples to even recognize him for being who he actually was.

Note: If the non-canonical Gospels are to be believed, Mary was far more inwardly awake than most of the disciples, and certainly more than Peter at that time.

The Second Coming of Christ

The Second coming of Jesus is a belief shared by Christians and Muslims alike. Similarly, the arrival of The Messiah is anticipated by Jews. However, like the announcement that the Kingdom is at hand, the Second Coming of Christ is widely misunderstood.

People are told to expect the historical Jesus, someone other than themselves, to return to this planet on some unspecified calendar date, because only Time&Space are "real" to the everyday worldly mind. Compared to a genuinely spiritual mind, our worldly mind can only be that swine which tramples pearls of wisdom into the mud. But what if this Return were an inner reality, one completely independent of Time&Space? As such, it could actually be experienced *at different times and places* by different individuals. In other words, some people have already experienced it, and others will do so whether you do or not, because hyper-luminous Christ is not limited to our Time-locked senses of perception.

The Kingdom of Heaven/God is at hand

There are two problems with how this pronouncement by Jesus is usually understood. First is that "repentance" must precede it in some manner. The second problem is that people are still waiting for it to come about.

During my college years, one of the big questions in Theology was, just what did Jesus mean by saying that the Kingdom was at hand? The typical theological debate focused on whether this meant that the Kingdom would soon come in calendar time, or did it mean that the appearance of Jesus was itself the appearance of the Kingdom? Both these explanations drove me nuts because they were so limited by the assumptions that made them seem so reasonable to the ordinary mind.

God as "I AM" is the Ultimate Kingdom, and God is never elsewhere or elsewhen, simply because there is no anywhere nor any when other than God. Time was never the issue when it comes to the Kingdom. The only dimension which separates us from our immediate awareness of God's Kingdom (BEING) is the limited awareness of our everyday worldly mind.

In learning to step aside from the illusions that this world of Flatland is "real", we discover that the Kingdom is always Here&Now for our Return to be accomplished. This awakening to God, to Reality, is the True Second Coming.

<u>An unsuspected significance to the "Virgin Birth"</u>

Until now, in January, 2018, it never once crossed this author's mind that the "virgin birth" of Jesus might be a topic for discussion in this Book. What caused a re-assessment were certain holiday TV shows presented in 2017, purporting to present the early years of Jesus of Nazareth. Typically, they attempted to define his presumed experiences he would have had as a child growing up in Roman held Galilee, experiences that molded the adult message of Jesus.

This approach is the approach that Social Science would be expected to take. And normally I avoided such shows because they always left me with a residual feeling of their having missed something important. Every year around the world, thousands of people are born and grow up in difficult circumstances, who choose to spend much of their life working for the good of others. But they don't usually end up inspiring a worldwide religion. So what was different here?

As for the Virgin Birth itself, I never believed it was a historical, literal fact. Virgin Births were too widespread for that of Jesus to be uniquely true. A short list will demonstrate this;

a) Horus—Egypt
b) Osirus—Egypt
c) Krishna—India
d) The Buddha—India
e) Mithra—Iran
f) Baal—Phoenicia
g) Balder—Norse
h) Quetzalcoatl—Mexico

Each of these were believed to be important agents for Religion, agents for the awakening and civilization of Mankind. A "Virgin Birth" is essentially a way of saying that one's Spiritual DNA is free of "hereditary" defects. In other words, it's a way of using a literal sounding description of a metaphorical condition, that someone is able to be a prophet because he is not heir to any sins of the fathers.

And that made me think of something…

The effort and process to Return Back to God can be thought of as a two stage affair. The first stage of our Return is the effort to climb out of this pit we fell into when we lost contact with our True Soul, soon after our initial incarnation here on Earth. Biblically, this was the consequence of the murder of Abel, when we lost ourselves to our worldly mind, to Cain the Wanderer. Abel himself didn't represent that Soul, he represented the potential New Mind which is capable of hearing the Voice of the Holy Spirit. Abel was therefore our proper channel of connection to our True Soul. Without that channel, we could only rely on our worldly mind to "guide" us through life. But with such guidance, we are essentially condemned to wander blindly throughout our lives. (I remind the reader that the land of "Nod" means "wandering" in Hebrew. Wandering is also the etymological meaning of the Sanskrit word Samsara, which refers to our entrapment to Recurrence, the wheel of Birth, Death, and Rebirth. Recurrence will be discussed in detail in the chapter about Man).

Without guidance from our True Soul, which ought to be the seat of "I AM" in us, our Will can only inhabit our worldly mind with its myriad conflicting impulses competing for primacy and supremacy. Whichever impulse prevails at some moment gets to write checks for a time, before another impulse is able to grab the pen. And then one has to make good paying off all those checks. As we ordinarily are, there's no single center in ourselves, able to speak or answer for the whole of ourselves. The ability to answer for the whole of oneself is the hallmark of the True Soul. When it is in genuine charge, nothing else within you argues with or even questions its decisions.

Therefore, the first stage of our effort to Return is to reconnect to our true sense of Self. Only having accomplished this allows one to make a promise that will stand, either to God or to oneself.

The second stage of our Return is that which concerns the "Virgin Birth". While the first stage is the uphill climb to reclaim one's "Birthright", the second stage is to offer that Individuality back to God as a Sacrifice. Here, one's true Individuality is the candle which allows itself to be consumed for the sake of the flame. In order to fully Return to God, we go through the Doorway of ADAM (the final SI-DO Phase Transition). ADAM is the seat for "I AM" (that inmost Zero within ourselves) while we exist, and as such, ADAM is a perfect circle. In contrast, our True Soul (our genuine individual Self) is some other shape, maybe a square, rectangle, triangle, or some other polygon, maybe a squiggle. The point to this visual imagery is that in order to get from your individual shape to the perfect circle we each bear as ADAM, all of those excess corners have to be rounded off, or the line has to swallow its own ending and beginning and become rounded out.

Anyone who completes this second stage is referred to in this book as a Saint. Another term could be Hero, because the individual fulfills his or her own Destiny, which is to say they actualize whatever service they were intrinsically designed for in the overall effort to neutralize the negative effects of the Biblical Dark (of the trapped Ahriman). That's what happens externally. Inwardly, this stage of Return is more like the insight given us by Meister Eckart, when he told us (paraphrased), "you see devils tearing your life away, only later to realize that they were angels, helping to free you from the Earth."

We can now return to the subject of the "Virgin Birth". An extraordinary quality of Being characterizes those who undertake the second stage of Return. This would have held equally true for every one of the saints listed above. Because they acquired full Authority over themselves, they could be sent into life to accomplish their last stage of Return Back to God, that of allowing their individuality to be ground away by their efforts to serve Mankind. In this context, the "Virgin Birth" would seem to indicate that these Saints and Heroes, including Jesus, were now Independent agents of God, free of all prior Karma, if you wish. In other words, this person would in effect be acting independent of any prior causes picked up in some prior life or generated by life circumstances, *including genetics, heredity, and parental influences*, which certainly exert profound effects on most of us. Remember, Will is defined as a Cause which is not the Effect of some prior Cause. In this sense, these are Virgin Births.

In the case of Jesus, this notion was first announced by the Angel Gabriel, and later emphasized by the Dove which descended as he stepped out of the River Jordan after baptism. Whatever he did in his life up to that point resulted in his full re-connection to his True Soul, resulting in full Self-Authority, hence the Dove. And the Baptism represented being washed of anything picked up from this specific life. All of this sheds a light on the message of Jesus, which runs completely counter to Social Determinism.

There's one final subject to be broached here. And that is, that Jesus had to be tempted in the Wilderness *after* the descent of the Dove. The word "tempt" derives from the Latin *tempiare* and has the root meaning "to try or test the strength of". Meanwhile, "to temper" (as in the process of tempering steel) and "temperance" both derive from *temperare*, which means to regulate, or to render free from admixture/impurities. In other words, it might be said that it's only temptation if you succumb; whereas, if you don't allow yourself to be sidetracked or deceived, it's just part of a tempering or refining process. That's because this point in a person's Ascent Back to God represents a point of *great possible danger*. A person should never see their Destiny through the eyes of, or while under the rule of, their worldly material mind. When this happens, Destiny is seen and acted upon as though it belonged to the ego. Hence, an Alexander the Great, an Oliver Cromwell, a Napoleon, a

Hitler, a politician who believes he naturally "towers" above everyone else. Enormous damage to Humanity, and to the entire world, is the typical consequence.

And by the way, the fact that Jesus could even be so tempted in the Wilderness underscores that he was a Man and not a Deity. His seeming divinity was merely the consequence of having successfully navigated this last challenge of Sacrificing his Individuality. Jesus was then an open doorway for God to act in this sub-luminous world. As a Muslim might say, Jesus had sold everything in his purse.

CHAPTER XXI

PERCEPTION

Hyper-luminous and sub-luminous minds; etymologies of words concerning knowing and transmission; avoiding (the doing of) harm; holy spirit

<u>The difference between hyper-luminous and sub-luminous minds</u>

The critical difference between these two different types of mind is a function of the Light Boundary, because from the Light Boundary downwards, one must always keep in mind that "the book itself is something other than the contents of the book." Hyper-luminous minds directly access the center of gravity of something, whereas sub-luminous minds can only access the exterior form.

<u>Etymology of several words concerning Knowing and conveying what is known</u>

(to) Formulate:

This means encasing (encapsulating) some meaning into a form which will allow it to be conveyed. Usually this means encasing that meaning into words, spoken or written, although many ideas and notions can more economically be encased in pictures, or, in formulas, such as mathematical or chemical formulas. Music also has its own unique script, one for expressing its notions in an agreed upon form. Formulation, providing meaning with a form, is indirect communication, something which became necessary for communication in this sub-luminous realm.

An aside: The word "form" itself is Latin, and is believed to be a transliteration, a transpositioning of sounds or letters, in this case of the "M" and "F" sounds of the Greek word *morph*, which also means form, as in the English word "morphology."

Intellect / Intelligence:
Both words are ultimately derived from the Latin word *legere* which originally meant "to collect", "to gather together". However, this word also came to mean "to read", most likely because of the monastic practice of having periodic gatherings for readings from scripture, hence the word "lecture."

The real meaning of the words "intellect" and "intelligence" *(inter-legere)*, would therefore seem to be the ability to "read between the lines." That is the meaning those words carry in this book. Intelligence is considered to be the ability to see the implicit hidden within the explicit; also the ability to see hidden assumptions, and the ability to see where the implications of something lead. The importance of this notion of Intelligence, when applied to Religion, is that it takes the intelligence of *Metanoia*, of a New Mind, to decipher allegories and metaphorical teachings.

(to) Interpret / Interpretation:
The *-pret* portion of these words is the equivalent of the English word "price". Interpret means to "negotiate a price", and by extension, to "negotiate a value, significance, or meaning".

Interpretation is the unavoidable complement to perception at the sub-luminous level of knowing. It is also entirely subjective. There will be subtle, often profound differences in how different people interpret the meaning of what they read, hear, see and experience.

(to) Know / Knowledge:

The reconstruction of this Indo-European word is something like *gene* or *gno* (hard 'g' in both). Its offspring comprise a huge stable of words, such as with the Sanskrit *jana* and the Russian *zhnat*. The Greek equivalent was *gnoskein*, which gave English such words as "gnosticism", "agnostic", "diagnosis" and "prognosis." And from the Latin *cognoscere*, which also meant "to know", English received the words "cognition", "recognize", and also "ignore / ignorance" and the French "quaint" and "acquaintance".

The corresponding Germanic root was *kna*, which gave English the word "can" (to know how to) and the simple word to "know." The German word *kennen* means "to be acquainted with someone"; to speak of knowing a fact, as opposed to knowing an acquaintance, one must instead use the word *wissen* (from *weid*).

(to) Mean / Meaning:

To mean something is basically to say that you have that something in mind. Both "mean" and "mind" come from the Indo-European word *men* (mind), which by the way, may also be the source of the English word "Man."

Mystery:

From the Greek word *mystes*, which meant the "closed mouth." The equivalent Latin word gave English the word "mute." A "mystery" is something one doesn't or can't speak about. Importantly, when it comes to Religion, it's usually more a case of "can't" rather than "won't." This is because the most important things in Religion simply are not amenable to words. According to research, the culmination of the Mysteries of Demeter was for the Priestess to wordlessly hold up a stalk of ripened grain.

In this same vein, in Matthew 7: 6, we were told by Jesus "not to give to dogs what is Holy, and not to cast pearls before swine, lest they trample them underfoot and then turn to attack you." This is usually interpreted as referring to people who've been labeled as sinners or infidels. However, that interpretation misses the real point here. Inwardly, the word "dogs" refers to the cynical part of the mind, and "swine" are a metaphor for the worldly mind's focus on personal advantage. At the same time, it is also the case that trying to talk about one's truest feelings and perceptions to people who do not yet have similar experiences will not go well for you. That too is implied in this word "mystery", because not speaking of something one knows to the wrong person also includes not informing them (whether verbally or by one's behavior), that you have anything special to know.

Note: Should this definition of the word "mystery" seem elitist to you, consider how much more dangerous our world has become, due to the availability of information to anyone on the internet about how to make or gain access to bombs, even nuclear ones.

(to) Notice:

This word also ultimately comes from the Indo-European root *gno* like the word to know. It comes more directly from the past participle of the Latin "nota", meaning a "mark." To "notice" something is to mark that something has come into your field of perception or awareness.

(to) Perceive / Perception:

The (Latin) -*cep*- of the word "perception" and also the -*ceiv*- of "perceive" are the very same word as the cap- in the English word "capture"; they all come from the ancient Indo-European word *kap* (with variants *kep* and *kop*), which originally meant to "take hold of into one's hands."

There are a substantial number of additional words which also derive from this, including "anticipate", "participate", "recuperate" and "concept." It also includes English words derived directly from its Germanic roots, such as the words "have" "heavy", to "heave" and "heft". The sound shifts in the Germanic languages, as documented by Jacob Grimm, are very apparent here:

k—> h; p—> v or f

Significance:

From the (Latin) word *sign*, which is also found in the words "assign" and "designate". It means to attach a meaning or value to something. For example, fingerprints only became significant in forensics when it was discovered that each human individual had a pattern of prints unique to themselves.

(to) Understand:

It took me a long time to decode this word, because I couldn't figure out how standing under something led to what the word "understand" means. Finally, after several decades, I learned the English word "under" (and its German sibling *unter*), was cognate to the Latin *inter*, and originally meant the very same thing. (In Latin and Greek, the meaning "under" is indicated by the prefixes *sub*- and *hypo*- respectively. Many prefixes which start with "h" in Greek start with "s" in Latin.) To "Understand" therefore really means to "stand inside" something or to "stand in the midst of" something, not underneath it. A bit embarrassing for an etymology aficionado to have to admit.

Weid

This Indo-European word combined the meanings of "to see;" "to know;" and "to understand." Its derivatives included many cognates:

i) the Sanskrit Vedas and Vedanta. The Vedas were the truths revealed by the gods, seen by those who knew.

ii) the Celtic word Druid, one interpretation of which is "powerful seer".

iii) the Latin *uidere*, which literally means "to see." English derivatives include words like "view", "vista", "video", "visual" and "visible". The Norman French word "guide" is even closer to the Latin.

iv) the modern German *wissen*, pronounced "vissen" and meaning to "know a fact"; and the word *Wissenschaft*, the modern German word for science.

v) the English words "wise", "wisdom", "wizard", and "witness". Also, by way of the Greek language, the words "idea" and "idol", as well as "eidetic".

<u>Perception as a kind of interpretation</u>

As stated above, to "perceive" essentially means to capture something, to take hold of it, either literally in one's hands or metaphorically via the mind. The words "perception"and "apperception" are sometimes used to indicate direct, wordless knowing the truth about something, including oneself. However, as I use the word, perception is a sub-luminous capacity, simply and precisely because the Light Boundary is where form separates from substance. Our brains "see" what light illuminates. We see the external forms of things, and the substance/meaning/significance must be inferred. Most of our life training is concerned with acquiring experience and learning how to interpret our perceptions with a reasonable chance of being at least close to correct. And this even applies to basic organic functions like sensations, which perhaps needs some explanation. Explaining how this works will be instructive, and we'll use color for our example.

Quite simply, there's no such thing as color outside of your head. What there is, is a tremendously wide range of electromagnetic radiation frequencies. Color is an interpretation the human brain has learned to make (over its millions of years of evolution) when perceiving differences within a minuscule range of those frequencies. And we primates are lucky. Mammals lost the ability to perceive green and ultraviolet frequencies during that long (roughly 135 million year) period spent underground while dinosaurs were dominant during daylight. Mammals could only safely emerge from underground at night, which is why smell is so important to most mammals. Tree dwelling primates regained the ability to see green, although by a different chemical mechanism from other vertebrates. Most birds, reptiles, amphibians and fish, as well as insects, can see ultraviolet.

Learning about this a few years ago (reading *Scientific American*), finally answered a question I'd had since childhood: How could the yellow of a lion or the orange of a tiger be camouflage within a field of green vegetation? Well, both yellow and orange are made by combining red light with green light (the reverse of combining pigments). Without the ability to perceive green, yellow and orange are perceived as different shades of reddish gray, just like the green of vegetation.

RELIGION REINTERPRETED

The inevitability of interpretation with regard to perception is critically important for this book because of how it applies to Religion. The notions of fundamentalism are based on the assumption that the words of scripture are always best taken at literal face value, that doing so is what scripture was intended for. There are places in the Bible where literal reading is absolutely appropriate: the laws with regard to preparing food protected observant Jews from many dangers; the practice of letting agricultural and pasture lands lie fallow every seventh year prevented the sort of blights and infestations that have ravaged croplands since that custom fell into disuse. It is worth noting that most if not all of the "take this literally and follow these proscriptions" portions of the Bible belong to the Old Testament. Even so, if this Cosmology has any validity, there is also a great deal in the Old Testament, especially the Torah, which I have argued calls for understanding ("standing in the midst of") that is hyper-luminous.

Material-minded perception of truth is based on form, on what can be directly perceived and taken in hand. This is why fundamentalism focuses on behavior, on the forms given to beliefs and actions. Fundamentalism tends to assume that God sees everything in the same way that you do—even though there are passages in the Bible which explicitly state that this is not so, such as when Jesus warns his listeners that there will be a lot of people who expect Jesus to personally welcome them to Heaven who will be told, "I know you not." Even more clearly, it is stated that the wisdom of men is folly in God's eyes. And visa versa.

There's a widespread notion here in Flatland that we can gain something of real worth by taking it from others by stealing or by "taking more than one's share". All crime rests on this assumption. However, that can only seem true in a material sense, when those of us who have lost in this sort of exchange believe that they have lost in truth. As long as this world alone is "real" to your perception, then religion can only be exactly what the ultimate materialist Karl Marx called it: "an opiate for the masses" which unscrupulous leaders use as a means of crowd control and social engineering.

Pronouncing your belief in God is meaningless while you still reject the equal status of Sonship in anyone else, because that very rejection is itself a rejection of God. This is not to say that one must leave oneself open to injury. It means instead that injury to another should be a last resort, and even when doing so, it shouldn't be done out of anger, hate or fear, nor for gain at the another's expense. There is an Islamic teaching story about a Sheik in battle who refuses to kill an enemy after that enemy had spat in his face. The Sheik turned away without killing that other man, rather than kill in anger.

A similar approach to this issue is presented early on in *The Bhagavad Gita*, where it's emphasized that one is allowed to do whatever is genuinely necessary without incurring any negative Karma (without incurring any negative moral rebound), so long as one does it without any attachment to the results. In other words, whatever must be done, must be done without concern for whatever might be gained or lost, without concern for whether it will be well received or not, or even whether one will be successful or not in one's endeavor. This certainly does not mean that being a psychopath, sociopath, or chauvinist is OK, only that doing harm to another is allowed *only* when equivalent or great harm will *directly* follow if you refrain. And yes, this is very difficult to reconcile with what was said earlier about the perception of harm. If it were easy, there wouldn't be any need for conscience or Will. Morality could be programmable, automatic, mechanical. It is precisely because decisions and choices are difficult this close to the boundary of the Biblical Dark that Mankind is endowed with Will and equipped with intellect and conscience.

The Holy Spirit is a concession made by God, so that we can receive help here in our struggle with the illusions of this world such as lack, illness, and being isolated. Learning to overcome illusion is why we were sent into this Hall of Mirrors, but it's understood that it's easy for us to become overwhelmed by them. But the need to win this struggle is precisely why we were created, and in God's view, we've all already succeeded, and Returned. We need but wake up to realize that this nightmare has already ended.

CHAPTER XXII

BEING HUMAN

The effect of fragmented being on will; analogy of crystals; the metaphor of the pyramid; evolutionary "tweaking"; ADAM and "the Woman"; brain convolutions; the brain-dependent self; laws which govern material being; continuity of self-awareness; Man #1, #2, #3; Man # 4: Natural Man; drugs as (dangerous) "amplifiers"; the laws which govern essence; the zodiac; 4-dimensional bodies; caves and incubation; reincarnation; the true soul; destiny; <u>The Journey to the West</u>; "No Self" of Bernadette Roberts

The effect of fragmented Being on Will

A question which may have already arisen in the mind of the reader is: "If each of us shares that very same Singular Will that is God as "I AM", then why do our so-called independent Wills seem to diverge so much from each other?" More even than that, why do the Wills of so many individuals so often seem perverted? How can that Will that is God Himself be turned to evil? The answer to both questions is the same: our genuine Will, which is consistent with "I AM" in oneself, is lost in the wilderness of Being (our many selves).

The lower a given level of Being is placed on the overall Hierarchy of Existence, the more differentiated it will be. And mineral crystals can easily provide an analogous example for the consequences that such fracturing of our Being can have on the manifestation of our Will.

Crystals like calcite or selenium which precipitate out of clear sea water, are themselves usually very clear. They will transmit light and images (such as the lettering of this page), largely without distortion. However, crystals must be without internal fractures, and also without inclusions for this to be the case. When they are fractured, they may still transmit some light, but not distinct images. An example of how this works can be shown with calcite (ordinary calcium carbonate). One can read a newspaper through an unfractured piece of calcite, but not through a piece that's been crushed and re-packed. Most everyone is very familiar with this, because crushed and compressed calcite is the chalk we use for our school blackboards (add a little flavoring, and you can call it Tums). Selenium crystals (calcium sulfate) when crushed and packed together is called gypsum.

The intended analogy here is that our lowest level of Being is intrinsically highly fractured: the multiple facets and impulses which in composite comprise our personalities. They disperse the singularity of our Will, the "light" which now cannot be transmitted undistorted through the resulting opacity. In our ordinary selves, very little of the light of Will can be transmitted as discernible illumination. And it's even worse if multiple inclusions are worked into crush.

Much of the selenium I found in northern New Mexico was loaded with iron oxide and pockets of mud or shale. Iron oxide is rust, and colors the crystals anywhere from a light yellow through medium red to almost completely black. These inclusions came about when those selenium crystals were forming as an ocean bed was rapidly drying up. If the water was frequently stirred up, the mud and rust would be included into those parts of the crystals which were then in the process of gelling and solidifying. The analogy intended to be made here would be the many negative thoughts (rust) and emotions (mud) we accumulate in the process of growing up, which are typically included as substantial parts of our personalities, as is the case for something like racism or chauvinism.

Our individual Will is just as subject to distortion and blockage as is light when passing through crystals which are fractured or full of inclusions. Furthermore, our bodies have their own agendas, which can further deflect our Will. Most of these agendas are legitimate, like eating food which provides essential nutrients when our body needs to maintain itself, sleeping and dreaming, preferring the smell of clean air to polluted air, seeking out creature comfort in companionship, taking part in exhilarating activities that strengthen and integrate our muscles. Still, anyone who had ever had a deadline to meet knows how these needs can interfere with accomplishing what we intend.

Furthermore, because of uneven education or other experiences, we become fractured in our feelings, having many impulses, desires, beliefs and such. It's largely a function of chance which of these will be in a position to "write a check or sign a contract" that the rest of you will have to pay for. Our feelings are gardens which grow up largely unattended, and are therefore usually full of weeds which distort our ability to discern reality. The proper aim of the entire process of our informal education, both social and moral, should properly be to find some balance between the animal we wear and the spirit (ADAM) which we bear. And it's precisely here that the variation in Will is to be found between individual Men.

In contrast to our personalities, our everyday social selves, ADAM is the direct creation of Spirit and is therefore the clearest possible self for the transmission of that Will which was God's gift to us. Individual and independent Will is what makes stewardship possible, and it needs to be individualized for Mankind to respond to different situations. Yes, there is the risk of Will getting "muddy", and we see how badly that turns out in examples out of history and our personal experience, but God decided the benefits were worth the risk. It's left up to us to prove God right.

Silent inner prayer is directly analogous to allowing that suspension which is our ordinary mind to sit quietly on an inner shelf until the impurities thereof have settled out to the bottom, thereby enabling the relative clarity of a solution (of your New Mind), to replace it. By doing so one can begin to see something beyond one's everyday worldly mind.

<u>A critically important reminder</u>: As I reported in the beginning of this book, I am nowhere even remotely near being a realized individual. The consequence of this is that much of what I write will seem theoretical and even fanciful, lacking the gravitas of one who can speak from Being. This doesn't mean that everything here is to be automatically discounted. Rather, it means the reader's own inner silence will be needed to determine whether or not there's enough of a kernel of truth to be found in whatever is being said to be useful to one's own understanding. This is possible because each of us already knows the Truth about everything, even though that Truth is rarely allowed to speak, and even more rarely listened to when it breaks through. We all need only find the sincere self-honesty and innocence to allow ourselves access to the quiet center of ourselves, in order to have genuine access to that inner reservoir of knowledge which can genuinely guide us.

The multi-storied pyramid or prism that is Man

This central-most Light at the center of every Man's Being is that singular kernel of Absolute Reality which we know to be God as "I AM". This inmost Light is the true Christ (by whatever Name one knows; for some it is Buddha or Tao or Great Spirit), the true anointed ONE which is "the way, the light, and the truth" which needs to be resurrected, the authentic "Second Coming". And we must both find this Light which is "I AM" in ourselves and free it layer by layer from the several sheaths of selves which surround and obscure and entangle it, which distort that Light (the "overburden of self"). And while the inmost sheath, ADAM, represents an absolutely clear layer of crystal self, with a unified Will that does not disagree with or oppose itself or God, each successive layer of "self" represents an increase in color and in distortion, and an increasingly diversified Will which is increasingly susceptible to deception and disagreement. The most external layer is our animal body. I am fairly sure that the social bodies, which consist of the many groups we belong to, also count as layers of color and distortion and of Will, but I do not see whether they count as more or less external than the bodies we live in. Certainly, our social groupings can be just as or even more demanding, even more "ravenous" than physical bodies are. This is why demons are so often portrayed in art and stories as ravenous beasts. These "demons" are the goals of our lowest selves, when we are possessed by those aims and purposes.

In the process of Return to God, the sense of "I am" displaces back inwards, all of the way back to its penultimate establishment in ADAM, which means the "extinction of all Self." This penultimate step of once again becoming ADAM is how Prince Siddhartha became the Buddha, and how Jesus became the Christ, the "anointed one". This attainment and anointment is the intended destiny for each and every one of us.

An aside: As the microcosm, Man encompasses the entire vertical dimension of Existence (the Macrocosm), as part of its Being. Whereas each of the Amesha Spenta, the six Seraphim that together make up the Elohim, are far greater in Horizontal Being than Man, Man surpasses them in Vertical Being. Only Man is able to change its status within this hierarchical stack of Existence. This notion was originally brought to my attention by Dr. Jacob Needleman in his excellent book *Why Can't We Be Good?*

First, a recapitulation

It would be useful to first repeat what this Cosmology has to say about the Human animal body as part of Man. Basically, Man is the result of combining the Idea of Man (ADAM) with a sub-luminous material Being. In our Human case, this sub-luminous material Being is a highly modified primate. This is the basic message of the first Chapter of Genesis, and by recognizing that our sub-luminous material Being was generated separately from that direct creation of ADAM, our hyper-luminous Ideal Being, one can reconcile the two differing accounts of Man's creation as presented in the first two Chapters of Genesis.

In Genesis Chapter One, Man, both male and female appeared last, after all other life was established on the surface of this planet. And note that in Chapter One there's no mention of the Garden of Eden. In other words, *Man's Human animal body was the end-result of a sub-luminous process of change,* subject to the laws of Time, Space, and also of evolution. Wallace and Darwin and Lamarck weren't the first to study evolution, they were just the Europeans whose work we have most ready access to. Darwin emphasized that there was a randomness to the process evolution, but he was not ruling out an original component of intelligent design. Lamarck was the one who emphasized the role intentionality plays. (Whenever scientists, or any group of personages seem to disagree about something, it's a good idea to remember the poem / fable "The Six Blind Men and the Elephant".)

This Cosmology acknowledges that there had to have been a number of instances of intentional, strategic genetic tweaking in the evolutionary process of Man's Human animal body, modifications directed by the Elohim—not directly by "I AM"— which were accomplished over a period of five to seven million years. An example of these modifications will be demonstrated in the Addendum below. These intentional modifications expedited the process whereby Mankind evolved to the point of being able to take pictures of our planetary home from the surface of our moon.

This merger of Soul with animal body is called "the Fall" in Genesis Chapter 3. This Cosmology instead calls it the Great Insertion, literally, the Incarnation, the descent of the Human Soul from ADAM. ADAM, directly made in the image of God, is the entire Idea of Man as both female and male, and is considered by this Cosmology to be part of the Elohim. ADAM is therefore immune from falling prey to illusion. That which "fell" had to have been something derived from ADAM, something subordinate, which is referred to in Genesis as "the Woman", which does *not* mean the female portion of humanity! Like ADAM, this "Woman" was also androgynous Man, both female and male. This Cosmology insists that it was only this "Woman" which "fell" to an intermediate position between Man's Ideal and material halves (at the Light Boundary), thereby becoming the True Soul for all Mankind, and also for each individual Man. As such, our Soul was now the Reconciliation between the Affirmation of our Ideal Self (ADAM) above, and the Denial of our material self below. This True Soul is also the medium by which our gift of Spirit and of Will could be transmitted from the Ideal (ADAM) into our sub-luminous material Being. Actually, it was only this Great Insertion which made necessary the partial differentiation of the female and male components of Man's Soul, in order to make possible incorporation into animal bodies of appropriate gender, the female portion being endowed with the separate name Eve, which means "the mother of all life".

However, Will is invested into both genders. The "I AM" of Mankind's female portion is identical to that of Mankind's male half, and must therefore be fully acknowledged and treated accordingly. In other words, females and males are properly full partners and companions in this affair called life, and **no** subset of humanity should **ever** be regarded as mere property or as "sub-human".

Addendum: brain convolutions

Amphibians were the direct descendants of the lobe-finned fish (like the present day lung fish and coelacanths), which first left the water for land near the end of the Devonian age. The cartilaginous fish like sharks and rays, and the far more numerous bony fish, were separate branches of fish. The lobe-finned branch alone led directly to all land-dwelling vertebrates. They had the anatomical architectural precursors that allowed their fins to be transformed into legs by the greater pressure from gravity when on land.

Reptiles descended from Amphibians by solving the problem of living permanently on dry land: dry, semi-permeable skin; advanced kidneys; the appearance of the colon to reclaim water which would otherwise be lost in digestion; and perhaps most importantly, the water-proof amniotic egg which allowed the larva to develop in its own private pond, instead of in an external pond like amphibian tadpoles. The amnion is the protein-rich egg white of a bird's egg, as well as being the water which breaks just prior to birth in a mammalian female.

Next, Reptiles diversified early into three primary branches depending on the number of holes found in their skulls (the holes in question do not include those for the eyes, ears, nose, nor spinal cord). They are as follows:

0—Anapsids: Skulls with no holes. These Reptiles became our present day Turtles.

1—Synapsids: Skulls with one hole (actually, a paired, symmetrical hole, one on each side, called the temporal fenestra). These Reptiles became our present day Mammals, which include our Human animal bodies.

2—Diapsids: Skulls with two holes symmetrically located on each side. These include all other present day Reptiles. From the Crocodilian branch came the Dinosaurs, and from the Theropod branch of Dinosaurs came Birds.

The reason for bringing all of this up is a specific genome which controls the number of convolutions of the brain's surface. In Humans, this gene (called "HAR1", an acronym for "Human Accelerated Region #1"), is responsible for the vastly increased number of convolutions of our brains, which vastly increase the surface area. When this gene is defective, a condition called Microcephaly ("pin-head-ism"), is the unfortunate result. (Microcephaly is a feature of the Zika virus.)

The important point to be made here concerns the evolutionary history of this genome. The evolutionary line of reptiles which led to Mammals (the synapsids) diverged from the line which led to birds (the most modern diapsids), some 300 million years ago. In all of that 300 million years since those two branches separated, there has been an accumulated difference of only 2 base-pairs in their respective HAR1 genomes. And yet, in the mere 7 million years since the line of Apes which led to Humans separated from the line which led to our nearest relatives, the Chimpanzees and Bonobos, Humans have accumulated a difference of 18 base-pairs. I find it extremely difficult to think that this occurred by nothing more than mere accident, by mere random mutations. Humans otherwise still share 98.8% of our DNA with our Chimp and Bonobo relatives. We're almost siblings genetically, save for that 1.2% difference.

<u>The material mind and its brain dependent material Self: the Personality.</u>

The reason why we were intentionally incarcerated into these animal bodies was to put us in a situation where our ability to differentiate between Reality and illusion would be compromised. Only in this manner would our efforts to reconcile the conflict between Reality ("I AM") and the illusion of discontinuity (anti-being), lead to something meaningful. However, we Human Beings have slipped even further away from Reality than we were ever intended to, resulting in our having lost the necessary connection to our True Soul. This means that we've slipped further into the grip of illusion than we were ever meant to. As a result, the Human animal is now the only part of ourselves that has any reality for most of us.

Religion, as intuited by individuals and as taught by many prophets, is intended to remedy this problem. However, because we have in fact lost so much ground, the messages of prophets has had to focus on behavioral instructions about how to live within this lowest part of our total Being in such a way that our animal side would interfere as little as possible with our ability to Return.

The Ten Commandments and the additional laws given by Moses are examples of this. So are the 16 Precepts or Pearls of Buddhism, which consist of 8 "Dos" and 8 "Don'ts".

What tends to happen is that our material mind, because it assumes its own knowledge and understanding of things to be complete and sufficient and "right", sees these behavioral laws as ends in themselves and not as a means towards that which is really needed: finding, freeing, and owning that Pearl of Great Price. The typical result of this common and persistent mistake is fundamentalism, in all of its forms. When behavior is your ultimate religious criterion, the intention of enforcing "religiously approved behavior", is not far behind. This enforcing of behavior includes determining what someone is allowed to think, to feel, and to believe, just as much as it means determining what someone is allowed to say or do or wear.

This is where religions (and most any "-ism") go wrong, eventually contradicting their own original intent because enforcing behavior invariably means the violence of overriding independent Will. This sequence of deterioration, having been repeated again and again in the course of Human history, is an example of why the material mind and the artificial self (the personality) have absolutely no business in deciding anything genuine about religion.

The brain of our Human animal became highly modified because it was necessary to have an intelligence capable of allowing us to act deliberately in this world. But the grade of awareness of which our brain by itself is capable is insufficient for anything other than navigating this material world. Only this world is "real" for it, and this is why our ordinary minds are unsuited for anything meaningful about religion. As Jesus told us in Matthew 7: 6, the animal part of ourselves can only trample the treasures intended for our spirit.

RELIGION REINTERPRETED

<u>The laws governing our everyday material being</u>

This animal side of ourselves, when it stands for "who" we are, is governed primarily by the "laws" of this material world, most of which boil down to Cause & Effect, and Accident—the laws which properly govern animal life and inert things. And in fact, these two "laws" are closely related. They are analogous respectively to the physical laws of directed (mechanical) force and of heat. Many of the effects we experience in life can be attributed to specific causes, like getting sick after being exposed to a contagious virus. Whereas the latter (heat) is the manifestation of innumerable atoms each having their own vectors of motion without any overall coordination. Accident is likewise the indeterminable result of innumerable vectors, including our not-so-free-will.

Although it's actually likely that there is some element of choice as to where and to whom one is born, once entering this world we usually begin our lives here at the mercy of almost everything. This includes large scale events like war and disasters; the many people we encounter growing up, starting with our immediate family; the culture we belong to; the religion (if any) we are raised in; and the language we speak. As a consequence, the personality which results from all of these vectors/conditions is usually only tenuously related to what is more genuinely ourselves (our Essence). And yet, we are typically brought up to take our personality to be our real selves, and we are typically slaves to the whims of the world around us and the impulses within us. If you doubt this, try setting a goal of your own, such as practicing silence for 40 days or following a dietary regime, and see what happens.

We mostly concern ourselves with appearances / possessions / popularity / and power, and we usually end our lives wondering why so much of what we've spent our lives pursuing and attaining eventually seems so empty. Only rarely do we come to a timely realization that this Flatland we seem to inhabit cannot be our true home and, by its very nature, cannot feed that which is most important to or about ourselves. Furthermore, we often come to believe that people who are of different races, from different cultures, or in a very different economic bracket are somehow intrinsically different from ourselves. In other words, we tend to believe that people who seem different from ourselves cannot be as Human as we are, and we act accordingly. Our sense of our common Sonship is corrupted into mere tribalism, a social form of schizophrenia.

To repeat, when manifesting through the personality alone, the "I AM" we each bear can only manifest as ego. Light, when shining through a filter takes on the appearance of that filter, and our personalities, when they stand in for who we believe ourselves to be, can be very dark filters— the "servant when he reigneth" that Solomon warned against. For present day Humanity, our "I AM" usually only manifests as having the goals of material resources, power, and status within one's pack or herd. But again, our animal selves and Being are not themselves intrinsically bad or wrong. It's only that they are unsuitable places of habitation for our Will. This therefore is why, when we dwell only in this level of ourselves, Nature cannot distinguish us from any other animals. We then remain subject to the laws of accident, which all too often means an accidental and meaningless death with no regard to whether we've led lives as morally decent people or not. When we live at this level of Flatland, we are living in the basement of ADAM's multi-storied home.

At this level or story, we experience our Human animal bodies as 3-dimensional.

But 3 dimensions can only be perceived in a context of 4 dimensions, just as a 1-dimensional line can only be "seen" when there is enough of a second dimension's depth to draw one—not to mention all the dimensions that make action and perception possible. And even here we fall short. Most of us are rarely in moment to moment touch with the experience of being alive in our bodies. Our memories of our physical sensations, and our habits of how to move our parts to perform various tasks of our living, have usually replaced the immediate experience of actually doing such things. For example, the few times long ago while in college that I "danced" with Mary Jane, the most immediate result for me was invariably becoming aware of how the clothes I was wearing felt against my skin. I would marvel at how I could live so unmindful of this pronounced, everyday, moment to moment experience.

This is the big reason why the first goal of many genuine religious practices are aimed at reestablishing a continuity of self-awareness of one's own physical presence. Often such practices involve repetition to the point of becoming uncomfortable, both physically and in mind—typically giving rise in the minds of novices to such questions like "What does doing this over and over again have to do with religion?". The point to all such practices is simple: if you can't be and remain concretely aware of the whole of yourself as a 3-dimensions Being, how do you expect to be aware of the whole of yourself as a 4 or 5-dimensional one?

Man #1, #2, and #3

According to the teachings I encountered in a Work group, Gurdjieff tried to point out that three kinds of Man live at the same basement level. The difference between them is perhaps best explained by the analogy of three people, each wearing goggles with a differently colored lens (like red, blue, and yellow), through which that person sees the world:

a Man #1 tends to experience everything physically and quantitatively, as substantial realities (perhaps with red lenses).

a Man #2 tends to notice and experience "sentiments", ordinary emotions (perhaps with blue lenses).

a Man #3 tends to see everything from the point of view of theory, from abstract generalizations (perhaps with yellow lenses).

Looking back: In the early seventies, I started going out with a girl whose parents were separated, even though they kept in fairly close touch. For the mother's birthday (in early October—a Libra), I gave her a dozen roses, which she accepted with a smile of genuine appreciation. Then her husband (an Aquarius) arrived, and gave her the present of a book about some philosophical subject, at which point the mother broke down crying. I don't know whether her husband ever really understood why she reacted as she did. But I saw that my girlfriend's mother was a Man #2, while her father was a dedicated Man #3 (fairly typical for an Aquarius), and that their mutual inability to communicate across that difference was a major part of the reason for their separation.

To properly understand these three types, one must understand that raw intelligence is an independent factor. While Man #1 tends to include most people invested in physical strength and accomplishments, it also includes many people who are very likely to commit white collar crime. Such people tend to be very intelligent, and yet their focus is on material values. Likewise, Man #2 can be very intelligent, yet will focus on manipulating the sentiments of others for whatever reason. As for Man #3, this includes many people who seem to be very smart, yet paradoxically seem to lack any common sense. Regardless of raw intelligence, all three types are equally stuck in the basement of themselves.

Interestingly enough, we tend to favor the language and vocabularies of our numeral. I tend to use words like "see", "know", and "perceive" to indicate my experiences; I see categories inherent in the objects around me, and I'd rather read a book than ride a bike. Some of my acquaintances rely on gut instincts and literally "sniff out" what's going on around them; they are happiest when doing something physical, both for work and recreation, and they talk about how things work. Other friends, who are emotional and quick to divine the moods of others, talk in terms of feelings and caring, likes and dislikes.

A true Man (female or male) must be and have a genuine balance between the three natures. The effort to acquire this balance leads us to the next level up: that of Natural Man. There is even a natural vocabulary of becoming more balanced. For me at least, a word that only comes to me when I am simultaneously sensing and feeling and seeing the truth of something is "realize".

The Natural Man / (Man #4)

Let me start here by first repeating that from here on, things will become progressively more theoretical. The reason for this is simple: I myself am not a realized individual. This is to say that I'm still very far from being a finished product, and therefore, I'm no Prophet, no Bodhisattva, Sheik, or Guru. I can only reasonably promise the reader to be as honest as possible, and that I will do my very best to say nothing that could do any harm by creating false expectations.

The most profoundly important thing about this next level up in ourselves, is that it's at this level in Man's total Being that the breach is to be found in Humanity. This is not necessarily the case for every other planetary species of Man. But Humanity (Man endemic to this planet Earth), has long been in trouble, and that trouble is because what belongs here is nowadays largely missing in us all, except in its most tenuous form. We all begin our lives with an intact Essence as the dominant aspect of ourselves. Yet the growth of this same Essence in most of us is soon eclipsed by our need to master this material world in which we find ourselves (as is pointed out to us in the many Biblical stories about "Two Brothers", starting with Cain and Abel). And because in modern times, we've collectively forgotten completely about both the existence and critical importance of this more interior part of ourselves (our Essence), it soon begins to starve because of the lack of the food appropriate to its needs. The typical result is the murder of Abel by Cain, or at best, the exile of Jacob by Esau (or of Joseph by his brothers), all of which is to say that this critical part of ourselves typically becomes stunted and even moribund by the time we reach our majority.

Under more normal circumstances, this Second Being in ourselves (our potential Double) would enable us to retain some significant access to our Birthright, that Birthright being a genuine connection to our True Soul, both as a secure access to our Will, and as an open doorway to our Return. This is important because only in this way can we be in any genuine and secure contact with that which is genuinely highest in ourselves, and therefore with that which is "I AM" in oneself. Our True Soul, our Ideal self as a specific individual, and our medium of contact with our *ultimate, common Ideal Self,* (ADAM), remains intact and active. But without the connection that this "ground level" self (our "above the basement" material Soul), we can't be directly aware of our higher selves except by some brief glimpse.

And yet, the substantiation and maturation of this second and "material soul" of ourselves is the only bridge that allows us to have a genuine connection to that which is higher in ourselves, and access to any genuine efforts to Return Back to God. It's the ground floor of our individual pyramids, the floor just above the basement where one can have a window which allows some natural "illumination" to enter, instead of the artificial "light" our present "civilization" has invented for us to live by in the basement of ourselves.

Looking back: While in high school, my class was shown a standard 1960s short film about drug use. Later in my third summer as a college undergraduate, I had a short summer job which required that I "council" high-schoolers on drugs, and I was given this very same film to show them. I myself had not yet had even one dance with Mary Jane. While watching this film this second time, one thing caught my attention which I had missed in high school. The film ridiculed how a person on drugs could become lost in fascination with ordinary everyday objects, such as an ashtray. Yet at that second viewing, long before I myself experimented with any mind altering drug, I came to understand that if one could genuinely see that ashtray for what it truly was, one would indeed be fascinated and captivated by what they saw. In other words, nothing about this stupendous Universe is truly trivial. I now believe this to have been the true underlying reason why experimentation with such drugs became so popular back then.

During my own later and single experience with mescaline, nothing I saw was dull or trivial. And yet the most important lesson I learned from my experiment, something which I was constantly and vividly aware of for the entire duration of that "trip", was that there was nothing there that I didn't see every ordinary day. In other words, the new vivid significance I then saw wasn't something added by the drug. The effect of the drug was only an "amplification" in some sense of my ability to perceive.

Addendum: This is in no way an endorsement of drug use. The effect of that mescaline was the equivalent of keeping the throttle of your automobile wide-open (aka flooring the gas-peddle), thereby quickly burning up whatever stores one had available of one's Noticing Being-Grade fuel. I was "lucky" because the only price I payed for that "trip" was to spend weeks thereafter in a fog of apathy. Later on, a similar after-drug experience of being a zombie prevented me from becoming permanently interested in cocaine, to which I had fairly easy access for a few months. Two experiences with cocaine's subsequent inner emptiness was more than enough of a deterrent for me. But the experience with mescaline did enable me to recognize what was happening those times that I came a bit closer to "waking-up" (without the help of any drug).

It's only rare that something is able to nudge us into waking up to the world around us, as well as to that world within us. For a brief moment when this happens, we notice things which have gone unnoticed right under our noses. We become aware of the vivid three-dimensionality of the physical world around us. Colors and sounds stand out as if we were just now seeing or hearing them for the very first time. We sometimes even become aware of what we actually mean when we say something. To give an example of such, one time after attending a marriage between Mary Jane and Juan Valdez, I had the very unusual experience, for a short while, of being able to recognize what I was automatically about to say, and judge whether it was worth saying or not. Something in me had become very much quicker than usual, and as a result, I could literally catch and judge the words as they traveled up my windpipe, and shut them off before actually speaking if I found them lacking. I've always been sorry that this experience was so transient, a half-hour at most, because it would have saved me considerable grief in my interactions with others since then.

Whatever happens to nudge us into a state of relative awareness is literally a gift from above. It's actually Grace in its most basic manifestation.

The laws which govern our Essence

The dominating Law which governs this second material body of Man is most likely Fate, which as best I understand is something like a script: a role in a largely invisible play that an individual soul has "auditioned for". And at this level, this includes Astrology. Both Fate and Astrology apply primarily to one's Essence. But to the degree that a person's Essence has become and remains stunted, neither Fate nor Astrology will have much bearing on that person's demeanor, behavior, or life course. Personality, one's socially acquired self, can almost completely override the manifestations of a person's essential inclinations. And that's what Astrology amounts to: inherent inclinations. Therefore, to digress for a moment...

An aside: the Zodiac

There are seven most basic questions we can ask: questions about Identity; about available Resources; about available Options; about Context; about Significance; about Method; and finally, about Timing. These seven basic questions correspond respectively to the seven following question words: Who; What; Which;

Where; Why; How; and When. When presented in that order (after excluding the last question about Timing), one then has the 12 signs of the Zodiac at their most basic. These 12 signs break down into six pairs of opposite signs starting with the opposing pair "Aries—Libra." When boiled down to their most fundamental, each pair of signs addresses each of the above basic questions in the sequence listed above. The first six zodiacal signs mainly concern the individual, whereas the second six address the connection and interaction between any two or more individuals.

The twelve signs of the Zodiac therefore attempt to organize how Human Beings address these six questions in both their forms, because every person must address all twelve questions in some way or another for a full life. The planets are points of emphasis within this Zodiac. For every person, the placement of those planets (along with several other factors), represents that individual's given strengths and weaknesses in dealing with those twelve questions during life. Fate enters this picture in that to become a truly realized individual, one must eventually acquire some minimal proficiency in all twelves areas of life.

Life will tend to confront every individual with those very situations which force her or him to move beyond the limits of their inherent inclinations. And here's where one's independent Will intersects: do you take the road of inertia and continue to act as you always have, along what for you is the line of least resistance, or, do you choose to confront your shortcomings and grow beyond your self-reinforced limits?

It's uncertain to me how this connection between planetary positions and the individual physically works. My own preferred picture is of a drama stage surrounded by a set of different colored lights (each light standing in for a planet) which move along separate circular tracks around that stage (Earth). This stage is surrounded by a series of 12 differently colored windows. The resulting combinations of those moving lights and the windows (filters) through which they shine would give a changing sequence of "moods" to the events which proceed in some drama on that stage.

At the point of birth (and / or of conception?), a person takes on the coloring provided by those lights, much like the iron domains in lava will align with the prevailing orientation of Earth's magnetic field at the time that the lava cools. This in turn affects how that person reacts or responds to the color combinations given to that stage from the outside lights at any later given time.

Our Time-body (our 4-Dimensional Being)

The Time-body of any sub-luminous entity is its trace through Time. If you can visualize how your entire life, at least your life so far, exists as a trace through time and space with all your changes and choices, you are glimpsing your own 4-dimensional body, and this awareness of our lives is proper to Natural Man. People with extremely vivid recall of past events are more aware of their 4-dimensional body. And because your entire life, including your "future" changes and choices are part of this line in Space&Time, it is possible to see or sense some events "before they happen" when what was perceived temporally (sequentially) is perceived spatially instead.

An aside: caves, and the process of incubation.

I first encountered the subject of caves in the writings of Carlos Castaneda. He spent extended periods of time in certain caves. Something about the inner configuration of those caves (they had been shaped intentionally), along with the surrounding mass of the mountain or ground in which they were located, supposedly enabled a person to bring his or her second body into greater focus.

Later I encountered the book by Peter Kingsley: *In The Dark Places of Wisdom*. The author spoke about the caves of Focal along the Aegean coast of present day Turkey. In the 600s B.C.E., that coast line was still part of the Greek world, and it was the home of the ancestors of Parmenides. Apparently, the caves there were important places of healing by means of incubation, and for the concentration and focusing of one's material Soul.

What all this brought to mind for myself was my first experience of a moonless night on a mountainside in Northern New Mexico. When I first went to New Mexico, I had never been anywhere near a real mountain, let alone near one at night. There was this unsettling physical sense of the immediate presence of something enormous. I felt the enormous mass of those nearby mountains as a bodily sensation.

So where is this leading? Well, there are the pyramids of Giza. They were supposedly built to be tombs for the Pharaohs. However, I've never believed this. They certainly could have eventually served in that capacity, but the notion that any people would make such an expenditure in resources and effort simply to house a dead body, never really made any sense to me. Others believe them to be astronomical instruments of some sort. That too has some merit, but only in connection with what I now believe their true purpose to have been. And Graham Hancock actually got quite close to recognizing this purpose in the video article he did where he actually entered the King's chamber.

Quite simply, I'm now certain that the Pyramids were built to be artificial mountains, constructed to contain artificial caves, that wouldn't become buried by sand. I am certain that it would have made far more sense for the Egyptians of old to spring for building those Pyramids for reasons of Healing and of Metanoia, far more so than simply to have a monstrous tomb for the dead body of a

Pharaoh. Again, burial would more likely have been an afterthought, a convenient additional function. Possibly, there was even a hope that the pyramid caves would somehow protect the souls of the pharaohs.

Reincarnation: Transference

There's an additional side to this issue about our Essence which concerns Reincarnation of a particular type (there being more than one). This type is called Transference. It concerns a specific kind of Conservation of Energy, which is similar to the Conservation of Matter. Water molecules can change form, becoming solid ice or water vapor, even becoming metabolized into other molecules in the body of a plant or animal. But the atoms persist. Energy does the same thing. It may change form, but it doesn't cease to exist. Where this has bearing on Reincarnation (Transference) is that sharp experiences, especially at the moment of death, can become energetically fixed as memories of those experiences for an extended periods of time, long after the person's mortal remains have become soil nutrients. This allows those memories to be picked up by a newly born person and reincorporated.

The person who first comes to mind in this regard is James Leininger of Louisiana who, from a very young age, was overwhelmingly possessed by the memories of a World War II Corsair pilot (James Huston Jr.) who had been shot down off Okinawa, and had been unable to exit his burning plane before drowning due to a jammed cockpit release. The fact that young Leininger's memories were genuine has been proved in a number of ways, something the reader is free to explore on their own on Google. And there are many verified examples of what is either reincarnation of a soul or acquired memories. I've had suggestions of "recycled" memories in my own life, though they were nowhere near as specific nor as pronounced as those of James Leininger's. (I had a pre-kindergarten fascination with the Pacific campaign of WWII, and with the very same F4U Corsair as he had.)

Fortunately for young James, his parents hit on a tactic which enabled the boy to establish the distance from those memories he needed for his own individuality. They took him to Okinawa, and at the very site of the 1945 crash, they bade "good-bye" to that pilot in a ceremony of acknowledgement.

The True Soul

This Cosmology has identified the "Woman" derived from the rib taken from ADAM (Genesis 2: 22), as representing the True Soul for Mankind as a whole, as well as for each and every individual. If ADAM were the alphabet of Man, then the True Soul would be an individual's name, drawn from that alphabet. For another such analogy. If ADAM were the Periodic Table of Man, then the True Soul would be the specific spiritual DNA for each individual. This spiritual individuality is the needed "helpmate" for ADAM; to continue the analogy, you cannot tell a story with just the idea of an alphabet; you need actual words. For ADAM to engage in the world in diversified ways, there had to be an individualizing agent.

Stated differently, this True Soul would now be the Holy Reconciliation between the Holy Affirmation that is ADAM and the Holy Denial that is the sub-luminous material body of Man, the "skins" put on when ADAM departed from the Garden.

The True Soul, the true source of our fate

ADAM, as the Idea of Man, is the collective whole of all logoi available as part of the Idea of Man. The same is true for the "Woman" as Man's True Soul. What this directly means for the individual person is that *one's True Soul is the Infinite matrix of all possible lives available to that individual,* as a single living, self-aware entity in its own right. In turn, one's actual life is but a trace through this matrix of possible lives, a trace of actualization from one possibility to the next.

ADAM, the overall Idea of Man, contains all of Mankind's virtual possibilities in the abstract. Our True Soul carries each individual's virtual life possibilities, because a single lifetime does not allow one to experience everything which is possible for Mankind to experience. One's actual life is a trace of actualization through that matrix of possibilities of one's True Soul. This does not mean that one's life is predetermined. One's life is infinite yet bounded, and which ones of those infinite choices are actualized depends on you. Doing something stupid that gets you killed at 12 years of age means that you no longer have any chance of becoming married and raising a family, at least for that particular lifetime.

Importantly, there are possibilities in everyone's life which support one's choice to Return to God if they are actualized. There are possibilities which retard that Return, or which can be considered neutral in this regard.

There is a particular kind of reincarnation which is not rebirth sequentially in time, it is rebirth into the same time, the same life, making it possible to make different choices within a life and change the line. This is the reincarnation of recurrence. When we begin to take responsibility for our lives, recurrence, spiritual growth, and change within and across a lifeline becomes possible. Otherwise, we cycle endlessly through mere variations on the very same life. This, by the way, was the intended point to the movie *Groundhog Day.*

HALE MICHAEL SMITH, M.D.

<u>Looking back</u>: Ever since I entered Medical school, I've been beset by this odd sense that I had finally negotiated some obstacle, and was now on a new life path I had never before taken. I've also felt that the people I've since met, people I could never have met by having taken any other life path, were in some way all people that fit in as a part of this new life path. Both feelings have continued to persist side by side in the background for me.

The dsimensions of the True Soul

The life path we take through the infinity of possibilities which define our True Soul is our 4-dimensional Time Body; our True Soul correspondingly is our 5-dimensional Body. Only at this level can *all* of the lives possible for a single individual be a single whole. In turn, everyone's True Soul is by itself much like a single "cell" in that over-all "body" that is ADAM. And because our True Soul contains all our possibilities, it is the source of innate wisdom and the self-authority which is the vehicle of genuine will power.

<u>Looking back</u>: Resorting again to my own experiences for examples, most of them have happened to me in moments of unexpected emergencies where there was no time for deliberation. There was the emergency, followed almost simultaneously by seeing the only way out. A momentary self-authority was manifest as the immediate ability to act according to what was seen and what was needful. More often than not, the failure to act accordingly would have meant that I would not now be writing this book. Several such moments involved driving at high speed on a busy highway. Curiously, several other moments occurred where I experienced being suddenly and literally stopped and physically held in place, immobilized, as if by some giant invisible hand, even before

RELIGION REINTERPRETED

I recognized that I was confronting some danger. But one specific experience of self-authority was quite undramatic.

That experience was how I stopped smoking. I started smoking late in college, and continued through Medical School and beyond, more than twenty years in all. It was a two pack a day habit, three packs a day if I was driving long distance. I even continued smoking after discovering that I had Type 3 Hyperlipidemia with cholesterol levels way beyond dangerous: reaching up to 1070 (literally, and documented by the V.A.Hospital in Martinsburg W.V. where I was working at the time). This was most likely a consequence of my Native American ancestry.

I'd wanted to stop smoking, but my efforts had always been undermined by tension and habit. Finally, a year after the diagnosis, I bought a carton of Benson & Hedges Menthols, but this time I knew I had to stop. So I tried to smoke each cigarette in that carton as mindfully as possible. I smoked the last cigarette at 9:00 PM of September 25, 1994 while I was cataloguing a number of rocks I had collected, mostly from out West, in order to give them to a local High School.

What made this attempt to stop smoking different from all of the previous ones was that, once that last cigarette was finished, I somehow quietly knew that I would never again be ensnared by that habit. There was no inner argument about this, nor any fear. I was simply and surprisingly free of any need to smoke. I had no cravings, nor did I gain any weight. Over that following decade, I did occasionally smoke several cigarettes, but never with any concern that I might once again be trapped by that habit. My last cigarette was more than ten years ago, as I write this.

I wish I could claim that this sort of quiet inner self-authority became the norm for myself. Many times it would have been so very helpful if I could have resorted to this ability at will.

Addendum: This inner self-authority did finally come into play once again in 2012, and it enabled me to lose 80 lbs I needed to lose. This was all within a couple of years, and largely without exercising (I was too busy writing this book). I simply followed Muhammad's rule of always getting up from the table before one is satisfied. And I still don't smoke.

It's important to repeat that the presence of this inner self-authority, when genuine, is quiet and is kept to oneself. There's no need for show or verbiage. Nor is such a person engaged in a struggle with her&himself, nor prey to fear or worry. That person understands that fear is merely the "belief in the power of nothingness" (an expression from the *Course of Miracles*). And the experience of encountering a person with inner self-authority (assuming one is awake to some meaningful degree), is very much like being that person oneself: nothing within you yourself is disposed to argue with him or her. Genuine self-authority is quiet.

However, a secure and permanent connection to one's True Soul is only possible when one's second body is at least in the process of crystalizing.

About Destiny

Many people have some sense of their destiny, incomplete as that sense might be. One's destiny includes the actualization of the gifts given you that define your individuality. My father, for example, knew from a very early age that he was destined to become a composer. (And it was a major problem for him when I had no such clear sense. I only knew that I needed to learn as much as possible about this world and how it worked.)

RELIGION REINTERPRETED

Beyond individual destiny, we may have a part to play in someone else's destiny, a social destiny, as it were. And as Sons of ADAM, we have the destiny of being stewards of Creation. Then there is the Great Choice, whether or not to pursue one's Return to God beyond the light boundary or whether to make the bodhisattva's choice and remain on this side of the light boundary to assist others.

As regards Reincarnation

It's very likely, and the Bible contains passages that allude to this, that individuals who've reached the option of Return yet choose to stay "where the action is" are able to be sent wherever they can be helpful in Human history. The limitations of perception and direction imposed by Time here in Flatland are like the walls of a maze which a 3-dimensional Man cannot see over. Being multi-dimensional allows one to not only see over, but to be able to pass through or pass over the walls.

The Great Chinese Classic *Journey to the West*

Knowledge of this book is unfortunately not widespread in the West. This is a great loss. It was only in 1977 that it was translated in full into English by Anthony C. Yu, Chicago University Press. Prior to that, the only available version, greatly abridged (only 30 of the original 100 chapters), had been translated by the Sinologist Arthur Whaley.

The basic story is about the pilgrimage of the Buddhist monk Hsuan-tsang (596–664 AD), who traveled from China to India to pick up Mahayana Buddhist scriptures during the Tang Dynasty. Over the following centuries, his journey became increasingly embellished with fanciful adventures, including encounters with magical creatures. Four of these creatures are assigned to help the monk; others want to eat him for the sake of the longevity his flesh and blood will impart. I will add here that no one is ever likely to read a more hysterically funny and entertaining book than this in their entire lives. But my reason for mentioning this book here is because it seems to me that the primary characters represent different levels of Man. In other words, there's more to this book than meets the eye. It too is a Sacred Construct.

The following diagram is an attempt to correlate the main characters of that book with the different levels of Man's Being.

Characters from *Journey to the West:*

(DO) UNITIVE "I AM"

—————————NEEDLE'S EYE

11) (SI) Ideal Man, the Buddha (ADAM level Man), Kuannon

10) Conscious Individual Tripitaka
_____

09) (LA) True Soul Pilgrim Sun Wu Kung ("Stone Monkey")

============ LIGHT BOUNDARY

08) Material Soul Sha-Monk (the Indigo-faced monk)

07) (SOL) Physical Self Chu Pa-chieh ("Pigsie")
Sentience, (worldly mind, the neurologic self)
_____

06) (Tritone) Human animal body, The (Dragon) Horse

And the "lower notes" are occupied by the ordinary people and by the hungry monsters, who always use illusions to deceive Tripitaka.

The "No Self" of Bernadette Roberts.

Let's return to the Image a spoked wheel, alone by itself. It represents Man, any Man, in that its outermost rim touches the ground beneath us, whereas at its very center one finds a hole, an emptiness meant for the axle. Around that hole one finds an inner rim from which radiates all of the spokes. The outer rim represents Man as a concrete entity, whereas the innermost rim represents ADAM. In effect, this entire wheel is a symbol for ourselves as existing Beings.

However, WHO we really are at our true center is that inmost Void that we experience as God. And when that entire wheel that is your total Being (self) has finally dropped away and been left behind, we discover that we too are that same emptiness at the center of everything.

I believe this to be the point which the former Carmelite Nun, Bernadette Roberts, has been trying to make. ADAM, while perfect in make-up and in proximity to God, still represents a "ME" that is other than God as "I AM". Unity between "ME" and "I AM" while grand, still implies an otherness from God which in turn, is still a manifestation of the illusion of discontinuity, a last remnant of the Biblical Dark. Instead, the "No Self" spoken of by Ms. Roberts, means "NO ME", no lingering shadow of individuality to mar the Absolute white of Biblical Light that is God as "I AM". Without the illusion of being a separate self, one can finally Return completely to the full awareness that the Prodigal Son only ever left home in seeming, in my illusions, and never in reality. We are then free to marvel over the ALL.

CHAPTER XXIII

WHAT DOES ALL THIS MEAN FOR ME?

S̲ub-luminous realities of sin and evil; revisiting the four tenets; a sad memory; a medical reality check on prejudice; free versus independent Will; etymological origins; two warning signs that a religion has "gone bad"; why we are here; why Jesus told so many parables; sorting

<u>Coming to terms with the sub-luminous reality of sin and evil</u>

For the most part, this book has made a determined effort to discount both sin and evil as being the central issues for Religion, simply because they cannot be the central issues for this Universe. It has also been emphasized that neither evil nor sin can have any genuine Reality, but instead, they can only be illusory Actualities for us, here in this Sub-luminous Flatland. This is simply because neither evil nor sin could have been created by God. Both were excluded by the Great Sacrifice.

But I have come to recognize that such a definition means little to someone whose life has been shattered by some evil done to them. As a consequence, I finally began to see that something more had to be said about both sin and evil, even though at the time of writing this Chapter, this book had already been submitted for copyright status. It was watching the news which finally forced my hand on this. So we might as well return to the beginning of everything to examine how this blight to Human existence called evil might have come to be (sin is something different). The intent is to demonstrate once again that the possibility for evil was an unavoidable consequence of the act of creation itself, and not the act of some independent wayward Will.

The Singularity that is God as "I" is the Absolute Collective Potential of all possibilities. And all "logoi" (all possibilities, options, potential, "thoughts of God") were morally neutral before the beginning.

This situation only began to change as a result of the act of Creation, that self-bifurcation that we call the separation of the Biblical Light from the Biblical Dark. Remember, the Biblical Light Itself was the True Creation, the Singularity of all that truly could *Be!* The logoi of order and continuity could now be bundled into a self-consistent whole, called a Cosmos.

But it was also here that a problem arose, because the Biblical Dark would now have to represent the antithetical logoi to those of the nascent Cosmos. Think of it this way; if you are going to create a world in which neighbors get along well, you exclude the ideas of certain actions, like stealing from each other and destroying each other's belongings. The trouble is, the closer you are to the boundary with the Biblical Dark, the more the excluded ideas "leak over" or "whisper" to us, and the more "reasonable" and justified they seem. The part of the Lord's Prayer when we ask to not be led into temptation and to be delivered from evil are prayers to keep us in the Biblical Light and apart from the Biblical Dark.

There is an odd aspect to several of the stories in *The Tales of the 1001 Nights* (aka *The Arabian Nights*): on numerous occasions someone is about to be put to death, usually by a Caliph or a Djinn, and the person bargains for their life with a story. If they tell a good enough story, their life will be spared. I suspect that there is a lesson here. Perhaps one way to engage with the Biblical Dark is to tell it stories, rather than let it have its destructive way. Perhaps that is one of the ways in which the Reconciling Force of God's Love, which ADAM also represents, is able to manifest.

Importantly, both sets of logoi (the Light and the Dark), remained equal halves of God as "I". In order to avoid becoming a Will divided in opposition to Itself, God as "I" therefore voluntarily limited Its access to Its full potential. God as "I" would now be God as "I AM". In this manner, the Biblical Dark would be reduced to an inert and passive state, even though it still remained a dangerous condition—not dangerous to God as "I", but to the Creation.

The Biblical Dark was contained by internment in Existence, but something was needed, something to play the role of the Independent Holy Reconciliation between the Holy Affirmation which was now God as "I AM", and the Holy Denial which was the Illusion of Discontinuity" (the Biblical Dark, anti-being), which could never be destroyed nor completely dispensed with.

This last necessity was the very reason for the creation of ADAM, and Man was given access to both sets of logoi (the Light and the Dark), as the necessary precondition for Man's independence of Will. One of ADAM's labors is to continuously renew God's choice and decision to hold separate the Biblical Light and the Biblical Dark—or not, as the case may be. And there you have your potential for evil: the proximity of the logoi of The Biblical dark. And there you also have your potential for sin: Man's decisions to allow the logoi of the Biblical Dark to be made manifest in Creation via our thoughts and actions.

The one limitation to Man's Will was that Man could not make those options and possibilities belonging to anti-being (the Biblical Dark) Real. They could at most become actual within sub-luminous Existence. Man was located within sub-luminous Existence by our incarnation into these Human animal bodies specially prepared for us by the Elohim (Gen. 3:21). This would be our starting place for our Return Back to God. What this means is that we are able to perceive the potential for evil (the "knowledge of good and evil") inherent in the antithetical logoi, the ones that say, "Hey, wouldn't it be a great idea to take whatever I want because I'm stronger than my neighbor?" And "Why not ignore the consequences of my actions? It doesn't matter to me if they hurt anybody else." *In short, evil is primarily the consequence of viewing other Humans and all living Beings as mere things, and treating them as such.*

In Chapter 19, as part of the explanation of "Christianity without quotation marks", four tenets were listed. All four of the tenets given for a genuine Christianity are actually the universal basis for every genuine Religion. All four are only of real worth when they are understood and practiced voluntarily; any attempt to mandate them is a sin of the first order, for that is a violation and usurpation of the activity of the True Soul in each of us. This is why forcible conversions are so wrong, whether by threat of death, or by making conversion a prerequisite for being allowed to enter heaven or live in a country.

The fourth tenet primarily refers to the method about how to get started one's Return to God when that goal becomes more than an idle wish. As for the third Tenet, violating this one is the real meaning of sin, that of making a mistake.

Understand, many sins are not "life or soul threatening." Most sins are done in ignorance, and the problem with them is that they lead you away from where you should be looking. Then again, such sins as anger to the point of hatred will usually eventually lead you to the evil of violating the 1st Tenet. Being willing to undercut others in any way is a violation of this 1st Tenet, as is elevating yourself above others (pride). Despair and *acedia* (giving up, usually translated as "sloth") mean that your faith has wrongly been placed in your own strength. Depression usually means that you were doing whatever you were for doing for the wrong reason, and are now unhappy because you didn't receive the reward you sought.

But there are also psychological needs, many of which are genuine, and many of which are not. Hence, every single religion in the world describes the need for sorting, for discriminating between what is genuine for oneself and what is unreal. (And this process may need to be undertaken more than once in most lifetimes, for needs can change.) Whether it is sorting speckled from unmarked beasts, sorting sheep from goats, sorting good thieves from bad thieves, or choosing a partner, discrimination—which does NOT mean prejudice—is an essential skill of the True Soul. Discrimination means the ability to discern who or what is right for the need at hand, based on the essential nature and the genuine need. Discrimination is, in fact, the very *opposite* of prejudice.

So just what are our real needs? Every Man needs to feel that they are significant in some manner, and when their upbringing fails to provide a basis for that, the person in question will seek out or invent a way to be significant. For example, difficult relations with their father is a very common motif among many of those American youths who gravitate towards White Nationalism and to other gangs. They invest their self-value in that which is most superficial about themselves, because it's most readily obvious: their bodies—and their color and their strength. Gangs are ultimately based on a demand for "respect."

Such a lack of self-respect is also responsible for much obesity, especially among women. While working at a clinic in North Tulsa, OK, it eventually became apparent to me that almost every markedly obese female who came to the clinic had been molested sexually by a family member. That was especially true for Caucasian females. For Black females, another reason was more influential. In their case, it includes the long cultural history in this country where Bantu facial features were not considered to be beautiful. This sense of insufficiency continues to be handed down generation after generation. Of interest, this perception conspicuously changes as these women become more significant because of their achievements in education and in public life. The reason for this is simple: these women understand that they've built themselves on a foundation of genuine self-worth, and therefore feel their own significance as a Human Being. That beauty shines through their faces, no matter what their features are. And that changes how others perceive them. Gradually, as more and more women (and men) discover their self-worth, our cultural standards of beauty become more and more inclusive.

Sad memory: I still remember a 14 year old girl I encountered during my last year of medical school, on my Obstetrics-Gynecology rotation. She was from Southeast Washington D.C., and she was pregnant.

HALE MICHAEL SMITH, M.D.

I asked her why she allowed herself to get pregnant. She told me that this way she could have someone to love. A sense of love was completely missing from her upbringing.

A sense of one's own significance is also a major part of finding a mate or companion. Lack of a sense of self worth, coupled to a lack of respect for women (which, tragically, is encouraged by nearly every fundamentalist version of religion) is why so many deficient men feel justified in injuring or even killing a woman who breaks up with them, even though the breakup is usually because the man in question has made it impossible for the woman to stay or live with him. Whereas, a healthy sense of self worth not only acts a sort of protection, it is what another person with a healthy sense of self-worth looks for in a partner.

Most of the prejudices which are used as dividing lines between "them" and "us", which perpetuate the social schizophrenia that lies at the root of most Human troubles in violation of all 4 Tenets, are based on superficial, external differences, because that is what the material mind can easily focus on. But upon death, the body of a Caucasian person rots exactly like that of an African person; the body of a rich person rots exactly like that of a poor person; the body of a Christian person rots exactly like that of a Jewish person, or a Muslim person, or a Hindu person, or a pagan person (etc.); and the body of a male person rots exactly like that of a female person. There's nothing pleasant or significant about a rotting Human animal body. We are all of us temporarily here in Flatland, and if anything in us is going to survive the inevitable separation from the flesh, it needs at least as much consideration as we lavish on our appearances.

RELIGION REINTERPRETED

I do believe that in some manner, we each choose the circumstances we are born into. Very few of us remember this because we all drink from the river Lethe before we return here. As for the circumstances of our lives, they are tailored to what we need for genuine growth. Therefore, we are born to those opportunities and obstacles that will encourage that growth, if encountered as opportunities. But there are experiences which are forced on us, not of our choosing, by people who are currently viewing other Human and living Beings as things, and treating them shamefully.

While we are here, this temporary body is all each of us has. Why would anyone ever wish to make things more difficult for someone else than they already have to be? Only someone blinded by their own pain and emptiness will see any "gain" in inflicting pain or a sense of insufficiency on someone else.

Acknowledging in your thoughts, emotions, beliefs and actions, that there is something far more important about each and every Man you encounter (regardless of gender or race) than that person's appearance is the price you must pay for that same recognition about yourself. Everyone needs to be nourished by everyone we meet in life. We genuinely owe this to each other. How you see (and judge) them, is how you will see (and judge) yourself. Although this was expressed above in the language of religion, you don't need to be formally religious to understand this. If nothing else, such honest mutual recognition alone would render it possible for us to live in peace. Without this acknowledgement, life becomes a "Me versus You" or "Us versus Them" question. From there on, it becomes a question of "How I can gain at your expense?" or, "How can I keep you from gaining at my expense?"

Our stumbling is just so sad.

"Free" versus an "Independent" Will?

This is probably a good time to explain why the expression "an Independent Will" is more widely used in this book than the more typical expression "free Will." We can begin this explanation with the etymological basis for having made this distinction between these two expressions, because they are not equivalent to each other. Quite simply, being independent does not necessarily mean being free.

a) "Independent." The central and most important syllable of this word is "-pend-", which comes from the Indo-European root "pen", meaning "to weigh." It came to English via the Latin words *pendere* (to be hanging, to be suspended), and *pondus* (a weight). The English words derived from these two are much too numerous to list here (pendulous; to ponder; appendix; suspend; compensate… etc.). Among all of these, the word "to de-pend" is presently most important to us because it literally means "to hang off of, or away from something", whatever that "something" might be. As a result, the expression "in- dependent" literally means "not to hang off of, or away from something, anything." In other words, being "independent" essentially means to "stand on your own two feet"; you no longer hang from the bough of the tree.

b) "Free." The "fr-" of this word is the Germanic cognate to the "-ber" of the Latin word *liber*, which gave English its word "liberty." Of interest here, the word *liber* was applied to the children of the well-to-do in ancient Rome. These children were usually "free" of the responsibilities typical for most such children while growing up. In other words, they were "free" from obligations, responsibilities, and restrictions, (something which both then and now is the perfect recipe for raising spoiled children).

RELIGION REINTERPRETED

Addendum: The Germanic word "free" has other connotations which are much less "irresponsible", because of its connection to words in Germanic languages which mean either 'love' or 'peace,' or both, such as in the name "Frieda." The English word "friend" is an important example. Being a friend actually means being free to be your (genuine) self with another person.

In short, the word "independent" means an absence of dependency, while the word "free" essentially means an absence of restraints or limits. In that sense, our Will as Man, as God's One Son, is not so much free as it is independent. We've already mentioned the fundamental inability of our Will to veto God about what's Real and what's not, and this is the ultimate point being made here. While our independence of Will allows us to choose for illusions to seem "real" to ourselves, we are not free to make illusion and deception Real in the eyes of God. Furthermore, our choices have consequences. Our independence of Will allows us to make this choice, but we are not free of the consequences of that choice. For example, when we choose to act towards this Earth as if we were the "liber" of ancient Rome, sooner or later, we will all pay the price for this irresponsibility, just as Rome did. Consider what global warming is costing us in loss of land to desertification and to rising oceans, or loss of homes in fires and storms aggravated by climate change.

Having been given an independent Will means we've been given the freedom to make mistakes—to "sin", in its original Biblical meaning of not aiming at the proper target and missing the mark. Freedom to make mistakes is not license to do harm. We were intended to be an asset to the well-being of everything that exists, co-creators.

The ability to make mistakes is the shadow of our ability to act independently and creatively. If God had needed machines to consistently and always "choose the right thing" that's what we'd be, and we are not. The (fractal) re-iteration of the Great Sacrifice, to choose, and live according to, and express the logoi that uphold Creation, to re-enact God's choice in our lives, is not easy when we are enmeshed in illusions, which include conflicting loyalties. There are times when any choice seems to have wrong or harmful consequences. But there are many, many teaching stories which show in some sense how listening to our True Soul, and not the urgings of our material mind, makes the best choice possible, and the best outcomes. It's meant to be a struggle, but one with intervals of joy and rest. Whether we interact with and "welcome in" the Biblical Dark, or whether we conduct ourselves as carriers of light, we are all God's One True Son, Man, and we are all here learning how to live according to our True Souls.

<u>Warning signs</u>

Religion, ALL religions, are intended to help us with this. However, since everything in the world, including religions, gets affected by separations and divisions, we have to exercise just as much care with them as we do with anything else important to us.

Here are a few warning signs that a religion is being interpreted in ways that violate the 4 Tenets previously described. (And for any Reader who seeks some really solid, clear examples of warning signs, I recommend C.S. Lewis's *The Screwtape Letters*. That man *nailed* the machinations of the material mind.)

Warning sign #1: This is the big one. Any time a religion or speaker for a religion urges, or worse, *orders* you to despise another person or group of people. This is in direct, indisputable violation of the injunctions given us by Jesus of Nazareth. There is no excuse, no mitigating circumstances, no wiggle room here. Prejudging others is, quite literally, a *diabolical* thing to do. "Dia-bo-los" means "one who throws across", and the image is of someone throwing obstacles or dangerous things not so much *at* another, but across their path so as to hinder or distract or scare them. And what is hands down the most dangerous thing that can be thrown? A malicious lie, one that is specifically intended to befuddle. Why is that? Because insofar as Creation is defined by logoi, by "the Word of God", then such lies are a "darkening" of the sub-luminous Creation.

The Greeks were quite precise in the construction of that word. The idea behind the word *diabolos* is that no matter how much diabolical harm is done in this sub-luminous realm of discontinuity, such attacks cannot be aimed directly *at* hyper-luminous realities themselves. Attacks can muddle our worldly minds, including our emotions and sensations, but not what is most real in us. Any person who retains or cultivates the ability to check in with their True Soul, to conduct a reality check from the perspective of their True Soul, develops a resistance to befuddlement.

Warning sign # 2: When the focus is more and more on appearances, more and more on rules for what you "must" do. (This substitution of dogma for living faith is nearly always accompanied by worldly benefits accruing to a small number of people.) Of course a religion will provide guidelines, because guidelines can help us develop good habits and congenial behaviors. The danger zone is when "musts" and "must nots" take the place of our independent Will, when they inhibit or actively oppose the promptings of the True Soul. Jesus made it quite clear on several occasions that rules matter less than kindness.

Why we are here

We as Man are a critical, essential part of the Return which all Creation eventually makes to God. Other than Black Holes, only Mankind, in whatever planetary forms we may occupy, has the capability of returning across the Light Boundary from this sub-luminous Realm, back to the infinity of the hyper-luminous portion of Existence. And this can only be accomplished by us by acts of Will on our part, which, paradoxically, are also acts of Love, as emphasized in the Christian and Hindu faiths, and acts of Submission, hence the name *Islam* ("Submission") for one of the world's faiths. A simple analogy which can demonstrate our part in this drama would be that of a ball dropped from a height. On hitting the ground, that ball will bounce back up, but never fully back to its original height. The final step of the Return back to the original height can only be accomplished by effort, by intentional and conscious intervention. This ever so important Cosmic task was given to Mankind to accomplish (and remember, Mankind includes far more than mere Humanity, the species of Man endemic to this single tiny planet). In so doing, we fulfill our role as the independent Holy Reconciling between the Affirmation of Reality (BEING), and the Denial of illusion (anti-being). Man (the entire Sonship), is the True One Son sent by God to redeem the cost of The Great Sacrifice.

This is how things were set up in the beginning. Man was created to do that which all of the intrinsic mechanism of Existence ("all the King's 'sub-luminous' horses and all the King's 'hyper-luminous men'") could not do, because that mechanism, encapsulated in the Elohim, cannot act by separate intention, being too close to and too continuous with God.

Yes, we are meant to Reconcile the conflict between the Light and the Dark by acknowledging the latter and choosing the former. We do so by seeking that very same Reality (the Biblical Light), aka "I AM", which is within ourselves. This kernel of Absolute Reality, for which we each must sell everything else about ourselves to possess, is the "Pearl of Great Price" which our teacher Jesus of Nazareth, and every other legitimate prophet, ever really spoke about. And this alone is what is meant by Salvation. It's the "salvation" of "I AM" from its dispersion within Existence, a dispersion within these material bodies, which was needed to make our choice for God ("I AM") meaningful.

This kernel of Absolute Reality we each bear within ourselves is WHO each of us really is: "I AM". It's precisely for this reason that every single Man, regardless of gender, race, or planetary species is the same God's True One Son. Everything else about us is merely some slight variation in the *what* that we are. As God's Son, we were each of us given an Independent Will, making it possible for each of us to do what nothing else within Existence was able to do, even though the whole of Existence is alive and self-aware in some degree.

We were intentionally inserted into these animal bodies, not as punishment, but simply because will only has meaning where there are choices to be made that have qualitatively different, definitive consequences. To be useful for "saving the world" (for Reconciling the Creation), any Angel expected to exercise an independent Will would have to be nailed down into this sub-luminous Realm where making mistakes, initially at least, is unavoidable.

But then, that's exactly what was done to us as ADAM. It's both how and why we came to be encased in flesh, literally, how&why we became "incarnated" and "incarcerated", which again is to say, "nailed" down here in this sub-luminous world. Existence itself is our "Cross." At the same time, having a meaningfully independent Will means that one can actually accomplish something, instead of having everything predetermined. But one must first learn that there are only ever two choices possible in any situation: choosing something (reality), or choosing nothing (illusion). Confusing the two was the result of "eating the forbidden fruit." We now have to re-learn how to recognize the difference.

Many believe that God will intervene in some manner and force people to behave, in the manner their own specific religion declares. But these descriptions of God's intervention are usually one of two things: either wishful thinking combined with revenge fantasies, which are the product of the worldly mind, or a metaphor for how our own inner process of metanoia transforms our inner reality. Each time one of us rediscovers and begins to live in the Kingdom of Heaven in the midst of life, it is a Second Coming on the scale of the atom of ADAM that we each are. And that's why Jesus of Nazareth told so many different parables, some of which almost seem to contradict each other, about what "the Kingdom of Heaven is like". No one story could get the message across every barrier of personality. We each get to find the parable (or parables) which is, for us, the golden key to our secret passage to the Kingdom of Heaven within. When we come across the parable we need, something in us recognizes it, with absolute clarity.

As for all those descriptions of sorting and consigning the unworthy to a place of "gnashing of teeth", which to me always sounded like a description of the Hungry Ghosts of Buddhism, that process of sorting is what happens whenever one of us dies, whether it's the death of the body or when we "die to the world".

RELIGION REINTERPRETED

During the life review, as described by people who have had near death experiences, we relive every mean, hateful, and derogatory thought and remark we've ever had or made about someone, and we'll even see how it affected their lives. Our inner reality, and the choices we've made all along, are what get sorted. Certain experiences, choices, and behaviors have no place in hyper-luminous reality because they literally belong to the Biblical Dark.

HALE MICHAEL SMITH, M.D.

Last Words

I hope that what is written here proves helpful. When I retired to focus on this work, I knew my health was such that I probably wouldn't get to reconnect with the world in any significant, active way. In that regard, you have the advantage over me.

What remains are the Appendix and a Bibliography. The Appendix is primarily intended for readers already familiar with the Enneagram symbol. It consists of my own musings, which might be of interest to some. As for the bibliography, this was never intended to be an academic book, but of course I wish to acknowledge the many, many writers who have influenced my life. If I hadn't found much that was good in the books named, I wouldn't be mentioning them.

Appendix

THE ENNEAGRAM

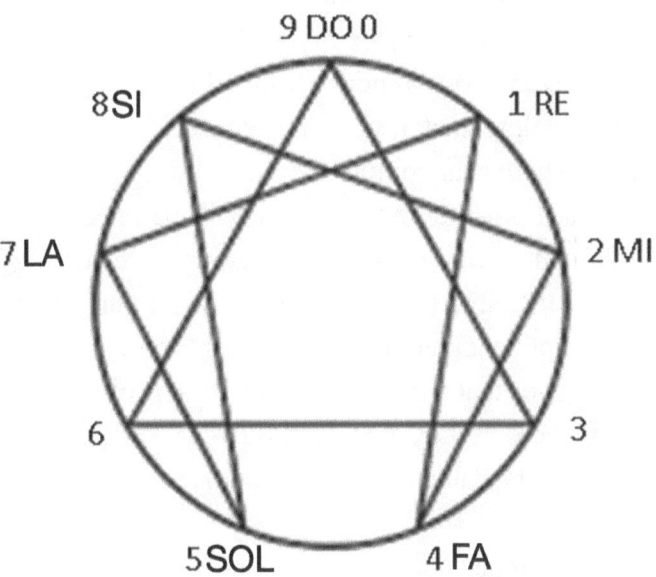

HALE MICHAEL SMITH, M.D.

THE ENNEAGRAM

This section is primarily intended for readers already familiar with this symbol, who have come to some understanding of their own. Rather than to attempt to explain its significance, what is written here is largely (though by no means entirely) the result of my personal efforts to understand certain aspects. My focus has been on how processes unfold in Time, and how to anticipate, prepare for, and deal with obstacles that arise, in the world and inwardly.

Although I do not believe that anything I've written here about the Enneagram is grossly incorrect, still, I would defer to any assessment by anyone with a more profound understanding than my own. It's a certainty that my own understanding of this symbol cannot be anywhere near complete.

In addition, I wish to add that what will be presented here has nothing to do with the so-called "Enneagram of Personality" which is popular in some circles. I can neither confirm nor deny whatever validity those applications may have, except to say that to the best of my knowledge, that particular interpretation of the Enneagram seems to have no currency among those who worked directly with Gurdjieff's pupil Madame Jeanne de Salzmann.

The Circumference

While Note RE is given the number One, this is not the true beginning of this Octave. The number One marks the emergence of the explicit from the implicit. The Note DO, which has traditionally been given the final number nine (accomplishment), must also be given the number Zero (Intent, Will).

The two Octave semi-tone gaps are given equal billing to the Notes themselves, thereby bringing the number of steps up to Nine. Notice that the second, higher semi-tone gap is placed between

SOL-LA. This is not the typical placement of the second and higher gap in a major key Octave (where it falls between DO—SI), nor does it represent its placement in most minor keys.

Octave Symmetry.

To really see the symmetry engendered by this displacement of the second semi-tone gap, we must look at the ratios which each Note represents. Note RE represented a frequency 9/8 times that of Note DO. The entire 12-Note sequence of ratios will be demonstrated here, with the five semi-tones. The central "Tri" represents the Tritone, the true geometric center of an Octave; its ratio to the fundamental Note DO being that frequency multiplied by the square root of two (1.4142135...).

```
DO—2.0————————————— 2 x 1 = 2
SI—15/8———————————— 15/8 x 16/15 = 2
si/la—16/9————————— the new SI 16/9 x 9/8 = 2
LA— 5/3———————————— 5/3 x 6/5 = 2
la/sol—8/5————————— the new LA 8/5 x 5/4 = 2
SOL— 3/2——————————— 3/2 x 4/3 = 2
Tritone— (1.4142135...). square root of 2, squared = 2
FA— 4/3———————————— 4/3 x 3/2 = 2
MI— 5/4———————————— 5/4 x 8/5 = 2
mi/re—6/5—————————— 6/5 x 5/3 = 2
RE—9/8————————————— 9/8 x 16/9 = 2
re/do—16/15———————— 16/15 x 15/8 = 2
DO—1.0————————————— 1 x 2 = 2
```

Note: This discussion of symmetry is not something especially critical to remember. It was presented here simply as a result of mathematical exploration.

The Middle Figure.

This internal figure represents the eternal sequence of anticipation. For example, if when taking a trip, Note RE represents your starting place, and Note MI will represent the preparations one must make. Note FA represents the actual effort that must be made to travel, but first one must look forward to how one will travel, in order to know how to prepare. Another example might be cooking a meal, where one must look forward to what the meal is to actually be, in order to know what utensils and ingredients will be needed.

The Inmost Triangle

This figure represents how Will enters this picture. Will enters at Note DO, as the Intent of the Octave. This means that Note DO is both the theme of a given process as well as the goal of its actualization. As the theme, as the intended purpose, Note DO is number Zero. As the actualized goal, Note DO is numbered as Nine.

As for the two semi-tone gaps, they represent two places of Crisis; the two places where something from outside of a particular process must enter and intervene, if that process is to continue to completion, something which will be obvious in the following examples. Because of this, nothing within Existence can be completely autonomous. Something substantive invariably enters, and everything that exists interacts with everything else that exists. This is also where Hazard enters every process. Here is where Chance participates as part of Existence.

Temptation

But where Will (read: Man) is involved, Hazard takes another name: Temptation. In other words, when Man is an intrinsic part of a particular process, these semi-tone gaps represent those places where a Human commitment must enter, or the process will go off the rails. For Man, the lower MI-FA represents the initial commitment to the necessary effort, to the necessary doing. If one is taking a trip, here is where the vehicle enters. And yet, one must actually enter that vehicle and actually begin to travel. If two people have encountered each other, and one wishes to become better acquainted, sooner or later he or she must stop dithering and take their best chance, or nothing will happen. This "gap" is therefore much like a drawbridge standing between the necessary preliminary preparation and the actual doing. This drawbridge must be lowered if the overall process is to continue.

And for the subsequent SOL—LA gap, this represents the need for a course correction if one is to actualize the original intention. In many cases, this represents the additional mile that must be walked. If the first "gap" is a drawbridge, then this one is like a switching yard, where each road or track represents a different final destination. For example, a seed which falls to the ground may germinate, or it may be eaten, or, it may rot because the ground was too soggy. Both these intervals are places of "temptation"—to not bother, or to settle for something other than the original intention.

Will, temptation, and metanoia

Let me say a word here about Will, temptations, metanoia. Yes, there are times when the only thing that will see you through is pure Will, "nothing in you except the Will which says…, 'Hold on.'" But these occasions are ordinarily quite rare, when *nothing else will serve*. But just as you shouldn't drive your car with the emergency brake on, we are meant to get through most of our lives by using the ordinary brake to slow down and stop where appropriate, and our ordinary brake corresponds to a combination of common sense, intelligence, awareness, skills and intuition, which see us through (or safely past) most situations and distractions.

When we live in Flatland, temptations seem to have all the reality on their side. They are appealing, or persuasive: they oh so reasonably seem to be (almost) the right thing to do; or they seem irresistible, or unavoidable. Resisting temptations in the dimensions of Flatland is like trying to walk against strong incoming waves on a shore. You can build up some solid muscles that way, but do it too long and it's exhausting, while you run an increasing risk of getting injured or swept out to sea. And here is where metanoia can enter the picture, because the kind of knowing that is possible for the Double, for the part of us which is our True Soul, sees Flatland with depth perception, from additional dimensions. Even a very small shift into the vertical can entirely change the way we experience the temptations of Flatland. All at once they lose their persuasiveness, their claim to being the only reality that matters. Seeing with the eyes of the Double, many temptations simply disappear. (You can even see this in small children who still live from their essence; they don't even notice certain things that seem terribly significant to most adults.) To return to the analogy of walking along the ocean, practicing metanoia is like bringing into play the iliopsoas muscles to lift the leg up, while also allowing the quadriceps femoris to relax so the leg can hinge at the knee. Suddenly, instead of struggling to resist the shove and pull of the waters, your leg is moving through the air above the water, and you can insert it through the waters to anchor your foot.

Regarding the individual Notes

From the time of my initial encounter with this symbol in perhaps 1970, I had no guidelines for arranging a process according to the Enneagram that did not seem arbitrary; neither had I yet seen

RELIGION REINTERPRETED

any such example that was convincing. Let's face it, one can divide up any process into any arbitrary number of steps. But I felt that there had to be some non-arbitrary sequence for arranging any process according to Octaves that was consistent, and which also made obvious sense, which would allow someone to see how the pattern of any one process paralleled that of any other, seemingly different process.

Eventually, I settled on the need to understand just what each individual Note might actually mean, as being my only chance to understand any importance this symbol might genuinely have. This finally (and surprisingly) happened for me in the summer of 1988, just as I was preparing to take a trip from Tulsa Oklahoma (where I was working at the time), to New Mexico. For some reason, while in the kitchen talking to my wife, it suddenly came into focus. Out of nowhere, I suddenly saw how the process of taking a trip naturally fell along the Enneagram in a non-arbitrary way. I also saw how this same process mirrored the sequential listing of the Astrological planets. This "Taking a Trip" has since been my prototype for all other Enneagram arrangements, and will therefore the first of my examples.

4) The meanings of the individual Notes.

0) DO: THE INTENT................................. SUN
1) RE: THE STARTING POINT..................... MOON
2) MI: PREPARATION (PLANNING / COST ASSESSMENT)
.... MERCURY
3) gap A: CRISIS A ("THE DRAWBRIDGE") .... VENUS
4) FA: ENGAGEMENT (STRUGGLE / EFFORT) MARS
5) SOL: APPROXIMATION......................... JUPITER

6) gap B: CRISIS B ("SWITCHING YARD") ..... SATURN
7) LA: THE REFINEMENT.......................... (Uranus?)
8) SI: THE ARRIVAL .... (Neptune?)
9) DO: THE ACTUALIZATION (CLOSURE / RENEWAL)

<u>A very important reminder before proceeding</u>: I have intentionally listed the planets along the side of each of the nine Notes of the Enneagram. They are generally intended to be understood according to their Astrological meanings. I do this knowing full well that in the eyes of many, this will automatically compromise any validity this work might ever have for that reader. Indeed, I've already encountered this problem.

But Astrology per se is not the point on trial here. Astrology, genuine or not, was but one system used to codify and convey knowledge, knowledge which was not so simplistic as what it has been reduced to for mass consumption. Equating the Astrology of the Ancients to what passes for astrology today in newspapers is as ludicrous as equating a banquet to a frozen burrito. For our ancestors, these systems were important templates for organizing the meanings they discovered in this world. Now to explain the Notes.

<u>DO—The Intent (as both a Theme and a Goal). {Sun}</u>
This is the basic Idea/notion of the process, as well as its purpose. In other words, this is the *name* of this process as both its theme and its goal. It is given the number Zero because even though it is the Source of the process, it is still only implicit because nothing is yet manifest or actualized. In short, Non-objective Will is the true Source of everything, whether directly or indirectly.

> Musically, Note DO (Dominus) is the Fundamental (the root) of the Octave.

RELIGION REINTERPRETED

> Astrologically (and Astronomically), the Sun is the Fundamental of this Solar system (as it is in Natal Charts).

> Note DO is metaphorically the white light which contains all of the diffracted colors.

RE—The Starting Point or Place

This represents that point of onset, that point where the recognition emerges that something is to start. It's an "illumination" of sorts, because this initial recognition is only the explicit realization of the inner light of intention. A starting point only becomes such when one realizes that one has somewhere to go from where one is. This is that knife edge where something has just begun to manifest, has just begun to become explicit.

> The Moon of course reflects the light of the Sun.

MI—Planning, Preparation, and Cost assessment {Mercury}.

Before setting out, one must plan for the intended undertaking, and make arrangements. One must also estimate what the potential costs might be. The stage must be properly accomplished for the effort to come.

> Here, Mercury stands in for Prometheus (forethought).

Gap A "Crisis A"— MI—FA {Venus}

This first crisis is the "Drawbridge." Something (very often something concrete), must enter here to bridge the gap between recognizing and preparing for what must be done, and actually doing it. One will either engage or not. In the three Biblical stories which speak about the inner transition from the "old mind & self" to the "New Mind & Self", and therefore from an "Older world" to a "New World", this gap is uniformly represented by crossing a body of water: respectively, the Flood; the Red Sea; and the river Jordan.

This gap also represents a need for a commitment to follow through, with the attending hazard being the temptation to avoid that commitment. It also represents a discrepancy between Will or desire and resources. You may wish to undertake a journey, but lack the means to do so. This crisis can only be resolved with outside help, hence Venus, which has to do with relationships of all kinds. Metaphorically, whoever (or whatever) helps you actually start on your way helps create the event.

— The Commitment: To actually commit oneself to the necessary effort / struggle.

— The Temptation: To avoid such.

— The Intervention: Whatever makes the effort possible. Usually, some form of love or shared goal is involved. In other words, it is not merely accidental.

> The Old World (Eurasian) Venus represents the drawbridge which connects the calculation of Mercury to the effort of Mars.

> In Greek mythology, this represents the point where a god intervenes to assist. For example, Hera decides to help Jason obtain the Golden Fleece because he demonstrates certain virtues. Athena and Hermes appear and advise Perseus how to begin his quest to rescue his mother. He ends up accomplishing a great deal more, but that is his goal, and he is completely stymied until the two gods show up and help him actually get started.

FA— Engagement: Effort, Struggle {Mars}

This is where the difficult but basic effort to actualize the process begins. It entails both the release and the use of energy in some sense, hence the need to calculate the cost beforehand. One is approaching the Tritone (between FA and SOL), and therefore one

RELIGION REINTERPRETED

is metaphorically and literally climbing uphill. In the above mentioned Biblical stories, this is where one has finally entered the "wilderness", be that the flood waters, or the mountain of Sinai, or the Wilderness of Temptation for Jesus. Here is also where the New Mind & Self must be nourished by a "New Food" (New Meaning). Looking back or turning back to the Old ways means that one risks being reduced to a pillar of salt.

The effort needed is rarely "heroic" or glamorous. It is most often dry, tedious, and ongoing; and either lonely or, when other people are involved, argumentative (Mars).

Note: The true meaning of Mars has always been that of struggle and effort, and not war. Equating it primarily to war was a later development as Humanity continued to decline in understanding. It is likewise with the Arabic word "Jihad" which is not very popular in the West nowadays. Muhammad, like Jesus and the many others who came before him, recognized that "salvation" (the recovery of inner peace and connection to God), required more than merely ingesting inspiring platitudes. This is because the effort to Return to God is literally an uphill climb out of the illusion and inertia of this everyday (sub-luminous) labyrinthian Flatland, where "God's Will" can never really be known, let alone actually done.

TRITONE

This is where nothing feels right, where something critical goes wrong, or where the whole project suddenly seems doomed to failure. It is the exact opposite of the Origin and Source DO (Zero), the nadir.

> It is a curious and eery coincidence that in our Solar System, an asteroid belt should be found at this place between Mars (Note FA), and Jupiter (Note SOL), the place of the Tritone in an Octave

and in our Enneagram. The asteroid belt is the region of maximum disorder, chaos, and danger to any traveler.

SOL—The Approximation = The Promised Land {Jupiter}

This stage represents the "Promised Land", where the results of the initial efforts in the previous stage pay off. However, this can really be only a temporary place of rest. Here one finds the rest, replenishment, reinforcement, and the reassessment so necessary for reaching the original goal of the process.

> Musically, this is the major fifth, the "Dominant" Note in an Octave. This Note is second only to the Octave Note DO in harmonious resonance to the Fundamental.

> Both Astrologically and Astronomically, this Note SOL is Jupiter, the Sun's gravitational second in command in our Solar System.

> In the second movie of the original *Star Wars* trilogy, this is where the travelers reach the haven of Cloud City.

The danger of reaching any Promised Land, even when there is not a risk of external betrayal, is the risk of internal betrayal, of mistaking this place of comfort for the actual goal. Perseus might have been tempted to stay in his new kingdom with Andromache and "forget about" rescuing his mother. That would have been a betrayal on multiple levels. Athena and Hermes had more in mind for Perseus than just helping him with his original goal. Hence:

Gap B— Crisis B—The SOL—LA gap {Saturn}

This is the second Crisis, the "Intersection" in the sense of "Which road do I take?" (The switching yard for you railroad enthusiasts.) The Approximation reached in the previous stage is rarely sufficient by itself, but it can seem that way. This gap represents the need for a course correction, one that sometimes entails starting over in some sense, or recommitting… hence the need to walk the extra mile. The obvious temptation being either to settle for the approximation, or to get side-tracked to another end-point (resort to another goal).

This point is one of crisis because something else must intervene which is consistent with the original goal. One has to remember the original goal and purpose, and more often than not there needs to be a shared sense of resolve. If one is lacking outside help, or in bad company, this is usually a place of subtle failure, of settling for a different objective.

> Saturn was represented by the Roman god Janus, the guardian of the doorway which could open onto either war or peace, degeneration into chaos or renewal of possibilities. In many ways, Saturn is Jupiter's opposite. From the perspective of modern storytelling, Jupiter is the god of heroes and patriarchal order, who overthrew the old order of the Titans, including his father, Saturn. However, it is well to remember just what Jupiter overthrew. Not only was Saturn the ruler of the Golden Age, the Titans were balanced when it came to the powers and domains of the masculine and feminine. So navigating the Crisis that Saturn represents can lead to a restoration in oneself of the energies of creation, of one's inner masculine and feminine. It also tends to signify some coming to terms with one's parentage.

> Failure at this point may involve some sort of failure or betrayal of something parental, whether one experiences this as the child or a parent.

> In the second *Star Wars* trilogy, Anakin betrays his children, his mother's hopes for him, and the potential his spiritual father Obi Wan tried to cultivate in him, when he aligns with his "stepfather" Palpatine. Parental issues all over the place.

LA—REFINEMENT {Uranus?}

One makes a commitment to return to the beginning in some sense. This means that this process becomes a spiral. Such a spiral may be intrinsically open ended, like the process of learning, or it may be an intrinsically limited one, as when polishing up something which was constructed or written.

> In Astrology, Uranus represents this beginning of something new on a non-trivial level.

SI—THE ARRIVAL {Neptune?}

This last stage is an echo of Note RE in its knife-edge subtlety. Whereas the starting point represents that infinitesimal point where the implicit becomes explicit, where an implicit intention becomes an explicit recognition, this point is the subtle moment of transition where the process in progress finally goes from doing to being done; from becoming to being.

> In Astrology, Neptune represents subtle shifts / changes / transformations.

DO—ACTUALIZATION / CLOSURE

The original Intent has been actualized.

> Astrologically, I wonder if this corresponds to the solar system as a whole. Something had become integrated.

The Middle Figure

Having examined the circumference of the Enneagram, we now inspect the intervening figure between the circumference and the inmost Triangle: the sequence in Notes is: RE—FA—MI—SI—SOL—LA—RE. The same sequence expressed numerically is: 1—4—2—8—5—7—1. This number sequence is the reciprocal of the number seven, the unending decimal fraction when any natural number (which is not an even multiple of seven) is divided by seven.

RE—FA—MI: (1—> 4—> 2)

From one's Starting Point, one must look forward to the Engagement so one can know how to Prepare. If I am to take a trip, it makes all the difference in the world to my plans if I will travel to a city or the open country, to a hot place or a cold place. How I plan depends on where I intend to go. Sequentially in time, the planning happens first, but the planning can only happen if I look ahead in time to both the actual setting forth AND the ultimate goal. Notice that SI connects to RE.

FA—MI—SI: (4—> 2—> 8)

Preparation is the means by which I reconcile my actual Effort with the Actualization of my goal. To merely work and struggle without some notion of how my effort is related to my ultimate goal is to waste my effort in ignorance. If I am driving somewhere, I must know beforehand which roads to take, otherwise I'm only asking to lose my way.

MI—SI—SOL: (2—> 8—> 5)

Arriving (Actualization) is the Goal of my Preparation. However, those initial efforts will most often only bring me to the general vicinity of my goal. I usually need to take new bearings after reaching the general vicinity (the Approximation) of my ultimate goal.

<u>SI—SOL—LA: (8—> 5—> 7)</u>

The Actual must be realigned with the Ideal, if that Ideal is to become Actual. The Approximation is a temporary place of rest. Having taken new bearings, I must start anew to reach my true Goal.

<u>SOL—LA—RE: (5—> 7—> 1)</u>

From my Approximation, I take my bearings and go the extra mile to reach my original destination, my real goal. Afterwards, I can start in a new undertaking. LA is not a resting place; it has a "Let's do something!" quality to it.

<u>LA—RE—FA: (7—> 1—> 4)</u>

I once again find myself Engaged.

EXAMPLES

1) <u>GOING SOMEWHERE (Taking a Trip)</u>
0) DO: Going Somewhere specific, both as a Theme and as a Goal
1) RE: The place where you start
2) MI: Planning the Trip
3) gap A: whether or not there are the means of travel (the vehicle, money, maps, and whatever else)
4) FA: Getting on or into the vehicle and actually traveling
5) SOL: Arriving in the general vicinity (the city, airport, train station)
6) gap B: Getting new bearings
7) LA: Your scale changes. You change from an Interstate map to a local one. Finding the street, you must look for the house number, etc. (You may also need to reorient inwardly. Why are you here? What are you here for?)
8) SI: You may encounter an unexpected obstacle before arriving at your destination
9) DO: A Trip has been accomplished.
Having arrived, this is your new starting place.

2) NOURISHING THE BODY

0) DO: Providing food to the cells of one's body, both as a Theme and as a Goal.
1) RE: Hunger; food is available.
2) MI: Food is purchased, prepared, ingested, chewed and swallowed.
3) gap A: Acid and digestive enzymes come in contact with the food.
4) FA: Food is broken down into molecules by the acid, by the enzymes, and by the muscular churning of the stomach and intestines.
5) SOL: Food is absorbed into the splanchnic veins. Food is not yet ready for general circulation.
6) gap B: Delivery to the liver. The food is subsequently "edited" by the liver, which removes ammonia and other toxins, and monitors sugar levels, turning excess into animal starch.
7) LA: Carbohydrates, fats, and proteins are released to the general blood stream.
8) SI: Food spreads to all of the body's cells
9) DO: The Body has been nourished.

3) SOLVING A PROBLEM / ANSWERING A QUESTION

0) DO: Solving a Problem (Answering a Question), both as a Theme and as a Goal.
1) RE: A problem (question) presents itself.
2) MI: The problem (question) is defined (formulated).
3) gap A: The problem (question) is deemed worthy of solving / consideration, or it is set aside.
 Compulsion or curiosity provides the necessary commitment.
4) FA: The problem (question) is studied / researched.
5) SOL: A solution (answer) is formulated.
6) gap B The solution (answer) is rebutted, or a false one is deemed acceptable. The Temptation: to abandon the effort, or to settle for an incorrect solution (answer).
7) LA: The solution (answer) is tested, refined / corrected.
8) SI: The solution (answer) is finalized and presented.
9) DO: A Problem (Question) has been Solved (Answered).
Every solution reveals a new problem, and every answer a new question.

4) <u>BUILDING A SCALE MODEL (actually, building any structure)</u>

0) DO: Building a scale model (structure) of something, both as a Theme and as a Goal.
1) RE: deciding on a specific scale model (structure) project, for whatever reason.
2) MI: Making preparations. Drawing up plans for a structure, or preparing a work space, figuring out strategies for construction, purchasing a kit.
3) gap A: The commitment to proceed with the actual building.
4) FA: Construction is underway.
5) SOL: The basic construction has been completed.
6) gap B: To review the rough copy in terms of what still needs to be done. The Temptation: to be satisfied with the rough work.
7) LA: Attending to details to be in genuine compliance with the original purpose / best standards. Sanding, polishing, painting, decals, etc.
8) SI: Presentation to the public. Adding the display format.
9) DO: A finished scale model (structure).

The structure is put to use; a new project is begun.

5) GROWTH OF A NEW PLANT.

0) DO: Bringing forth a new Plant, as a Theme and as a Goal
1) RE: A mature Plant.
2) MI: A Plant in bloom (reproductive readiness)
3) gap A: Pollination, whether by wind, insects, birds, etc.
4) FA: Embryonic development within the seed.
5) SOL: Completion of the seed, and ripening of any encompassing fruit.
6) gap B: Release from the mother plant, and subsequent dispersion by whatever means. The nature of the switching yard is most obvious here, because of the many possible fates of the newly dispersed seed.
7) LA: Germination: breaking through the seed capsule and sinking a root.
8) SI: Independence: putting forth a shoot. (The plant can now make its own food.)
9) DO: A new plant.

6) A NEW HUMAN BODY—OR ANY ANIMAL

0) DO: Having a Child, both as a Theme and as a Goal

1) RE: Physically mature female and male

2) MI: The female is physically receptive (ovulation has occurred).

3) gap A: Sperm becomes available to the egg via copulation or by dispersion.

4) FA: Fertilization and Implantation. First and second Trimesters. Larval (Embryonic) development and elaboration of basic organ systems.

5) SOL: The third Trimester. Maturation of embryo approximating completion; if there were a premature delivery, the infant has a chance to survive. In mammals, this is attended by changes in the female physiognomy in preparation for birth.

6) gap B: Coming to term. The exact time is ideally a decision made by the newly incarnated Soul; but there can be interference or accidents, such as adults who want to hurry or delay a birth for any of a number of reasons.

7) LA: Birth process.

8) SI: Independence: the first breath is drawn, and a new life is started.

9) DO: A child, human or otherwise, begins its life

7) GROWING UP

0) DO: The psychological maturation of a Human Being, both as a Theme and as a Goal
1) RE: Birth of a human Infant.
2) MI: Infancy. Gaining autonomous control over the body.
3) gap A: Impact of the world beyond biology (first family, then peers and schooling).
4) FA: Childhood. Development of the personality, the social "mask" (per-sona).
5) SOL: Coming of age, physically, psychologically, and socially. (These almost never coincide in Time.)
6) gap B: The presence or absence of Responsibility. The potential birth of Character and true Individuality. The Temptation: to avoid being responsible, whether by allowing others to make all the decisions, or by resorting to "rules" that obviate any exercise of responsibility.
7) LA: Young Adulthood. Learning to handle responsibility.
8) SI: Awakening: the moment the person fully realizes that he or she must pull his or her own weight, and accept the consequences of his or her own actions.
9) DO: A mature adult Human Being.

The continual learning that a mature adult goes through for the rest of his&her life.

8) HELPING SOMEONE.

0) DO: Helping someone, both as a Theme and as a Goal.
1) RE: Seeing that someone needs help.
2) MI: Cost appraisal. One not only calculates the cost of what help is needed, but also the cost to oneself.
3) gap A: Urgency (seeing the consequences of a failure to help). The Temptation: to avoid putting one's own self at risk (this may or may not be justifiable).
4) FA: Struggle. The effort to stabilize the situation.
5) SOL: Stabilization. Not the final solution, but a reprieve or place to catch one's breath.
6) gap B: Relinquishment. It is critical that the initiative at least begins to be returned at this point to the person being helped.

The Temptation: to encourage dependency by retaining the initiative.

7) LA: Reworking the situation. One continues to help, but the person being helping should now shoulder most of the responsibility.
8) SI: The problem is solved, or at least, the person is now able to do what is needed for himself.
9) DO: A Person has been helped.

9) A TRUE MARRIAGE (Not intended as a statement on religious, social, or political law)

0) DO: A true Marriage (the establishment and recognition that both share a common Will), in other words, the effort to practice love, as both a Theme and as a Goal.
1) RE: recognizing that Marriage is a valid and worthwhile possibility.
2) MI: <u>Courtship</u>: The attempt to become better acquainted both with each other, but also the attempt of each partner to become better acquainted with themselves, as much as possible.

The need to be sure that each genuinely wishes to commit to this other person, and the Marriage.

3) gap A: The Wedding Ceremony. The word "to wed" originally meant "to promise." This promise is properly made to both God and to Mankind (which has a tremendous stake in a successful marriage), as well as to each other. The inner commitment: to spare no effort in learning how to genuinely love each other.
4) FA: Cohabitating. Finding one's role in this partnership. Children usually enter here.
5) SOL: Accommodation: A status quo has been established.

Both adults have their roles and manage to live together in some sort of equilibrium. Children are growing up.

6) gap B: The Reencounter: Facing oneself and each other anew after years of cohabitation.

The Temptation: To look elsewhere for Love.

> Here's where many marriages break up or die without either partner understanding why: mere accommodation in mar-

riage is ultimately a dead end, because it is no substitute for genuine intimacy and unity in Will.
7) LA: Recommitment and reconnection, to each other and to Marriage, and to what is possible together
8) SI: Finding unity beyond differences, even while retaining those differences
9) DO: A true Marriage.

12) THE BEATITUDES (Matthew 5:3—12)

0) DO: The Path of Blessing for those who wish to Return to God in this lifetime, both as a Theme and as a Goal.

1) RE: <u>Blessed are the Poor in Spirit, for theirs is the Kingdom of Heaven.</u>

The Poor in Spirit are those who have come to see themselves as they really are, and not as they wish to be seen either by themselves or by others. In other words, they have begun to understand that appearances don't add up to reality.

2) MI: <u>Blessed are those who Mourn, for they shall be Comforted.</u>

As the Buddha said, "Existence is suffering." "Ex-stasis" is the illusion of "standing out" or apart from everything else. The price for this illusion of distinction and individuality is the sense of inner isolation we suffer from, and the need to find some sense of completion beyond ourselves. It's this very sense of loss and absence which prepares the ground for a sustained effort of Atonement with ourselves, with Mankind, with the entire Creation, and ultimately, with our true Source, God as "I AM". As long as we believe we can fill this inner isolation with the illusory affairs of this external sub-luminous world, there is no impetus for us to reject those illusions, or seek that "Pearl of Great Price" within.

3) gap A: <u>Blessed are they of fine spirit, for they shall inherit the Earth</u>

The Greek word usually translated as "meek" is πραΰς, *praus*, which does not mean "meek" at all. On the contrary, it referred to horses who were too spirited yet responsive to be used as mere work-horses. We as Humans cannot fulfill our responsibilities towards Creation and God as mere plodders.

> Most breakthroughs and real advances are made by approximately 5% of the human population. These are the people of fine spirit. Even living ordinary lives, they are the ones who are immune to herd mentality. In terms of the individual, "praus" is that in us which is capable of choosing metanoia over both the stale old mental ploddings and the excitement of revolt.

4) FA: <u>Blessed are those who Hunger and Thirst for Righteousness, for they shall be Satisfied.</u>

Having crossed from our old world into a new one (by changing how we see things), we find our self in a Wilderness. The "food" (aka meaning) that fed us before no longer nourishes us. New "food" (meaning) is provided, and yet, because we are unaccustomed to it, it has yet to seem satisfying. So we go hungry while old self within, which seemed to thrive on the older "food" (meaning), is being starved to death. If we return to our old habits, we are like Lot's wife, who wants her former home and turns to a pillar of salt. Our hope lies in continuing to persevere in spite of our seeming hunger. The temporary repose of the "Promised Land" awaits, the Oasis where "milk and honey" will make up for what seemed to be a long lack in nourishment.

5) SOL: <u>Blessed are the Merciful, for they shall be given Mercy.</u>

Here we find rest and nourishment. However, there's a price to pay, which is to accept that all who search to reach this place are also deserving of all it provides. This is true because of that which we each bear within ourselves as WHO we really are: "I AM".

6) gap B: <u>Blessed are the Pure of Heart, for they shall see God.</u>

The people of fine spirit make the world a better place, usually in visionary yet practical ways. The pure of heart make the world a better place in ways that are closer to mystical. Internally, being pure of heart means that what used to be difficult has become simple. It's the difference between having to walk miles to a well for water and having a spring of fresh water by your home.

7) LA: <u>Blessed are the Peacemakers, for they shall be called the Sons of God.</u>

The peacemakers are the whole package: they possess the combined virtues of *praus*, mercy, and purity of heart, and they give rise to these same virtues in others.

However, since most of us are not the result of a "virgin birth" as defined previously, it is nearly impossible for any of us to eradicate every vestige of "the sins of the fathers" that "infect" us. Consequently, even peacemakers typically have their flaws, sometimes quite pronounced. This does not invalidate their work. Refer back to "Blessed are the Merciful...."

8) SI: <u>Blessed are those who are persecuted for the sake of righteousness, for theirs is the Kingdom of Heaven</u>

I confess to having a problem with this one. It sounds too much like the "repentance" substitution for metanoia, but I haven't found the etymological solution for this one. Following as it does the mistranslation of *praus*, I am more than a little suspicious. I doubt that Jesus of Nazareth was urging his listeners to become martyrs, especially in the light of his own efforts to avoid being brought to the attention of the Romans. Recall how he repeatedly told those whom he healed to not talk about him, and on more than one occasion he relocated when there was too much "buzz" about what he was doing. But there was too much expectation for a worldly messiah for people to hold their peace. The stage was set for a Mystery

Play which, unfortunately, resembled Aesop's fable about a goose who laid golden eggs.

But doubt aside, there is a danger inherent in becoming unworldly. Flatland will eventually figure out that you no longer belong to it, and it will treat you like your body treats a foreign object or foreign tissue within its midst.

9) DO: <u>Blessed are you when men revile you and utter all kinds of evil falsely on my account.</u>

<u>Rejoice and be glad, for your reward is great in Heaven, for so men persecuted the Prophets who were before you.</u>

> It was from J.G. Bennett that I first learned that the Beatitudes of Matthew could be arranged as an Enneagram. Especially important to me was to have pointed out the inner "Triangle of Will". Eventually, this enabled me to finally understand what was so different about this last Blessing, compared to the one preceding it. Whereas there was one obligation to God and another to Existence, this final obligation is actually about how we are to be towards each other.

The idea here is that keeping a genuine smile on your face while cultivating inner quietude will actually accomplish far more than martyrdom.

This Sermon is done.

13) Enneagram Related Events in the Bible

Noah's Flood:
Noah was instructed to build an ark and collect therein the animals (MI). Importantly, certain legitimate aspects of our ordinary, worldly mind must be preserved, even those represented by the "unclean animals" which were also saved, just in smaller ratios. In this story, the Flood is the Wilderness which must be endured (FA). And the forty days it took to do so refers to the time it took for the older mind and its thoughts, emotional reactions, and values (the people lost to the flood) to die off.

The Exodus:
In this story, Egypt takes the fall by representing Flatland, specifically, Flatland that has been debased by human error. This is, after all, where the descendants of Joseph, the very man whose counsel saved Egyptians from famine, wound up enslaved by the descendants of the people their forefather saved. Here, Egypt represents what results when Humanity "gets the letters wrong".

Having gathered everything and everyone together, the Hebrews headed East, which means that they headed towards the Source of Inspiration and Knowledge (MI). The way was cleared for them to cross the Red Sea, during which time they were saved from being destroyed by the Pharaoh's Charioteers (MI—FA). They then entered the Wilderness for forty years (FA), until the generation who keep "looking back" towards their old life in Egypt die off. Then Joshua can lead rest into the "Promised Land" (SOL).

Note: The name Joshua is the same name that is later translated as Jesus.

There's something in this story that wasn't emphasized in the story of the Flood: the question of "food." The Hebrews were instructed to eat only "manna", a word which in Hebrew is essentially a question meaning "what the **** is this?" (fill in your own four-letter word)" The Hebrews did not initially even recognize "manna" as being food. This anticipates the parable of not putting new wine in old bottles. The adult Hebrews adhered to their old thoughts, emotions and views, which derived from their experiences as slaves in Egypt. But these mindsets were incompatible with the metanoia. A New Man with a New Mind must be nourished with new food, if that new Man is to enter and function in the new Promised Land.

Jesus in the Wilderness

All of the learning that engaged Jesus as a child and young man was the preparation (MI). Jesus was then baptized in the Jordan river, during which the Heavens open up for him and the dove descends (MI—FA). So why, after the descent of the Spirit, would Jesus need to go into the Wilderness to be tempted (FA)? Well, it means that Jesus was no less Human than you or I. The temptations had to be genuine for his refusals to mean anything. The Buddha, along with the Prophets Moses and Muhammad, were similar in this regard, they all endured periods of temptation and separation from the world.

Jesus fasted in the Wilderness for the full term, while all in him that looked back to the old died off. His conversation with the Tempter is significant in that he is not merely shunning the Biblical Dark. When the spokesman for the rejected logoi presents arguments for how he should live in the world. he doesn't just redraw the line, he explains how he will live in accordance with the Biblical Light so that the Word of God as "I AM" reaches even into that Dark.

And once again there is the issue of food. By being tempted to turn stones into bread, Jesus was being tempted to nourish His inner Man with the hard, concrete ideas of the external, worldly mind. Finally, Jesus dispenses with the temptation to use divine power to stay safe from harm. Real immunity from harm comes from learning to see that this sub-luminous world cannot harm anything genuinely Real. It was only after this struggle that Jesus was free to start his ministry (SOL).

It is my hope that this reinterpretation of these three stories demonstrates to some small degree how the Bible can be better understood by those who are genuine in their wish to find and Return to God… in this lifetime.

HALE MICHAEL SMITH, M.D.

Bibliography

The books listed here are those I've read over many years, which in one way or another have influenced my overall outlook on the subject matter of this book. What hasn't been included are the many books and textbooks on math, physics, chemistry, biology, anatomy, physiology, astronomy, history, linguistics, and yes, astrology, which I've read in the course of my life.

A

A Course in Miracles
Margaret Anderson, *The Unknowable Gurdjieff*
Muhyid Din Ibn Arabi, *The Wisdom of the Prophets*
A. J. Arberry, *The Discourses of Rumi*
Karen Armstrong, *Muhammad: A Bibliography of the Prophet*
Farid Ud-din Attar, *The Conference of the Birds*

B

Richard Bach, Jonathan Livingston Seagull
Helen Bacovcin, *The Way of the Pilgrim* and *The Pilgrim Continues His Way*
John G. Bennett:
    A Spiritual Psychology
    Conscious Labor and Intentional Suffering
    Deeper Man
    Enneagram Studies

RELIGION REINTERPRETED

Exploring Aspects of the Subud Experience
Gurdjieff—Making a New World
Gurdjieff Today
How we do Things
Intimations—Talks With J. G. Bennett at Beshara
Is There Life On Earth
Sacred Influences
Studies From the Dramatic Universe
The Dramatic Universe
The Enneagram
The Sermon on the Mount
The Sevenfold Work
The Sherborne Theme Talks Series
The Way to be Free
Transformation

Eric Berne M.D, *Games People Play*
The New Oxford Annotated BIBLE with Apocrypha
Mary Boyce, *Zoroastrians—Their Religious Beliefs and Practices*
Ignatius Brianchaninov, *On the Prayer of Jesus*
Dannion Brinkley, *Saved by the Light*
J. A. B. van Buitenen, *The Bhagavad-Gita* (in the *Mahabharata*)

C

Ron Cameron, *The Other Gospels*
Carlos Castaneda:
    A Separate Reality
    Journey to Ixtlan
    Tales of Power
    The Active Side of Infinity
    The Art of Dreaming
    The Eagle's Gift

HALE MICHAEL SMITH, M.D.

The Fire From Within
The Power of Silence
The Second Ring of Power
The Teachings of Don Juan: A Yaqui Way of Knowledge
Kenneth K. S. Ch'en, *Buddhism*
Thomas Cleary, *The Essential Koran*
Franz Cumont, *Astrology and Religion Among the Greeks and Romans*

D
Rene Daumal, *Mount Analogue*
Paul Deussen, *The Philosophy of the Upanishads*

E
Riane Eisler, *The Chalice & The Blade*
Mircea Eliade, *A History of Religious Ideas*

F
Gia-Fu Feng/ Jane English: *Tao Te Ching by Lao Tsu*

G
Kahlil Gibran, *The Prophet*
Frederick C. Grant, *Hellenistic Religions: The Age of Syncretism*
Karlfried Graf Von Durckheim, *HARA—The Vital Center of Man*
Liz Greene, *SATURN—A New Look at an Old Devil*
A. Guillaumont/ H. CH. Puech, *The Gospel of Thomas*
G.I. Gurdjieff:
    Beelzebub's Tales to His Grandson
    Life is Real Only When I AM
    Views from the Real World

RELIGION REINTERPRETED

H
Thomas A. Harris, *I'm OK You're OK*
Thomas de Hartmann, *Our Life With Mr. Gurdjieff*
Thich Nhat Hahn:
    The Miracle of Mindfulness
    The Sun My Heart
    Transformation & Healing
Anna Butkovsky-Hewitt, *With Gurdjieff in St. Petersburg and Paris*
Kathryn Hulme, *Undiscovered Country*

J
St. John of the Cross, *Dark Night of the Soul*
William Johnston, *The Cloud of Unknowing*

K
Karen l. King, *The Gospel of Mary of Magdala: Jesus and the First Woman Apostle*
Peter Kingsley:
    A Story Waiting to Pierce You: Mongolia, Tibet, and the Destiny of the Western World
        In The Dark Places of Wisdom
        Reality
Paul Kriwaczek, *In Search of Zarathustra*

L
P. Lal, *The Dhammapada*
Lao Tsu, *Tao te Ching*
Ursula K. LeGuin, The Earth Sea Trilogy
Jean-Yves Leloup, *The Gospel of Mary Magdalene*
Meyer Levin, *Classic Hassidic Tales*

C. S. Lewis:
> *The Great Divorce*
> *The Screwtape Letters*

M

George A. Maloney, *Man: The Divine Icon*
P. D. Mehta, *Zarathustra: The Transcendental Vision*
Marvin W. Meyer, *The Secret Teachings of Jesus*
Lama Mipham, *Calm and Clear*
Raymond A. Moody, *Life After Life*
Melvin Morse M.D.:
> *Closer to the Light*
> *Transformed by the Light*

N

Seyyed Hossein Nasr:
> *Ideals and Realities of Islam*
> *Islamic Life and Thought*
> *Muhammad—Man of Allah*
> *Sufi Essays*

Jacob Needleman:
> *A Sense of the Cosmos*
> *Consciousness and Tradition*
> *Lost Christianity*
> *Money and the Meaning of Life*
> *The New Religions*
> *Time and the Soul*
> *The Way of the Physician*
> *The Wisdom of Love*
> *Time and the Soul*
> *What is God*
> *Why Can't We Be Good?*

RELIGION REINTERPRETED

Maurice Nicoll:
    Psychological Commentaries
    The Mark
    The New Man: An Interpretation of Some Parables and Miracles of Christ

S. A. Nigosian, *The Zoroastrian Faith*

O

A. R. Orage:
    Consciousness
    On Love
    Psychological Exercises and Essays
    Madam Ouspensky: Talks with Madam Ouspensky

P. D. Ouspensky:
    A New Model of the Universe
    Conscience
    In Search of the Miraculous
    The Strange Life of Ivan Osokin
    Talks with a Devil
    Tertium Organum
    The Fourth Way

P

Elaine Pagels, *The Gnostic Gospels*

G.E.H. Palmer, Philip Sherrard, Kallistos Ware; *The Philokalia*

Parabola

Eric Partridge, *ORIGINS—A Short Etymological Dictionary of Modern English*

M. Scott Peck M.D.:
    A World Waiting to be Born: Civility Rediscovered
    People of the Lie

The Different Drum
The Road Less Traveled

R

Sarvepalli Radhakrishnan, Charles A. Moore:
A Sourcebook in Indian Philosophy
The Principle Upanisads
Bernadette Roberts:
The Path to No-Self
What Is Self?
The Experience of No-Self
Hugh McGregor Ross:
The Gospel of Thomas
Thirty Essays on the Gospel of Thomas

S

Scientific American (Since late 1950s)
Idries Shah:
Tales of the Dervishes
The Sufis
The Way of the Sufi
The *Nasrudin* collections
Hasan Shushud, *Masters of Wisdom of Central Asia*
Margaret Starbird, *The Woman with the Alabaster Jar*
Claude Steiner, *Scripts People Live*
Yuri Stoyanov, *The Other God*

T

St. Teresa de Avila, *Interior Castle*
Edward Tripp, *The Meridian Handbook of Classical Mythology*

RELIGION REINTERPRETED

<u>W</u>

Bishop Kallistos Ware, *The Orthodox Way*
Timothy Ware, *The Orthodox Church*
E. H. Whinfield, *Teachings of Rumi*
Whitney's Sanskrit Grammar (12th Edition, 1971, Harvard Press

<u>Y</u>

Arthur M. Young, *The Geometry of Meaning*
Anthony C. Yu, *The Journey to the West*
Lin Yutang, *The Wisdom of Laotse*

<u>Z</u>

R.C.Zaehner:
> *The City Within the Heart*
> *The Teachings of the Magi*
> *Zurvan: A Zoroastrian Dilemma*

HALE MICHAEL SMITH, M.D.

About The Author

Hale Michael Smith was born in Cleveland, OH in 1949, the oldest son of renowned composer Hale Smith and Juanita Smith. He attended Brown University and earned a medical degree from Georgetown University Medical School in Washington, DC. As a doctor, he worked in DC, New Mexico, and Oklahoma.

He was a man of many interests and abilities. As a child he studied sciences, including geography, astronomy, cartography, and read world literature. As a young man he studied the history of languages and world religions. Later, he taught himself organic chemistry in order to qualify for medical school. His hobbies included geology (he was an avid rock hound), origami, collecting sea shells, cultivating cactus plants, each in its pot with a small zen stone garden, making exquisitely detailed models of WWII ships and planes, and studying the mathematics of fractals.

RELIGION REINTERPRETED

His lifelong quest to understand the purpose of religion and spirituality led him to work on the material that comprises this book for over five decades.

HALE MICHAEL SMITH, M.D.